A Time to
HEAL

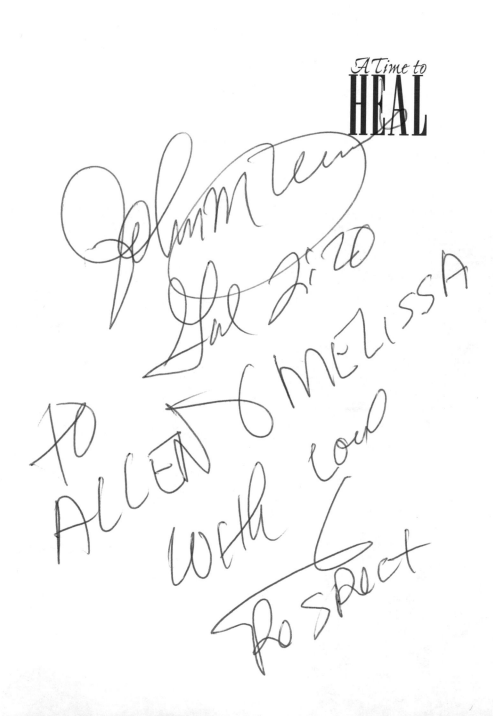

TO ALLEN & MELISSA
WITH love & RESPECT

A Time to
HEAL

JOHN PERKINS,
COMMUNITY DEVELOPMENT,
AND RACIAL RECONCILIATION

STEPHEN E. BERK

FOREWORD BY SPENCER PERKINS

Baker Books
A Division of Baker Book House Co
Grand Rapids, Michigan 49516

Published by Baker Books
a division of Baker Book House Company
P.O. Box 6287, Grand Rapids, MI 49516-6287

Printed in the United States of America

Library of Congress Cataloging-in-Publication Data

Berk, Stephen E., 1944–
A time to heal: John Perkins, community development, and racial reconciliation / Stephen E. Berk
  p. cm.
Includes bibliographical references.
ISBN 0-8010-5756-6 (paper)
1. Perkins, John, 1930–. 2. Afro-Americans—Mississippi—Biography. 3. Civil rights workers—Mississippi—Biography. 4. Mississippi—Race relations. 5. Afro-Americans—Civil rights—Mississippi—History—20th century. 6. Voice of Calvary Ministries (U.S.)—Biography. I. Title.
E185.97.P48B47 1997
976.2′00496073′0092—dc21   97-11672

For current information about all releases from Baker Book House, visit our web site:
http://www.bakerbooks.com

For my son,
Adam Nathanial Berk
L'hayim!

A time to kill,
and a time to heal

Ecclesiastes 3:3

Contents

FOREWORD

On Monday afternoon, April 21, 1997, I visited my father in his hospital bed. Sedated to the point of semiconsciousness, he still groaned from the intense pain only moments after surgery for prostate cancer. My mother cried off and on. It was only the second time in over forty years that I've seen my father in a helpless state.

The first time was on February 8, 1970. And on this terrible occasion my mother and I were visiting my father, not in a hospital but in a jail cell. The night before had been one of the longest nights of our lives, especially for him. He and several other demonstrators had been arrested and beaten all night nearly to the point of death for their involvement in our quest for equal rights in a small Mississippi town.

The image of my father that day, and the reaction of my mother to seeing him, will always be seared into my memory. On his head was a lump the size of my fist. His eyes seemed as big as silver dollars. His clothes were tattered and bloodied. But the thing I will remember most about him was the expression of humiliation on his face at having his sixteen-year-old son see him in this helpless condition.

My mother was reserved and stoic, almost as if in shock. They embraced and I could faintly hear my father desperately whisper to her, "Git me out of here. If you don't, they gon' kill me tonight." Those are the only words that I remember being spoken.

Only after we left the jailhouse and were out of view of the police officers did my mother's true feelings surface. Bursting into tears, she sobbed over and over, "I didn't want them to see me cry."

Thank God that is not the end of the story. God used something that was meant for evil and turned it into good. To complement my father's driving passion for the poor, God used this horrific night in a smalltown jail to instill in him another message. That momentous night John Perkins began to realize that racial and economic justice, though a battle that must be continually waged, was not a high enough ideal for Christians. For those who claim to be new creatures in Christ, reconciliation must be the goal.

Today and for the past thirty years, God has used my father to stir up a grass roots movement among the poor that he calls Christian community development. And from Seattle to Syracuse and in inner city neighborhoods from Pasadena to Peoria, Christians rich and poor, black and white, and every shade in between are planting themselves and their families in at-risk communities as a visible demonstration of the hope that Jesus intended to offer to the poor.

I have had the privilege of watching and participating up close as God has used my father to offer evangelicals a fresh new way to, as he says so often, "authenticate their faith." By coming out of our theological tower and living among those we minister to, we offer a practical gospel of "good news to the poor."

Over the years I have helped my father greatly with his own writings. Consequently I am very protective of what is written about him. So when I heard that a white college professor, Steve Berk, was going to write his biography, I have to admit that I was a little concerned. But trust came easy for me with Steve. I quickly sensed his passion and could see the excitement in his eyes for this project. And what was even more important for me was seeing his honest respect for my father's lifework. I'm sure the last chapter has not been written on John Perkins. But if nothing else is ever written, I can rest in the fact that there is an accurate account for history's sake. And for this I will be eternally grateful to Steve Berk.

Less than three weeks after visiting my father in his hospital bed, my extended family sat and listened as he became the first African American to give the commencement address and to receive an honorary doctorate from Belhaven College in Jackson. With less than a fifth grade formal education, my father was receiving his seventh honorary doctorate. It was another moving moment in history, especially in the fragile annals of our home state, Mississippi.

No one will ever be able to convince me that God does not have his hand on my father. The fact that I know the everyday John Perkins with all of his faults and weaknesses only says to me that God can and does use any cracked or broken clay pot that is willing to submit their will to his.

Spencer Perkins
President, Reconcilers Fellowship

PREFACE

During the 1970s a church renewal movement was plowing over fallow Protestant and Catholic fields and planting new forms of Christian life. *Community* was the word on the lips of people radically committed to serving the poor and building a just order. I had long professed belief in social action and I was newly Christian, so I decided to write about the diverse styles of community that renewal was breathing into life. I visited intentional communities and transformed urban churches around the country. But it was the first stop I made that June of 1977, as I started my fieldwork, in steamy, buggy Jackson, Mississippi, that made the deepest impression on me.

John Perkins was just turning forty-seven then. They had a little party with a cake for him in the Samaritan Inn, an old stucco and wood house where his Voice of Calvary Ministries sheltered volunteers, people-in-need, and guests like myself. I merged for a time with a group of college-age volunteers from Second Presbyterian Church of Memphis, Tennessee. Toward the end of my week in Mississippi, I was riding with them back to Jackson from Mendenhall, the site of Perkins's original community building, when the VW van we were driving in broke down. We found ourselves trudging miles down the highway into the city in the middle of the night. There was something about breaking down and walking that distance together in the warm Southern night that felt richly bonding.

Likewise I felt a warmth and closeness toward the workers at Voice of Calvary. The impossible tasks they had taken on—the raising of opportunity and hope in black Mississippi, the reconciling of white with black in a place notorious for its racial hatred—stirred something deep in me. Meeting John Perkins and driving into Mendenhall for the first time with him, listening to him talk about his ideas and his work, I caught something of the inspiration and enthusiasm that was animating the people who had come around him.

Arriving in Mendenhall, we drove across railroad tracks into a low, swampy section of town. Edging down the narrow road, we passed a row of dilapidated shacks and shabby storefronts. We turned off, and two, three bright new houses came into view, interspersed among more shacks. As we went on, I could see lumber, cinder blocks, and a partially constructed building nearby. At the far edge of the winding little streets in lower Mendenhall, fronting an open, mown field, stood Voice of Calvary's compound—a row of neat, redbrick, one-story buildings and a little up-and-down house with two dormer windows poking out of a sloping front roof. This modest white bungalow had housed the Perkins family, which had expanded to eight children during the sixties when they had lived there. Across from the compound, next to the field, stood a large, high, barnlike structure with a metal roof and painted cinder block walls. Over the big double doors was lettered R. A. Buckley Gymnasium.

John Perkins had grown up amid Mississippi's poverty and segregation in the thirties and forties. When he returned there from a materially abundant life in California, his purpose had been to teach Bible. He was full of newfound faith and learning and he wanted to impart these things to people he knew were among the most disadvantaged in America. His own experience had taught him how the degradation that black people had to live under in Mississippi impoverished their lives. And as he addressed their spiritual needs, he knew he would have to address the whole battery of their need. People are not disembodied souls, and John knew he needed to work to set them free materially as well as spiritually.

As Perkins confronted issues of economics and justice, he inevitably ran afoul of the custodians of white supremacy. He had been changing the consciousness of the black community in Mendenhall as he and the people who joined him dealt with issues of hunger, health, employment, and shelter. It was the sixties, and Mississippi had become a civil rights battleground. John Perkins brought his organization behind voter registration, and Mendenhall's black community began to use politics and economic pressure to challenge the white power structure. This brought violent reprisal, and Perkins would come close to paying with his life. But he escaped martyrdom and lived to build a movement that brings races and resources together to build community life from the ground up at the local level.

We live in a time when consensus has died, public discourse has soured, and public institutions are failing, a time when chic cynicism supplants healthy idealism among the young. But away from the jaded public eye, in out-of-the-way places abandoned by affluent America, a movement is thriving, a movement that contains the potential to heal our deepest wounds and divisions. It had its beginnings in 1960 when one obscure black man left his prosperous life to return to the place of hopeless poverty and pain where he had grown up. John Perkins's decision violated the canons of the American success story. But Christianity, when it is practiced with integrity, has this upside down and backwards look to the world.

In telling John Perkins's story, I have tried to avoid academic jargon and the buzz words of the Right and Left. My hope is to give the ideas embodied in the man and the movement he began the broadest possible application. This work is essentially a biography, though in part 3 Perkins is progressively absorbed within the movement he pioneered. That is the way he would have it, since his purpose was to fall to the ground as seed and bear abundant fruit.

My broader purpose has been to set Perkins and his movement in the context of American and African American history. Hence, I have included general essays on such events as black migration out of the South and the postwar boom in California, the civil rights movement, the rise of a social (or progressive) evangelicalism, and the persistence of an urban underclass. These subjects are interwoven with the distinct events and periods of Perkins's life. In the case of civil rights, I use an entire chapter, chapter 8, to describe the work of Martin Luther King Jr. and Freedom Summer in Mississippi as necessary background to Perkins's work. I have also included an essay on the African American church, a subject that comes up as Perkins becomes a Christian and decides to set up a mission in Mississippi. This essay I have placed in an appendix, however, so as not to interrupt the continuity of that part of the book.

In the last chapter, The Beloved Community, I compare Perkins's ideas with those of other pivotal African American reformers of the Left, the Right, and the Center. In so doing, my aim is to show the dynamic interrelationships of these diverse points of view within the evolving African American community. If America has bequeathed anything worthwhile to the world, it has come out of our humanitarian reform movements. African Americans, uniquely oppressed in American society, have created what is perhaps our most vital and complex reformist tradition. John Perkins's lifework forms one important point on the spectrum of that tradition.

Getting to know John Perkins and the people in the movement as I researched and wrote this book has been a wonderfully transforming experience. Without many people's help, I would not have enjoyed this opportunity. I have most appreciated the many hours spent in conversation with John Perkins. This is really John's book. He has lived the remarkable life described herein and he very much continues to live it. Thanks are especially due to Vera Mae Perkins for her help with many details and for her gracious hospitality. The six grown Perkins children in the ministry have also been most helpful in giving me access to their lives. They are Spencer Perkins; Joanie Perkins Potter; and Derek, Deborah, Priscilla, and Betty Perkins. Spencer's wife, Nancy Perkins, of Reconcilers Fellowship, was of great help to me in getting seemingly endless details straight. I would also like to thank the Antioch Community in Jackson.

In The Mendenhall Ministries thanks are due to Artis Fletcher and Dolphus Weary for working my project into their busy schedules. In Jackson, Melvin Anderson, Phil and Marcia Reed, and Chris Rice made time for me to get the information and insights I needed. In Pasadena, Julie Ragland was especially helpful, providing her unique perspective on the Perkins family and their work. Phil Schaafsma, serving as John Perkins's appointment secretary, helped me track down this man in constant motion so I could get the interview time I needed. And H. P. Spees, a man much like John Perkins, who started the Jackson ministries with him and has remained an integral part of the movement, has been a most vital general resource to me.

To aid in funding this work, I had a spring sabbatical leave from Cal. State, Long Beach, in 1995, which enabled me to make early progress with writing. A special word of thanks is due the Louisville Institute for awarding me a stipend, which enabled me to devote full time to completing the work in the summer of 1996. Along the way I have also had generous assistance from my friends Jan and Rod Dornsife.

In the early stages of this project, Elizabeth Lurie of the Brady Foundation and David Blankenhorn of the Institute for American Values gave me helpful advice and warm encouragement.

Augustus Cerillo Jr., my friend and colleague of many years and specialist in American evangelicalism, provided me with many vital resources, including a full run of *Freedom Now*, the fundamentalist civil rights periodical of the sixties. Keith Collins, in Southern and African American history, gave me useful insights. Graduate assistant Linda Johnson helped me with research. Elise Miller gave vital assistance in legal research. Arek Pfeffer spent many patient hours providing invaluable computer help.

I would also like to thank the people at Baker Book House for believing in this work and especially my copyeditor, Mary Suggs, who made many useful suggestions.

In more general terms, my father, the late Morton Berk, stirred an early love of social and racial justice in me. My mother, Shirley Berk, taught me to value perseverance. Finally my wife, Mollie, has been my chief source of encouragement and moral support throughout this project. I have relied, and not always gratefully, on her helpful criticism and her patient endurance of my mercurial and sometimes annoying temperament.

There are many others who have helped me in various phases of this work. I acknowledge them and I salute the valiant people of the Christian community development movement, whom I believe to be among the best hopes for America.

PART 1
MAKING IT
1930–1960

1

The Outlaw Family

The hot air hangs densely over the cotton fields during Mississippi's long, languid summers. Lying awake in the sweaty nights, you can hear the relentless screech of thousands of cicadas rubbing their legs together in the swampy thickets. In a tiny, sparsely furnished sharecropper's shack in June of 1930, a tired black woman was dying of pellagra. Maggie Perkins had just given birth to her sixth child, the fifth to survive. She called him John. She was an intelligent, strong-willed woman who had taken good care of her four older children, two boys and two girls. She had a girl by an earlier marriage who would die young, and Cleveland, her oldest child with her present husband, had choked on a piece of lean meat and died as a baby. Clyde, the oldest surviving child and a born leader, was twelve. Then came Mary, Clifton, and Emma Jean. Emma Jean was a little more than two years old when John was born. The elemental conditions of life for black folk in the rural Deep South had taken their toll on Maggie's overworked, malnourished body.

The Perkins family were all sharecroppers in and around New Hebron. They worked mainly cotton on the smaller white plantations that characterized south central Mississippi. The land was cultivated in cash crop; there was no space or time or money for subsistence farming. So vegetables that could provide the nutrients to help stave off diseases were not a regular part of the black sharecropper's diet. The staples were cornmeal and fatback and they provided few nutrients for the body's defenses. Typhoid, malaria, hookworm, and rickets were facts of life in the rural South.

Pellagra is one of the diseases of poverty that used to be commonly found among blacks and poor whites in the days of Jim Crow, the system of racial apartheid that characterized the South for much of the twentieth century. It is a painful, drawn-out disease that includes lesions of the skin, severe diarrhea, and mental disorientation. Since it is caused by vitamin deficiency, it can be remedied by an enriched vitamin diet. But such luxuries were not available to people like Maggie Perkins. She died seven months after her last child's birth, a young woman, leaving her infant son to the care of other women in the family.

Death was all too familiar a presence for these people, who had drawn close to one another to cope with the severities of poverty and oppression. Maggie and her husband, Jasper—everyone called him Jap—did not have a cow, so they had to get milk from a neighbor who had one. The women carried pails of milk to the house so that little John could have what he needed.

After his mother died, John and the other children went to live with Jap's mother, Aunt Babe, there in New Hebron. The Perkins family matriarch, who had reared nineteen of her own children, eventually gave Mary, Clifton, and Emma Jean to other extended family who lived nearby. As they grew up, the children would live as part of the families of different aunts who were Aunt Babe's daughters and in-laws.

Emmaline Barnes, known to the community as Aunt Babe, was born in slavery. Her mother, Rose, told her that her ancestors, two sisters and two brothers, had come from the West Indies some time in the early nineteenth century. These Caribbean slaves had not been bought as field hands but as people to work in some higher capacity. One of the brothers was said to have graduated from college in Johannesburg, South Africa. Coming to the United States, they were originally sent to Williamsburg, the stately old tidewater capital of colonial Virginia. During the early nineteenth century, when cotton was beginning to supplant tobacco as the main southern staple and the Mississippi Valley was becoming the place of the new plantation fortunes, Rose's owner, Mr. Bass, migrated west and settled in what would become Bassfield, Mississippi. At any rate, Emmaline's ancestral kin had been intelligent, accomplished people who had been enslaved in the relatively recent past.

Aunt Babe's husband, Dennis Perkins, and their son, Tom, had gone into the bootleg whiskey business in the early part of the century, distilling and distributing moonshine through rural Mississippi and Louisiana. Even during the most terrible period of the southern caste system, there were ingenious, enterprising blacks who were able to carve out a bit of independence for themselves. Bootlegging was always profitable in the South. Abstinence from alcohol remained an integral part of the evangelical religion that had become the backbone of regional culture. As a result, dry counties were common throughout the South, including the piney woods area of central and southern Mississippi. Bootlegging had become a way of life among both blacks and whites by the Prohibition era.

In characteristically American terms, black entrepreneurs like Dennis Perkins found a way to cash in on the great thirst Prohibition had created. He did the usual sharecropping and built his covert liquor operation on the side. Sharecropping, called farming on halves since half of the crop went to the plantation owner, was a poor means of livelihood. By the time a farmer paid for his seed, fertilizer, and implements, he was lucky to break even. A small minority of black farmers managed to acquire their own land. The Perkins family probably could have gone in this direction. They had the fiercely independent spirit and the ability to stand up for themselves in a society that relentlessly pressed them to bow and scrape before white power. But their adventurous, oppositional temperaments and the opportunities that presented themselves drew them into trafficking in moonshine. And since their business was illegal and could so easily get them in trouble with the law, it was important for them to also be sharecroppers.

Sharecropping gave them legitimacy and the appearance of submission to the system. The Jim Crow South tried to make blacks dependent on whites for their very identity. Whites liked to have blacks identify themselves by saying whose plantation they lived on. When John Perkins was a child in the early thirties, some of the first words he learned to say were "the Fred Bush place." Fred Bush was the plantation owner for whom his grandmother and her family sharecropped at that time.

Farming on halves made black farmers dependent on not only the white plantation owner, but also the merchant who sold him supplies. Generally they ended up in debt to these white bosses who paternalistically controlled their lives. Dennis Perkins and his family were able to live better than the typical sharecropper due to their bootlegging.

Some time around the First World War, Dennis got cancer and became so weak he fell out of bed and hurt his little daughter Ethel, who was helping to care for him. After he died, his family continued the business, which gave them a bad reputation among church members, who formed the respectable element of the rural black community. But because of their bootlegging, the Perkins clan avoided severe want; this at a time when deep poverty and hunger were the common life of the black South.

Dennis's wife would outlive him by more than twenty-five years. She took over and ran the family. In those days women did as much as men and shared power with them in a rough-hewn equality of the sexes. In the Jim Crow culture, black women were less of a threat to whites than the men were, and so they had more license to confront. The strong ones like Aunt Babe did so commonly. When she was an old lady, the sheriff's deputy Gene Cliburn stormed the house one day, brandishing a half-pint of whiskey he had planted. He tried to take Grandma to jail, but she refused so forcefully that he relented.

Young John Perkins witnessed this incident. It was the first time he had seen anyone stand up against the police and it affected him deeply. This display of his grandmother's sense of her personhood in resisting the white authority would stay with him and would help to embolden him in years to come.

The sons and daughters of Aunt Babe carried on the family business for more than two generations. Like their white counterparts, black bootleggers generally got caught up in lives of risk and passion. Blacks also carried a deep, smoldering anger inside, the result of having endured centuries of grinding oppression. Since whites controlled the means of force and effectually cut off all black access to power and accomplishment, black men were apt to vent their rage only in brief bursts of self-destructive violence. They wore side arms and commonly died of gunshot wounds or killed others, sometimes whites but more often other blacks. One of Aunt Babe's sons, Sam, died as a result of an argument that escalated into a shoot-out with another black man.

When he was in his early teens, Tom Perkins went to prison for killing a man. Tom certainly carried the barely suppressed rage common to African American men but he was able to turn his energies in a more profitable direction. He made and sold whiskey while incarcerated, got out just before the Great War, picked up his share of the proceeds, and bought a horse and buggy.

Tom was always a good businessman, seeing possibilities and taking expert advantage of them. While the country was trying to dig itself out of the thirties' depression, he was paying his little niece, Rosie Lee, to roast peanuts for him. He trucked them to town in New Hebron and sold them to eager customers who were even more eager to purchase the moonshine deftly concealed beneath the neat rows of peanut bags. Tom served three terms in federal prison for illegal manufacture and sale of alcohol. His time at Leavenworth and Fort Benning was not idly spent, however. He was able to link up with an underground network and continue to make and sell whiskey from prison. Besides the profits, Tom surely enjoyed the satisfaction of reaping his ill-gotten gains right under the Man's big nose.

Aunt Babe's home was an outlaw house. People living there, including the children, were all involved to a greater or lesser extent in the family business. The life of enterprise, profits, and putting one over on the Man carried a powerful satisfaction. It was the closest thing to living free that you could do in the Jim Crow South if you were black. It was addictive, like its alcohol product, and inevitably carried with it other risky addictions—like gambling.

Tom's brother Bill bootlegged mainly to serve his appetite for gambling. The Perkins men were high riskers; it was a dominant trait that could lead to great acts of courage or it could lead to a wild, violent life of reckless thrill seeking. Bill was known by blacks and whites alike as "the crazy nigger." He had a great temper, and no one was anxious to mess with him.

Like the rest of his family and most black farmers in the South, Bill was a sharecropper. In his case, farming on halves served mainly as a cover for his gambling activities. During the winter, when there was no farmwork, sharecroppers, including Bill Perkins, worked at sawmills and logging. Aside from cotton, timber was Mississippi's biggest crop in the thirties.

During the hard winter rains, when the rivers would rise and there was no work in the sawmills, Bill would get a poker "skin game" going. He would never quit until the end; he would either be broke or he would win it all, seven or eight hundred dollars, quite a tidy sum of money for that time and place. But as with any compulsive gambler, his winnings were generally the stake for his next game. They didn't serve any constructive purpose.

Bill Perkins was one of the few blacks in Mississippi who had the nerve to stand up to the boss man. To monopolize power in the Jim Crow South, whites believed they had to totally control blacks, and to retain that control they often resorted to terror, epitomized by lynching. They were the law. They owned the plantations and bent every aspect of black life to economic and emotional dependence. Most blacks lived in fear of the white authorities and outwardly accepted the severe restrictions on self-assertion required by the system. But people like Bill were constitutionally unable to shuffle. He was always challenging and trying to muscle or outwit or outrun the white power structure.

One time when he was in jail in Prentiss, the jailer left his little boy alone with the prisoners. Bill began to talk animatedly with the child and told him to get the key and let him out so he could play with him. The boy eagerly did so, and Bill freed himself and the other prisoners who wanted to leave. He hid in the woods that night and went to his mother's house the next day. He was preparing to leave the state along with some outlaw cronies when he heard the sheriff coming. Hiding behind the barn, he heard the sheriff, accompanied by his deputies, vowing to take Bill back to jail or kill him when he found him.

Just then Bill stepped from behind the door with his gun drawn saying, "You're not going to take me anywhere." The sheriff backed off and Bill fled to Louisiana. It was customary in the black outlaw culture of the time to leave the state when things got hot and wait until there was another sheriff or enough time had passed so that the incident had blown over. This time Bill was gone seven or eight months. These scrapes with the law flowed directly from his way of life. Eventually the law caught up with Bill, arresting him for killing a man, and he went to prison and died a natural death while still incarcerated.

Aunt Babe's house was known to the black outlaw community as a safe house. People on the run would stay there for a night or more, sometimes as much as a week. And at the opportune time one of the Perkins men would take them someplace else, helping them to escape. During World War II they would strip cars down and leave them in the camouflage of the dense woods, efficient transportation for the flight out of state. The Perkins family helped black men who had killed whites to escape north to places like Detroit. In this way they channeled their anger into covert resistance to the system.

Young John Perkins was raised in this atmosphere, and it became quite natural for him and the other children to imagine killing some white folks and hiding out in the woods. In this way their minds learned to gnaw at the pain of resentment they always felt toward the southern whites who lorded it over them.

Bill and the other Perkins family members, who could challenge the symbols of white power, proved the resilience and resourcefulness of the African American spirit. Strong black men and women reared amid strongly supportive families found ways to defy the system and assert their individuality. It was hard for blacks to wrest more productive lives from an order so weighted against them.

When Maggie Perkins died, Jap gave the children to his mother and left the area. He would likely have stayed with his family had his wife survived, but without her it was easier to move on. He too had been trained in the family business, and it was easy to give in to the foot-loose life of the outlaw, which was all around him. He was a quiet, less aggressive man than Tom, Bill, or Sam. He left his children and went to live in another part of the state, returning only rarely to see them. Sometimes they would go to Columbia, where he lived, and stay with him. John and his big brother Clyde grew up in their grandmother's home, and Toopie, as John was called, was nursed by his Aunt Ethel, whose daughter, Rosie Lee, was about two years older.

Ethel had been married at thirteen to a man whom she had met picking cotton. He was very light skinned, educated, and old enough to be her father. He had taken her away from her people to live at his place in Bay Spring, Mississippi. He had a way with words and would type out letters to con corporations out of suits of clothing, record players, and a variety of other goods. Hustling of one kind or another had become a common way of life among black men during the years of Jim Crow because it was the only way they could get in on the American success game. But Ethel was a woman of simpler tastes and close family ties and she became lonely with her husband. The marriage broke up, and she returned with her baby, Rosie Lee, to her mother's home in New Hebron.

While Ethel nursed little Toopie, it was Grandma's bed he and Rosie Lee slept in. Space and privacy were nonexistent, and the rural poor lived and slept communally. Often there were eight or more people arranging

25

themselves on a shuck bed, which was just a big homemade cotton-stuffed mattress on the floor. Rosie Lee became the big sister, helping Ethel, who was only fourteen years her senior, take care of Toopie.

Toopie had the Perkinses' strong will and a tenacity that made him combative and even downright mean. But the family was warmly indulgent with him, feeling sorry for him because he had no mother. When he was little and she was bigger, he would pick on Rosie Lee and see how much he could get away with. Emulating her elders, she was especially forgiving of him, and he took advantage of her. Sometimes he got into real fistfights with her over something they both wanted and he would keep at it until he would fall from exhaustion.

In traditional rural American culture, discipline was often meted out with a switch from the tree in the yard. If not carried to excess in frequency or duration, this manner of correction was quite effective. It provided immediate painful consequences for obnoxious behavior. And it administered a simple justice, setting clear limits on a child's aggression. Toopie, however, due to his privileged status, was almost never whipped for his misdeeds, as the other children were. This probably served mainly to increase his natural willfulness.

Rosie Lee, for her part, knew how to capitalize on the soft place the grown-ups had for Toopie. One day she and Toopie went into the watermelon patch and cut one melon open to see if it was ripe enough to eat. Finding it deep red and juicy, they polished off a good portion. Toopie then had the task of going to Rosie Lee's mama with a ripe piece of melon. Rosie Lee knew that Toopie would not be whipped. If Toopie thus ran interference, no one else would be whipped either. As it was, her mother was pleased that the kids had discovered that the melon was ripe enough to pick. Toopie did not, however, manage to get through his whole childhood without corporal punishment. There were times when his antagonistic nature went too far to be winked at.

Aunt Babe's youngest son, Sylvester, who was always called Bud, acted as head of the household while Toopie, Rosie Lee, and her younger brother, Jimmy, were growing up. When they earned money, they gave it to Bud. He was also the one who imposed limits on their behavior. Jimmy, a quiet, passive child, was three years younger than Toopie and five years younger than Rosie Lee. Toopie often picked on him. One day he was tormenting Jimmie so much that Bud finally called him over and whipped him. Toopie never resented this. It was the natural order of things. In fact Toopie felt particularly close to Bud, who was the nearest thing he had to a father.

Like his brothers Tom and Bill and his sister Rosetta, known to the family as Aunt Coot, Bud successfully plied the family business. And like his brother Bill, Bud liked to gamble, but unlike Bill, he knew when to quit. For Bud gambling was more to win the money than it was for the excitement of the play. Toopie loved and admired Uncle Bud. He admired him because he was so respected in the community.

Like the other Perkins men, Bud got into scrapes but he was able to bridle his temper more effectively than Sam or Bill had. Once Toopie saw him crying because he was so angry. It didn't make him lose respect for his uncle. Bud's crying made him seem more human, more accessible to his little nephew. Adults did not often show this kind of feeling to the children around them. The men in particular were not apt to hug or give open affection to the children. But Toopie knew Bud loved him because he took him fishing and hunting. He showed him how to do things and he would lift him onto the back of a mule while he walked and talked with him. Uncle Bud was the man who was there for him.

Toopie's big brother Clyde was second to Bud as the male authority figure. Twelve years Toopie's senior, Clyde was the oldest of the children and the hero of his generation. He had the same tough, determined quality that characterized most of the Perkins family. As the oldest, he assumed the responsible role, often playing the protector of the younger children.

Once when Rosie Lee was being taunted by a boy at school, she picked up a stick and hit him with it, causing him to bleed. The boy's family had to take him to the doctor and they told Rosie Lee her family was going to have to pay the bill. She in turn told Clyde, then in his late teens, and he said he would take care of it. Nothing further was heard from the boy's family. Clyde's quiet strength helped to give the Perkins children a sense of security and stature in the community. His example would have a powerful influence on his little brother, who felt especially close to him.

When Toopie was about four years old, his father, Jap, came home overnight. The little boy was awakened in the middle of the night by his

27

daddy, who took him on his lap and called him his baby. Toopie was embarrassed at being called a baby. He was already doing his share of work around his grandmother's place and had a strong sense of his value.

Not long before, on a chilly day when four of the Perkins women were quilting together on four sticks of wood, their fire went out, and they asked Toopie to get them firewood. He took a good half hour to cut the limb off a nearby tree and proudly carry them his prize. They were grateful and thanked him for it.

Nevertheless, Toopie could forgive his father for calling him his baby, because it made him feel so good to have a daddy of his own. It was good to have uncles, but it was special to have a father. He knew he had a father and he had waited and waited for him to come and see him. Now at last he had his daddy, and it was the best moment of his life.

The next day Jap was going to return to Columbia, and of course Toopie was going to go with him, because a boy belonged with his daddy. But when Toopie tried to follow him down the railroad track, Jap told him he couldn't take him. Toopie wouldn't believe it. He continued following his father. Finally, Jap plucked a switch from a tree and struck his little boy with it to make him go back. Toopie was crushed and he was confused. He couldn't understand why his daddy, who loved him and had come here to see him, could be leaving him behind. And he couldn't understand why daddy would be whipping him for wanting to be with him.

This experience kindled a deep sense of loss and grief in him and renewed a powerful longing for acceptance. While his aunts and uncles loved and indulged him, he would always feel like he didn't quite belong. He labored mightily to overcome that feeling. Throughout his life he remained especially sensitive to issues of fathering and family.

As with other rural families, the Perkins children put in dawn-to-dusk days of farmwork during planting and harvest seasons and they had a full load of chores to do in the off-season when they attended school. The children worked alongside their adult relatives and received hands-on teaching from them. Hard work was strongly valued, and though the children liked to play and avoid toil as much as any other kids, they learned to respect accomplishment.

When Toopie was not in school he was usually doing some kind of work: cutting fence line, chopping (weeding) cotton, picking corn, or another of the thousand tasks of farm life. He learned to like work. His ever gnawing desire for acceptance and love made every job he was given an important job, which he would do well to show what a valuable person he was. And as he worked the long hours from dawn to dusk and felt the deep weariness in his bones and muscles, a sense of his worth and competence grew.

When the children were working in the fields, rain was a great relief to them. When the sky began to darken and the wind picked up, they would pray that the rain would get there quickly and rain hard and long so they wouldn't have to work. But they couldn't show the grown-ups how happy they were for it to be raining. They would make a great show for their uncles of wanting the rain to go away, so they could all get the cotton crop in.

Not all of childhood was consumed with work. There were times of play also, the richly imaginative, improvised play of country children unfettered by the passive diversions of modern urban life. As with children in all times and places, getting and eating sweets was a worthy object of playful energies. On the back roads of an older America, the door-to-door peddler was a common sight. Farmers sometimes sold produce this way, and women would inspect the collections of cooking implements spread out for them by the pots-and-pans man, as curious youngsters looked on. But the peddler whom the children really got excited about was the candy man. This familiar figure, who was a white man, recruited women of the black community, like Rosie Lee's mother, Ethel, to sell his candy.

One day in later childhood when Toopie and Rosie Lee were left alone, Rosie Lee spied the candy man coming toward the house. Because mama wasn't home, she had to think fast to get the candy man to leave off a box. Toopie would have to be Mama. She tied a big handkerchief around his head and put an old dress on him. He willingly went along because he wanted to figure a way to get his hands on the candy. When the candy man knocked, Toopie, following Rosie Lee's prompting, opened the door in his disguise and asked him to leave off some boxes for sale. The peddler laughed but he played along and left a box anyway, and the children riotously celebrated their victory.

Money went a long way in the thirties. You could buy little toys and candies at the mom and pop variety stores for pennies or nickels. The uncles would frequently give change to the children, and Toopie, always mindful of the value of saving, resisted exchanging his treasure for such transient pleasures. He would hoard his stacks of coins in an old snuff box, and like a Caribbean pirate, he buried it in a sandy hill close to the house. Rosie Lee, who was freer with her wealth and ended up commonly paying for both of them, became resentful of Toopie's miserliness. She told him she was hoping and praying to the good Lord that it would rain and wash away Toopie's money.

Sure enough, one of those torrential rains that regularly inundate the South came, and rivers of water formed everywhere, washing sand and soil away, together with Toopie's precious treasure. Rosie Lee felt terribly guilty as she and Toopie cried while fruitlessly digging all over trying to uproot the missing stash of coins. While the children were often rivals, they felt a strong familial loyalty to each other and would support one another in times of crisis or in the face of a common enemy.

Because the Perkinses were better off economically than many in the black community, the family usually had enough to eat. Unlike many black sharecroppers they often had meat, usually chicken. But even though there was enough to go round, the children got stuck with the chicken feet, which were mostly gristle. The black farm culture was mired in want, and it was common practice among poor rural folk to favor the adults. When Rosie Lee was eight, she began to help cook and she saw to it that the children got some of the good pieces.

After harvest time, when work and profits became more scarce, there was sometimes not enough food. They would eat up everything in the house, so they had to rely mainly on the vegetables they grew. Cutting sugarcane and sucking the sweet juice from it, roasting potatoes, and consuming handfuls of the plentiful wild hickory nuts, they made do over the cold winter months. Toopie, Rosie Lee, and Jimmy would crack so many nuts their fingers would ache but they'd never really get full.

Their mainly vegetable diet was supplemented by a few animal products like fatback pork. During the winter, when the children were walking many miles to school over the icy path, they would cut down to two meals a day, with green peas and buttermilk at night. There was enough to keep them from the deep gnawing pain of relentless hunger, but their provision was often meager.

2

COMING OF AGE

Schooling in traditional rural America was not the child's whole life. The school was there mainly to teach youngsters to master written and spoken language and to figure. In the great stretches of family farm acreage where the majority of Americans used to live, schools commonly adjusted their schedules around the seasons of farm life—planting and harvest. Traditional farm families were large. Lots of children were considered a blessing since there would be more hands to labor in the fields. Farmwork was indeed the primary activity of the rural child. In the thirties things had not changed much from the nineteenth century in rural Mississippi. Modernity arrived at a torpid pace that matched the lackadaisical lifestyle of this part of the country.

The high rate of illiteracy in rural Mississippi was a factor of its poverty as well as of the Jim Crow system. Ironically it was during the Great Depression that rural Mississippi received its first exposure to twentieth-century technology and its accompanying development and prosperity, as Roosevelt's New Deal created the Tennessee Valley Authority (TVA) and the Rural Electrification Administration (REA). These agencies began the lengthy process of bringing electricity and modern industry to the rural South.

At the bottom of the southern economy stood Mississippi, which had only 1.5 percent of its farms electrified in 1935. Alcorn County, in the northeastern part of the state, a good distance from New Hebron's south central location, was the site of a pilot electricity cooperative run by the

TVA. But full electrification would not occur in rural Mississippi for several decades to come, and the state continued to lag economically.

At the bottom of Mississippi's rural peasant economy stood black farm life in hamlets like New Hebron. Work—long and tedious labor, hoeing, picking, cutting, chopping, and carrying—took the better part of the children's energies. Nevertheless, primarily in the winter months, schooling was marginally available, and most children attended, though often only sporadically.

The white South eschewed investment in black literacy. The system was geared to keep blacks from all forms of advancement, which would inevitably make them "uppity," as it expanded their sense of personal ability. Consistent exposure to the disciplines of formal education from an early age has always been a key to building one's confidence and firing success in a free and open society. But freedom and openness were anathema in segregationist Mississippi. As late as the World War II period, the state was spending ten times more for white education than for black and paying white teachers more than three times the salaries of their black counterparts.

Black teachers and children were crowded into one- or two-room cabins with crude benches and an occasional table. It was cold and drafty in the winter and stifling in the warmer months. Commonly the girls received more schooling than the boys. Rosie Lee and Toopie's future wife, Vera Mae Buckley, both finished high school, though they had to travel some distance and board away from home to do so. Toopie received the equivalent of only about five years of schooling over his first fifteen years of life in Mississippi. He would not gain any real literacy until he served in the army during the Korean War period. Still his grade school experience was a positive and memorable one for him, since it was dominated by a strong, dedicated teacher.

Maybelle Armstrong made a powerful impression on her young students. She was a strict disciplinarian whose conductor's baton was a switch applied liberally to the hand or backside of any wayward or inattentive young scholar. She even used it to goad the children to performance in spelling bee competition. The message she conveyed was that school was serious business and learning and literacy were important for black people.

Hers was one of the most powerful presences in Toopie's life. She taught him respect and love for his people, their travail, and their accomplishments. She introduced to him heroes of the struggle against slavery, like Nat Turner, Frederick Douglass, and John Brown, whose body she had the children singing about. While Toopie barely learned the rudiments of reading and writing in her schoolroom, she built his self-confidence by giving him encouragement. Miss Armstrong assured Toopie that he had a brilliant mind and that he was a natural leader. Such affirmation helped to fortify his heart, building his self-image and giving him a sense that he could really accomplish things in life.

Toopie's belief in his own creative powers came to the forefront of his mind in an experience he had when he was eleven and working as a hired hand for a local white farmer. It was common for older black children to hire themselves out to whites to get extra spending, or in Toopie's case saving, money. He was visiting a friend about fourteen miles from his home. Since rural Mississippians did not move around much, this was considered far away. It was haying season, and a local white farmer needed some help getting hay into his barn before the rains came.

Always ready to exchange his hard work for a good wage, Toopie spent a grueling day hauling hay. Expecting to be paid somewhere between one and two dollars, a respectable sum for the time and place, he was dumbfounded when the farmer handed him only fifteen cents. His shock quickly gave way to anger but he had to stifle his feelings.

The ironclad etiquette of the southern caste system required a black person always to appear grateful for white "largesse." Even the slightest hint of black self-assertion or confrontation in the face of a white would get you in big trouble. And if whites thought of you in those terms, they would not hire you and they well might hurt or even kill you.

Yes, Jim Crow etiquette demanded total subordination of blacks, and sometimes a white would even test a young black male to see if he really understood what was expected of him. For it was strong, independent, assertive black men who constituted the potential threat to the white male overlords. White bosses had to drive home the message of self-effacement to black underlings from time to time, and what better time than when a young black male was just coming into the first sense of his power and competence. A decent sum of money for a day's hard work might build up this boy's sense of himself, and it was the whites' desire to do just the opposite, so as to render the black male down and dependent. So here was the white farmer's cruel object lesson.

Toopie choked down his appreciable pride and accepted the fifteen cents without comment, as he knew he had to. And he did get a lesson from the bitter incident but it was not the one the farmer would have desired. This was a marking event in Toopie's young life. He had known since he was small and hoarding coins in the little snuff box that accumulating money would give him power. Now he began to understand just what kind of power the man who owned the farm and the team of horses had.

He understood that if he could get to own the house and the barn and the fields himself, then he could exert greater control over his own destiny and he would not be vulnerable to the kind of treatment he had just suffered. Toopie's economic-mindedness was beginning to crystallize into a burning desire to advance himself and gain independence through acquisition. These were dangerous thoughts for a black boy in Mississippi in 1941. But they were characteristic of the cantankerous Perkins clan. Young John Perkins had been born into and reared amid a family of fiercely independent entrepreneurs. And now that spirit was beginning to bud in him.

In the fall of 1945 just after the Second World War had ended, when Toopie was spending a few days away from home, Uncle Bill summoned him back to his grandmother's place. Aunt Babe was dying, and all the kinfolk were gathering there. About thirty people moved in and around the little house for three or four days keeping vigil. They had never, of course, had any electricity, so they were all adept at stepping around and taking care of things in the dark. When the doctor said she would die within thirty minutes, Toopie slipped outside. He didn't want to be there when she breathed her last; it was his way of dealing with the loss.

When someone finally said "Maw is gone," Toopie absorbed the shock of it. The stolid old woman had been the linchpin of the family. She had bathed him and he had slept in her bed as a child. Her presence had provided a powerful reassurance and stability amid the poverty and oppression that so cheapened the lives of black people in Mississippi. He felt the loneliness of the loss of a great mother figure. Aunt Babe's death was another benchmark in his life. It pushed him toward adulthood, giving him a sense of being more on his own and having to make his own decisions.

With Babe's passing, her daughter Rosetta—Aunt Coot—would take over her function. Traditional rural farm families were held together by strong, nurturing women. Besides caring for and rearing the children, these women did some of everything to insure the family's survival. And the black family was very much an extended one, a clan, with a compound of related houses. Blacks in the agrarian South had continued much the same pattern of clan life and mutual aid that had existed in Africa. African families were commonly matrilineal, with husbands going to live in the wife's family home, and the Perkins family, gathered around the home of Aunt Babe and then Aunt Coot, were in keeping with that tradition.

Aunt Coot was perhaps the most versatile entrepreneur in the Perkins family. She plied the family business, specializing in the retail end of it. Selling gallon, quart, and pint jars of moonshine directly to the public yielded readier profits than distilling and wholesaling, which drew more competition from both white and black dealers. Aunt Coot also ran a rooming house, which put up transient men. She generally boarded about twelve men at five dollars a week. During the latter New Deal period, many of these men were government employees, digging out right-of-ways, cutting down trees, and putting up posts for power lines, as the REA commenced the gradual process of electrifying rural Mississippi.

These boarding houses, which were commonly run by black women, played an important part as temporary housing for black people in the Jim Crow South. The hotels, inns, and restaurants, which whites frequented as a matter of course, were entirely closed to the black population, thus making travel over any distance an onerous task for them. Not until the Civil Rights Act of 1964 made it illegal to discriminate in public accommodations would blacks traveling in the South begin to gain access to them. In the meantime, the black women who opened rooming houses met some of the need. In the Perkins family Aunt Lilly Mae, another of Babe's daughters, who was called Sister, also took in boarders. During the Second World War, Jackson became a military depot, with a recruiting center, an air base, and a military hospital. At this time, Sister opened a rooming house for black men in Jackson. Like Aunt Coot, Sister sold whiskey but she was also well known in the black community for the big games of Georgia skin she organized.

Georgia skin, which Uncle Bill also specialized in, was a variety of poker in which the deck was shuffled and each player drew a single card and held it. Then the "heavy cut" would proceed as the cards were continuously cut and players bet after each cut. You lost when your number card came up. The beauty of this game was that it could accommodate large numbers of players and a big pot. Sister became another successful Perkins family entrepreneur with her boarding house and her popular skin games.

Aunt Coot sold whiskey to boarders and others around town. She was well known for her cooking and she was able to gain ready access to the white plantations and please their owners with her culinary arts. With her various enterprises, she never got visibly rich but in all likelihood she did acquire wealth. It was dangerous for blacks to display any sign of prosperity in the southern caste system, so those who had money became adroit at hiding it. Aunt Coot was known to be one of the biggest retailers of moonshine in the area. Family members would talk of her treasure trove of five-dollar gold pieces.

Toopie went to live with Aunt Coot in 1945, just after his grandmother died. During a brief period, when Toopie was fifteen, he had visited his father in Columbia and stayed with him for a while. He had never lost his longing for a father. But it didn't work out, in good part because Jap's girlfriend didn't really want his teenage son around. Somehow, the bonding with his father that would have satisfied Toopie's deepest yearnings never occurred. He had to content himself with his close relationships with Uncle Bud and his big brother Clyde. Jap never played much of a role in his life, and it left him with a certain sadness.

Aunt Coot lived on the farm of her second husband, Mr. Cooter. She had split up with her first husband, Willie Cox, before the war. They had gotten into an argument and she had shot him in the leg. The marriage did not survive the incident. It was some time during the war that Aunt Coot remarried. Mr. Cooter was pretty well fixed for a black man in Mississippi. His father had managed to get some land and send his children through school. So Mr. Cooter gained the refinement of a little learning, which helped him gain favor with whites.

The family farm was wedged into a plantation that was owned by a family of five brothers and two sisters named Smith. Mr. Cooter's father had hired him out to the Smiths when he was a young boy and over the years he had grown close to them. He became the trusted family servant who, were he not black, would have been considered a relative. In the segregated South the only way for a black man to acquire status was through white patronage. Aunt Coot's marriage to Mr. Cooter was an economic boon to both of them. It brought him into her lucrative liquor business, which now received the protection of a prominent white plantation family. The Smiths were good customers and their influence pretty much kept the law away.

While Toopie was at his father's, Aunt Coot offered him a job working for the Smiths for twenty dollars a month. He knew he was worth a lot more than that, but there was nothing holding him in Columbia, so he returned to New Hebron and took the job. He hated working for whites. Racial etiquette dictated that he mold his whole outer being to the demands of the white boss, and to do so constricted his free spirit. He didn't mind working hard; in fact he liked it if it was for his own people. His work in the family was an integral part of their support. Toopie drew a sense of his significance as an individual and a Perkins from that work. But working for the whites did not carry these intangible benefits; it was strictly for a wage, and inevitably an insultingly low one. Nevertheless he took the job Aunt Coot had proffered—he needed the money. He had this job, which he hated and was always ready to quit, when something occurred that would radically alter the course of young John Perkins's life.

Clyde Perkins returned from the European war a celebrated hero within New Hebron's black community. The family, which received that distant, fearful kind of respect sometimes given to outlaws, could now gain a more legitimate respect, based on Clyde's decorations. But while martial valor could elevate a man's status in the black community, it could at the same time expose him to hostility and violence from the whites. The derogation "smart nigger" was reserved for black men who would be men, that is, they would exert some form of power outside the black community. The caste system organized the whole pattern of race relations so as to degrade black men, to make them act and feel less than men. To enhance and feed off the tonic of their power, white men set up a system that was totally geared to reduce black men to fawning, cowering impotence.

A black man could raise a white's hackles if he looked him in the eye or if he passed him on the sidewalk without removing himself to the gutter. Everything he said or did in relation to whites had to exhibit subservience. The second a black man conveyed to a white in conversation or any transaction a spark of self-respect or self-assertion, he was suspected of harboring thoughts of equality and judged uppity. Further marks of insubordination, even what would appear the most inconsequential—a look, a tone, an offhand remark—might earn him the label "smart nigger." Many black men learned to display a servile demeanor and use it to take indirect advantage of whites.

But having to constantly maintain the servile, self-abasing pose invariably took its toll. The tension created by so having to hide your real self to conform to others' scapegoating rules became hypertension or high blood pressure, and early death from stroke and heart attack became and still is epidemic among black men. The Perkins men and others like them, who were constitutionally incapable of playing the Sambo role, ran the risk of death at the hands of whites for their uppity ways. They had survived, when they had, by becoming outlaws and having as little contact with whites as possible. Because outlaws had no formal status, they were tolerated, though of course they were often jailed or killed in shoot-outs.

Black men, who had had the legitimate means of livelihood and power cut off to them by a racist system, resorted to the many and varied forms of hustling. And hustling, whether it was bootlegging, gambling, or whoremongering, was not as much a threat to white supremacy as the simple assertion of one's manhood was. For to be a man was to be equal as a person with other men, and social equality was the primary taboo.

Before Clyde Perkins had gone to war, he had already pushed the boundaries of racial discretion. In fact the local draft board had discovered his eligibility following an incident in which he had had the temerity to argue with a white man. The draft boards in Mississippi were using their office to get potentially troublesome black men out of the state. By speaking up instead of acquiescing, and thereby asserting his manhood, Clyde had marked himself as a "smart nigger."

The man Clyde had challenged had become mayor of New Hebron during the war and the mayor strongly influenced the sheriff and his deputy. These men were on the lookout for any sign of insubordinate behavior from Clyde after he returned to New Hebron. Local white men burned with resentment because of black soldiers who came back from service to their country with a new sense of their personal dignity. The military in the world wars provided black men with the most important avenue of advancement in the first half of the twentieth century. War may be an evil, but paradoxically it became the means for black men to reclaim their manhood.

A black soldier who had made sergeant got a little rowdy one night in a tavern near New Hebron, and a group of whites clubbed him to death with an axe handle. The racist system was born in and enhanced white men's addictive appetite for total domination of black men, so much so that many whites could become filled with murderous rage whenever a black man rose and displayed his personality. And it was this kind of sick anger that was festering against Clyde on a hot summer Saturday night as he and his girlfriend waited in line at the Jim Crow entrance in the alley beside the Carolyn movie theater.

The fuse had been lit and the explosion was about to occur on that Saturday, for Clyde had returned from the war determined to stand up for himself. He raised his voice while waiting in line for the theater to open and inspired a typically controlling response from the deputy marshal: "You niggers quiet down." Instead of silently acquiescing, Clyde tried to speak to the law officer. The deputy reacted to this hint of insubordination by clubbing Clyde. Moving to defend himself from further attack, Clyde grabbed the baton. The deputy, now completely overtaken by his rage, stepped back and shot him twice in the stomach.

**New Hebron, John's hometown, in the 1970s. Between the store
(*left*) and the old Carolyn theater (*right*) is the alley where Clyde
Perkins was shot in 1946.**

The shots were fatal. To get proper treatment Clyde had to be driven forty miles into Jackson. Toopie had been visiting with a friend who had a store in New Hebron. He came quickly when he heard Clyde had been shot and he cradled Clyde's head as he rode in the backseat, along with Uncle Bill, and his cousin Joe drove as Clyde's life ebbed away.

This was the bitter event that marked the beginning of young John Perkins's adulthood. While males in diverse cultures have experienced more nourishing rites of passage, this is the kind of searing trauma that was not uncommon for a black youth to undergo in the years of Southern apartheid. John was only sixteen. He had never experienced the strong sense of personal identification that life with one's parents can give a child. He had, however, been reared in the midst of a close, nurturing, extended family, and that experience had strengthened him.

Big brother Clyde had been John's model, his mentor, his hero, and his companion. All the children of his generation had looked up to Clyde. He had donned his country's uniform, had been wounded several times in the bloody war against the Germans, and had returned with ribbons and a Purple Heart, to celebrate the Allied victory among his people. Having proved his manly valor on the battlefield, he came back to a racist system that denied him his very personhood. Having helped cleanse the world of Hitler's racism, he had returned to a place where he received treatment similar to what a Jew would experience under the Nazi regime. This was the supreme irony for the black soldier in World War II, and that fact of life was not lost on the African American people after the war as they began to coalesce to put an end to the evil Jim Crow system.

But young John Perkins had more concrete thoughts about the white tyranny that had killed his brother. A deep, primal anger flared up within him, a rage that burned for retribution. Anger at whites was no stranger to him. He used to imagine how he might design a bomb that would blow up all the white folks in New Hebron and how he could time it so he could get back to where he was supposed to be when it went off. His aunts and uncles, who dealt daily with their own rage, knew that Toopie might do something after Clyde's murder that would cause him to end up like Clyde. So they arranged for him to live in Jackson with his Aunt Sister.

Sister's daughter, Willie Mae, had recently gone to Southern California, as many black Mississippians were doing in the postwar period. Bud and Sister thought it would be a good idea for Toopie to join her

out there. She had a place in Monrovia, near Pasadena, in Los Angeles County, where she worked as a domestic. In the fall of 1947, when
John was seventeen years old, his aunt and uncle got about fifty dollars together for him and said their good-byes as he boarded the train
to go west. And young John Perkins became a part of the great postwar black out-migration from the South. He became a part of the postwar population surge and economic boom in Southern California.

3

CALIFORNIA

The murder of his brother Clyde left a deep root of angry bitterness in John, but his great drive for personal advancement activated a pragmatic quality, which was partly innate and partly taught him by strong family mentors like Uncle Bud and Aunt Coot. John's pragmatism, his deep sense that he needed to do what would work out best for him, would serve him well throughout his life, helping to give him resilience and adaptability. As he sat in the railroad car on the long train trip to California, he had a gut-level sense that he must focus on his future and not on the painful past in Mississippi. Younger members of the Perkins family were beginning to leave a stagnant, stifling South and wend their way to this sunny, surging land of promise.

The two decades that followed the end of the Second World War were a period of tremendous economic boom. The United States reveled in the prosperity it enjoyed as the world's leading producer of nearly everything. Years of pent-up demand had caused the generation that had endured the thirties' depression and the war to yearn for the good life. Henry Ford's car culture had begun to produce suburbs in the 1920s, and postwar America was churning them off the assembly line. Middle-class American utopia consisted of a machine-driven pastoralism, a split-level "ranch" with one- and then two-car garage, and a wide green lawn with shrubbery and shade trees. No vegetable plots were needed because you could get all you needed at one of the new supermarkets, which punctuated the wide commercial boulevards of the new suburban utopias.

A more masked but economically virulent racism persisted in this clean new world of racially homogeneous suburbs in the form of restrictive covenants that kept blacks and other ethnic minorities like Asians and Mexicans from moving in. The Supreme Court outlawed this practice in 1948, though it would be decades before housing would really begin to open up. But definite opportunities for the minorities did exist, albeit lesser ones than for the whites. And so minorities came in ever greater numbers.

Blacks had first poured out of the South during what has become known as the Great Migration, between 1915 and 1929. They were escaping a farming depression that had caused a great many landlords to evict their tenant farmers, and 75 percent of southern black farmers were tenants; sharecropping was the most common form of tenancy. The depression was initially caused by a temporary decline in European markets due to the outbreak of the First World War, but then it was compounded, as depressions so often seem to be, by natural disasters. As if God were pouring forth his wrath on the South's oppressive way of life, boll weevil infestations and floods followed and caused a crisis in southern agriculture. And black farmers with starvation heaped on their already weighty burden of troubles now began moving north in ever increasing numbers.

As favorable reports filtered back to others, the incipient trickle of migrants swelled to floodtide, and cities like New York and Chicago, with their expanding job opportunities, absorbed them. Thus northern cities like these gained an infusion of black labor, and black cultural life germinated in the Harlem Renaissance and enriched the bubbling cauldron of creativity brewing out on the midwestern plains in Chicago. The northward migration flourished through the twenties and then slowed with the Great Depression as employment opportunities dried up.

But economic possibilities had persisted during the depression in the West and particularly in the American dream capital, Los Angeles. During the thirties, for diverse reasons, black people were leaving the rural and urban South and even the cities of the northern promised land and making their way to California. These were the years of the dust bowl and the westward-trekking Okies and Arkies. The South was in transition. Cotton prices had been falling since just after the Great War, and with the onset of the depression they really plummeted. The plantation owners were turning from cotton to other more profitable commodities like cattle and dairy products and they were introducing tractors and harvesters.

As they thus moved away from the old cotton culture, they found less use for their tenants, and many a sharecropper suffered eviction or they were degraded to transient wage laborers and renters. Many of these people, now feeling detached from their traditional moorings, floated into southern cities like Memphis. There they would take jobs mainly in the traditional black service occupations: janitor, porter, maid, and the like. With little to keep them in such environs where they still were bitted and bridled by Jim Crow, they were often the ones most open to California migration.

Those who continued in sharecropping had a desperately hard life always at the edge, having to borrow for subsistence and pay the Man upwards of 35 to 40 percent interest. And Mississippi was always at the bottom of the southern economy. In the Delta, in the northwest corner of the state, where cotton persisted and black men and women were trucked in en masse to do seasonal labor, the average annual income was ten dollars per person in the mid-thirties. The New Deal's largesse, distributed through the Agricultural Adjustment Administration, gave the lion's share to the farm owners with precious little for the croppers. And in the northern cities, blacks, at the bottom of the economic ladder, experienced the most unemployment.

California, with its inviting dry warmth, its expansive new cities, and its high wages seemed a bright ray of hope, and blacks migrated there in sizable enough numbers to carve out neighborhoods amid Pacific urban life. Oakland in the north and Los Angeles in Southern California housed the largest black communities.

It was the distinct hardships of the depression then that shifted African American attention from the South and from the northern cities like Chicago, Detroit, and New York to the West and California. In the immediate decades to come, that was the place where blacks would most frequently seek a better life. Even though most black people in Los Angeles worked at unskilled jobs, their material life was far better than in the South; indeed it was better than any place else in the country. In mid-depression, ever larger numbers of blacks in Los Angeles were buying homes, cars, and insurance. Even though they were still poor and the depression limited their opportunities, they were moving and some were even beginning to enjoy a little progress toward a better material life. As World War II exploded, the depression and the war industries began to mushroom. It was the West Coast, particularly Southern California, which experienced the biggest boom.

With their traditional rural culture gradually eroding, southern blacks looked increasingly westward. Despite the poverty and the miseries of the caste system, there had been a close, personal quality to life in the South. Being a ghettoed, pariah people was hard and oppressive, but as with the European Jews, it forged deep bonds of shared experience.

Black families and communities of the South huddled together around farm and church life. To move out of this familiar setting into the unknown dangers and anonymity of the big city was a venture fraught with too many imponderables for many to contemplate. But the promise of much better wages, less discrimination, and good education in California lured many. A steady stream of depression migrants grew to an exodus as the war economy expanded.

The war years completed the transformation of a once lazy, palm-studded coast into a throbbing urban beehive. As black migrants arrived in the burgeoning Los Angeles area, they did not initially find easy entry into the aircraft and munitions industries. Although they could frequent most public places and they no longer suffered the straitjacket of southern apartheid, they still had to put up with a good deal of discrimination. Many racist whites from the South and Midwest were also relocating in California, bringing their prejudicial folkways with them. As they had been in places like Chicago and Detroit, blacks were bottled up in the most dreary and dilapidated parts of town, as restrictive covenants kept them from moving out and up. But as demand for labor spiraled and the shortage became acute, black workers found their lot improving.

The voracious defense industries digested them in growing numbers, though they rarely obtained jobs that gave them much responsibility or any authority over white workers. Progressive unions like the CIO were also a strong source of support, as they pressured their affiliates to adopt antidiscrimination policies. By the end of the war, a booming California economy, paying the nation's highest wages, had engineered a population shift to the West that would continue and expand for much of the rest of the century. Blacks relocating from the South were and would continue to be a significant part of that migration.

The postwar period at first saw some slowing down of California's growth, but the wartime industries matured into those of the defense establishment as the ever lucrative Cold War took hold and "fortress California" was created. The war had been a powerful fulcrum of material advancement for African Americans, and in the aftermath its momentum would propel them into their most sustained and comprehensive campaign for equality with whites. Intimations of this movement were already present as black veterans filtered back to their southern homes harboring ideas of their right to human dignity. Mississippi, which together with Alabama and Georgia formed the backbone of the white resistance, erupted in sporadic racial violence in 1946, when blacks began to push for the right to vote. Not only were whites nervous about black veterans getting uppity notions of who they were, but they also found themselves competing with blacks for a declining number of jobs as the war ended and the economy slackened.

Lynchings had been declining in the South during the second third of the twentieth century. There were twenty-nine across the region during the war decade, but five of them occurred in 1946 in Mississippi within a few days of an election primary, which had seen blacks trying to vote. That year black men were beaten bloody, tortured, and murdered around the state, as white men became ever more sensitive to infractions of etiquette. The police, symbols of the white command, acted most zealously in defense of the system, and numerous black men, Clyde Perkins among them, lost their lives as a result.

When John Perkins arrived in Los Angeles on a fall day in 1947, his cousin Willie Mae met him at the train station. She had come to California as the war was ending in 1945. She lived and eventually bought a house in Monrovia, a suburb of Pasadena, east of Los Angeles at the foot of the San Gabriel Mountains. In the forties the San Gabriel Valley was still a picturesque place with its wide arroyos and new tracts of homes climbing into the foothills. Pasadena was one of the prominent cities in the Los Angeles orbit and it proved to be a place where blacks could get a toehold in the good suburban life.

Willie Mae got John space with her brother, Tommy Davis, in Mr. Lee's rooming house in Monrovia. He was surprised to find two of his first cousins on his mother's side that he didn't even know about living there. Mr. Lee charged four dollars a week rent for one, and six dollars for two in a room. It was easy to get work; they learned of jobs through a network of black workers.

John got a job in a steel foundry in the lower coastal part of the Los Angeles basin at South Gate. He commuted to work with someone who owned a car. Those who didn't have their own cars got to work this way. It was 1949 before John had his first car.

In the foundry John was able to exercise his drive to succeed. Hard work felt good to him, especially if it paid dividends in rapid personal advancement. The company was automating its production of steel pipes, and John's crew was given the task of digging the ditches where the machinery was to be put in. The foreman, impressed with John's energy, made him the lead man. Such an act of favor would turn many workers into company men, but John's experience of working for whites in the South had taught him that currying favor with the boss kept you shuffling, hat in hand. Greater independence from the owners, made available through the union, meant real power for the workers. This attracted John.

Unionism was strong and growing in the postwar period. The foundry became affiliated with the United Steelworkers, part of the racially progressive CIO, while John was working there. The organizers came and talked to the black and brown men and the minority of whites who did the gritty manual labor in the company's trenches. John identified on a deep level with the union's belief in strength through solidarity. He had never had a chance in the South to gain that kind of bargaining power against the white bosses. His assertive nature led him to play an active role in the shop's unionization, standing up to the company's threat to fire those voting for the union. When the union won the election, John became shop steward for his department.

So here he was in this seemingly contradictory position: lead man and union man. But for John it was not contradictory. He wanted to do the best job possible, one that would please his employers and help his advancement. He was warm and affable, though at this time in his life he was a bit shy. He was like an immigrant from a peasant society, deeply conscious of the disadvantages of his southern roots. He was only marginally literate and much less educated than the average worker, black or otherwise, who had grown up in California. His consciousness of this handicap hammered at his self-assurance, giving him a stuttering speech, which further lessened his confidence. But his tremendous drive for success, coupled with his native intelligence and his strong desire to please, made him a likable asset to the company even as he became a leader in the union.

The foundry was making the steel pipes for plumbing the multitudes of new housing tracts that were blossoming all over Southern California as the economy expanded. These pipes were traditionally tooled individually and workers were paid piecework wages. But to raise production to meet voracious demand, the company was automating. John worked hard for the better part of a year constructing and getting the new mechanized system into operation. It would take some time to work the bugs out. It also took time for the workers to learn to operate the assembly line effectively. The inevitable breakdowns occurred, and initially mechanics had to be called in from the outside, but eventually the foundry's own workers mastered the new production process.

Such changes and the workers' need to adapt to them rapidly created a good deal of job stress. And, as so often happens when industrial plants introduce more automation and production increases, the workers lost ground economically. They didn't lose their jobs, but the change from piecework to an hourly rate cut their wages by a third, from one hundred fifty to one hundred dollars a week. John led his shop out on strike for a more equitable wage, and he was able to negotiate a settlement in a few days. Management agreed to put the whole system on a piecework rate, so that workers would get a percentage for so many pipes produced. This restored incentive and acted as a spur to productivity.

John was only eighteen and barely out of the South. He was making more money than he ever dreamed about as a child and he had already begun to exercise his gifts for organizing and moving people forward. Despite many formative years under the yoke of Jim Crow, he was not afraid of confrontation. Indeed, he relished it, and in this fluid western environment he could use it effectively for his own and other people's advancement. The foundry's workforce was largely black and Hispanic. John was in a position to challenge the white managers to improve these minorities' economic livelihood and he succeeded. Such positive action would have been unthinkable in Mississippi where the Perkinses' ability to confront and grow was blocked by a life-denying system. They had had to thrive, as much as possible, outside the system. But in California there was genuine opportunity, and John found himself able to make full use of his faculties for the first time.

John, his family, and the people they respected back home had never bought the black inferiority ideas of the white South. They uniformly thought that given the chance, they could perform equal to or better than the whites. That's why they so identified with Joe Louis and Jackie Robinson and why they were glued to their radios when these powerful athletes, who had crashed a thought-to-be impenetrable race barrier, were performing.

John found the racial waters of the Pacific Coast warm and inviting. Despite the persistence of institutional racism in hiring and housing, the possibilities for self-improvement were so much better than in the South that John discovered a heady new sense of freedom. He did come across a few racial incidents in these early years of adulthood. Once some southern white boys had passed by his company softball team as they played a rival in a local South Bay park and had taunted "the niggers." But nothing of any consequence occurred that would hamper John's freedom to go and do and be. The times were good and California was basking in a growth boom that was stimulating such a demand for labor and such a climate of optimism that the old racial antipathies were for a time shunted aside. Like a strong, young runner at the starting blocks—his muscles taut, his energies wholly absorbed in the race, his joy in the open competition, the prize—John was bursting with ability and desire to realize his potential. He loved California!

In 1951 when John was twenty-one, he found himself turning in the direction of marriage. John was basically a monogamous person. He had a healthy sexual urge but it was not all-consuming, as it so often is with young men. If anything was all-consuming, it was his drive for success and respectability. For him manhood meant the responsibilities of a good job with lots of growth potential, a devoted, practical-minded wife, and a good home with healthy children. He hungered after the American middle-class dream, which had always been dangled before black people but cruelly denied them.

Despite his love of California, he was most comfortable around black Mississippians. Their lives had familiar touchstones with which he could identify. So when he wanted a wife, it was natural for him to find one in Mississippi. In 1949, when he was back on a visit, he began to court Vera Mae Buckley, whom he had played with as a child in New Hebron. Vera Mae's family was among the minority of black farmers who had managed to acquire their own land.

The Buckleys were hardworking people, more cautious and conventional in their habits than the Perkinses. They were Christians—Vera Mae had an uncle who was a preacher—and church involvement gave them a respectability in the black community that the Perkinses did not have. In fact when John made known his interest in Vera Mae, it raised some eyebrows in her family.

Vera Mae's first memory of Toopie Perkins was at the Oak Ridge Missionary Baptist Church; that was the one her family attended. It was the biggest of the black churches in the New Hebron area, with between two and three hundred worshipers on a given Sunday morning. The fact that the Perkins family were not churchgoers did not mean they took no part in church life. In black society throughout the country, but particularly in the hamlets of the South, the church was the hub of community life. It was usually Baptist, though blacks were represented in most denominations.

Besides the usual weddings and funerals, the churches orchestrated annual week-long revivals. Also known as protracted meetings, these events, spawned in the periodic revivals and camp meetings of frontier America, had both spiritual and social dimensions. Featuring many hours of dramatic pulpit exhortation, protracted meetings were means of gaining new church members, while renewing and strengthening the commitment of old ones. But after meeting came the celebration, featuring heaps of well-prepared food and warm conviviality. Booths were set up and every kind of sumptuous edible was hawked: big steaming chicken pies, yams sizzling in molasses, fruit pies, fried chicken, fried okra, tender white catfish, and lots of well-seasoned black-eyed peas.

Unchurched people like the Perkinses were attracted to these events with their carnival-like atmosphere. Inevitably a good deal of gambling and drinking went on, apart from the church's blessing but right under its nose. Revival time had much in common with the great feast days of rural society from ancient Israel through medieval and renaissance Europe. Joyous family reunions gave it an especially celebrative atmosphere as relatives came from increasingly dispersed parts. The church presided over and served as the gathering place for the community's festivals. It drew these people of deep common experience together and conferred meaning and continuity on their lives. And it was on church grounds that the black community gathered to give witness to the joyous and grief-filled passages of people's lives.

The time Vera Mae remembers seeing her future husband at the Oak Ridge Church had been another tragic marker in the life of the Perkins family. The year was 1943, and Toopie's sister Mary, eighteen years old, had been killed by her husband. After their mother died, Mary and her sister, Emma Jean, had lived with various relatives. For part of their childhood they lived with Aunt Babe's oldest daughter's family in Bassfield. But they lived with different aunts at different times, and in all likelihood, Mary was never strongly rooted, grounded, and nurtured in the family. She was a beautiful, spirited girl who had to grow up too early. She drifted to Louisiana where she married. The circumstances surrounding her husband's killing her are unclear but it was known that he stabbed her to death.

The deep, violent rage was ever seething just beneath the surface of the black South, a rage that blacks knew they had to contain if they were to survive. But occasionally it would burst outward and when it did, it would almost always be turned destructively against members of their own community, even their own household. This is the ugly, destructive rage, simmered in the heat of southern oppression, that slashed out Mary's young life.

Thirteen-year-old Toopie was filled with uncomprehending grief. Why would anybody want to kill Mary? She had been a warm, affectionate big sister to him when she had come to his grandma's, and he had looked forward to his visits to Bassfield where he would see her. He loved her and now she was gone. He felt sad and empty. He didn't understand why her husband had killed her, violently, with a knife.

When Vera Mae saw Toopie, he was standing under a tree in the churchyard quietly weeping as they were burying Mary. Something about him struck her, and she asked her grandmother who he was.

Though Vera Mae's family had been more respectable than the Perkinses, she and John actually had much in common. They both grew up with a strong work ethic. They knew what it was to get up in the silent predawn chill and labor in the fields until the daylight receded many hours later. They sensed that such hard work conferred purpose and value on their lives and they would always feel uncomfortable if they didn't have something useful to do. Vera Mae's parents had separated when she was a little girl of five, her father had gone away, and her mother sent her to live with her grandparents. Grandpa Williams died when Vera Mae was eleven, and like John she was raised by her grandmother.

Grandma Brillie Williams was a devout, praying Christian, who taught the Bible in church. Her religion did not make her rigid and moralistic as it does with some. It filled her with a quiet strength and resolve that helped her become a positive molding force in Vera Mae's life. On the surface she seemed wholly different from Aunt Babe. But Toopie's grandmother was similarly a strong, nurturing woman, devoted to providing for the well-being of those around her.

While church people looked askance at these bootlegging outlaws, from Aunt Babe's view the family business was what they did to survive and have a little something in the midst of a hard, poor life. She too in her distinct way had labored to make the individuals in her charge strong, resolute, and resourceful. While standing apart from the church, she always acknowledged God and saw to it that the children said their prayers before bed. From their differing perspectives these strong women imparted a sense of hope and a belief that hard work and determination paid off. In Jim Crow Mississippi this was no small accomplishment.

While John was visiting his family in Mississippi in 1949, he went over to the Pleasant Hill Church during revival festivities. He saw Vera Mae coming out of church and was immediately attracted to her. He knew right away that he wanted Vera Mae for his wife and told her so. Despite Toopie's family background, Vera Mae's grandmother liked him. She quickly became aware of his earnest disposition and his lack of bad habits—he didn't drink or carouse. Yes, Toopie Perkins would be a responsible man and a good provider for his family, a good husband for Vera Mae. Vera Mae thought so too.

For about a two-year period, John corresponded with Vera Mae. It wasn't easy because John had trouble writing then. He intended to bring her to California as soon as he could gain a bit more economic security. But Uncle Sam intervened, and John was drafted. Most young men considered the draft a nuisance, an unwelcome interruption of their all-important life plans. Invariably it interfered with courtship, coupling, career building, and the personal freedom that young American men have always so valued.

John, with career advancement and marriage center stage in his mind, was no exception. He possessed the self-propelling, entrepreneurial quality that was so much a part of the Perkins makeup, and the military's inhibition of personal ingenuity tended to throttle his energy. But while

John was too much his own man to ever consider making the army his career, his time in the service turned out to be of real benefit to him.

Of course it didn't begin well. It never does. The military always wants to emphasize the unit and deemphasize its component parts. Persons who have grown up having their individuality valued suffer through embarrassment and a certain shock and outrage as they are told to strip naked and submit to poking and prodding by medical personnel who leave no bodily orifice inviolate. They line up to be shorn like so many sheep, receive their unimpressive fatigues, and in short order—gathered in rude formation—get hounded and barked at by a sergeant who tells them they are the sorriest bunch of misfits he's ever had to look at.

While southern black men were subjected to endless indignities from whites, they did not live with whites and they did not get their essential self-image from them. Black extended families like John's were able to confer a strong sense of personal worth on their young. The army's initial ceremonies were likely to be almost as jarring to him as they were to sheltered middle-class suburbanites. But he recovered quickly and learned as he trained to profit from the army's emphasis on discipline and chain of command. Physical exertion was an old friend to him, so he adapted well to the rigors of basic training.

John trained at Fort Ord in central California. The military was the advance guard of integration, having begun to integrate during the Second World War. John found himself in close personal contact with white men for the first time in his life. He became friends with a young man from Bell, California, one of the small industrial communities growing out of Los Angeles. He found no sign of bigotry in this person and it surprised him. California white people did not seem to have the deeply racist attitudes that southern whites always displayed.

Training's basic purpose was to toughen up these draftees and make them an efficient fighting unit with strong adherence to chain of command. The Korean War was going on, with the United States providing the lion's share of men and material for the U.N. "police action." Many of those who led the training were battle-hardened veterans of the island campaign against Japan. They were intent on impressing these young men with the seriousness of their mission.

"You're not here to fool around," roared the master sergeant. "You're here to learn to kill people and kill them dead." That one got John's immediate attention. There was a tough, war-seasoned lieutenant who headed his unit. Most of his World War II division had been wiped out. He was a skilled and strongly supportive leader who inspired a warm response from the young men he was training. One of the exercises in the last part of basic has you crawl under actual rifle fire. As the lieu-

John on Okinawa, 1951.

tenant led them through this exercise, something went wrong and the bullets were coming in too low. One hit the lieutenant and killed him, and two others got wounded. Here was a sad, ironic lesson in just how seriously they needed to take the things they were learning.

A black captain replaced the lieutenant. Because of advancement during World War II, there were a good number of black officers by the time of the Korean War. John was impressed with this hopeful sign of his people's progress and he worked all the harder to excel. Some of the maneuvers were particularly grueling, like the fifteen-mile, five-hour forced march in the hot California sun. Loaded down with pack and rifle, John began to experience a dizzying weariness as the march wore on. He noticed that seven black soldiers had already fallen out and he was afraid he would be next. Suddenly he became aware that the captain had come alongside him. The black officer, wanting John to finish the march, reached out and lifted his rifle from him. John felt a surge of warm gratitude and felt a close camaraderie with the captain. It gave him the energy he needed to finish the march.

In the early fifties African Americans in the service were in the forefront of the black common man's advancement. Conscious of their visibility in this first locale where they were working beside whites, they were anxious to surmount the old white racist image of their inferiority. John's captain felt the need to extend himself for a fellow black man as he strived to succeed. In doing so he forged the kind of bond of racial solidarity that would be needed for the mammoth undertakings of the civil rights movement.

John profited in a number of ways from his stint in the service. He learned to work with people from widely divergent backgrounds. Military life helped to discipline him, and he learned how to work efficiently, carrying out orders in chain of command. He became comfortable working with and under a commander. This would stand him in good stead as he moved back into civilian life and began climbing the corporate ladder.

It was also the military that gave him his first opportunity to really improve his literacy. He read constantly, feeding his curiosity about economics, politics, and current affairs. With Cold War issues dominating the news, he took it on himself to become better informed about what communism and capitalism were and how they differed. He had a mind that wanted to grasp and evaluate the ideas, issues, and practices that undergird and run societies. He wanted to understand how the different systems—the varying degrees of public and private ownership—could create or detract from opportunity and the chance for people to gain wealth and advantage.

He wanted to understand what made powerful leaders successful. He identified with the populist leaders who dethroned kings. At this time Gamal Abdel Nasser became the premier of Egypt, successfully opposing British colonialism and the monarchy it supported. John thought Nasser was a courageous man. The black experience as a whole and his own experience with American white racism gave him a feeling of identity with peoples struggling against colonialism.

By the time he left the military, he had thus gained some knowledge of public affairs and had broadened his vision. He had also developed his basic skills, and his self-confidence had grown. His unit could have gone to Korea but they shipped out to Okinawa, and John never saw combat, at least not of the military sort.

In 1951, before he left for the Orient, John got a three-week pass. He brought Vera Mae to California. They were married, and enjoyed a brief honeymoon in the Los Angeles area.

Vera Mae returned to Mississippi afterward and stayed with her grandmother while John was in the service. In February 1953, just after John was discharged, she moved to California. They settled in Monrovia, and John took a job with Shopping Bag, an up-and-coming supermarket chain, which had started in the San Gabriel suburb of Eagle Rock. He began as a janitor but he wasn't about to stay in that position for long. John had a single-minded, industrious quality that inevitably moved him in a successful direction at work.

John and Vera Mae's marriage, however, began to unravel almost as soon as they moved into Willie Mae's house in Monrovia. The reasons for their trouble went back to John's time in the army. After their marriage Vera Mae returned to Mississippi, and they lived apart until 1953, when John was discharged and finally able to bring her to California. The courtship had been brief, their time together was very limited, and there had not been enough of it for real marital bonding to occur.

So John had fallen into living the bachelor life, continuing to chase women with his army buddies just as if he were not married. What was even more damaging, he continued to run around and cheat on Vera Mae after he got out of the service and they were together in California. Vera Mae was deeply hurt and a lot of bitter words were exchanged as their marriage quickly deteriorated. Finally Vera Mae decided to leave and she went back to her grandmother's place in Mississippi. At the time she was a few months pregnant with their first child, Spencer. She stayed in Mississippi for eighteen months, during which time she and John sporadically corresponded. John really did love Vera Mae and he wanted her back but he was living single and footloose.

John and Vera Mae came close to divorce. In fact if things had continued to drift in the direction they were going, they both would have gravitated into other relationships. But Grandma Brillie, who sensed that Vera Mae and Toopie really needed to be together, encouraged her granddaughter to go back to California and settle things with him one way or the other.

For his part, John continued to have strong, loving feelings for Vera Mae despite his unfaithfulness. He would listen to Louis Armstrong's gravelly voice pleading for "a kiss to build a dream on" and long for wife and home and children. Family had always been important to him and in his gut he knew he needed to be married and he needed Vera Mae.

In September of 1954, when Vera Mae arrived back in Monrovia with eight-month-old Spencer, whom John had never seen, he was about ready to commit to her. When he saw his son and took him in his arms and loved him, that cinched it. John and Vera Mae came together, as if it were the first time, and their wounded marriage began to heal.

The hurt didn't just evaporate. It would leave its painful residue. But as John's new commitment took root and they began to grow together as they shared their lives, the pain he had caused Vera Mae gradually receded. Initially it was hard, and John felt his wife's maternal closeness to Spencer and her guarded emotional distance from him. But about a year after they got back together, Vera Mae gave birth to Joanie. It was this second child that really broke down the barrier between them.

John experienced a real sense of joy in Joanie's birth and babyhood. His love for both the children became a source of nourishment for his marriage. And so the family grew quickly. By 1957 they had added Philip and Derek and they were ready to move into a big house of their own. John was doing well, and they could afford to make a down payment. He was now a family man, a husband and father with a good job in a growing company. The good life and middle-class respectability were within his grasp.

When John Perkins went to work for Shopping Bag, it was a family-owned company with somewhere between fifteen and twenty stores. William "Rube" Hayden was one of the many entrepreneurs who struck it rich in the California postwar boom. Mr. Hayden was a self-made man who ran his company on a very personal basis. He made the rounds of his stores and talked with the employees. John found out quickly about Mr. Hayden's store visits and he seized the opportunity to meet the boss. He wanted to convey his eagerness to work hard and move up in the company. They talked at length, and John had the chance to fill in Mr. Hayden on the details of his life.

Hayden was impressed with this young man's energy and intelligence. He set him to work in the welding shop. One of Shopping Bag's distinct assets as they competed with other larger supermarket chains was the fact that they made much of their own equipment. Grocery carts, for example, and customized racks and baskets for the bakery trucks, were products of Shopping Bag's elaborate welding operation.

Working as a welder's helper, John rapidly assimilated the essentials of the craft. He became good friends with his supervisor, Norris Thompson. Norris was Rube Hayden's brother-in-law. Hayden had come to California from Kentucky back in 1930, and his wife had come from a poor Kentucky family. When his business really took off after the war, he brought a good many of her relatives to California and gave them jobs in the company. John's supervisor didn't have a lot more formal education than John, but given his big break, he had capitalized on it and worked his way up to his management position. He and John hit it off immediately.

As their friendship grew, John gained easy access to Mr. Hayden through his brother-in-law. He became a valuable man in the welding shop as his skills improved and he discovered he had the ability to read complicated diagrams and a growing interest in industrial design. He worked with his accustomed total commitment and he was scrupulously honest, never taking anything home from the shop. A prosperous future with Shopping Bag seemed assured as John began to reap some of the material benefits of his ambition.

John put his full energy into working and advancing. He was ever striving to get as far as he could from the two-room shacks with eight to a bed he had grown up with in Mississippi. Vera Mae, who had gone a year beyond high school in Mississippi and received training in cosmetology, was bringing in a second income working as a hairdresser. They both worked hard but they didn't mind. In California they could study, learn, work, and move up. This was a far cry from the oppressive atmosphere of Mississippi, where everything a black person tried to do met the staunch resistance of a hard, controlling white power.

It was good to be in a place where they could move ahead quickly by their own efforts, where nobody blocked their path. Yet moving up had its costs. So bent on carving out his niche in middle-class utopia was John that he found himself often running on his anxiety. Deep within was the old part of him that said, "They won't let a black man have real success . . . be in charge . . . be his own man." It was that sharp little doubt that clawed at his stomach. He ignored it and kept his mind on his work and he progressed. But he was restless and he had an ulcer by the time he was twenty-seven.

4

F_{AITH}

Despite his stalwart commitment to success and respectability, there was something in John that knew intuitively that life is somehow bigger than those things. He had a probing intellect that was never quite satisfied with the platitudes and pat solutions that most people settle for. So he began to explore a number of different religions. He wasn't sure what he was searching for but he longed for inner peace and a deeper sense of meaning to his life. The spiritual intensity and total commitment that members of some of the sects demonstrated sparked his interest.

He had known some black Jehovah's Witnesses in Mississippi. They had a powerful sense of mission and had endured a good deal of persecution from whites who called themselves Christians. When they knocked on his door with their tracts, he invited them in and asked them questions. They taught religion from the Bible rather than merely telling stories about God, as was common in the southern black church, and that impressed him.

Another sect that attracted his attention was Science of Mind. With his intellectual bent, the idea of a thinking man's religion held much appeal for him. The unreflective emotionalism of the religion he had grown up around grated against his nature. Science of Mind appeared attractive because it emphasized study and promised knowledge of the mind of God.

As John continued his spiritual search, he received a book from a follower of Father Divine. He read about the spiritual mogul who had risen in depression Harlem, preached racial equality, fed the poor, and started a worldwide movement of avid followers. A black American preacher with these kinds of accomplishments was certainly impressive. But Father Divine claimed to be God, and John figured he was probably just a very good hustler.

At the same time as he was looking into these religions, he was going with Vera Mae when she occasionally attended Second Baptist Church. John had grown up with a certain prejudice against the black church. The Perkins family had rejected it as something that makes you weak and dependent. He thought of all those good, churchgoing black people in Mississippi, how they would get to shouting in their emotional meetings, and how the preacher drove a new Cadillac, and ate what he liked, while the people were dirt poor and scraped and saved to put their money in the collection plate. He thought of how church people shuffled, how they always humbled down to the white bosses, postponing all good living and all self-respect until the sweet by-and-by. These things made him wince at the thought of being a Christian.

But he knew Vera Mae was a strong, intelligent woman. He loved her and he respected her family. He understood that the Christian beliefs that Vera Mae and her grandmother professed made them better people and helped them through the pain of life. So he went to church with Vera Mae, and with his penchant for really getting involved in whatever he was doing, he even did some ushering. Despite John's critical attitude toward it, Christianity in its black American Protestant expression was ever prominent in his mind.

It was about this time that Vera Mae began sending Spencer, now three years old, to Sunday school at a little church near their house. They now lived on Pomona Street in Monrovia in a little house with a white picket fence. The church was in the neighborhood, so Spencer could walk there with his mother. It was a lot different from most of the churches in the black community. It was called the Protestant Catholic Church, and it was a white church with a smattering of blacks in the congregation. John would later find out that this church was a mission of a denomination founded in Illinois. They had built their own town there, which they called Zion, and they had named all the streets with biblical names.

This pietistic little sect had sent its missionaries to California, where it had planted a church in the black community in the San Gabriels. As they opened the rudiments of faith to the little children, they touched their spirits. And when Spencer came home from church, he acted different. Something seemed to be lighting him up and he wanted to pray and recite Bible verses. At Sunday school they gave the kids prizes for bringing someone to church, and Spencer thought he might be able to get his daddy to come.

John was curious about a church that could have such an impact on Spencer. He decided to go over there and see what they were teaching. On a September Sunday morning, during that time of the year when Southern California bakes in the hot dry sun before it slowly cools down and ambles into the rainy season, John walked down the street holding Spencer's hand. John's interest was aroused as he sat in on the Sunday school and worship service at the Protestant Catholic Church that day.

He had a friend, Calvin Bourne, who had been trying to get him to go to church with him over in Pasadena. Calvin wasn't like the stereotype of the weak southern black churchgoing man that had been fixed in John's mind years before. Calvin was intelligent, hardworking, and really excited about his faith and he wanted to share it with John. John decided to take Calvin up on his offer to take him to his church, a little Church of Christ Holiness in northwest Pasadena. It was a black church, and John thought he would feel more at home there than he had in the Protestant Catholic Church down the street. So one Sunday he and Vera Mae packed the children into their fifty-six Chevy and drove over to Calvin's church.

When John Perkins walked into the Bethlehem Church of Christ Holiness with his wife and two children that day in 1957, he wondered if it would be much different from Second Baptist. Calvin was there and he introduced John and Vera Mae around. John found a close community of people there who really took an interest in his life. They invited his family to their homes for dinner and they earnestly discussed Bible teaching. Other than the Jehovah's Witnesses, John had never met Christians before who wanted to talk about the Bible in any depth. And these people were so warm and friendly. They were like a big family and they wanted him to join them.

John began attending a Bible class at the church. He had never heard the Bible presented in a way that elicited real personal commitment. Hearing and reading about the apostle Paul's experiences moved him deeply. Here was a man who had hated and persecuted Christians and then he was suddenly and completely turned around. He became so sold-out to his faith that he devoted his life to spreading it despite all kinds of persecution. What could cause such a radical change in a man? John was captivated by Paul's drive and motivation.

The person who could completely focus himself and his energy on a single, productive goal always attracted John. People who overcame great obstacles to achieve success were the ones he admired most, some of his own people like Joe Louis, Jackie Robinson, and Ralph Bunche. John knew that, given a chance, black people could achieve greatness, just as these men had, and he burned for his own achievement. But it wasn't the achievement, the money, the house, family, and respectability in themselves that drove John. There was something deeper, and it was that deeper longing that opened him to the experience of faith.

The family John had grown up around in Mississippi—his grandmother, aunts, uncles, and cousins—had given him strong, solid roots. He knew his kinfolk had loved him, but there had always been something missing, a hole in his heart. He hadn't had a mother and he hadn't had a father who was there for him. He had never felt that natural sense of belonging that a child can feel with a real father and mother.

As he worked to build his own family and be a husband to his wife and a father to his children, he was always moving against a deeply embedded sense of his own inadequacy. It made him anxious, and gnawed at his stomach, so he worked all the harder. He went to Santa Anita and bet on the horses, losing his anxiety for a moment in the excitement. But when he was alone with his thoughts, lying in bed or commuting to work, his sense of inadequacy haunted him. It seemed like all his work and success, his family, and the things he was able to buy could not fill the void and give him a feeling of belonging.

It was the overpowering need to belong, to fill the emptiness that came from never having been cherished as someone's beloved son, that drew John toward the familial warmth of the people at Bethlehem Church of Christ Holiness. But it was more than the people, as nice as they were. He was learning as he went to the Bible classes and read and studied more deeply, that God can meet us on a personal level. He began to understand that if he gave himself to Christ, he would actually be able to walk with a fatherly God and have his presence inside. He would belong to God.

A line in the letter Paul had written to the Galatian Christians struck him at the core of his mind and reverberated there. Paul so closely identified himself with Christ that he said he was crucified with him, and Christ loved Paul so much that he lived in him and worked through him. Paul was saying that his faith, the faith that gave him the drive to plant churches all over the Roman Empire, even while they were throwing him in jail and beating him and trying to kill him, was the actual presence of Christ in him. John was awestruck by that possibility. It was an amazing idea that he could have that kind of deep connection to God, that God would give that to him. He would belong to God, as Christ lived in him, loving and motivating him to do good.

When John Perkins became a Christian in Bethlehem Church of Christ Holiness, he felt for the first time that sense of belonging he had missed all his life. It filled him with a new feeling of warm joy, and the old ache went away. He grew close to the people in the church and he threw himself into Christian work with the all-encompassing energy that propelled him in everything important to him. John didn't get involved in Christian activity to make himself acceptable to God or even so much out of the gratefulness to God that he deeply felt. He plunged into the Lord's work because it flowed out of him naturally, just the way that verse in Galatians said it did for Paul.

He understood on an intuitive level that Christian faith meant letting go of his life so that the Lord could get hold of it and work through it. As a child John had gone to church once in a while and he knew that people getting happy was supposed to be caused by the Holy Ghost. But now he had a whole different understanding of the Holy Ghost. He knew that when he gave himself to God that it was God's Holy Spirit who began to work in him and motivate him to live the Christian life. Now he could understand what it was that drove Paul to do the selfless things he did.

John had believed in himself. He had believed that he could be successful—have a good job with good money, a wife and family, a nice house in a nice neighborhood—if he just worked hard enough for those things. Like successful Americans back to Ben Franklin's time, John Perkins was a bright, positive, hardworking young man who bent all his energies toward self-advancement. He was very much in the process of achieving something but he had no inner peace. He felt a deep-seated loneliness that he tried to escape through work, playing the horses, or whatever could take him away from himself. But suddenly God had broken into his life, and he no longer felt like he had to run from himself. He could begin to accept who he was, because he knew God loved him and wanted him in his family.

So John could let go of his need to achieve, prove himself, and acquire respectability. He knew he was accepted and loved by the One who created the whole universe. What else could he do but let that great Father God work in him and use him to build his alternative kingdom in the world? What kind of kingdom that was, John was just beginning to learn. He knew it was based on loving others and giving self to them. In that kingdom John knew he could no longer strive for power and success.

As John thought about the alternative values of God's kingdom, as opposed to the values of the world, he began to realize that when he joined himself to God he took on "a whole new structure of life." That's the way he put it years later when he reflected on the heady days of his conversion. He wasn't sure yet what form this new life would take but he knew he would live it for God, and that thought both excited him and gave him a sense of contentment he had not known before. John would retain his tremendous drive to advance and achieve, but it would be absorbed into his newly born passion to serve a God who loved him.

5

CALLED

The brothers and sisters in the Bethlehem Church of Christ Holiness, with their strong commitment to a biblical faith, provided John with a good nurturing community. The older women acted as mothers of the church, and they mothered him, feeding an ancient need in him. He became close to Calvin Bourne and the other men at church. With his hunger for knowledge and love of ideas, John eagerly consumed the Bible lessons in Reverend Howard's Sunday school class. Reverend Howard was the assistant to Matthew Richardson, the pastor of the church, whom John also got to know.

Having two pastors in such a small church was a clear indication that this church was serious about the Lord's business. John was aware that back in Mississippi one pastor usually served three or four churches and preached at each one only about once a month. There was never anyone with a preacher's credentials to teach the Sunday school.

John thrived as his appetite for knowledge of the Bible was stimulated. He had previously absorbed the point of view common among modern secular people that the Bible is a book of stories, myths, and superstitions irrelevant to life in today's world. In the South it seemed that the ones most active in church and apt to quote the Bible were mostly old women and men who kowtowed to the whites. His view of the Bible changed radically once he encountered the living Christ. Now his eyes were open to the impenetrable depth of Scripture and he found he just couldn't get enough teaching.

As John's desire to learn and to get involved in Christian work grew, he talked about these things with his wife. Vera Mae had felt pangs of guilt when John had first experienced conversion. Here she was a committed Christian who had married an unbeliever and she had neglected to pray for his salvation and hadn't done much to encourage his faith. In fact she was as caught up in the pressures of making it as John had been. Working at the hairdressing salon and caring for her little children made it easy to let spiritual disciplines slip into the background. But when John began to apply his intense, active temperament to matters of faith, Vera Mae felt a strong rekindling of her own. She came alongside him and they began to work together.

A neighbor friend, Wilnora Price, who had been attending classes in Child Evangelism Fellowship, encouraged her and John to get involved. This brought back to Vera Mae a flood of warm memories, which she shared with her husband. Back in the Oak Ridge Church when she was growing up, a Child Evangelism teacher had come to her Sunday school class. He used brightly colored illustrations and flannel figures that he stuck up on a big flannel-covered board resting on an easel. He had told the salvation story this way, and Vera Mae traced her first real faith commitment to this experience.

The flannel graph was and is the basic tool of Child Evangelism Fellowship. For well over fifty years they have been putting out materials and training people to start little Good News Clubs in their neighborhoods, teaching the gospel to children after school. John responded enthusiastically to the Child Evangelism concepts, as he and Vera Mae took the training and began having regular children's classes in their home. Vera Mae, who had a knack for working closely with children, would make child evangelism her special province.

As John moved into ministry, his appetite for greater spiritual knowledge was stimulated. Through the Child Evangelism network he began to meet people who could feed this desire. Mrs. Price put him in touch with two white Christians, Mary Feastal and Wayne Leitch.

As he expanded his circle of association in the Christian world, John was coming in contact with a number of white evangelicals. At first he felt uneasy at the prospect of being around white Christians. White church members had never seemed like real Christians to him in Mississippi. He knew how religious and Bible-quoting white people were in the South, and they were the same sorts who kept blacks poor and hungry. They were the same people who lynched and castrated black men, the same kind as the deputy who had shot Clyde. Old, bitter feelings welled up in him when he thought of white churchgoers. But now, as he ventured into wider circles in response to his spiritual hunger, he was meeting a very different kind of white Christian.

Mary Feastal had been a missionary in Brazil. She had a Christian bookstore in Pasadena, where she guided John to a treasure trove of resources ranging over the many aspects of Christian faith. He pored over in-depth Bible commentaries, biblical and church histories, books about foreign missions and missions to the poor, personal stories of faith, and books about so many different kinds of evangelism. John read voraciously in all these areas. But he wanted to go deeper. He wanted to study the Bible formally. He thought about enrolling in Bible college, though an accredited one would have demanded a high school diploma or the equivalent for his admission. Both Mary Feastal and Wilnora Price encouraged John to go to Wayne Leitch's Bible classes, so he decided to sit in on one at Mr. Leitch's Child Evangelism Training Center in El Monte.

The class was held on Tuesday nights, and John could easily go there from work at Shopping Bag's welding shop, which was right there in El Monte. He arrived a little late that first night. They were singing choruses before the teaching began. John slipped into a seat at the back of the room. He quickly noticed that the class was all white and mostly women. As he focused on the teacher, he saw a man in his seventies speaking with quiet authority. He listened intently as Mr. Leitch taught Bible and he was enthralled at the depth to which the teacher went as he explained the background and content of a passage.

At the end of the lecture John made his way to the front of the room. He wanted to ask if he could come regularly but he felt a bit hesitant, not sure if this class full of white people really wanted him there. As John approached Mr. Leitch and was reaching out to shake his hand, Mr. Leitch threw both his arms around John and hugged him. This spontaneous display of warmth immediately brought down any barriers John was feeling.

Mr. Leitch welcomed John to the class, and when John told him of his desire to go to Bible school, he asked John if he would consider letting him take him on as a student to personally disciple him. For some years he had been trying to reach out to the African American community with some false starts and not much success, but in John he had

John and Wayne Leitch, the Child Evangelism Fellowship missionary who discipled him, were reunited in Pasadena, 1981.

finally found the eager, supple young mind he had long been seeking. The two men developed a warm, close relationship, as John drove over to the Child Evangelism Training Center twice a week after work.

The training center was a storefront that Mr. Leitch and his wife also used as living quarters. They had built a little apartment in the back, so the atmosphere was homey, with Mrs. Leitch serving drinks and snacks, as her husband dipped deeply in the well of Scripture and offered John the waters that would slake his powerful thirst. Mr. Leitch had the serenity, the kind and gentle manner that flowed out of a lifetime of learning to give himself to others. John had never felt so close to a white person. They became best friends, and John would eventually name one of his boys after Wayne Leitch.

John Perkins's adult education thus became a tutorial, a practical, hands-on experience that satisfied emotional as well as spiritual and intellectual wants. This personal approach would actually work to increase the effectiveness and originality of his thinking. John's Christian education never had the canned quality that institution-bound learning usually has. There was none of the pompous theorizing that academic people, whether sacred or profane, love to indulge in. As he was learning the principles of faith, studying with Wayne Leitch, he was constantly seeking to apply them in his life, with his own family and with the children in his Child Evangelism classes. Mr. Leitch was always there to give John the close personal counsel he needed. He was one of the two father figures who guided John at this pivotal point in his development.

This was a period in John's life when his old unmet childhood longing for a father would be at least partially filled. Some years earlier, not long after he had gotten out of the service, Aunt Coot had telephoned him in California to tell him of his father's death. Jap had become sick with a heart condition and had moved in with her. While John was back in New Hebron for the funeral, Aunt Coot told him that his father had really wanted to see him. This was a surprise to John. Suddenly he realized his father had always cared about him.

He asked Aunt Coot why she hadn't told him Jap was sick and wanted him. She explained that Jap had expected to see John when he came back to Mississippi to get Vera Mae after his discharge from the service. But John didn't go back to Mississippi, and Jap didn't feel free to ask him to come just to see him. John was sad, realizing that his father had really loved him, but they had never had a chance to get any closer, and now he was gone. He thought about how his father's second wife, Miss Susan, who had no children, never really wanted John or his brother and sisters around. Jap had passively gone along with her feelings, and as a result his children never developed a relationship with him.

Men really need their fathers not only when they are growing up, but after they have attained adulthood. In the clans and tribes of traditional societies, fathers mentor their sons and initiate them into the growing responsibilities of male adulthood. Just as young women need the advice and teaching of older women of the extended family and the community, so young men need to receive the wisdom of male elders. These mentoring traditions have atrophied among both genders in America for a complex of reasons. The absentee parent, particularly the father, is a common malady of contemporary life. The problem of the absent father was evident earlier in the African American family because racial discrimination closed off a good livelihood to the men and made many of them transient.

John Perkins gained a good deal of stability from his extended family while he was growing up. His uncles, particularly Bud, loved him and provided him with examples of courage and resourcefulness. But the lack of a continuous, close involvement of a responsible father set him on his own early, making his transition to husband and father very difficult. He was always a good provider but he had to learn as he went along how to be a good husband and father.

After his conversion he began to develop a sense that God was the Father of a family of the faithful, and in that family he had placed people who could take on fatherly responsibilities. In John's life Wayne Leitch was the man who gave him spiritual fathering. The one who became the complete father in his life was "Papa" Wilson.

Mama and Papa Wilson were matriarchal and patriarchal figures to the young black Christian community in Monrovia. Jimmie Wilson came to California in the thirties from New York, where he had grown up. He had been involved with horse racing in the East, exercising the horses of wealthy men who liked to invest in the excitement of the track. His compact, light physique made Wilson a perfect jockey and he acquired a good bit of experience in the saddle before coming to the West Coast. He came to Pasadena chauffeuring one of these racehorse-owning employers.

With the coming of the Second World War, he was one of the African Americans who got "drafted" into the defense industry. Again his stature worked in his favor. Douglas Aircraft employed him to wedge himself into small spaces in the planes to do the riveting. He could have stayed at Douglas after the war and prospered with the postwar defense boom but he was a born entrepreneur and he couldn't wait to get on his own.

His original idea was to get some land, start a chicken farm, and open a fried chicken restaurant. While still working at Douglas during the war, he borrowed money and added it to his own, investing in a big piece of real estate, fifteen or twenty acres, in Monrovia. The land was still cheap at that time. He built the chicken ranch but he never opened the restaurant. Instead, he worked the ranch while still crawling around the planes at Douglas and he sold chickens and the vegetables he raised on his acreage to retailers. When the boom came and the city subdivided the land, he was able to sell the lots at a sizable profit, buy houses, and rent them out. With capital from his real estate interests he started a lucrative janitorial service, which would service shops and office buildings in Monrovia, Pasadena, and Arcadia.

By the time John Perkins met him, Papa Wilson had long been a well-established businessman, respected and very visible in the San Gabriel Valley's black community. He was a pillar of Second Baptist Church, the black church with the most prestige—even if its worship wasn't the most inspiring—in the area. With his abiding belief that a black man had every bit as much right to success as a white man, Wilson became a vocal civil rights advocate and served as the local head of the NAACP.

Jimmie Wilson met his wife, Elizabeth, just before the start of the Second World War, when they were both well along toward middle age. After they married, he moved into her home in Monrovia. John had met Mrs. Wilson before his conversion, through Vera Mae. A leader at Second Baptist, Elizabeth Wilson was the popularly acknowledged senior woman of the Monrovia Christian community. She had a habit of visiting people who had just received Christ, and when she heard about John, she went to see him and Vera Mae. This was on a Tuesday morning. John was doing shift work and working nights at the time. He enjoyed her visit, and when she was getting ready to leave he asked her to pray with him. This turned out to be such a moment of inspiration that Mrs. Wilson came back every Tuesday morning for some weeks following to pray with John.

The Wilsons' only child, a son, had been killed in an automobile accident. The death left a painful void in their lives, one that business and church work did not satisfactorily fill. And so Mama and Papa Wilson found themselves becoming surrogate parents to John and Vera Mae, neither of whom had had their own parents involved in their lives. Much of the Perkins family's spare time was spent with the Wilsons.

They went to the Wilsons for Sunday dinner after church, and John would sit and listen to Papa Wilson hold forth on a variety of subjects. He talked a lot about people, but not in an unkind or gossipy way. He used them as examples of success and failure, good habits or bad habits. "You see, Bill Smith thought he was somethin' special, didn't take a good look around before he invested his hard-earned money, didn't take advice from older guys who'd been 'round the block a few times. So he invested it in fly-by-night schemes and lost it all."

Papa Wilson's stories of people were lively, concrete object lessons, like the gospel parables. "Don't be like this preacher, let me tell you 'bout him," he would say, and then talk about how the preacher exploited his people. And he would go into detail talking about the good habits of the people he helped financially and the bad ones of the people he didn't. John admired Papa Wilson deeply. He was a hardworking black man who understood economics and he had made it in a white man's world. He was smart but he was also a moral man, a good Christian who dealt plainly. John thought he had the wisdom of Solomon, so he sat and listened to him and expected him to be right about most everything.

John had a need for an older man to take authority over him in this way. Papa Wilson gave him a clear sense of how to conduct the business of life: what was right and wrong, and why it was important to be truthful and open. It was especially important to John to have such close, loving counsel from a strong, accomplished black man of the previous generation. His father had been neither strong nor involved with him. His uncles had demonstrated strength and had shown him how to do things but they lacked the intensive, caring involvement and staunch morality that Papa Wilson showed him.

John became something of a celebrity in local evangelical Christian circles, both black and white. Not long after he had been converted, he was asked to speak at Second Baptist Church's mission conference. The people of Second Baptist were amazed by this young migrant from Mississippi, amazed that he had gotten converted in the first place and amazed that he was literate and could communicate gospel truth so well. There were some not so subtle class divisions in the black community. People at Second Baptist represented a more educated elite, and like the children of immigrants who look down on "green horns," these urban church members looked down on recent arrivals from the South.

The white evangelical churches' prolonged battle against modernism and secularism had made them defensive, and out of that defensiveness they had largely cut themselves off from most Americans unlike themselves. Evangelical insularity had had its benefits. It had shored up Christian orthodoxy and stimulated strong group identity and cohesion and it had been a powerful way of resisting negative influences from society at large. But the price had been the formation of a homogeneous cultural community that had become white, middle class, and largely suburban. In so ghettoizing themselves, American evangelicals had increasingly lost contact with and sensitivity to blacks and many of the other ethnic cultures.

There was little interest in evangelistic outreach among most of these status-conscious church members. As John became known to people in the white evangelical churches, whose lives had kept them separate from and ignorant of black Christians, they too acted surprised and curious.

Because of the evangelical basis of his faith and his involvement with Child Evangelism and Wayne Leitch, John began to make contact with a number of white evangelicals, and it was in evangelical churches that he was invited to speak. In the late fifties, when John became a Christian, liberal seminaries were responding positively to Martin Luther King Jr. and the black civil rights movement. King took doctoral training at the Methodist Boston University School of Theology.

Fundamentalists and evangelicals, on the other hand, either ignored or out-and-out rejected King, his Southern Christian Leadership Conference, and the black church–based civil rights movement because of the liberal influences on them.

This animosity between the evangelical churches and the civil rights movement eventually became an issue that John would come to deal with frontally, but in his early years of faith he spoke as a fellow evangelical. Because he was black and a migrant from the rural South, he was inevitably a curiosity in white evangelical churches. His racial and class background contrasted with that of these white middle-class folk. The Bethlehem Church of Christ Holiness, Child Evangelism Fellowship, and Wayne Leitch were intensely evangelical in their orientation, and so was John. His Christian experience led him to focus on the necessity of personal conversion and this gave him kinship with white evangelicals.

Working with the children almost every afternoon at his house and seeing them respond with growing enthusiasm was deeply gratifying to John. As was his way, he went into a new project with both feet and as he got results he went in deeper. His interest in sharing the message that was transforming his life spread to new areas. He linked up with four friends—Mrs. Wilson; two preachers, Curry Brown and George Moore; and another layman, Jim Winston. They called their little group the Fishermen's Gospel Crusade and their purpose was to go door-to-door in the black community, sharing the gospel with the unchurched. They went about this task with a sense of commitment and regularity that got them good results.

Some of the people they visited became interested and took the first steps of faith. This fired John's enthusiasm and he looked for other avenues of evangelistic activity. One of the Christian bookstore owners he met put him in touch with the Christian Businessmen's Committee of Arcadia-Monrovia. This was an all-white group of men who were involved in evangelistic activities. Among them was John McGill, who was a board member of Child Evangelism Fellowship. Beginning with their common passion for working with little children, he and John became close friends.

It was through his involvement with these Christian businessmen that John became aware of the prison work camps that had been set up in the San Bernardino Mountains by the California Youth Authority. The young convicts in these camps were teenage boys between the ages of thirteen and seventeen. John had discovered in his evangelistic work that he was particularly drawn to working with boys and he was effective with them. After his conversion and the growth of his relationships with Wayne Leitch and Papa Wilson, he became deeply aware of the need that young boys have for men who can love and guide them. And when two men in the Businessmen's Committee asked him to go with them to do evangelism with the boys in the work camps, he jumped at the chance.

When he got there, he noticed that the majority of these boys were black and many of them had come out of the Deep South. This gave him pause. He remembered what murderous feelings had gripped his mind after Clyde was killed. He remembered the tinge of hope mixed with his bitter grief he had felt on the long train ride out of the South to a more promising California. He remembered the chance he had been given to prove himself at the foundry, and again at Shopping Bag. He had been fortunate, fortunate to get these breaks, and even more fortunate now to have this relationship with God that was changing his life. Why hadn't these kids had these kinds of breaks? Surely God must love them too.

These are the thoughts that went through John's mind as he prepared to preach to these troubled youngsters. They looked suspiciously at this black man who had come with the two white men. John told his story with an intense feeling that was a response to the kinship he felt with these teenage convicts. He knew only too well that but for the grace of God he could have been one of them. Many of the boys connected with John's deep feeling for them. Some of them broke down in tears and some of them asked to receive the Lord into their lives.

Something happened to John that day in the mountains with the boys. He had looked in their faces and he had seen himself. He knew that these black kids who were coming out of the South had much the same inadequate education he had had. They came west with their parents, or maybe only one parent, and it was difficult to compete with these Californians who were always better educated. John himself, despite his very real accomplishments, always carried a sense of inferiority due to his lack of schooling. He had compensated well for it but he had stomach ulcers to show for his efforts.

John thought long and hard about why these southern black kids were failing in free and sunny California. He knew their minds, how they'd been conditioned by the Jim Crow system. And he knew how much energy it took to push against the idea, hammered in by life in the South, that if you're black, you'll never amount to much. It was always easier to get into some kind of hustle. But then came the trouble and the police record. The inner voice that insisted you were nothing got louder and more forceful. You figured the cards were stacked against your making it legitimately, so you might as well get yours the other way. John understood these things on a level that his two white evangelical companions from the Christian Businessmen's Committee couldn't begin to relate to. He guessed that was why they'd brought him.

John reflected that if these kids had been exposed to the gospel through Child Evangelism and if they had had the kind of discipling that Mr. Leitch was giving him, they would have been less apt to fall into crime. He knew the problems they had were complex and weren't going to be solved overnight but he couldn't help thinking that somebody needed to go to the source of these problems. If young men in the South could get real conversion and sound Bible training instead of emotionalism and if they could get some solid education, then they'd have a better chance of making it in life. As he turned these ideas over and over in his mind in the weeks after he went to the work camps, he found himself thinking about going back to Mississippi. His heart had been burning for evangelism since his conversion and he began to think Mississippi was a good field for it.

There were lots of churchgoers there but few who really understood and lived by the gospel. He thought maybe he could make a difference among the people he had grown up around. There were lots of big, prosperous, urban black churches here in California, and there were black people who had college degrees who had what it takes to do evangelism here. But Mississippi was a place where his people still groaned under terrible disadvantage, and when they came here to California in search of opportunity, their boys didn't have what they needed to compete successfully and they often ended up in trouble. More and more as he thought these things over, John thought God was calling him back to Mississippi.

Going back to Mississippi, back into the ugly racist system that had held him down and spit on him, was not an easy decision. John and Vera Mae were doing well in California and they had carved out a good life for their children. John was making good money, and his bosses liked and respected him at Shopping Bag's welding shop, where he was now learning to do industrial design and enjoying it. And Vera Mae was adding to the family's income with her hairdressing. Two more boys, Philip and Derek, were born in 1958 and 1959, and now Vera Mae was pregnant with their fifth child, Deborah. It was a good thing the family was doing so well, because they had certainly outgrown their little white cottage on Pomona Street. They were proud of their accomplishment and hopeful about their future as they made the down payment on a rambling twelve-room house on Los Angeles Street.

What's more, John had a meaningful Christian life, a ministry right here. He and Vera Mae were making a big difference in the neighborhood children's lives with their daily Child Evangelism classes. And there was the close fellowship of the Fishermen's Gospel Crusade, which was finding a willing audience among many adults in the area. John's association with the white Christian businessmen was further broadening the scope of his work. By most people's standards, including those of most devout Christians, John and Vera Mae were leading exemplary lives, and God was blessing them.

Yet the strong sense of a call to go back to Mississippi and help his people wouldn't go away. John shared his vision with Vera Mae and met with her strong resistance. Back when she had married John, there had been mixed feelings in her family and even in the back of her own mind. After all, she was marrying an unbelieving Perkins, from the outlaw Perkins family. Yet they had gotten through the rough period when it looked like they might break up, and John had become a strong Christian. They were doing well, they were doing meaningful Christian work, and this was a good environment for the children.

There was nothing in Mississippi but poverty and white folks who stood in the way and would harm the family if they should step out of line, which Vera Mae knew they would. Her powerful need to protect and nurture her family kept her firmly committed to their present course and shielded her from being able to catch John's vision. John and Vera Mae reached an impasse as they pulled in opposite directions.

Then a strange thing happened. John began to lose weight and become weaker day by day. He went to the Veterans Hospital where they treated him for ulcers, and the ulcers healed, but John continued to grow weaker and thinner. With his powerful drive, he kept going to work until one day in early November of 1959, he was so weak and frail that he couldn't get out of bed. As he lay there, Vera Mae was becoming more and more worried about his condition. Her fervent prayers at last led her to let go of her own will for John, the children, and herself.

This is a place to which people come in the midst of life-threatening crises, when they reach the end of their resources and they discern that they can't control their own lives or the ultimate fate of their loved ones. They have no choice but to let go, giving themselves and their whole situation to God. In this way, Vera Mae released her will and she received a profound sense of peace. She felt free to tell John that she would no longer oppose his going back to Mississippi.

As they became reunited in purpose, John began to recover rapidly. He felt well enough by the end of the month to make what would be a six-week trip to Mississippi to prepare the way for his family's move. His sense of his mission was so strong that he had let no time elapse between his recovery and this trip. Arriving in Mississippi in late November, he went straight to New Hebron and began to speak in the local black churches. He told the people that he was coming back from California to teach Bible and do evangelism with their children and youth.

As the year and the decade ended, giving way to a new and turbulent era in American life, the civil rights movement was heating up. In a few months a group of black students in Greensboro, North Carolina, would begin their sit-ins at segregated department store lunch counters. The Freedom Rides were about a year away. White supremacists in the South had committed themselves to "massive resistance" to school desegregation and any other kind of "race mixing." And John Perkins was getting ready to give back his own piece of the Great Migration and the American Dream. He was about to go back into a southern volcano that was on the verge of eruption as civil rights leaders mobilized vocal protest, demonstration, and nonviolent confrontation on southern streets.

John was moving his prospering family to the poorest state in the country, a state that had long been corroding in the acids of racism and was again about to be a bloody battleground for this latest phase of America's ongoing civil war. By any normal standard of logic what John was about to do made no sense. His progress had been a sign of hope, a vindication of the ancient American ideal of opportunity and advancement for the downtrodden, a reaffirmation, proclaiming that black people can make it in America. At least that's the interpretation that could have been made of John's life since he left Mississippi. But John had a whole different view of it.

He had what the Quakers like to call an Inner Light telling him that if he failed to address the problem among his people in Mississippi at its source, any further evangelism he would do in California would be hollow. He had only a general idea of what he needed to do; it awaited his subsequent action to be fleshed out. But he had a deep sense that he could do something back there that would make a much greater difference than all the success he could garner in the promised land.

He began to take the first steps, gaining support for his mission and scouting out the territory. This is where John's association with white evangelicals and their churches began to take on real significance. Many of his friends among the Christian Businessmen's Committee were prominent men and influential church leaders. John McGill, with whom he had become so close as they shared involvement with Child Evangelism, was chairman of the Mayflower Food Stores, one of Shopping Bag's big rivals. McGill introduced John to his pastor, Glenn Zachary at Arcadia Union Church. Zachary in turn put John in touch with a number of the evangelical luminaries in Southern California.

John met J. Vernon McGee, pastor of Lincoln Avenue Presbyterian Church in Pasadena. McGee would later shepherd the well-known Church of the Open Door in downtown Los Angeles. He received John warmly, expressing interest in his work. With his thick Texas drawl, he was a popular radio Bible teacher. Fundamentalist preachers had pioneered religious radio programming almost as soon as the medium had been invented back in the twenties. On his international daily broadcast, *Through the Bible,* McGee would wend his folksy way from Genesis to Revelation, in a five-year period over and over again as the second millennium moved toward its end. After his death in the late eighties his ghostlike voice continued in taped syndication.

John also met Bob Pierce, the founder of World Vision, the interdenominational foreign missions organization that would become singular in its economic-development work among Third World peoples. Zachary introduced John to Jack MacArthur, pastor of Calvary Bible Church in Burbank. MacArthur also had a radio program, a weekly gospel message called *The Voice of Calvary.* MacArthur's became the first white evangelical church to make a sustained monetary commitment to support John's vision of evangelism among African Americans in Mississippi. Out of his gratitude John would christen his new work Voice of Calvary.

After he returned from his exploratory trip to Mississippi, as he was getting ready to move his family there, MacArthur's and Zachary's churches committed seventy-five dollars a month between them to help with his support. John McGill and another businessman named Dave Peacock, whose fortune was in air-conditioning and refrigeration, also made contributions. Peacock took up an offering from the Christian Businessmen's Committee and gave it to John just before he left. These white evangelicals were few in number and their financial commitment was limited but, joining with John at the beginning of his mission, they became pioneers in drawing evangelicals out of their isolation from African Americans.

It was significant that in a racially divided America, this nascent black ministry was starting out with some white backing. It was because of John's own evangelical orientation and commitment that white evangelical churches were offering their aid. If he had given them any notion that his ministry would become deeply involved in the fight for social justice and black equality, he might have had to go elsewhere for white support.

John's initial vision was within the bounds of child evangelism and Bible teaching, safely consistent with mainstream white American evangelicalism. But as John began to relate to his people in Mississippi as a Christian, seeking to better their lives, he began to see that their spiritual needs were intertwined with all the rest of their needs and that to work effectively he would have to do more than teach Bible. He would have to address the needs of the whole person. This insight, which would come quickly, had momentous implications.

The black holiness church John attended as he first came to faith was a part of the broader holiness movement that began in the nineteenth century and encompassed both black and white churches. The same evangelical movements and divisions that molded the various white denominational traditions also influenced the course of development among African American churches. But while black church beliefs had much in common with white evangelicalism, its practice grew out of the distinct needs and cultural expression of the African American people.

The preacher and his church as they had arisen on the plantations in the days of slavery, had addressed two essential needs, the one more emotional and otherworldly, the other more material and immediate. The passionate emotion that came to characterize black preaching grew out of an oppressed people's need for catharsis and for release and redemption from the pain of life. The other need, no less emotional at its base, was the need for freedom and justice in the here and now. In the civil rights era, preachers like Martin Luther King Jr. would combine emotional crescendo with the prophetic call for justice to galvanize the movement. John Perkins, more Bible teacher than preacher, would combine preaching for social justice with biblical exposition. To appreciate the religious currents and cross-currents that flowed around him, it is useful to have some historical understanding of the African American church. An essay appended to this work attempts to provide the rudiments of that understanding.

PART 2
THE MISSISSIPPI WORK
1960–1982

6

FATHERS

obert Archie Buckley was born in 1889 in Smith County in the piney woods region of south central Mississippi. His parents were a part of the resilient minority of black yeomen. They were tough people who retained their pride and determination to get and hold onto their own land. When he was about eight years old, his daddy was put in prison on a false charge. A man had come to stay with them and had broken into a local general store. The sheriff came out and accused his daddy of being in on it. There was no evidence, no stolen goods, no witnesses, but they imprisoned him anyway.

He hired a lawyer to plead for him, but that did him no good, and he sat in the penitentiary at Parchman and he drank the bad water, got malaria, and died. That was in 1901. During that period strong black men in Smith County were trying to take a stand against whites who were raping their daughters and kicking black people around. But the whites overwhelmed them. The Klan came out and burned down their houses and many were killed and others were falsely imprisoned.

Mrs. Buckley held onto her land and eventually paid off the mortgage. Young Archie got about four years of schooling, enough to learn a little reading and writing and not much else. But he had a sharp mind that always wanted to dig to the taproot of a subject. His mother was a churchgoing woman and, from the time he was little, he had heard the emotional calls to be saved and had seen people get worked up, happy with the Holy Ghost. He was fourteen or fifteen when he was sitting in a revival meeting where the preacher had been exhorting the people to repent and be saved. He felt moved to go down front and sit on the mourners' bench. He wasn't sure what exactly to pray, so he said: "I don't know how to present myself to you, Lord, but what this man has said, I want that. I want it."

And he prayed that same prayer as he sat there three successive nights on the mourners' bench. The old folks had told him about all variety of ecstatic experiences, describing what had happened to them when they received Christ. Some said they had looked at their hardworking hands, and their hands had looked new. He looked at his, and they didn't look even a little bit newer. He sat and waited and waited for some kind of overpowering spiritual experience, and none came. On the last night of the revival, somebody said to him, "You got all you'll ever have. What you holdin' back for? You ain't never going to get no more than that."

So he asked if he could be admitted to the church. He simply made a decision, a commitment with his mind. He was never swept up in a wave of emotion nor did he have any supernatural experience at this time. This was in keeping with the kind of person he was.

As a man, Archie Buckley was not one to bend the truth or water it down to accommodate people's wants. When they asked him to be a deacon, he at first turned them down. He had read the qualifications for deacon that Paul listed in his first letter to Timothy and he knew he didn't come up to those requirements. He was drinking and not walking with the Lord, so he didn't feel right about being a deacon.

But while he was in his field, leaning against his plow one day, the Lord came to him, like a vision, and he lifted his head and took notice. God told him that when he had joined the church, he had signed a contract to live under the church's rule of life. And now he was breaking that contract with the way he was living. If he was going to continue this way, he had better resign from the church. But then God led him to hear a preacher in another church nearby, and that preacher was explaining the difference between law and grace, the kind of preaching you rarely heard in black churches in Mississippi. He found out that he had been taking God's call on his life to mean that he had to obey a set of laws to be saved. The way this preacher explained it, he wasn't saved by the works he did for God; he was saved simply because God had chosen him; he didn't have to work for it. And now God, who was with him and would not leave him, would give him the power to let go of drinking and wrong living.

He really under-
stood for the first time
that it was God's power,
not his own, that saved
him and kept him
saved, and that he now
had to choose whether
or not he was going to
give the control of his
life over to God. Right
there he made a vow to
do that. And so he came
back to the Lord and
quit his drinking. And
God came to him again
and showed him the
difference between the
deacons he had chosen
and the ones of the
world. So Archie Buck-
ley received his second
calling from God, the

Robert Archie Buckley, at his farm.

one to become a deacon. He took it seriously and he often rankled the
preachers and the other deacons because he refused to support anyone
for deacon who wasn't leading the godly life required in Scripture.

Over the many years he served in the church, he never did get to sit
under the kind of preaching he valued. Black congregations in the rural
South were often too poor to support a regular minister and so they
had preachers who itinerated on circuits of four or more churches.
Buckley would get to hear the preacher maybe every fourth Sunday,
and the service would be an occasion for emotional exhortation and
release rather than the learning experience he coveted. And since the
preacher only visited the community and didn't live in it, he wasn't
around to pastor, teach, or disciple the people in the church. Buckley
longed for a man who would come and live among his people, teach
them the Bible, and be a real spiritual guide to them. It wasn't until he
was more than seventy that his long-frustrated dream would be ful-
filled, when John Perkins appeared in his community.

John and Vera Mae loaded their five children into the family's fifty-six Chevy and drove east across the hot deserts of California and Arizona into the dry mountains of New Mexico and across the endless stretch of flat Texas prairie that June of 1960. John was just then turning thirty.

It was hot and uncomfortable driving across the country, and they had to eat and sleep in, on, and beside the car, because the motels, roadhouses, and restaurants were all segregated. When they finally arrived in New Hebron, they all crowded into Vera Mae's grandmother's house, a little three-bedroom cottage near the Oak Ridge Missionary Baptist Church.

The Oak Ridge Church became the first nursery for their vision and work in Mississippi. John began to teach the men the way Mr. Leitch had taught him and he showed them how to teach Scripture to their families. The people at the Oak Ridge Church grew close to John and his family. They became his mainstay as he ventured out into the churches and schools and as he walked the narrow dirt roads and sat and talked with the people on the sagging front porches of their tumbledown wood-frame houses. John was never one to move slowly. In the fall, when they were enrolling Spencer and Joanie in school, he met Mr. Gray, the principal, who was preaching to the parents, exhorting them to give the school their active support.

The schools in black Mississippi had improved some since the crude cabins of John's childhood, but it was hard to get parents, who'd had so little schooling themselves, involved. This was a ready-made opportunity for John, who warmly introduced himself to Mr. Gray and volunteered his services to do child evangelism. In the South, evangelism and evangelical Christianity are as much a part of the folk culture as baseball. Making hairline distinctions between the provinces of church and state was something for Yankee city folk, not Southern country people.

In the black community, with the church at its heart, no one would have ever thought religion should not be taught in public schools. It was food for the spirit, as necessary as the black-eyed peas and okra that nourished the bodies of rural black people in the South. So in the fall of 1960 a couple of times a month saw John journey off to the elementary school in New Hymn with his easel and flannel graphs. There he animatedly talked Bible with the children. Word of John's enthusiastic teaching spread rapidly, and a number of other schools across the county invited him to give lessons to their children.

Centrally located in Simpson County, Mendenhall is the biggest town and the county seat. John found it convenient to relocate his family there from New Hebron in early 1961. Mendenhall's layout reflects the common pattern of regional town centers in the rural South. Main Street, lined by retail stores, climbs straight uphill to the crowning courthouse, with its dome and heavy neoclassical, turn-of-the-century look. This public building presides over Mendenhall, a brooding reminder of the ironclad legalism that buttressed southern caste.

If you drive down from the courthouse across the railroad tracks, the street narrows and angles off to the right, and you come into what is still called the "quarters." It was once the slave quarters and continues to house the greatest concentration of black families in town. In 1961 the street was a poorly lit dirt road, fronted by patched-together housing and tiny stores in varying states of weathered disrepair.

The people lived in the meanest conditions imaginable. There was no indoor plumbing. Hunger always dogged them. They boiled their greens and fried their lard and corn meal and tried to be satisfied with their small portions. They might walk down to the store and spend a dime or two on some junk food, Twinkies and such, that would momentarily sweeten their existence and divert their attention from their rumbling stomachs. But there was little to really satisfy there in the quarters.

This was the community John moved his family into, a far cry from the twelve-room house in Monrovia and the solid middle-class lifestyle they had had there. Black Mendenhall, like so many of its rural and urban counterparts, was saturated with the dank atmosphere of hopeless resignation. Idleness and escapism pervaded the lives of its young people.

There wasn't much to the quarters—a number of narrow streets melting into one another around a creek bed, an open field, and a swampy wooded area. There were only a few hundred residents, but there were five honky-tonks. These were single rooms, some crudely built onto the ends of houses, where youths gathered, drank moonshine, and danced. The contrived warmth of booze, beat, and physical closeness eased them toward casual sex.

Pregnancy and the dead-end world of single motherhood followed, and the teenage mothers and fathers would often move, independently of one another, to the crowded northern ghettoes in search of an elusive escape from poverty's traps. They'd leave their children with the grandmothers, and another generation would grow up without parents.

John reflected sadly on these grim realities of black life and he had to stave off a bitter anger that came up in him. As he walked the streets of the quarters and talked earnestly with the people—his people—he grew more and more determined to do something about these conditions.

When they moved to Mendenhall, John and his family became part of the local Nazareth Missionary Baptist Church, where John began teaching Sunday school. Since the pastor had five churches he preached at, he was present at Nazareth only infrequently. His preaching was traditional, arousing emotion and aimed at a generalized personal spirituality.

Unlike the pastor, John had become a part of the local community and he didn't see how someone could believe in the truths of the gospel without applying them to real immediate issues. He spoke out with heartfelt concern about what was happening to the local youth as they hung around the honky-tonks. But when he proposed tearing them down and converting an open field to a playground, he didn't get the kind of reception he might have expected. These seedbeds of alcoholism and teenage pregnancy were actually owned by church members who complained about John to the pastor. The pastor, in turn, asked John to stop teaching in his church. John felt hurt and he was angry at the church's hypocrisy. No wonder the youths who came to California, many of whom had church backgrounds, were ending up in trouble.

John had known right along that many black churches were not nurturing an active faith and healthy morals in the young, but experiencing this kind of corruption firsthand was still something of a shock. The vision of change that was beginning to take form in him was generating new wine, which quickly burst the old black church wineskins. To really change people's lives, he decided he was going to have to start his own church. Mrs. Effie Mae Tyler, a local Christian woman attracted to John's mission, volunteered her home as the place for Bible study, and seventeen people began to meet there. These people became John's core group.

John squeezed his family into a little two-room house in Mendenhall. The owner rented him a storefront along with the house. This was to become John's first little mission. It was also where they could hook up their washer and dryer, remnants of their California affluence. Thinking fondly of his little evangelistic group in California, John called the storefront the Fisherman's Mission.

As John was thus planting the seeds of what would become his church in Mendenhall and sowing his child evangelism in the schools, Archie Buckley heard about him, came to a class John held at the storefront, and liked what he heard. Mr. Buckley told John that he had waited most of his life to hear the kind of Bible teaching John was doing. In short order he would become the elder statesman of the infant mission. Besides being a kindred spirit with the wisdom of years, he was able to provide the Perkinses with land to work, vegetables and fruit, and milk from his cows for the children.

The old yeoman was called by his surname, "Mr. Buckley," though Vera Mae began to affectionately call him "Uncle Archie." In the sixties the northern college-age men and women who flocked into the South to help with the civil rights movement respectfully called black adults "mister" and "missus." One of the innumerable ways that southern caste tradition had demeaned blacks was to use only their first names, refusing to allot them the symbols of power and authority that come with age. The use of "mister" and "missus" caught on, and blacks began to use these appellations to assert their dignity. It was a sign of respect and not cold formality then that caused the people of Simpson County to say "Mr. Buckley," rather than Archie, or R. A., though many of his friends called him by those names.

The missionary-like work John was doing paid precious little. Individual churches and denominational and interdenominational missionary societies among white American Christians give bountiful support for missions in "darkest Africa" but they have rarely recognized the hungry needs in darkest Mississippi. John essentially took on the labors of the old

Voice of Calvary workers on Mr. Buckley's farm.

frontier farmer-preacher when he arrived back in the South. He found himself chopping cotton, cutting wood, and hoeing beans again, doing all the familiar field labors of his childhood.

In California he had believed this work was happily gone from his life forever, but when he came back to Mississippi, it held a strange comfort for him. He knew this work and he liked to work alongside the people, to be one of them. As he worked planting and harvesting on the local plantations, he began to build strong and warm relationships with the people who worked there with him.

John enjoying farm work.

Mr. Buckley liked to peddle his eggs and vegetables around the countryside. He had regular customers and he'd find out what they wanted for the week. Then he'd take them their orders. He had been out peddling when he first dropped in on John's little storefront Bible school and that was when he got so excited about what John was doing that he left him a full dozen out of his twelve dozen eggs.

He sometimes accompanied John on his speaking engagements and used his influence to line up some of those engagements for John. On rainy days he accompanied John as he taught in the schools. And John got up early on a Saturday morning and helped Mr. Buckley milk the cows and do the other farm chores. They'd drive around together on his peddling route and then they'd go back and work Mr. Buckley's land.

During the time John and Mr. Buckley spent together they talked. John spoke his vision of an advancing black community, nourished in the Word of God, and Mr. Buckley shared his life experience with the young Bible teacher. John admired Mr. Buckley's ability to take a stand and his stolid determination to have his own and to do it honestly, in the face of controlling whites. John had his own brand of determination, inherited from his family and blended with the sweet waters of success he had been drinking with such satisfaction in California.

John believed in that success and he fiercely wanted it to be available to these people around whom he had grown up in Mississippi. He wanted them to realize the full power of the gospel. He believed that the gospel lessons he was illustrating with his brightly colored flannel figures actually had the power to change the quality of people's lives in the present. Because John saw the poverty, the alcohol, and the teenage pregnancy and because he knew of those things firsthand, he burned to change them.

His evangelism could never be restricted to pie in the sky. It meant social change now. And his ideas of change were raising a storm of controversy among vested church members who profited from the status quo and didn't want things stirred up. Mr. Buckley observed John raising hackles as he talked about how whites exploited blacks and how black church people were bought off by the whites. He agreed heartily but he wished John had turned the bright light on a bit more gradually and had not scared off so many people.

Talk between John and Mr. Buckley was not restricted to such weighty topics. Deep comradeship grows as people share their whole life and personality with one another. Humor has always provided relief from care-filled lives for oppressed peoples. And black people in the land of Jim Crow were no exception. They developed a rich vein of humor that Mr. Buckley liked to mine from time to time. He would constantly illustrate his points with little jokes where the doughty black farmer bested the poor white or the city white.

One was about a black dog trainer. This man trained dogs for people far and wide. They'd come and leave their dogs for him to train. "And in trainin' the dog you gotta train the person how to do the things you been trainin' the dog in, so he can do that himself. And a white man lived up the road from him, and this white man can't get his dogs to do nothin' he wanted them to do. So what he'd do on a Saturday, he'd come down and look at this black man trainin' these dogs, so he could learn what he was doin'. And of course he don't wanna ask no black man how to do things. But he wanna get his dog trained, so he finally breaks down and asks the black man how he got this dog to do that. And the black man says to him, 'You gotta be smarter than the dog.'"

Then there was the one about the black farmer and the white man from the city. "The city man was comin' along the road. The country man was plowin' corn in a field. The city man says, 'If you keep plowin' this corn as deep as you're plowin' it, you gonna end up coverin' half of it up, and you gonna get half a stan'.' The black man says, 'That's what we're farmin' on—halves.' The city man thought about it and he says to himself, 'This boy's pretty dumb. How can I communicate with him?' He says, 'If you keep plowin' it as deep as you're plowin', the corn is gonna turn yella.' The farmer says, 'That's what we're plantin', yella corn.' He came back next time and he says, 'Son, I can see you ain't far from a fool.' And the farmer says, 'There's just a fence between us.'"

Many years later as John recalled these jokes Mr. Buckley had told, he would still chuckle over them. Working and talking and joking together drew him and Mr. Buckley close to each other. John felt a warmth and camaraderie with Mr. Buckley that he had never quite known before. As they worked the rich dark soil and talked about their lives, John felt strengthened and affirmed. Mr. Buckley was not merely a valuable asset to him in his nascent ministry; he was his best friend and another important father figure in his life. The two men shared a common ability to think in terms of economics. They were born entrepreneurs, and as John began to plan out his projects, Mr. Buckley was the one he would usually bounce them off first.

R. A. Buckley was not the only older man who helped to clear a path for John when he came to Mississippi. When he first got to New Hebron, Isaac Newsome, an elder in the Oak Ridge Church who ran the Sunday school program, gave his adult class to John. This forum provided the sturdy base of personal support that he needed as he was getting started in Mississippi. Sunday school was actually more important than preaching in the week-to-week life of the church. All the black churches followed the International Sunday School Lesson format for the week. But since literacy was low, and few if any had received any real Bible training, the typical Sunday school class had little substance. Isaac Newsome's was something of an exception. He was about eleven years younger than Mr. Buckley but like him was a strong, independent black farmer who found himself gravitating toward this fiery young preacher.

Isaac Newsome had first experienced faith in about 1908, when his mother died. He had been very close to her and he felt the cold embrace of grief and aloneness after she was gone. He was only about eight years old when he decided he would ask the Lord to come and be a mother to him. As he reflected back on it as an old man, he thought, yes, the Lord had really been mother and father to him. He remembered how he'd fallen away and started rough living. He was living the life of a drunkard when the Holy Spirit came and convicted him. He felt ashamed of the life he was living and how badly he was treating his wife. So he gave his life back to the Lord and that's when he started to grow spiritually and he became a deacon and a Sunday school teacher.

Then John Perkins came back to Mississippi and began to teach a gospel that reached out beyond just the "good" people to the destitute and the drunks and to the unchurched teenagers walking the streets and wasting themselves in the honky-tonks. Isaac Newsome had known John and his rough family, but this was a whole different John Perkins that he saw here in New Hebron. He liked what John was saying and he was happy to let him teach the Sunday school class he had taught for forty years at Oak Ridge Church.

There were other men of his father's generation at Oak Ridge who came around John and helped him in these early hardscrabble days when he was just starting out. Isaac Newsome's cousin Jesse was about sixty-four years old, four years older than Isaac, when John began his work in Mississippi. He also became a close friend who gave him strong support as he was pushed out of the Nazareth Baptist Church and began his little Fisherman's Mission. Jesse was convinced that the Lord had given John the courage to return and start something new that would really help his people. Jesse had had to retire from his farming in 1950 because of his rheumatism, so he had the free time to help John as he began to expand the activities of the Fisherman's Mission.

Eugene Walker was one of the original students in John's Bible classes at Oak Ridge and he was an enthusiastic one. When John moved to Mendenhall, Walker followed him there. He was a hardworking farmer who sacrificed for his children and would eventually put ten of them through college, no mean accomplishment. In the early days of John's ministry, Walker's house burned down, an all-too-common occurrence among those little wood tinderboxes, and he fell into debt. He thought he was going to have to take his children out of college. He had them in Mississippi Valley State, Alcorn State, and Prentiss Institute.

John came by one day and Walker shared this concern with him. They talked and stood together in prayer about it. John happened to be friends with Mrs. J. E. Johnson, one of the founders of Prentiss. The black educational community was fast availing itself of John's teaching gift and he had become chaplain at Prentiss. During his first year in Mississippi he had participated in a vacation Bible school there and had impressed Mrs. Johnson with his command of Scripture. John contacted Mrs. Johnson, who had relatives at Alcorn and at Mississippi Valley State, and she interceded with them on Walker's behalf. The outcome was that he was able to keep his children in college. Such networks of mutual aid have long worked to insure black survival and steady advance in the South.

John was the first preacher that just about anybody in Simpson County and most of rural Mississippi had seen actually living among his people. They all wondered at his not taking an offering when he taught. The preachers they knew all emphasized the offering. John, however, had his black and white donors in California providing a small monetary allowance. And he supplemented that with what he earned with his farm labor. Archie Buckley and Eugene Walker gave him a lot of in-kind support. Walker gladly gave John vegetables, fruit, and eggs. He told John that if he came around when he wasn't home, he should just go out and get whatever he wanted.

A warm association developed between John and the older men in the community who supported his work. People respected John because he had come back from a prosperous life out West to share the knowledge and skills he had acquired with the people to help them improve their lives. He lived and worked alongside them and shared their needs, their joys, and their sorrows. As he taught them and their children and sweated in the fields with them, they grew close to one another.

It was a good thing that John acquired the support of these solid older men who had stature in the community. They established his credibility while providing an important base of support. This would be particularly important as he expanded his ministry and incurred the anger and opposition of most of the local black ministers. John had a totally different idea of what pastoring was about than they did. He was seriously concerned with addressing the besetting sins of the community that were hurting the people and holding them back. In prophetic manner, John specifically addressed the real things people needed to do to change their lives and bring themselves in line with biblical mandates.

Most of the other preachers just tried to make people feel good. John, on the other hand, was interested in developing the character and integrity that go with genuine conversion and discipleship. That meant taking biblical standards seriously. He upheld marriage by speaking out against casual sexual relationships. He spoke out in favor of the civil rights movement to give blacks genuine equality and he told his audiences that they needed to get out and register black people to vote.

As John understood his Bible, justice is always an integral part of God's will for humanity. The things he enjoined people to do called for commitment, self-discipline, and personal risk. And so he became controversial. People who wanted to feel safe and who had made their peace with the segregated order, coaxing what petty favors they could get from the white establishment, were rankled by his message. But the tough old farmers, the ones with their own land, who had never taken much interest in all the church hoopla, were coming to John's meetings and getting interested in what he had to say.

7

Sons

In a nation of religious stereotypes John Perkins was something of an anomaly. His approach to matters of faith and the conduct of life drew on a number of sources. He wove them together to form his own unique garment. Wayne Leitch and the other pastors, teachers, and businessmen he had met through his association with Child Evangelism were influenced by the popular evangelical theology called dispensationalism.

This school of biblical interpretation that began with J. N. Darby and the Plymouth Brethren movement in nineteenth-century England jumped the Atlantic and became the theological basis of modern Fundamentalism as the popular and influential evangelist Dwight L. Moody adopted it. Subsequently much of its basic worldview pervaded the broader evangelicalism and the charismatic movement. Dispensationalism divides history into seven ages in which God deals with humanity in different ways. The three most important ages, the ones that most significantly affect the dispensational worldview, are law, grace, and the kingdom.

In the first of these periods, which falls between the giving of the law at Mount Sinai and the death and resurrection of Christ, God held the Jews to obedience to the law as the basis of receiving all temporal and eternal blessings. In the age of grace, which we now experience, people are saved entirely by their faith in Christ, not by works of the law. In the kingdom age, following a personal return of Christ, people will be able to obey the sublime ethics of the Sermon on the Mount because Satan and sin will have been banished, and God will rule the earth personally. Hence war and strife will cease, and the lion will lie down with the lamb.

Fundamental and evangelical churches that see through dispensational eyes tend to take a dim view of human effort to change the world for the better. They believe that the world is growing worse and the mission of the church is simply to evangelize as many people as possible so that they will inherit eternal life. In practice, these beliefs have generally led their evangelical adherents to view God's call on them narrowly in terms of personal morals and verbal evangelism. The ancient prophetic outcry against social injustice and the attempt to reform society by making its structures more equitable are not dispensational concerns. The world is aflame, and the church's task is to pull people from this charred, collapsing conflagration to heavenly safety.

One might think that this dour view of the world would create otherworldly ascetics who go about in sackcloth and ashes proclaiming, "Repent. The end is near." But modern American evangelicals, while professing spirituality, tend to be as dedicated to the pursuit of affluence and pleasure as everyone else. Success fills the vacuum that the lack of a social ethic creates. With its negative view of this world, dispensationalism inhibits sensitivity to the poor, the hungry, the oppressed, and the ravaged state of the earth.

Dispensational piety is individualized and spiritualized, having no incarnation in social structures. Because it so divides spiritual from material concerns, it does not have a vision of the Spirit of God permeating and transforming the living earth. With God and his Spirit so separated from the world and its structures, believers are free to treat the world as mere commodity to be consumed or used and discarded, and the result has been full-throttle evangelical participation in the American culture of self-centered consumerism.

As he pondered the relationship of God's Word to the condition of black Mississippians, John Perkins quickly recognized the glaring omissions in dispensational Fundamentalism. While he believed fervently in evangelism and conversion as the means and ground of faith, his deep personal awareness of poverty and oppression led him back into the world. He veered away from the dispensational separation of spiritual from worldly concerns. Instead, he found himself attracted to Reformed theology, which dates back to John Calvin and the Reformation.

Leitch and many of the other white ministers John came in contact with were Presbyterians. In the early part of this century that denomination split apart, leaving a deep chasm between liberal Social Gospelers and conservative evangelicals. Because the whole Fundamentalist movement was awash with it, dispensationalism began to seep into conservative Presbyterianism, and many students attended the new dispensational Bible colleges in Los Angeles and Dallas. But the foundation of Presbyterianism is in Calvinism, and the Calvinist Reformation bequeathed a powerful legacy of commitment to transform society. The English, Scots, and Scotch Irish Puritans brought it to America, where it flourished and was carried to new heights in the revivals of the First and Second Great Awakenings.

In those movements, there had been none of the fissure between evangelism and social action that later developed. Believers were the heart and soul of the antislavery movement and most of the other movements to recast society. This earlier evangelical consensus is the one John Perkins drew on as he set about the mammoth task of responding to what he called the felt needs of black Mississippians. By the time he went back to Mississippi, a few other evangelicals, such as the ones around Fuller Theological Seminary in Pasadena, were beginning to articulate a more socially conscious theology, untainted by dispensational spiritualizing of the Christian mission.

The positive influence of the dispensationalists on John was in his Bible teaching. Dispensational theologians laid heavy emphasis on the verbal inspiration of the Bible, so it was important to them to thoroughly study and teach the exact meaning of every line of Scripture. Under that influence, as originally mediated by Wayne Leitch, John always did expository preaching and he used dispensational sources as his guides. His Bible was a Scofield Reference Bible, which places each passage of Scripture within the dispensational framework. His verse-by-verse commentaries were by Harry Ironside, M. R. DeHaan, G. Campbell Morgan, Merrill Unger, and Dwight Pentecost. The dispensationalists gave John a deep appreciation for the biblical text that enriched his teaching and preaching. People with an intellectual bent, who felt alienated from black church emotionalism, were drawn to John.

Despite any influence of Reformed theology's social interest or dispensationalism's strong biblical foundation, John's ideas grew mainly out of the hands-on work he was doing among the people. Because he was so bothered by the teenage pregnancies and the aimless, passion-driven lives of the young, he directed his early energies mainly at them. In his first years, he became a familiar inspirational presence in the black schools, academies, and community colleges.

At the Bible studies at Effie Mae Tyler's home in D'Lo, a hamlet bordering Mendenhall, he began to gather a core group of youth that included two young men, Leonard Stapleton and Excel McGee, who would recruit many of the youth who first populated John's little Bible school at the Fisherman's Mission. The three Quinn sisters—Lucille, Sarah, and Eva—who would later play such an active role in expanding John's base among the local youth, were young children when they first began to attend John and Vera Mae's Bible classes. Using the flannel graphs of Child Evangelism, their teaching took in all age groups, and it wouldn't be long before they would need something more roomy than the little storefront for their classes.

Herbert Jones was a big, rotund man with a drooping mustache and a gentle smile. He was twenty-three years old, had just gotten out of the army, and had taken a job pumping gas. One day a woman drove up to his gas pump in a station wagon. It was Vera Mae. They talked and she asked him if he was a Christian. He thought about how his mother had always taken him and the others to church and Sunday school. The preacher had come up from Bogalusa, Louisiana, every two weeks, and it had seemed to young Herbert that he was only interested in stirring the people up and taking a big offering.

These memories left a sour taste in Herbert's mouth. So when Vera Mae invited him to the Fisherman's Mission, he smiled politely but he did not intend to go. Yes he was a Christian and yes he sometimes went to church, but church wasn't a very inspiring place for him. Herbert was more focused on getting out of Mississippi. He was saving his money so he could go out to California and get a good job. Then John Perkins came to see him.

This new preacher had something about him that attracted Herbert. John was really interested in his life. He was excited about what God was doing there in Mendenhall and he wanted Herbert to come over and see for himself. So Herbert went over to the mission on a Saturday night in the winter of 1963. John had brought a bunch of teenagers over in a pickup truck with the sides built up. Herbert was surprised to see old Mr. Buckley there. He had gone to the same church as Mr. Buckley and had heard him give talks there. Mr. Buckley always seemed to have more to him than the other church members.

That night at John's little mission, Mr. Buckley spoke about his life as a Christian. Then John Perkins preached a sermon about how God had protected Daniel and how he had protected Shadrach, Meshach, and Abednego. He said God protected them because they had given their lives to him and God had something important for them to do. Then John told the young people that they could also give their lives to God and that he loved them and would protect them. John said that God had something special for them to do too. As he spoke, a deep intensity flared in his eyes and resonated in his voice.

Herbert had never heard a preacher talk about inviting the Lord into your life this way. The idea that he could have a personal relationship with a God who would give meaning and purpose to his life astounded him. He had never heard it explained that way in his church. So on February 16, 1963, Herbert Jones found himself praying with John Perkins to receive Christ into his life. That event changed his focus and he no longer wanted to leave Mississippi. Instead, he wanted to be around John Perkins and he wanted to help him do the Lord's work.

John wanted to rapidly expand his work. His mind was percolating with all kinds of projects. Vera Mae was getting into day care and nutrition for the neighborhood children. John wanted to expand the mission into a real Bible institute, a solid building with the space he needed. So in 1962 he decided to take the money left in his savings and invest it in five small lots on the outer fringe of the quarters. In the spring of the next year, he began building a house from a prefab shell he bought. This was when he first began to work with the young men who were coming to the Fisherman's Mission. Herbert Jones was among them and by helping build John's house, Herbert got a good basic education in putting up Sheetrock. The house was never quite finished but it became the Perkins family's home and the original building of John's ministry, a warm gathering place for many different groups of young people in the years to come.

During this formative period in the early sixties, John was blowing his evangelistic trumpet loud enough to gather a good-sized community of committed Christians. In the summer of sixty-one Reverend Wallace of the Bethlehem Church of Christ Holiness had come from Pasadena and put his formidable preaching skills at John's disposal. John had taken him around to the churches, Wallace stirred the people's hearts, and many of them came forward to receive Christ.

A church long established in any community, whatever its level of wealth, does not commonly rock its boat. Were the preacher to identify and preach against the prevailing sins of the neighborhood, he might risk losing a good part of his congregation. This was no less true in lower Mendenhall, where some of the honky-tonk proprietors and patrons were known to attend church. It was even something of a threat for an outside evangelist like Reverend Wallace to come in, since his preaching might stir up discontent with regular church practice. All the same, the local preachers gave him access to their pulpits the first year John was in Mississippi. This was before John had really begun to shake things up in Mendenhall, when they began clambering over the pews to slam their doors to him.

Vera Mae in the 1960s.

Reverend Wallace had been a big success in 1961. He did not have the practical, entrepreneurial side to him that John did. In fact he was an otherworldly man, extremely gifted in preaching and capable of drawing huge crowds. So when he arrived again in 1963, without notice, John looked for a place with a big enough seating capacity to conduct a major evangelistic event. He found what he was looking for when some white businessmen offered to lend their rodeo stadium to him free of charge.

101

This was one of those rare times when white southern culture, in this case southern evangelical culture, actually served John's needs.

Reverend Wallace's evangelistic preaching at the rodeo stadium was a big success. John liked to be able to reach large audiences and when he discovered an opportunity to purchase a used circus tent, he jumped at it and laid out four hundred dollars. The giant green and white tent stood out boldly, a canvas convention center there on Effie Mae Tyler's property in D'Lo. John set Reverend Wallace up inside, and they drew capacity crowds of two hundred nightly.

Mama Wilson and her close friend Sister Carroway had come from Monrovia to work with John that summer. Sister Carroway was a preacher herself and she and Mama Wilson were not exactly smitten with Reverend Wallace. Reverend Wallace was a stalwart traditionalist who didn't believe that women should be up front in the church. So John was in the unenviable position of having to mediate between the two strong-willed women and one old hellfire holiness preacher.

The circus tent remained up well after Reverend Wallace returned to California with John converting it to his own theater for Bible teaching and expository preaching. It became a popular gathering place for the children and teenagers in the area. Parents who wanted their children to get good, moral teaching sent them there, and children and teens who were wandering around looking for something to do were attracted to the goings-on at the big tent. John's little band of young, enthusiastic supporters was ever on hand and scheming all the time to get others to come. The tent and John's style of preaching gave religion a different look and content that attracted people who wouldn't otherwise be interested in organized Christianity.

Johnny Budhalter was a successful black farmer, owning somewhere between three and four hundred acres—a big spread for a black man in Mississippi. He was one of the strong, independent men who came to the tent to hear John talk. And he brought in a whole segment of successful older men who normally wouldn't have anything much to do with church. These men absorbed John's earnest call to faith and his Bible teaching and they eventually began to get involved in the local churches. John moved the tent around Simpson County and caught a good many fish of all ages and backgrounds during 1963 and 1964.

By the time of the tent evangelism, John had renamed his mission. It was now called Voice of Calvary (VOC), another name taken from

California. It was the name of Jack MacArthur's weekly radio program. MacArthur's church in Burbank had been John's principal backer, so John thought it was appropriate to take the same name as the radio ministry. Just before he bought the tent, John had gone back to California to raise money. He was focused on getting a few thousand dollars to build his Bible institute building. In California he managed to raise six thousand dollars—a substantial amount and thousands more than he had hoped for. Again it was his white donors, including MacArthur's church, who provided most of the support.

The biggest gift, two thousand dollars, came from Mr. Hayden, John's former employer at Shopping Bag. John had worked for Shopping Bag right up until he left California. After his conversion, he had vocally shared his newfound faith with his friends at work. The Hayden family were active Catholics, and John's glowing enthusiasm had fired up their interest in his ministry. So the Haydens had become active supporters of John's mission in the South, and when John returned to California in 1963, Mr. Hayden, now retired, was happy to help out with the Bible institute.

So John and four young men from the community—Herbert Jones, Leonard Stapleton, Melvin Weary, and Artis Fletcher—built a solid single-story brick building next to John's two-story white house on the edge of the quarters. They were holding classes there by 1964, and with some of the money John had raised in California, they were able to buy a secondhand bus. Herbert, who had moved in with the Perkins family, became the driver, and the children loved this soft-spoken giant of a man who carted them back and forth to the Bible institute and to the meetings in the big tent. And he loved them.

Melvin Weary's younger brother Dolphus was at that time a seventeen-year-old junior at the local black high school, Harper High, named for Annie Bell Harper, its retired principal, who would teach for a while in an adult education program John was just starting up. Dolphus was getting a haircut one day when the barber, his friend Leonard Stapleton, asked him if he was a Christian. A bit startled, he answered, yes, he thought he was, but the question had disquieted him. It poked into some old unsettled feelings he had put aside.

The Weary family had been desperately poor during the whole time when Dolphus was growing up. His father had left his mother, Lucille, with eight children. She did day labor—whatever she could get—to support her family. The children learned very young to pick cotton and corn with their mother on their grandfather's four acres. They would drag their tired, achy bodies back to a dank three-room shack that had no electricity or indoor plumbing. The stinging winter cold leaked through the cracks of the uneven walls and up through the floorboards.

Dolphus grew up in the fifties, a generation after John's childhood, and a time of supposed affluence. But his family was poorer than John's had been and had fewer resources. When Dolphus bit into an Eskimo Pie at about eleven years old, it was the first ice cream he had ever tasted. Still Lucille Weary was a good Christian woman, completely given to the survival and well-being of her children. She took them to Sunday school and church every week, even when the cold rain soaked them through and the mud splashed about their ankles as they walked together. And she made sure that all her children finished high school so that they might have more opportunities than she had experienced.

Despite Lucille's heroic efforts, churchgoing had not been a positive experience for Dolphus. With a certain bitterness he remembered singing, "I'm working to make one hundred, ninety-nine and a half won't do." You always had to be doing things at church and being good and giving more and more money to the church. God never seemed satisfied; he wanted perfection from you. That's the way they had taught it and preached it and Dolphus had absorbed it. Now his friend Leonard urged him to go with him to the revival that was going on in the circus tent. All his old frustration with the church and with what seemed its endless list of requirements now flooded his mind. He thought, yes, I think I'm a Christian, but I sure don't want to climb back on that treadmill.

It was the time when they'd first put up the big circus tent, and Reverend Wallace was preaching there. Dolphus knew that his brother Melvin was involved with John Perkins and he was struck by Leonard's enthusiasm, so he decided to go to the tent revival. John taught the Bible lessons using his Child Evangelism flannel figures as visual aids. His audience was all ages, and the bright cloth figures caught the children's attention. The others were charmed as John wove his story together with these colorful images. Then Reverend Wallace got up to preach. He preached about the need for salvation, a classic call to be saved. The old holiness evangelist stressed the idea that you can't earn salvation. It's a free gift from God to everyone who believes. And then he asked all who wanted to receive eternal life to come forward.

Dolphus suddenly experienced an awakening to what the gospel is really saying. After all the years of "trying to make a hundred," feeling a failure, and finally casting the church aside in painful discouragement, he began to see some bright rays of light as Reverend Wallace poured out the message of grace. Suddenly it dawned on him what free grace was, and as with Archie Buckley, the experience enabled him to begin letting go of his life. He let God get hold of him to do good through him, instead of his having to work for salvation. Suddenly all his creative energies and his dormant enthusiasm were bubbling over as he felt the secure warmth of God's unconditional love.

Dolphus began to get active in Voice of Calvary's Bible institute. John held Bible classes for all ages twice a week and every Saturday evening they held Youth for Christ rallies. These were more like social gatherings, with lots of singing and talking. People got up and gave personal testimonies of faith, and John taught the Bible. John taught Bible in a personal, informal way, the way he did everything else. If there was too much starch in the white collars of some pastors, there was none at all in John's blue one. He was always among the people, and nobody called him Reverend, just plain John. Because he was just one of the people, he and his family also suffered the hardships of the people.

Early on, when he was still in New Hebron, his son Philip had started to run a high fever and limp when he tried to walk. The local doctor treated him, but his condition only deteriorated. Due to their poverty it was some weeks before they could take Philip to Louisiana to get him properly diagnosed. He had polio. In 1961 the Salk vaccine was available, and polio was becoming a thing of the past, but you wouldn't know that in rural black Mississippi.

John and Vera Mae both became immersed in the pain of their little boy's illness. They thought of how they would have had access to good medical care if they had stayed in California. As Philip worsened, John sadly began to resign himself to his son's impending death. But suddenly Philip began to improve a little, and they were able to get the money to take him to a treatment center in California. The doctors there examined Philip and said he had begun to heal.

John saw this crisis as a major test of faith coming at the beginning of his ministry. When he and Vera Mae surrendered Philip to God, as Vera Mae had surrendered John and his vision back in California, Philip began to improve. He would eventually make a complete recovery. But

for weeks, as they prayed long and hard and tried to care for their little boy, they were not certain whether he was going to live or die. This
is the kind of suffering John experienced with his family in Mississippi
that would have been less likely amid California's affluence. Experiencing the people's wants sensitized John to them and as he moved to
expand his work in the direction of people's material needs, good medical care would be a priority.

Artis Fletcher was about sixteen when he first saw John Perkins at
Prentiss Institute, speaking in a chapel service. Artis grew up in
Mendenhall, twenty-six miles away from the black academy. His father
had had a good-sized farm, and his mother was a school teacher. This
background placed his people among the more well-off black families
of the area. Mr. Fletcher had had a large family—twelve children—
with his first wife and then three with Artis's mother. He died when
Artis was only ten, and a much older brother, with a farm in nearby
Rankin County, took over much of his raising. Artis learned the satisfaction of working hard and accomplishing a goal at his brother's farm.
As might be expected in a land-owning family with a teaching mother,
the Fletcher clan was bent on personal accomplishment. If you had
what it takes, you were expected to go as far as you could in school.

Official white Mississippi always threw as many obstacles in the path
of black advancement as could be dreamt up, and this meant making
it as hard as possible to get a real education. High schools were scattered around the rural countryside. By the fifties the white children had
bright yellow buses with flashing lights to take them to school. Black
children like Artis had to make do with clunkers that were so old and
raggedy the children could see the road through the worn-away floor-
ing. The buses belched sooty, smelly fumes and broke down all the time.

The children never knew if they were going to make it the fourteen
miles to the high school. The trip was long, slow, and exhausting with
many stops along the way. Because of the transportation hardships and
the overall poor quality of public schooling, education-minded blacks
tried to scrape together the money to put their children in the black
academies like Prentiss. So Artis's older sister, a ninth grader, and Artis,
an eighth grader, were sent to Prentiss.

While he was in school at Prentiss, Artis came back during the summers. During one period, just after he had been badly burned in a gaso-
line fire, he was back home to go for medical treatment in Jackson,

and it was John Perkins who often drove him there. Artis got to know John in Mendenhall, and John took him along while he did errands around town. They would start out early, and Artis would often be at John's house for family devotions and for breakfast.

Being with John all day gave Artis the chance to absorb his life and his example. They'd go out to Mr. Buckley's farm together and pick vegetables, and then when they came back to the mission, Artis would help John prepare the flannel graph lessons. John talked Bible to him. As they went about the day's tasks and experienced the day's events together, John made them the fuel for his teaching on many subjects.

If John and Artis were crossing the track to go up to the bank, John would contrast the muddy potholed streets they had to put up with in the quarters with the smooth pavement in white Mendenhall, pointing out the injustice. They'd get to the bank, and John would move into a talk on how to save and manage money wisely. They'd be talking to some church members, and John might comment later to Artis on their having more of a churchy religion and not the personal relationship to God that is necessary to propel real faith. Everything was grist for John's mill as he used the stuff of his daily life to teach young Artis. Artis got to feel something of the inside of John's life as he saw him rejoice and play and dream and work. He saw how John related to Vera Mae and the children and he listened while John talked with other ministers and people in the community. He quietly pondered what he saw and heard.

Artis was eighteen when he actually went forward in a chapel service and dedicated his life to the Lord. He was a quiet, gentle youth and he had always wanted to be a preacher. Preachers and teachers were the ones who were really looked up to in the black community. The younger children in families don't usually get a lot of respect, especially in big families like Artis's, so maybe that had played into his desire to be a preacher. At any rate it was fun when he was a kid going about the tedious farm chores to practice preaching to the livestock. Those forceful moos made righteous amens. As Artis moved into young adulthood his sense of his calling deepened, and he found himself getting very involved with Voice of Calvary.

Young men like Artis Fletcher, Dolphus Weary, and Herbert Jones, along with women of their age like Lucille Quinn and Carolyn Albritton, became part of an active nucleus of young people at Voice of Calvary. They came to John's Bible institute and helped him organize a ministry that would reach out to people with in-depth teaching, something they had never had. Throughout much of the decade of the 1960s, John and Vera Mae were working with young people and training young adults and teenagers to work with little children.

John never restricted himself to Bible teaching alone. The Bible was the basis of what he was doing, because it sets people in contact with God and teaches them how to live wisely and abundantly. John was concerned, as he knew God is, with the whole fabric of people's lives—their minds and bodies as well as their spirits. Before long he and Vera Mae started a tutoring program and then adult education. From the beginning John wanted to get young people involved in athletic competition. He recognized sports as a healthy outlet for youthful energies, and before long Voice of Calvary would be fielding strong teams in softball and basketball.

Much of John's concern revolved around the deeply embedded poverty of the black community and all the multitude of evils that flowed in its wake. Disease and chronic poor health due to malnutrition and substandard living conditions sapped the people's vitality, burying them in listless resignation. Lack of money and gainful work caught and stuck them in a moment-to-moment life, and they'd spend a dollar almost as soon as it came into their hands. Planning for the future and deferring gratification, values of the suburban middle class, are rare among the oppressed poor. To plan for the future, people have to have some measure of optimism, some sense that they can advance through their own effort. Centuries of lower caste living had destroyed that hope among the black poor of Mississippi.

John wanted to get capital, businesses, and jobs into the black community. He pondered how to stimulate enterprise that would give blacks power over their own lives and a chance to grow and thrive. Economic ideas were always churning somewhere in John's mind. But the center of John's attention, particularly in these early years, was on the little children. Without adequate nutrition, they would lack the capacity to learn, play, and grow properly. This was the era of John F. Kennedy, Lyndon Johnson, and the flood tide of welfare liberalism. The Perkinses saw an opportunity to make sure Mendenhall's little children received the nourishment they needed through Head Start.

Vera Mae had been providing day care and food for children who came from as far as ten miles away. She had started it in the Perkins home, and as it grew in response to crushing need, she moved it over to the Bible institute building. She served the children the vegetables, grains, and dairy products that came from the surplus foodstuffs the federal government distributes to the poor. People in the area were donating these goods to the Perkins family in appreciation of what they were doing. John and Vera Mae gave most of what the people brought them back to the children, thereby recycling it into the community.

Providing day care and nutrition led right into their involvement in the government-sponsored Head Start program. In 1965 Vera Mae went to Tuskegee Institute in Alabama to learn more about early childhood development and nutrition programs for children. This is what brought about Voice of Calvary's involvement in Head Start, which was at its base a nutrition program. The Perkinses didn't have to actually administer the program, so they were able to concentrate all their community resources on involvement with the children. Administration, that is the financial end of the program, was done through the Sophie Sutton Mission. Sophie Sutton was a white woman who had been a missionary in Africa. Her family had owned a big piece of land in Mississippi that she gave as a mission to aid local blacks.

With Voice of Calvary's expanded nutrition program at its hub, Head Start became a powerful stimulus to training and job creation in the black community. People who had been forced to quit college because of lack of money and people who had finished high school and wanted to go on to college but couldn't go for the same reason were given a boost by Head Start. They were hired on as teachers' aids and assistants in the schools.

This was a way up for many black women who were tired of being stuck in the white folks' kitchens. The pay was much better, and the Head Start–financed positions helped to instill more hope and self-confidence in the employees as well as to provide them with the wherewithal to get further education. So Head Start was a boon to the black communities in rural Mississippi, and John and Vera Mae Perkins were in the thick of it.

John never artificially separated out spiritual things from all the other parts of life. God is the God of everything, and if you are interested in people's eternal salvation, you need to be interested in the rest of their lives. He saw the Spirit of God, who gives hope to the downtrodden, rest to the weary, and comfort to the brokenhearted, as needing to permeate the community. That meant loving people around their "felt needs," and because people have bodies, these needs were by and large material. Nutrition and Head Start made a beginning.

John was working at developing health care, housing, and black-owned businesses at the same time as he continued to do evangelism and mentor the youth. But something else was looming ever larger before him and before every African American. That was the civil rights movement. The summer of 1964, Mississippi's "long, hot summer," focused the whole nation on the bloody beatings and the venomous murders and the bombings of black houses and churches, as whites vented their fury at those who would disturb the racial status quo.

All the anger and bitter pain that John had felt when Clyde was murdered came back up in him. But now he could pour his feelings out to God and seek direction from him. With the Lord's help John was building something that would give hope and dignity and progress to people long battered into cruel submission by racism's truncheon. But the people would have to take a stand so they could get the human power that had been so long denied them. They needed to wrest control over their own lives from the white tyrant so they could create, grow, thrive, and become who they were. John knew deep in the pain of his gut that before black people could gain real economic power and before they could begin to tap into their real potential, they had to lay the ax once and for all to Jim Crow.

8

Civil Rights

The term *racial etiquette* sounds as if it contains the essence of southern propriety. It suggests columned porticoes of stately white mansions with properly attired black servants politely serving good Kentucky bourbon to genteel lords of the manor, who respond in paternal warmth. In reality, *racial etiquette* encompassed total white control over African American behavior.

A black person did not dare express an opinion of his or her own around whites. His or her house had to remain dingy, unkempt, and unpainted. If a person should fix it up, make it into a neat, attractive little cottage instead of a tumbledown shack, even this act of simple cleanliness, aesthetic taste, and self-respect branded the person a threat to the established order.

If a black person had any personal enterprise or ambition, he or she was never to show it around whites or that person would be judged uppity, and men might visit him at night and would speak strongly about how it is best for all concerned when people remain "in their place." If a black person persisted in the stubborn pursuit of the American Dream and started a business and made it grow, he or she might be burned out, run out of town, or even lynched, depending on the whim of the white men who were affronted by the success. Should a black person attain such a level of literacy that he or she entertained ideas about things, he or she was being dangerously subversive. Such forays of the intellect would inevitably lead to belief in the inherent equality of blacks with whites. And that would make it all the harder to retain a safely servile composure.

To be black in the Jim Crow South meant constantly pretending to be the stupid, grinning, shiftless, thieving fool that whites wanted to see. If blacks played this game, though it made them sick to do so, the Man might let them have a little something for themselves and their family. As part of the racial mystique, southern whites of every class could feel superior, magnanimous, and firmly in power by "taking care of [their] niggers." Upper-class whites did so by doling out work and money and by selectively endowing black education. Such paternalism made blacks dependent on the personal largesse of whites and secured their control. Lower-class whites had no such resources but they would commonly make grandiloquent gestures that bespoke their status over blacks. A poor white man might come by a group of black children and buy them all cokes, and the children would thank him kindly for his beneficence.

Blacks learned to accommodate Mr. Charlie to get favors from him. But they maintained their sense of personhood by keeping their own counsel, and so they were entirely different around whites than they were in their own community. Whatever small things they found room to do that showed enterprise or ingenuity, they had to hide from the Man. Like Jews who had faked conversion during the Spanish Inquisition, African Americans could only be who they really were underground. Also like the Jews within European Christendom, blacks were ghettoized and scapegoated in the evangelical Christian South.

The relationship between white and black functioned like an addiction, a mutual dependency. White people, from the genteel planter or banker to the lowliest laborer, had license to exalt themselves over blacks. Such domination was intoxicating, and the white lust for power over blacks grew obsessive. The need to control fed on itself, growing greater as whites increasingly feared retribution from the blacks they were so victimizing. For their part, blacks who stayed in the South mainly accommodated the whites, trying to work the system for what little it could yield them. The black church developed as an accommodative institution, preaching the deferral of gratification to the hereafter. In this way it placated ruling whites and thereby carved out a limited autonomy. Similarly, blacks were permitted modest higher educational institutions, so long as they emphasized "humility" and "character building," and a tiny, strictly segregated black elite, made up of small businesspeople, teachers, clergymen, doctors, and lawyers plied their skills mostly in urban locales.

Blacks submitted in order to survive, telling whites what they wanted to hear and showing them what they wanted to see. The small, educated black middle class, having some stake in the system, acted as its conservative prop. But African Americans in the Jim Crow South yearned for freedom, just as their enslaved forebears had. They knew that in the United States, with its egalitarian pretensions, its worship of success, and its relatively fluid society, their own status was a scandalous anomaly.

During Reconstruction the federal government had attempted to guarantee the civil rights of blacks. And for some years after the South was left to its own devices, the ruling gentry class had not seen fit to ostracize them. Until almost the end of the nineteenth century, blacks had retained the vote, and segregation was not the all-encompassing system it would later become. But during the Populist revolt of the nineties, poor whites temporarily aligned with blacks and threatened to upend upper-class rule. This scared the gentry into inflaming the race issue, playing to the fears and prejudices of lower-class whites. Black disfranchisement and strict segregation in all walks of life would follow as the means for making peace between classes. The first two decades of the twentieth century would see a virulent racism spread throughout the nation, as the mystique of the Old South was restored and Reconstruction denounced. Black progressives responded by creating the NAACP in 1910 to battle for black civil rights in the courts.

Things began to improve some as the New Deal and the Second World War opened opportunities to blacks. This was the setting for a number of court victories that chipped around the edges of the hard Jim Crow structure. In 1954 the Supreme Court ruled on *Brown v. the Board of Education,* boldly pronouncing school segregation anathema. This watershed event energized blacks, giving them new hope and the will to begin active resistance.

Thus began an epic folk movement, replete with heroes, anthems of freedom, and landmark battles and martyrs. The civil rights movement that began with the call to desegregate the schools was actually a latter phase of an African American exodus from slavery to freedom that started with the abolitionist movement in the eighteenth century. *Brown* was the catalyst needed to turn pockets of resistance to segregation, which were increasingly appearing after World War II, into a mass movement. The Montgomery bus boycott, which thrust Martin Luther King Jr. into national prominence, started the following year.

The Supreme Court would void segregated busing after the successful boycott was more than a year old. But the significance of this and other boycotts, as with the sit-ins and Freedom Rides, is that southern black people en masse were at last beginning to stand up and move against their oppressors and out of their accustomed role as victims. When the African American people rose up to challenge the old order and claim their rightful heritage, they gained new strength and the underpinnings of the segregation fortress began to give way.

Martin Luther King Jr. became the Christ-like prophet of southern black liberation. His vision and his language were in the biblical, evangelical idiom that the South had made distinctly its own. He conceived and articulated his cause as one of redemption of black people and their reconciliation with white people. He held that black men, women, and children who boycotted the buses and those who marched in the streets of Birmingham and Selma were to love the white police who beat and jailed them, unleashed dogs on them, and sprayed them with firehoses. They were to respond in nonviolent forbearance to those who shot at them and bombed their churches and homes. In so doing they were drawing on the gospel command to love and forgive our enemies and do good to those who hate us and pray for those who persecute us.

This is a Christianity that the racist white southerner did not want to acknowledge, but when the black Christians around King lived it out in the civil rights movement, it ultimately would call them to account. King did not believe that southern whites were peculiarly evil but he saw that their culturally engrained racism numbed them to institutionalized persecution and blinded them to blatant injustice. His movement's sublime moral basis would not prick the Klansman's conscience but it would establish the ground for eventual changes in the law and the overall pattern of racial relations.

King appealed to the conscience of white Christians in his *Letter from Birmingham Jail*. He was responding to the clergymen who suggested that his civil disobedience in that city was "unwise and untimely" and that he was acting as an extremist in pushing so hard to end segregation all at once. They thought he was upsetting an orderly evolution of racial relations in the South. Masterfully he set forth his rejoinder to their criticisms, setting the movement within a prophetic context. To the frequently heard white denunciation of "outside agitators" who come in to stir up trouble, he responded by likening his mission to that of the biblical prophets, who traveled the land to speak God's judgment against injustice.

And then he named Birmingham as a city where the gross injustice of segregation was at its most flagrant. He argued that the direct action of marching and challenging iniquitous Jim Crow laws brings underlying racial tension to the surface. Once racial iniquity is brought out in the open for all the world to see, pressure for change will occur and ultimately healing will come.

The Alabama clergymen whom King was addressing liked to think of themselves as enlightened moderates in the racial struggle. But King in his letter cut the ground out from beneath them, stating that the moderate counsel to wait and let time pass did more evil than the violent resistance of the white supremacists. Their pretense at reasonableness gave sanction to the perpetuation of ongoing racial atrocities and degradation into an uncertain future. And he catalogued these abuses in vivid, moving language to shake these white critics of his movement out of their self-serving complacency. "I guess it is easy," he said, "for those who have never felt the stinging darts of segregation to say, 'Wait.'" He went on:

> But when you have seen vicious mobs lynch your mothers and fathers at will and drown your sisters and brothers at whim; when you have seen hate-filled policemen curse, kick, brutalize and even kill your black brothers and sisters with impunity; when you see the vast majority of your twenty million Negro brothers smoldering in an airtight cage of poverty in an affluent society . . .

And then he told them how discrimination creates "clouds of inferiority" in the "mental sky" of a little black child. And he spoke of the southern black man, whose "first name becomes 'nigger' and [whose] middle name becomes 'boy' no matter how old [he is]," living constantly at tiptoe stance never quite knowing what to expect next and plagued with inner fears and outer resentments." Such language was calculated to sear the consciences of these sheltered white ministers.

Moderates like the men he was writing to valued the preservation of order over the creation of a just society, said King. Courageous people were needed who would take a stand to bring about human progress; it would not come about as a result of the mere passage of time. King went on to deal with their accusation that he was an extremist. He contrasted his nonviolent direct action with discouraged inaction on the one hand and a militant black nationalism, like that of Elijah Muhammad, which casts all whites as devils, on the other. King's was the middle ground. But if white moderates wanted to insist he was an extremist, he would not refuse the mantle. Jesus, he said, was an extremist for love, and Paul for the spread of the gospel.

In concluding, King directed a prophetic blast at the white evangelical church, which considered the crusade for Negro freedom and justice an inappropriate field for its involvement. He confessed his disappointment with the contemporary church, which remained wedded to the status quo. God's judgment is on the church because it has lost its mission to heal the most wounded of society, the poor and oppressed. Recalling the transformational role of a "God-intoxicated" early Christianity, he warned the churchmen he was addressing that the institution they represented was decaying into an "irrelevant social club." King spoke as a fellow believer and one with a deep love of the church, having been the son and grandson of ministers. His purpose was to open the hearts of these men to the divine cause in their midst so that they would join arms with him. Reconciliation of the races and what he termed "the beloved community" was always King's deepest intent.

The civil rights movement of the fifties and sixties was very much a religious crusade, deeply rooted in the black church, which provided its mass base. As effective as it had been in getting the black cause before the courts and gaining favorable decisions, the NAACP could not get the black masses into the streets. Martin Luther King was able to bring together a practical theology based in nonviolent civil disobedience together with a strategy for bringing about national awareness and social change. He and his pastoral associates in the Southern Christian Leadership Conference (SCLC) would conduct workshops on nonviolent protest. People who took part went through a deeply spiritual experience in "self-purification." They learned to extend love to their tormentors by not returning blow for blow. King believed that the very violence of the white segregationist response to the demonstrations would become the means of redemption.

The act of offering oneself in sacrifice to reconcile people to God and to one another is the essence of Christian love. King had come to believe deeply in this kind of enactment of love and he based his whole movement on it. He would march in the face of police orders not to, and this would provoke violence from the police and from white supremacists in the community, and the violence would draw national media attention. The country would react in shock and outrage as they watched peaceful black marchers—men, women, and children— attacked, clubbed, and beaten bloody in the streets of Birmingham and then again in Selma. The result would be federal intervention.

Both the Kennedy and Johnson administrations responded by sending in federal troops and introducing civil rights legislation. The Public Accommodations Act, which passed Congress in 1964, and then the Voting Rights Act, which sent federal registrars into the South beginning in 1965, were the direct results of King's Birmingham and Selma campaigns.

King and the Southern Christian Leadership Conference set the spiritual tone of the civil rights movement and established its base in the black church. The black churches formed the main communications network of the African American people, especially in the South. As the traditional centers of verbal proclamation and all forms of organization in the black community, both urban and rural, the churches became the natural disseminators of the civil rights movement. That is why they were so often the targets of segregationist bombs and Molotov cocktails.

As the movement spread from the visible urban centers of the South to a backward rural hinterland, characterized by the small towns and hamlets of Mississippi, King's tactics of mass mobilization were less relevant. A long-term, house-to-house, grass roots organizing effort that spread over a number of years was needed. In this extended campaign, the Student Nonviolent Coordinating Committee (SNCC), staffed, as its name implies, by younger people than those in SCLC, became the prime mover. The churches provided the spiritual touchstone and the base of operations in SNCC's voter registration drives as they did for SCLC's campaigns.

SNCC had its origins in the student-led F. W. Woolworth's lunch counter sit-in, which took place in Greensboro, North Carolina, in 1960 and then spread over much of the South. The young men who first mounted this audacious challenge to southern racial etiquette were well-mannered, well-groomed college students. Like King, they saw their world through the prism of southern evangelical values, which were common to black and white alike. They sought to call their white Christian neighbors back to the heart of their professed faith.

Reconciliation of the races, realized in full black participation in southern life, was their intent, a warmer and more humane goal than the mere acquisition of power.

Along with King and SCLC's work and the sit-ins, a third form that direct action took in the early sixties was the Freedom Rides. With the purpose of desegregating the terminals of the interstate bus lines, the Congress of Racial Equality (CORE) sponsored Trailways and Greyhound buses that were set to go from Washington, D.C., into the Carolinas and Georgia and on through Alabama to Jackson, Mississippi. They encountered Klan-led mob violence in Alabama. Black and white passengers were attacked and battered, and the buses were damaged, one of them firebombed.

The Kennedy administration Justice Department became involved to secure the safety of the riders. After an angry, taunting mob descended on the remaining bus in Montgomery to keep it from leaving the terminal, CORE reluctantly called off the last leg of the trip. But with federal protection arriving, SNCC took over with its own volunteers, and the bus traveled from Montgomery to Jackson surrounded by National Guardsmen. SNCC, with its militant, young leadership, was propelling itself to the dangerous outer edge of the civil rights movement.

It was in the Freedom Rides that the black civil rights organizations first began to join in formal cooperation. As the movement continued to grow in the first half of the 1960s, many northern blacks became involved. One was Bob Moses, a New Yorker with a Harvard master's degree in philosophy. In 1964, as a leader of SNCC, Moses re-formed the Council of Federated Organizations (COFO), the civil rights umbrella that had first come together during the Freedom Rides. SNCC was the spearhead for the drive to register black voters in the South, and Moses was about to lead his volunteers into the most rugged theatre of civil rights warfare, the hitherto impregnable apartheid of Mississippi.

With the endorsement of all the civil rights organizations, united under the COFO banner, Moses journeyed to elite universities like Stanford and Berkeley in search of idealistic white youth, the kind who were asking what they could do for their country and joining Kennedy's Peace Corps. He was aware of how effectively Dr. King had involved the media, thereby speeding up federal involvement in his Alabama campaigns. Moses figured that drawing white youth from a privileged sector of America into Mississippi would instantly fire up the media.

Moses had led a previous voter registration campaign in Mississippi's Delta. Thick with an impoverished black migrant population and a cruel racial atmosphere, the Delta had proved a most inhospitable environment for Moses' organizing efforts in 1961. It had crunched on his voter education project for a while and then spit it out. For Moses, having endured beating and every sort of harassment, this earlier expedition into Mississippi's closed society had been a vital learning experience.

During 1961 and 1962 Moses had been beaten, jailed, bombed, and harassed in the worst racial tarpits of Mississippi. He had valorously, maybe even a bit naively, descended into McComb in the Jurassic southwestern part of the state and was lucky to emerge with his life. Drawing on these experiences, Moses imparted his wisdom to the college students as he taught them tactics for staying alive and reasonably healthy while conducting a campaign to register black voters throughout Mississippi.

White resistance to black civil rights reached the peak of its crescendo in Mississippi in the early sixties. Terrorism was a long-established practice for keeping blacks fearful and submissive. And when white supremacists felt particularly threatened, the Ku Klux Klan rode, burning, bombing, and lynching. By the sixties other racist organizations like the Association for the Preservation of the White Race and the National States Rights Party were thriving in the Deep South. While not directly participating in Klan violence, these disseminators of white racial paranoia made the atmosphere hospitable for it.

The white citizens councils, formed in the fifties in reaction to *Brown,* became the main fount of segregationist orthodoxy. Harboring the most influential elements in southern politics, they were essentially the Klan in dress suits. They produced the fire-breathing politicians of the Deep South like Governor George Wallace of Alabama and Governor Ross Barnett of Mississippi.

When a steely-nerved James Meredith, backed by a court order, enrolled at Ole Miss in 1962, Barnett did nothing to stop the ensuing riots in Oxford, which killed two and injured scores of others. The following year, Wallace tried to block integration at the University of Alabama, shouting "Segregation forever!" But black enrollment proceeded there, as it had in Mississippi, and Wallace would live to recant and eventually become a strong supporter of black advancement.

The segregationist establishment redoubled its efforts in Mississippi during COFO's voter registration campaigns there in the sixties. Local politicians and pundits railed against "commie, race-mixing, outside agitators who come into our state and stir up our niggers." A best-seller in Mississippi during this period was the John Birch publication, *Color, Communism and Common Sense,* which blended white supremacy with Cold War Americanism. Legislators had put as many barriers as they could think of in the path of black voting, among them literacy tests that gave local registrars power to demand recitation of state constitution minutiae before voter registration could take place.

James Eastland had inherited former Mississippi Senator Bilbo's mantle as the chief exponent of white supremacy in the United States Congress. A seniority system that elevated obstructionist Dixiecrats to the most powerful positions in Congress had conferred chairmanship of the Senate Judiciary Committee on Eastland. With power over nationwide federal judicial appointments, this devout believer in black incapacity would see to it that only people of similar racial sentiments occupied the bench. One of Mississippi's circuit judges, Tom Brady, had made Eastland's case in *Black Monday,* a diatribe against the *Brown* decision that made all the familiar claims of inherent black inferiority.

The increase of terrorism and overall oppression by Mississippi's white supremacists in the 1960s actually worked to draw blacks out of their accustomed role of passive submission. They got to the point where the tactics of fear mongering no longer worked to hold them down. People who had long borne the beatings and the killings and the moment-by-moment humiliations of their scapegoat status at long last began to stand up and fight back. The triggering event was the murder of NAACP leader Medgar Evers in 1963. He was shot in the back while standing in his front yard. The perpetrator, Byron de la Beckwith, was freed and not imprisoned until more than thirty years later when he was an old man.

Evers had always been one to take positive risks for the betterment of his people. He had tried to register to vote back in 1946 and had been marked for assassination since the mid-fifties. He was a veteran of the Korean War, when the armed services of the United States were first integrated. Like Clyde Perkins after World War II, Evers had come back home with hope for positive change in racial relations. The Evers brothers—Charles would serve four terms as mayor of Fayette, Mississippi—

were strong, determined men, who had wrested college education and middle class status out of an environment heavily weighted against them. For years Medgar had traveled the state ceaselessly organizing, recruiting people for, and engineering the protests of Mississippi's civil rights movement. His murder suddenly galvanized black anger and brought about a newfound determination to make changes happen.

The summer of 1964 became "Freedom Summer" in Mississippi. COFO's leadership had designated it as time for the big push for black voter registration and other civil rights. White students on their summer vacations came into the state and joined with Moses' SNCC workers. They found a ripened discontent and receptivity among Mississippi's beleaguered black population. The white volunteers included social action–minded Christians as well as idealistic young liberals and radicals, many of them of Jewish heritage.

Bedding down on the rough floors of black people's homes, they shivered as they washed at outside cold water pumps in the early morning, and then they sat down to eat simple food together with their hosts. These children of a different, affluent America shared their lives with black Mississippians that summer. They worked with them in COFO's Freedom Schools, teaching basic skills like reading, typing, nutrition, and child care, and they helped to build and staff their community centers, which offered libraries, preschools, and social services.

The voter registration drive proceeded slowly and painfully amid much violent resistance from recalcitrant, raging whites. Black churches all over the state—where meetings were held, literature distributed, and the word spread—were the constant targets of dynamite and firebombs. The summer was barely under way when three young workers, two white and one black, disappeared after having been arrested in the town of Philadelphia. James Chaney—a volunteer with CORE—Andrew Goodman, and Michael Schwerner—two young New York Jews—had been working with a black congregation whose church had just been burned down. Later in the summer their decomposing bodies would be discovered by FBI investigators under a recently built earthen dam.

Over the years whites had murdered and lynched blacks as a matter of course in Mississippi with little national attention. White-on-black crime there inevitably went unpunished. But the killing of two white men, this twenty-four-year-old social worker and this twenty-one-year-old college student, brought the press and television cameras to Mississippi in force. The disappearance of Goodman, Schwerner, and Chaney brought in federal police power and precipitated greater federal action against illegal racist acts in Mississippi.

Despite every form of intimidation, from howling mobs and police clubbing to various forms of murderous terrorism, as well as a legal system that refused to treat blacks as human beings, voter registration proceeded. Blacks continued to stand up to be counted. Nineteen sixty-four was the year of the Civil Rights Act that integrated public accommodations, and there was no shortage of blacks willing to enter restaurants, hotels, public libraries, and the like to put white proprietors and authorities to the test. Similarly blacks fought back when whites fired them or refused them services as reprisal for their civil rights activity. They boycotted offending white businesses and marched and picketed.

The most impressive organizing effort to come out of Freedom Summer was the Mississippi Freedom Democratic Party (MFDP). Among the key organizers were Aaron Henry, a black druggist from rural Clarksdale, Fannie Lou Hamer, an eloquent black farm woman from the Delta, and Edwin King, the white chaplain of Tougaloo College. These three people represented the firm, determined stand that increasing numbers of black Mississippians were willing to take.

Henry had replaced Medgar Evers as the NAACP's leading figure in the state. He paid for his activism by suffering harassment, which included firebombing his store. Hamer had done voter registration in the Delta. Her gender afforded her no protection from police brutality. She was beaten more than once and permanently disabled, but this did not stop her. Edwin King had helped make the black Congregational college in Jackson the only truly integrated institution in the state. The college's racial liberalism drew the ire of state legislators, who tried unsuccessfully to get its accreditation removed. King and Henry toured the state together seeking to build support for an alternative slate of delegates to the 1964 Democratic National Convention. Their contention was that the all-white slate the party was fielding was obtained fraudulently, since the process excluded blacks.

The MFDP's challenge proved an embarrassment to the national Democratic Party, whose leaders' professed liberalism on civil rights took a backseat to their felt need of Dixiecrat support. They offered a "compromise" of seating two MFDP delegates. This alienated both sides. The white supremacist delegates stormed out, and the MFDP leaders decried the party's tokenism and refusal to recognize the constitutional question that made them the legitimate delegation. But while losing the battle, the MFDP would win the war. President Johnson was effectively pressured to introduce a new Voting Rights Act and twist arms as only he could to get it through the southern dominated Congress in 1965. This was the first such act with any force behind it, since it would send federal registrars into the South.

The tide was finally beginning to turn as an insistent black stand for freedom worked together with massive media exposure, an aroused public opinion, and federal action in two strong civil rights acts to make the difference. COFO's voter registration campaign, the MFDP, and the Voting Rights Act wrenched Mississippi politics open to black participation. All these elements that served to expose the dark violence of a closed and isolated society to the light of day also brought the more reasonable, moderate element to the surface.

Some of the gentler white folk began a long process of soul searching and change in response to the dogged demand of the people their society had so long victimized. Members of the business community and educated, genteel women now began to speak out for compliance with federal law. They wanted their rabid countrymen to stand aside and let blacks vote and frequent restaurants, hotels, and parks. They began to speak out for these things and they spoke against the segregationist effort to close down the schools, rather than integrate them. Freedom Summer was a bloody, murderous experience for the courageous people who participated in it but it marked a turning point in Mississippi's racial relations.

9

SIMPSON COUNTY

The confrontation and bloodletting that occurred in the traumatic summer of 1964 marked the beginning of the end of white supremacy in Mississippi. Together with the Voting Rights Act, which passed the following year, this stand for freedom cleared a path for progress toward eventual healing and reconciliation. But it would be some years before Mississippi's hinterlands would adapt to these changing realities. White domination and persecution of blacks continued in rural outposts of the state. Both school integration and voter registration first came to Simpson County in 1966.

John Perkins and Voice of Calvary eagerly anticipated and even prayed for the coming of the civil rights movement to Mendenhall. John believed strongly that without the affirmation of black identity and without the freedom of movement and association conferred by civil rights, other forms of black advancement could not occur. To his way of thinking, the freedom that Christians should uphold and fight for was not just an inner, spiritual thing. God lives in people, and the need for freedom applies as well to our bodies and minds as to our spirits. Racial discrimination is outside God's will because it interferes with the ability of people to grow, thrive, and actualize the gifts God has given them. So when the opportunity to integrate the schools and to register black people to vote finally came to Mendenhall, John and his people would be at the center of the action.

The states of the Deep South, where the chains of racial hatred bound most tightly, used a number of subterfuges to get around doing real school integration. State officials tried delaying tactics that would make integration nominal and postpone the real thing into a vague future. Like the alcoholic who cuts down on his drinking rather than going into recovery, white Mississippi used these ploys to avoid the inevitable reckoning. In 1966 the state offered what it called freedom of choice, a plan that left to individual black and white families the choice of which school their children would attend. White families of course would never send their children to the black schools, and only a tiny minority of hardy black souls would risk the well-being of their children in the white schools. John and Vera Mae decided that theirs would be one of the black families that would put themselves forward in this painful pioneering work.

Eleven-year-old Joanie was ironing her clothes in the downstairs back room when she heard Daddy say, "You can go to any school you want to next year." She knew he meant that black people now had a choice and that he wanted her and the others to integrate the white schools. Spencer and Philip, wanting to please their father, acted bravely compliant. They had a sense that their family was doing something special for black people. And though it often stung, they felt a sense of pride at being in civil rights leadership.

The significance of what they were doing was not lost on Joanie but she was a child who deeply valued personal relationships. Her vivacious personality had made her popular at school and she had been made class queen several of the five years she had been there. Mama and Daddy, with their fundamentalist leanings, had scruples concerning dancing, though, so Joanie wasn't at liberty to dance at the ball she reigned over. But it had been lots of fun anyway. She had close friends at school and she was a model student. She knew she would be losing all this at the white school and that it would be a harsh, lonely experience there, so she cried bitterly.

Joanie's tears were a poignant prediction of what was to come. Being the only black in a white Mississippi classroom was an ordeal of continuous and scalding humiliation. Spencer and Joanie were of middle school age, in the eighth and sixth grades. Philip, Derek, and Deborah were in elementary school. Wayne and Priscilla were not yet in school. The last Perkins child, Betty, was born that year. She was named after Vera Mae, but they all called her Betty.

The older children endured sharper barbs of racism at school than the younger ones. Spencer was in the early throes of adolescence, a

Vera Mae and children in the late 1960s. *Front row:* **Betty, Priscilla, Wayne, Deborah.** *Back row:* **Philip, Derek, Vera Mae, Spencer, Joanie.**

time when children, especially boys, can behave with exquisite cruelty. Skill in using a whole arsenal of verbal and material assault weapons is the special prowess of that age group. A natural, competitive jockeying for power goes on all the time, and authoritative teachers of superior character are needed to rein in the more aggressive youngsters. Introduce the despised "nigger" into a class of white Mississippi adolescents, and there is an open field for white predatory activity. And that is what Spencer experienced on a daily basis in his early teen years.

During the summer just before he was to descend into this arena of torment, Spencer attended a Freedom School in the nearby hamlet of Rose Hill. The black and white COFO volunteers who staffed the school attempted to fortify him emotionally for the abuse he was about to receive, much as Bob Moses and his staff had done with the white college students. Developed by SCLC, they taught the principles and techniques of nonviolent response to provocation. Spencer absorbed their training. He was proud of the historic stand that his family was taking but he was only thirteen years old and he needed security, companionship, and validation. At the white school he certainly got none of those things. He was completely isolated. No one sat in any of the desks adjacent to him. And he became the inevitable object of relentless abuse.

The evil of racism is in its reduction of persons to things. Dr. King, in his *Letter from Birmingham Jail,* had referenced the Jewish mystic Martin Buber's contrast of "I, Thou" with "I, it" relationships. "I" and "Thou" are loving, giving, receiving equals. In an "I, it" relationship the controlling person uses, exploits, and degrades the other, reducing her or him to a thing. When people have the power and license to treat those of a different race as if they were mere things, a whole train of sadistic horrors follows. And the familiar, ugly ritual of racism played itself out on a small scale, like so many little murders, in the white classrooms of Mississippi as a consequence of freedom of choice.

As Spencer sat at his quarantined desk, he became the constant target of spitballs the young white predators shot at him with rubber bands. They didn't hurt him physically, but each one pierced him emotionally. He was called all the usual racial epithets, and the white boys told crude jokes about him within his earshot, as if he were not there. He responded to these abuses with outward composure, saying things like "Glad I can entertain y'all." But he burned and ached inside. He would go home and sit in his upstairs front bedroom and stare at the police car two streets away, thinking how he'd like to shoot into it and no one would know where the shots came from.

At long last one of his teachers managed to overcome his own damaged sensitivities and hauled two of Spencer's boldest assailants along with him down to the principal's office. One of the boys defended his behavior, saying, "He's only a nigger." Spencer had learned to expect that kind of thing and he had steeled himself against it. But the child's ejaculation found a familiar frame of reference in the adults, which was why he had said it. It served to disarm the principal, who backed away from punishing or warning the offenders. The message Spencer received, and it devastated him, was that he would get no justice, no recognition of his personhood, in this white school.

One of the factors that made the integration so difficult for Spencer and for Joanie was its intense loneliness. Neither child had a black comrade-in-arms while doing combat duty at the white school. In the early months of this period of tokenism, Joanie did enjoy the companionship of two black classmates, Patricia Showers and Erskin McGee. But their families did not have the deep sense of mission of the Perkinses and they were soon gone, and Joanie was alone, really alone. As with Spencer, no one sat at a desk near her. No one talked to her. She was shunned as if she were a leper, always on the outside of things, never invited to participate. Other children would brush themselves off should they happen to touch her. Spencer also endured this particular insult.

At recess the children played games or danced and sang along to records of pop vocalists like the Monkees and Herman's Hermits, and

127

Joanie sat watching them, longing to participate. The sixth grade teacher tried to get her into class activities, but there were major barriers between Joanie and the white girls. Aside from the monstrous chasm that racism had created between white and black, Joanie saw in her white classmates a whole different way of behaving that was foreign to her. Black sixth grade girls down in the quarters were clearly still children doing children's things. But these white girls were wearing bras and hosiery and flirting with the boys and talking about them all the time. The mass commercial culture that sexualizes younger and younger children in order to excite their appetites for ever more consumption was only available in limited amounts to poor rural blacks, and so their children remained children a bit longer.

Day after day for two long years the Perkins children trudged into the white school. At the beginning the school bus picked them up, but all the seats were always taken, and they had to stand for the trip with the hostile white children glaring at them. Then the bus stopped crossing the tracks into black Mendenhall. So Vera Mae began to drive the children to school, and every day the crossing guard would ask to see her license. That was his own little contribution to the family's harassment for exercising their freedom of choice.

After the school year ended in 1968, John and Vera Mae decided to place their children back in the black school. They knew that the abuse had hurt them severely and that they needed time to recuperate and mend. Joanie's needs were particularly acute. The constant stress and the need to internalize her anger had taken a toll on her body. She ate in response to her anguish and struggled with a weight problem and she developed phlebitis, a painful inflammation of the blood vessels in her leg. Phlebitis was virtually unheard of in someone so young. It is a dangerous disease because it can cause a blood clot, which can break free and lodge in the head or lungs.

She spent about half of her eighth grade year getting medical care in California and staying with the Wilsons. It took her the better part of a year to recover from the phlebitis. One thinks of Richard Nixon, who would suffer with the same ailment just after he was driven from office in the Watergate affair: the common denominator, protracted trauma. Joanie continued her schooling in an integrated setting in California. She wasn't subjected to harsh treatment there, but the experience in Mississippi had hurt so much that it was hard to be with the white kids, even when they accepted her. Then in about the middle of the school year, Mama Wilson got sick, and Joanie had to go back home earlier than John and Vera Mae had planned.

One of the most damaging aspects of the freedom of choice episode was the miserable learning environment it created for blacks attempting to integrate the white schools. The hatred of the white children coupled with the biases of southern white teachers against black intellectual abilities was a perfect setup for failure. Philip and Derek were held back and Joanie worked below her ability. Recovery occurred when they returned to school in the black community. Joanie was sent to Piney Woods, the nearby black academy founded by education innovator Lawrence Jones early in the century. Dolphus Weary was a graduate of the Piney Woods Junior College. In this environment of academic nurture, Joanie was able to thrive again, though she picked up some rowdy habits from the teenage misfits who were sent to board there.

Spencer compensated for the indignities he had suffered by excelling in sports. He became a star basketball player in his junior year and went on to become all-state. In 1970, his senior year, when genuine integration finally took place, he played football with some of the same white boys who had abused him back in the eighth and ninth grades. Philip and Derek with their stocky, powerful builds, would eventually star in football for Jackson State.

The traumatic experience of the sixties certainly took a toll on the Perkins children. The three oldest were left with deep emotional scars. For the most part they buried their experiences deep inside. Spencer wouldn't mention them until he talked about them with a girlfriend in his senior year of college. And Joanie would recall them with sharp anger well into her adulthood. Philip preferred to remember how he had bested the white teachers who tried to get him to cut his bushy Afro. He simply started washing his hair before he went to school, and the water tightened the curls, which lowered his 'fro, and the white folks believed he'd gotten a haircut.

The younger children, Deborah and Derek, were less traumatized by the initial attempt at integration. Deborah was the only black girl in her first and second grade classes but she didn't experience any of the scornful rejection that her older siblings did. Her teachers were pleasant and they worked her into the class activities. The other kids didn't avoid her. The song in the Rodgers and Hammerstein musical says, "You've got to be taught to hate and fear," and these first graders hadn't yet had the full course in racism. Once when a boy said something derogatory to Deborah, the girl who had been chosen class queen spoke up, saying, "Don't you call her that. It isn't nice." And that little girl became Deborah's friend. Another time a boy marked the back of his shirt with a pen and told the teacher Deborah had done it. When she pleaded innocent to the crime, the teacher didn't believe her and disciplined her. But later some other children spoke up and told the teacher Deborah hadn't done it. It was the older kids who made little Deborah cry when she was waiting outside after school for her big sister and brothers. They took her books and started kicking them away, but Spencer and Philip rescued her.

While the children were going through their ordeal at the white school, John was working his way through Simpson, Lawrence, Smith, Rankin, and Jeff Davis counties registering black voters. Civil rights preoccupied his mind during the tumultuous late sixties, and he wanted to do everything within his power to pry the closed society open to full black participation. Voter registration was just the beginning though; for John it was a means to political and hence economic power. He knew that blacks in Mississippi could become a big, powerful voting bloc that could get people elected who would start funneling some of the patronage in their direction. And he also knew that whites jealously guarded the entrances to political power because they wanted to keep all that patronage for themselves. When John began registering voters, he was joining battle with a tight cabal of old boys that did not wish to be intruded on. And they would make it as rough as they could for any "smart nigger" who would dare challenge them.

John's work in voter registration was part of the Voters' Rights Project, which took place during 1966 and 1967 under the auspices of the AFL-CIO. Vernon Jordan, later president of the Urban League, led this action to put the 1965 Voting Rights Act into effect. Claude Ramsay, head of the AFL-CIO in Mississippi, had courageously stood up and brought the union umbrella in behind the voting rights drive. Ramsay was able to provide access to a substantial fund the AFL-CIO was making available in support of the effort. And he made John one of his supervisors, with authority over four counties in central Mississippi.

So John went out and told people that if they would get a local voter registration drive going, he could hire them at two hundred dollars a month for two months. Fifty dollars a week was a healthy sum for a black person in Mississippi in the sixties, and so the money made it easier to get workers. But money was also a potential corruptor, and John had to be careful to hire really committed workers and not people who were going to filch from the campaign till. John made that mistake in Jeff Davis County, where the man he hired undermined the campaign by spending the campaign expense money on himself.

In Simpson County locales John paid homage to the local NAACP leader, Nathan Rubin. But it was John's relentless energy that really propelled this theater of Mississippi's civil rights movement. In Mendenhall, when the white powers-that-be made it impossible for voter registration workers to get office space, a VOC crew built one on the loading dock of the post office, the only piece of federal property in town. As John traveled around central Mississippi organizing voter registration, he found that most of the local authorities were choosing to comply with the law. When this occurred, he and his coworkers found they could register people without incident, and the federal registrars, authorized by the Voting Rights Act, didn't have to be called in.

Progress was made, but whites were getting a good long look at who it was that was politicizing black folks in central Mississippi. John's image was most sharply silhouetted in Simpson County during the tumultuous election year of 1968. During the same time that the war of hawks and doves in the national Democratic Party was building toward an inferno in Mayor Daley's Chicago, John and VOC were leading a campaign to unseat John D. Smith, the mossback highway commissioner for Mississippi's southern District. A white man, William "Shag" Pyron, had the temerity to court black support for the Highway Commission, and he was promising jobs to blacks in exchange for votes.

During this first election campaign to draw intensive black involvement, racial tensions around Mendenhall increased. Klansmen were driving provocatively by the front of John's house and they were telephoning late-night murder threats. And now it was time for Mendenhall's black community to mount its own defenses. Armed men surrounded John's house and they gathered around the wood and redbrick buildings of Voice of Calvary: the one-story church, the Bible institute, and the newly built cooperative store, which was regularly used for civil rights and election-strategy meetings. These were hardened men, many of them, who lived at the fringe of black community life. They expressed no interest in spiritual matters but they respected John and they liked the seeds of hope and progress he was planting. So they took up arms to keep him alive and his mission intact.

Perhaps it is a current of fear in official America, just below the level of consciousness, that explains why histories and journalistic accounts of the black civil rights movement avoid mention of southern black measures of self-defense. Whites have feared that blacks, having endured centuries of white atrocity, might seize the day to wreak murderous vengeance in thousands of twentieth century Nat Turner–style rebellions. White fear of black violence was an ironic theme in media coverage of the civil rights movement, since blacks had endured centuries of white violence.

Children and staff of VOC, c.1966.

Dr. King knew well that it was in the establishment's self-interest to give saturation exposure to his nonviolent crusade. And thus his March on Washington for Jobs and Freedom on August 28, 1963, the year of the hundredth anniversary of the Emancipation Proclamation, drew more white support than any other single event in the civil rights movement. Militant blacks castigated the March as having an aura of petitioning the Great White Father for their rights. Wanting and demanding more black self-assertion, Malcolm X had derided it as the "Farce on Washington."

The March drew involvement from a nation of sincere white liberals, who supported black civil rights but who also had a stake in King's nonviolence—safe as it was for whites—as the most effective way to freedom. Because of white fear of black violence, particularly after the Watts riots in the summer of 1965, a myth was created that the black civil rights movement was built entirely on Ghandian pacifism. It is true that King believed in and taught such passive resistance—and he, like the Hindu leader, ended up martyred. But blacks as a whole in the civil rights movement throughout the South upheld the hallowed American practice of taking up arms in self-defense.

Guns had been in the African American community since the days of slavery, and the need of blacks to counter spiraling violence from the Klan and other white terrorist groups during the civil rights movement led to the formation of the Deacons for Defense and Justice. The Deacons came to Mendenhall in 1969 and 1970, when the civil rights movement there turned to economic boycott and public demonstration. They were a strong, quietly effective force organized to protect blacks in the South from white terrorism. Created in 1964 in Jonesboro, Louisiana, the Deacons would retain a formidable presence throughout the Deep South until the tide of southern racism turned in the seventies, as law enforcement agencies began to hire large numbers of blacks.

While most of them were not likely to be churchgoers, the Deacons sprang out of the deeply religious southern black culture. When they chose their name, they had the New Testament concept of "overseers" and "protectors" of the faith in mind. Blacks as a whole saw their civil rights movement as an expression of their faith, since God desires justice for poor and oppressed peoples. A popular expression among blacks in the sixties was "Keep the faith, baby."

Martin Luther King and the Southern Christian Leadership Conference and its affiliates in other parts of the country decried the Deacons and other black self-defense associations, fearing that self-defense would turn into aggression. The Congress of Racial Equality strongly endorsed them. CORE's national director, James Farmer, went so far as to commit his organization to a "partnership of brothers" with the Deacons. Not that CORE in 1965 was eschewing non-violence in favor of some kind of racial warfare. But Farmer and Floyd McKissick and the other CORE leaders recognized that only when blacks seized the initiative and took up arms to defend themselves in concerted action could they halt a growing plague of southern white terrorism.

Bogalusa, Louisiana, which housed a giant paper mill of the Crown Zellerbach Corporation, was crawling with Klansmen. Some of the most active KKKers were members of the police department. Redneck mill workers foamed with rage against blacks and their quest for equality. The mill workers paraded their cars and pickups through the ghetto, burning crosses, shooting, and firebombing at will. When blacks sought to eat at restaurants to test the local public accommodations' compliance with the law, they were accosted and pummeled by angry white mobs. The police didn't lift a finger to protect them, and snarling white cops looked for the slightest excuse to bash a black man's head.

This was the situation in Bogalusa as it was in much of the rural Deep South in the mid-sixties and this is what made the Deacons necessary. Not wishing to operate as a band of outlaws, they took out a charter and articles of incorporation under Louisiana law. Their leaders were often independent black shopkeepers and professionals, men with some education and a sense of their self-worth. A. Z. Young, the leader of CORE's Bogalusa affiliate, the Civic and Voter's League, eagerly embraced the Deacons. He and most of the other black inhabitants saw them as the best insurance of black safety and civil rights.

Men like Ernest Thomas, the civil rights worker who first organized the Deacons, wanted to make it a nationally based civil rights organization. Deacon spokesmen responded to King and SCLC, saying that they were supporting nonviolent demonstrations by protecting black demonstrators from white violence. And despite the opposition they drew from tactful civil rights leaders and nervous white authorities around the country, the Deacons' membership expanded rapidly. By the middle of 1966 they had close to sixty chapters, mostly in the Deep South.

They operated like trained undercover police or secret service personnel. Using walkie-talkies, they monitored mass civil rights gatherings, and their restrained presence protected an ever vulnerable black community from violent white reprisal. Though Deacons went north to Chicago and west to Los Angeles in 1966, seeking black financial support and involvement, they never became an important presence outside the South.

As the Deacons mounted armed resistance to racist terrorism, black men, who had been emasculated by southern racism, were now taking back their power by protecting their parents, brothers, sisters, and children. This was a milestone of healthy self-assertion in the African American revolution and it drew expressions of grateful support from Mississippi's black leaders, like Charles Evers in Fayette and John Perkins in Mendenhall.

The Deacons struck a responsive chord in John. He had more than a little of his uncles in him and he knew better than he knew his name that when a black man finally takes a stand and says, "Enough! Y'all come after us and a lot of y'all are goin' down with us," that's when he takes back his personhood. Taking that stand restores self-respect and brings a new if grudging respect from the white antagonist who begins to have second thoughts about his night riding, head bashing, and terrorism. John knew that, contrary to the worst fears of the Deacons' detractors, their stand actually worked to prevent violence and not to foment it.

The men who guarded John's house and the VOC compound during the 1968 election campaign were not Deacons, but they were men of similar background and commitment. They were joined by Deacons when the civil rights movement in Mendenhall escalated during the following year. John was more than pleased with the results of the election. A large turnout of newly enfranchised black voters elected Shag Pyron highway commissioner.

The white power structure of Mendenhall, feeling injury to itself, began to look harder and more resentfully at this preacher who had come back from California and was now stirring up trouble for them. After the election, relations between Mendenhall's white and black communities chilled. In neighboring counties too, where John and his organization had worked hard registering voters, white authorities were now aware of them and set against them.

Along with the voter registration and election campaigns, blacks in the Mendenhall area, as throughout the South, moved to test locally the Public Accommodations Act. Again it was VOC that provided leadership. Big, gentle Herbert Jones was the bearlike figure who led many of the teams that went out to integrate the restaurants and the hotels. He mapped out strategy at the meetings they held in the cooperative store, deciding which places to hit and when to hit them. Integrating public accommodations, like most civil rights activities in Mississippi, was very dangerous, and if a person went out alone he or she could easily get beat up. So Herbert organized teams and they went out together. Herbert often landed in jail, and Vera Mae, who was easier to get hold of than John, had to go get him out.

Integrating public accommodations was a battle and it could be pretty scary. Largely for that reason, this form of combat carried a badge of distinction. Herbert became fabled among VOC staff for his daring feats in this field, but most of the workers were eager to volunteer for public accommodations duty. The young, white civil rights workers, many of them northern Jews, would stride through cafe doors together with black Christians from Voice of Calvary. John was often involved in these missions to open white commercial establishments.

One of the tenser moments in this campaign came at a truck stop in D'Lo, between Jackson and Mendenhall. John, Herbert, and Leonard Stapleton were driving a young soldier, Private Norwood, home for his furlough. Norwood didn't know the others were planning to integrate this watering hole of good old boys until they started talking about it in the car. He went along willingly but a little nervously. As the four men entered the truck stop together, John's eyes took in the tables of rough-looking men lifting their heads to stare at these black intruders. He felt his heartbeat quicken as they walked to a table and sat down.

The place filled with an eerie stillness. The rough-looking men were now glaring hard at John and his party, and the waitress was saying she wasn't going to serve them. John had to sit on his hands to keep them from shaking. Just then, the owner told the waitress to go ahead and serve these customers. Slowly people turned to resume their conversations, though they would shoot hard and ugly glances at John, Herbert, Leonard, and the young man in uniform as they sat, ordered their meal, and ate.

Integrating the places of commerce that had long been white only was a fearful experience but it was something that blacks and their progressive white allies knew they had to do, like landing at so many enemy-occupied beachheads. Once a party of black pioneers had penetrated a restaurant or motel, others went in their wake to keep it open. It was an empowering experience that forged close, resilient bonds among southern blacks as they laid claim to their civil rights.

You can get the best food in Mendenhall between twelve noon and two P.M. at a two-story house in the lower part of town, near the tracks you cross to get to the quarters. The dining room, on the main floor as you walk in, has a number of big round tables with revolving lazy Susans in the center. On them are dishes heaped with fried chicken, catfish, mashed potatoes, fried okra, and other delectables. This family style house of southern cooking was of course closed to black clientele until the mid-sixties.

The woman who owned Revolving Tables paid a visit to John and Vera Mae one night and pleaded with them not to integrate her restaurant. She told them it would kill her business. But people from VOC ate at the restaurant, and the blacks who worked there felt uplifted as they got the opportunity to serve their friends and families for the first time in public. The owner acceded to integration, and Revolving Tables continued to dish up its delicious southern fare for an eager public, now in black and white.

By the end of 1968 the civil rights movement in central Mississippi had produced many tangible results. African Americans had a long road yet to racial equality but they had begun the process of building a more positive identity and assuming their rightful place in southern society. John was encouraged by what blacks were accomplishing for themselves in Mississippi. When he thought of his own and VOC's role in the recent election, he smiled with satisfaction. Public accommodations were opening up rapidly now, though real school integration was still two years away, and it had been sadly necessary to take the children out of the white schools. Much more needed to happen, but the accomplishments of the civil rights movement were giving new hope to a long-suffering people.

Civil rights would remain a major absorption of John and Vera Mae and Voice of Calvary to the end of the decade but it was not the chief purpose for their existence. That continued to be the spiritual reclamation of rural southern African Americans. John was always cognizant that spiritual transformation could not occur without paying attention to the whole range of their human need. In the late sixties, together with a changing and growing number of white supporters and volunteers, he would discover new ways to meet these challenges. And the focus of his work would broaden and deepen.

10

Co-ops

The civil rights movement acted as a potent force for bringing together black leaders and everyone else committed to African American advancement. In 1966, as the voter registration drive was going on, John and Vera Mae compiled a list of the hundred people in Simpson County most active in the area of civil rights and invited them to an organizational meeting at their house. Close to seventy showed up and they organized the Simpson County Civic League, with Nathan Rubin of the NAACP as their chairman. This was the core group that pushed against the white power structure and supported measures of self-help that would liberate the black community from dependence on white paternalism. They planned the campaigns for integrating public accommodations and they supported John's drive to improve conditions among poor black folk with such programs as Head Start.

John brought Head Start to Mendenhall not only to feed black children, but to buttress the black community with federal money and power. The southern white establishment had always been able to exert absolute power over blacks by holding the economic means of their survival. John was keenly aware that ownership of whatever generates wealth was the only way blacks could get out from under the heel of whites. That concept had been burned into him back when he was eleven years old and the white farmer had paid him fifteen cents for a day's hard labor. Now he would pragmatically use any federal program, foundation grant, or charitable contribution that he could obtain to help bring about black economic independence and development.

Immediately he observed the limitations of Head Start and most of the federal antipoverty programs in generating black development. Head Start enabled young black mothers to get quality care and nutrition for their children while they worked outside the home but it was federally based and did little to help blacks take real control of their own lives. Reliance on federal largesse rather than on that of white Southerners might be helpful for the moment but it could create a more benign form of dependency. John had a belief rooted in his entrepreneurial spirit that when African Americans could at long last build enterprises of their own, they would gain immeasurably in hope and personal dignity. So federal programs were a good way to begin the process of setting blacks free, but real progress would come only as blacks began to make creative use of their own resources.

John was a busy man in the summer of 1967. He was still making his teaching circuit through the schools, and then there was all the civil rights work and leadership development with the youth at VOC. Still he was ever alert and casting about for anything that would further the cause. He was particularly attuned to economic opportunity and when he came across a flyer publicizing a talk on how to start your own cooperative business, it drew his immediate interest. He attended the meeting and was exposed to some ideas there that fired his enthusiasm. Immediately his mind began to work overtime thinking about the kinds of cooperative enterprises he could introduce among the people Voice of Calvary was serving in Simpson County.

The younger, more militant black activists of the sixties were concerned about African Americans getting control of their own lives and developing their own culture and commerce. That is what was meant by "black power," as sociologist W. E. B. Du Bois, black nationalist Marcus Garvey, and novelist Richard Wright had developed the term. Jesse Morris, who was close to two of the most controversial black nationalists of the sixties, Rap Brown and Stokely Carmichael, was one of the leaders of the cooperative movement in Mississippi.

At the meeting advertised in the flyer, John met Morris and other organizers of Liberty House, a poor people's sewing and handicrafts enterprise. Using the cooperative model, Morris and his fellow entrepreneurs had built an operation that trained rural blacks to follow sewing patterns and make clothing, handbags, and other accessories. Liberty House bought the finished goods and marketed them all over the country. This was a successful, cooperatively owned venture, staffed largely by CORE and SNCC personnel. As John learned about Liberty House, he became impressed by the cooperative's effectiveness in putting people to work and increasing their income and independence.

John also met A. J. McKnight, a Roman Catholic priest who had attended seminary in New York and gone south with other members of his order to aid in black rural development. McKnight, who was based in Lafayette, Louisiana, was one of the most prolific users of the cooperative idea. John was excited by McKnight's work and by cooperatives in general because they were a way that the poor could pool resources, generate capital, and build real enterprises of their own. McKnight's story in essence paralleled that of John and Voice of Calvary. He was trying to minister to the felt needs of the people and had begun by training a staff to do adult education to enhance literacy in the parish. But it was hard to get people to attend the reading classes. They felt a more pressing need for jobs, and so McKnight gravitated in that direction and hit on cooperatives as a good way to generate jobs. He spent some time in Canada studying co-ops before beginning in agriculture, forming a cooperative to buy fertilizer.

Agricultural co-ops were a familiar way of doing business in rural America, dating back to the Populist era in the late nineteenth century. Farmers were always in debt, cash poor, and dependent on the big railroads and corporations to market their goods. They found that joining together with their neighbors to form cooperatives increased their purchasing power and cheapened the cost of supplies and machinery. During the Great Depression and the New Deal, the federal government's REA used the cooperative principle to spread electrification through the rural South. Cooperatives kept control at the local level, giving the users who participated in them an active voice in their management. Thus overdependence on bureaucracy had been avoided and grass roots participation encouraged.

McKnight's fertilizer cooperative was successful in generating capital and its success inspired a bakery and then a gas station run on the cooperative basis. He began to champion the cooperative principle as the best way to bring economic development to the impoverished rural South. The Ford Foundation agreed and gave him a hefty grant in 1967 to do cooperative development in four southern states: Louisiana, Mississippi, Alabama, and Tennessee. And it was this grant that had sent him into Mississippi to spread the cooperative gospel.

Father McKnight was looking for people he could train and provide with seed money to start cooperatives throughout the state. This was a godsend for John, who was always on the lookout for an idea that could help bring independence and prosperity to his people. He jumped in with both feet, heading down to Louisiana in the fall for an intensive three-week training workshop McKnight was running.

As John walked the streets of black Mendenhall and drove through the countryside and sat with the people in their cramped little hovels, a pained sense of the need for decent housing was ever stirring in his mind. And so housing became a natural place of focus for John's first cooperative venture. As he began to lay out the economic possibilities inherent in cooperatives, he kindled people's hopes. With the dream of good housing nurtured by John's efforts, forty people chartered the Simpson County Development Corporation with each person putting ten dollars into a common fund. Forming this housing cooperative made them eligible to receive a loan from the Farmers Home Administration (FHA), which enabled them to build five duplex houses.

This project was the first major stimulus for black housing development in the area. It led to the appointment of the first black FHA administrator in the area, and he in turn made home loans more easily obtainable. In the late sixties and seventies you could hear the sweet sounds of hammering and sawing and muddy wet cement being mixed, and soon a number of tidy, warmly painted, little houses blossomed amid the general decay of the quarters.

Mendenhall's housing cooperative gave the renters a chance to invest their rent money in a fund that would pay them dividends. A prime attraction of cooperatives for John was the opportunity they gave the poor to build enterprises of their own. African Americans had been so poor and dependent that, having little concept of self-help, they tended to live from day to day, spending what little came into their hands. There had always been the Archie Buckleys and the Jesse Newsomes and the Aunt Coots but they were the exceptions.

Cooperatives offered the possibility of revolutionizing grass roots economic values by bringing working capital into the community and getting a large number of people involved in the empowering process of enterprise building. The housing co-op did not make much of a dent in the vast problem of black housing but it stimulated other cooperative ventures as well as a good deal of black-run housing construction, facilitated by the friendly FHA administrator. One thing good about Mississippi was the relative ease with which a man could become a general contractor and hire subcontractors and build houses for people. No bureaucratic gatekeeping or torturous testing procedures stood in the way.

In the latter sixties, as the civil rights movement was expanding throughout Mississippi, so too was the cooperative movement. Father McKnight came often to Mendenhall, and John became his right-hand man in spreading cooperative development locally and around the state.

For John the heart of the cooperative movement was not an objective set of ideas and practices to bring economic advancement and greater independence to blacks in the South. It certainly contained those purposes, but like everything else in John's orbit, it was woven into an expanding community, based in rich personal relationships. The thrift store, a Mendenhall cooperative built in 1970, illustrates the forming of deep familial bonds around John's work. He and Herbert Jones and the others put up the structure that housed the store near VOC's buildings. The back room of that facility was used for planning sessions during the boycott and campaign for a broad spectrum of black civil rights that would go on in Mendenhall that year.

**John and Mitchell Hayes in front of the first cooperative store
in Mendenhall.**

Mitchell Hayes, who was one of the tough-minded old farmers who were the bedrock of John's support network in the early years, became the manager of the store. Mr. Hayes loved John and his family. Like Mr. Buckley, Isaac and Jesse Newsome, and Eugene Walker, he was deeply affected by having a preacher who lived among the people. And he wanted to do everything he could to help John and the movement. His background was a rougher one than that of most of the old churchmen at Voice of Calvary. He had been convicted of premeditated murder and had done a long stretch of prison time. But when he came out, he had his passions under control, and his life became marked by a plain-dealing honesty and integrity. For Hayes, lying about anything would be the coward's way out.

Hayes became active in the civil rights struggle, though he remained at the edge of VOC's church life, never learning the religious language that punctuates the speech of other Christians. You could say he stood midway between those who were being converted and coming in Christian faith into VOC and the people committed to John's work whose involvement was not based on religious motivation. With the men in the latter group, Hayes was one of the people who had guarded John's house during the tense days of the 1968 election campaign.

Of course Mitchell Hayes was a most conscientious store manager who kept an eye out for anything untoward going on about the premises. One morning after a civil rights meeting in the back room had continued late into the night, he was informed about a broken pane of glass in the door. Normally he would have been ready to apprehend the culprit, and woe to that person, but this time Mr. Hayes was smiling. It seemed that during the meeting the two little Perkins girls, four-year-old Priscilla and two-year-old Betty, had fallen asleep on a back bench unbeknownst to the adults. When the meeting ended, they walked out and locked up with the two little girls still sleeping inside.

Hours later Priscilla and Betty woke up in the dark storeroom. Betty began to cry, but Priscilla comforted her little sister, saying "Don't cry. We'll get out of here." She was able to break the glass and open the door, and the children scurried out of the store and over to the Perkins house. When John and Vera Mae became aware of what had happened, they were thoroughly unnerved, but at the same time relieved at the sight of their little girls. As Priscilla told her parents how she and Betty had gotten out of the locked store, they felt proud of the little girl's courageous ingenuity.

And so did Mr. Hayes when he heard about the incident. He loved the Perkinses and felt like a father to John and Vera Mae and a grandfather to the children. These were the kinds of personal ties that underlay all the evangelism and economic development John and VOC were doing.

One of Voice of Calvary's early cooperative ventures was a farm they used to provide much of the food for the volunteers who staffed the ministries. This little farm was more for the subsistence of people directly involved with VOC than for any commercial market. But it served well to train its participants in the workings of cooperatives in agriculture. By the late sixties VOC's growing adult education program was drawing many white Christian volunteers from more affluent parts of the country. The United Brethren Church sent modest young men and women down to Mississippi to help.

They were Germanic plain folk, many still inhabiting the Pennsylvania farmlands originally settled by their eighteenth-century Pietist ancestors. Coming from agricultural backgrounds, they worked with knowledge and efficiency on the cooperative farm. These young Brethren volunteers also served as staff in adult education and helped out in the construction projects and the other programs. They were clean, earnest young people. The women, without makeup, wore loose-fitting dresses, falling well below the knee, and tiny gauzy caps perched on their heads, a sign of their submission to God.

The central thrust of Father McKnight's cooperative movement was the planting of commercial farming co-ops throughout the South, and John got deeply involved with him in this effort. In 1967 and 1968 he spent a good deal of time traveling in Louisiana and Tennessee in addition to Mississippi, supervising rural cooperative projects. Working as a partner in McKnight's Ford-endowed Federation of Southern Cooperatives, he taught, organized, and gathered information for the ongoing in-depth study they were doing. As part of that study, Ford sponsored Father McKnight, John, and four others to fly to Israel to research the kibbutzim, Israel's highly touted version of cooperative agriculture.

John flew out of New York on a nonstop flight to Tel Aviv. Flying was becoming a familiar and rather comfortable experience for him as he had started to travel regularly, speaking at churches and Christian gatherings about his work and raising support. But this was the first of his travels abroad. It was to be a thirty-two-day crash course in coop-

erative economics, Israeli style, and John, with his inveterate curiosity, was brimming with excitement about it.

This flight, an El Al charter, was going half-way around the world,
a lot longer and more tiring than anything he had yet experienced. In
fact the pilot announced to the passengers that they were on the longest
nonstop flight in existence.

As they were making their way out of the plane in Israel, John could
hear the festive sound of bands playing. The music relaxed him, making him feel warmly welcomed, even though he knew it was to honor
an American delegation that came annually on the charter to deliver
a big check for Israeli schools.

After John and the others had recuperated for a day or two at their
hotel, they began a whirlwind tour of the kibbutzim and their elaborate support system in the banks, universities, and government. Israeli
public and private institutions were integrally connected in a well-
wrought process of economic development, and there was much to
learn from them. The six Americans were given a limousine with two
alternating chauffeurs and an interpreter. One of the chauffeurs told
them that he had been in the terrorist Irgun, which had played a role
in wresting Palestine from the British. John's days were jam-packed
with activities as the limousine carried him and his colleagues from
place to place on their educational tour.

On a typical day they might start out visiting a cooperative bank
where they would receive an elaborate overview of the principles of
cooperative finance. Then they were off to a university to talk with one
of the professors who was on loan from a kibbutz. The Israelis liked
the idea of combining theory with practice, and the professors, most
of them in agriculture and the sciences, longed to be back out on the
kibbutzim, where they could get their hands dirty. Life on the kibbutz
embodied the reality of what they were teaching, and the fact that they
were practitioners as well as theoreticians gave vivid immediacy to
their academic presentations. As the day ended, John's group would
typically find themselves on a kibbutz, where they would spend the
night and then rise early the next day to tour and gain familiarity with
the intricate workings of Israeli communal life.

They visited a number of kibbutzim, and John caught something of
the collective idealism that powered them. Most were quite diversified, though they usually had a main industry, like cotton growing or

cattle raising. Some had small-scale factories and enterprises turning out finished products for market. Holding their land and goods in common, the people on the kibbutzim had developed strong bonds of unity and a lofty sense of purpose. John wondered if it would ever be possible to generate such productive enthusiasm in Mississippi.

The tour served to immerse John in the specifics of a diversified, well-coordinated economic development process. A key object lesson it drove home was the primary need for a bank that could finance long-term development. The Israelis, with their strong commitment to the way of life in the kibbutzim, used banks to finance kibbutz industry and agriculture, providing five-, ten-, and fifteen-year loans. With the backing of the government and the banks, the cooperative enterprises had five years to start up and grow before they had to begin paying on their loans.

The experience in Israel gave Father McKnight and John the insight to develop the means of financing long-term funding for the co-op movement in the American South. They created the Southern Cooperative Development Fund (SCDF), a cooperative investment and banking agency. It would take them about a year and a half, from 1968 to 1970, to get the SCDF up and running, but in the long run it would prove to be a highly successful and durable means of financing new co-ops.

John was immersed in the cooperative movement into the early seventies, expanding Voice of Calvary's operations to Jackson and locating an SCDF office within the facility. He planted and nourished all kinds of co-ops, co-op organizers, and participants throughout Mississippi. Within the Mendenhall operations as well as around the state, wherever John brought the cooperative movement, he saw it as a means to give the people excellent practical training in economics. Teaching cooperative economics to help African Americans emerge from poverty and dependence fired John's enthusiasm and he taught in a lively, engaged manner, much as he taught Bible to the children. For John, development was holistic; you get freed from self-destructive sin by giving your heart to the Lord and you climb out of poverty and hopelessness by tapping into your God-given resources.

In his schoolmaster role John expounded four principles at the base of cooperative development. First, he emphasized open membership. The mere act of buying the product makes you a member of the community of producers. You're paid a periodic dividend based on the amount you spend. Your investment through your patronage gets you involved. As you get more and more involved and learn the economic principles, you may be motivated to move into management. John preached co-ops because they were an open system and not controlled by some outside authority. To an oppressed, dominated people this was a thoroughly liberating ideal.

John's second egalitarian principle was democratic, one-person-one-vote control. This is the bulwark of open membership. No matter how much or how little of the product a person buys, he or she has only one vote. So those with money can't steal control of the enterprise. In a credit union, for example, you can borrow the maximum amount of money available, but you still have only one vote.

The dividends or users' refund was the third cooperative principle John emphasized. Everybody shares in the profits, based on his or her patronage of the co-op. This is the built-in incentive to use the co-op. Again using the example of the credit union, the more you use it, the cheaper you get your money. If it's a supermarket, the more you buy there, the more dividend you get back from it. Because of the dividends, spending becomes a personal investment program, and it connects the consumer with a growing enterprise.

John was always harping on the need for community-based businesses that keep the people's money within the community. And in the rural South, where few individual blacks could amass the capital to start a business, the co-ops were a means to use people's spending to generate capital to build community-controlled enterprises.

John, like Francis Bacon, knew that knowledge is power and he saw the cooperative movement in the South as a practical way to give a deprived people a continuous education in economics. This educative function was his fourth principle of cooperative development. The education was a holistic process. People were drawn to the co-ops because the co-ops were based in the community and had reasonable prices. Other important factors were that people could spend and invest at the same time and that they could belong to the co-op.

Gaining a sense of belonging had been a crucial element in John's own development, and the co-ops were one way to bring people into a sharing, growing, community experience. People experienced economic improvement, hope, and camaraderie all at the same time. These advantages were a powerful means of people getting in fruitful contact with one another. Such personal connection naturally attracted people, so the co-ops didn't have to spend precious resources on advertising.

John saw the cooperatives actually changing the consciousness of the people from passive consuming to active saving and investing. The self-perpetuating poverty of the black community has always been reinforced by poor spending habits. John observed that poverty causes people to dwell on instant gratification. When they have a little money, for example, they buy a cheap table and chairs that will soon turn into junk rather than saving money until they have enough for a nice dining room set they can will to their children. With co-op participation, John saw people's habits begin to change from instant gratification to saving for better things. As they got involved in real economic development, they gained hope and they began to see the possibilities in investment, accumulation, and growth.

In the late sixties, as the black power movement was gaining ascendancy and Martin Luther King's nonviolence was pushed to the periphery, the pent-up rage from hundreds of years of oppression became a spontaneous combustion that exploded the cities in flame. After King was killed in 1968 while he was campaigning for Memphis sanitation workers, another round of conflagration engulfed cities throughout the country. A great fear of black violence and destruction spread among whites, and black power, in the public mind, became equated with vengeful mayhem. Translating civil rights victories into real power for blacks, however, was only the logical next step in the movement. It was true that Rap Brown, Stokely Carmichael, and the Black Panther movement sounded angry and threatening, much as Malcolm X had, but anger among black men was inevitable, for America had marginalized them, reducing them to impotent poverty. And as they had moved to claim the common rights of Americans, they had seen their most effective leaders killed.

The essence of black power was not in rage or violence. It was in securing the opportunities for advancement supposedly afforded all Americans and in gaining a greater measure of control over one's own life. John Perkins embodied a constructive black power as he worked to end segregation, built cooperatives to bring capital into the community, and trained and motivated young black leaders.

Discipling, educating, and empowering young men and women to assume leadership roles in developing the black community was at the heart of John's vision for the future. And Dolphus Weary had the natural drive, intelligence, and leadership potential to become the fulcrum of John's program. Despite the grinding poverty of his fatherless family, Dolphus had managed to get in two years of junior college at Piney Woods, and with John's encouragement, Dolphus received his bachelor's degree at Los Angeles Baptist College (LABC) in Newhall, California, on a basketball scholarship.

LABC was a small parochial institution with a student body made up of white suburban evangelicals. It was perched in the dry hills at the remote northeast end of the San Fernando Valley, the sprawling chain of smoggy suburbs just above Los Angeles. In 1968 Newhall was probably home to a lot more lizards than people. Its isolation characterized many suburban evangelicals, who tended to cluster in their own churchy ghettoes, well away from blacks and other ethnics. Dolphus and his childhood friend Jimmie Walker were the ones who integrated LABC, and the experience, to their grim surprise, had some things in common with integration in Mississippi. Many of the white students stereotyped Dolphus and Jimmie as dumb because they were black, and some would look through them as if they didn't exist.

Dolphus was particularly jolted by the reaction of a group of students gathered in his dormitory corridor as they heard about Martin Luther King's assassination. He and Jimmie could hardly believe what they were hearing. When the radio news reporter announced the great black leader's death, a loud cheer went up from these young white Christians. Dolphus had been only dimly aware that evangelicals disliked Martin Luther King.

Stuck in reaction against liberalism and the social gospel, many evangelicals tended to view social justice issues as somehow subversive. Fundamentalist spokesmen commonly wrapped themselves in the ideals of nineteenth-century rugged individualism and they tended to view King and other social reformers as dangerous rabble-rousers with socialistic or even communist agendas. These biases, together with their physical isolation from blacks, served to alienate many white evangelicals from the African American cause. So Dolphus found the racial atmosphere at this evangelical college in Southern California different only in degree from what he had known in the South.

Rather than leaving the college or remaining silent and building up resentment, Dolphus decided to respond frontally to the racism he encountered at LABC. He resolved to be bolder in speaking out about prejudice on campus. And in the months to come he lost no opportunity to raise the issue of the existence of racial discrimination on campus and in the nation-at-large. He took it on himself to educate the white college students around him about African American culture and achievement. As a result of his efforts, he found some people becoming friendlier and more sympathetic toward his position. Racism was not ingrained in these young people as an integral aspect of their culture, as it was with southern whites, and they were open to changing their attitudes as they were more exposed to a black point of view.

When Dolphus and Jimmie returned to Mississippi for the summer, they talked proudly about the "pioneering" work they had done at the West Coast college and they tried to persuade others to join them out there. Two of the people they succeeded in recruiting were Carolyn Albritton and Rosie Camper, who were working in Voice of Calvary's summer programs in Mendenhall. Rosie would eventually become Dolphus's wife, and Carolyn would marry Artis Fletcher. Artis had gone up to Chicago to Moody Bible Institute, where he was working to turn his old interest in preaching into a divinity degree. Carolyn and Rosie were among the seven black Mississippians broadening the white students' horizons at LABC during Dolphus's senior year.

One day during that summer, Dolphus found himself sitting in the Voice of Calvary office talking with John Perkins about creating a new ministry. John had a passion for getting young black collegians to locate back in the poor community of their origin after graduation. Early on in his Mississippi work John realized that the "up and out" phenomenon that so characterizes the American pattern of individual success acts to leave the poor community, whether rural or inner city, even more economically devastated. The natural leaders were moving out to the suburbs, and so their leadership and skills would not become available to their community of origin.

Dolphus was the first of these achieving youths whom John was able to persuade to bring his skills and his commitment back home. As the leader of VOC's lively youth group, he had been a big brother to many, including the older Perkins children. And now John wanted Dolphus to be the key person in organizing a cadre of young Christian leaders to go into the churches of nearby communities and do Bible teaching and discipling.

During that first summer, Dolphus led a group of six Voice of Calvary youths in teaching week-long vacation Bible schools in local churches and other settings within a thirty-five-mile radius of Mendenhall. One of the places they went was the Oakley Training School, a reformatory for juveniles who had been in trouble with the law. The churches they went to all had preachers who lived forty to sixty miles away, so it was the members who made the decision for the VOC team to come.

Strange as it may seem, the preachers and elders commonly perceived such an educated team of Bible teachers as a threat to the church. The Voice of Calvary youths, in keeping with what they had learned from John, stressed the Reformation message that you don't work for salvation; God gives it freely to all sincere comers. But as Dolphus had experienced as a child, churches in the area often used works and guilt to motivate their congregations, and it came out sounding like people are saved based on what they do for the church.

Now as he and the others of Voice of Calvary came into the churches teaching that God saves you unconditionally, and then you let God do good for others through you, they were in fact challenging the old system of works. Some of the pastors sent them away, but many of the people were eager to receive their teaching. With the preachers living so far away, they were little involved in the day-to-day life of the churches and they usually exerted little immediate control over the actions of the church members.

Dolphus and his vacation Bible school team found lots of spiritual hunger among the black church people and they were kept very busy that summer as they set up ten different schools in ten different church communities. This was hands-on, meaningful work, and Dolphus's warm, outgoing personality thrived on it. It was exciting to see people transformed and full of joy as they experienced the vitality of newfound faith. Among the young people they served, they were planting seeds that would sprout into a new generation of productive Christian leaders, many of whom would be developed in Voice of Calvary's programs.

The following year, Dolphus came back as director of VOC's entire summer program. He saw the size and scope of the ministries grow as they developed a tutoring program to supplement the work of the schools. John had always stressed education, and this period also saw VOC move into adult education in a major way, helping people get their high school diplomas and training them in clerical and vocational skills like typing and printing.

"I ain't never comin' back," is what Dolphus had said when he first left the poverty and degradation of Mississippi behind and made his way west. He had hoped that going to college in California would open opportunities for him, and indeed it had. In 1970 he went on a six-week exhibition basketball tour through Asia. He was playing with a Christian team, the Overseas Crusaders, who played exhibition basketball as a vehicle for doing evangelism. Dolphus received much flattering personal attention as a touring basketball star, and when the coach offered him a permanent place on the team, he felt a thrill and an eager desire to sign right away. But the words of John Perkins echoed in his head, and he could see the enthusiastic faces of the black children he had been working with back home.

The glory, glamour, and fun of having people fuss over him as the single African American on a team of white athletes held almost irresistible appeal. But in the end, like his mentor, he felt drawn back to the cruel place of his origin. Dolphus had thought of all kinds of places other than Mississippi where he could go and enjoy a little American success. His older brother Melvin was doing all right as an electrician in Washington, and for a time Dolphus had thought of joining him there. But like John, he felt a deep sense of calling and he had caught the heart of John's vision. So in the end he turned away from the lure of individual success and he chose to return to Mendenhall, where he moved in as head of Voice of Calvary's outreach ministries. That was after he graduated in the spring of 1970. But while he was still in college, a series of events occurred in Mendenhall that would heat to the point of eruption the racial antagonisms that were always smoldering just below the surface.

11

Cops

The thrust of the work John had been doing in Mississippi since 1960 was toward the rehumanization of his people. That meant giving attention to all their needs and not splitting off spiritual conversion and growth from political empowerment and economic development. The voting rights campaign and the ensuing election of Shag Pyron and the cooperative movement that made possible the building of new homes and enterprises, injecting hope and slowly but steadily transforming the black community, these things together with genuine spiritual renewal were setting the people free. John called it "holistic development," and his mind worked overtime thinking about new projects and the improvement of ongoing ones. People were moving into the new housing co-op apartments in 1969, and John planned to help farmers cope with inflated fertilizer costs by starting a new co-op to sell fertilizer at prices significantly below retail.

These enterprises and the leadership development program, together with the steady pressure and progress of the civil rights movement, all meant that Mendenhall's black community and blacks throughout the county and south central Mississippi were beginning to stand up and assert themselves. Black independence was a threat to white domination and it filled whites with rage. They and their ancestors had held all the power as long as Mississippi had existed. Blacks were not fellow human beings and neighbors to them. They were like obstreperous beasts of burden that sometimes threaten to stampede or run wild. Then they had to be corralled and forcefully shoved back into "their place." Their place must always be apart from and beneath that of the whites. If they were moving toward independence by starting businesses of their own and asserting political power through the vote and if their young leaders were teaching them self-respect, these things were all a grave threat to white control.

In interpersonal relations, in the family, and in human institutions—religious and secular—certain individuals or elite groups sometimes become dictatorial, petty tyrants seeking absolute control over the behavior and even the thinking of others. The object is power and domination; power is the drug, the intoxicant. Along with greed, the thirst for power is a dominant malevolent theme in human affairs. When an individual, commonly a man, becomes obsessed with total control of his mate, he becomes violent and abusive, and when the victim tries to save herself by leaving the relationship, the abuser stalks her. If she breaks away completely and gets involved with someone else, he becomes filled with rage, goes after her, and beats or kills her.

One person's obsession with absolute control over another can occur on a greater scale in cults and in societies-at-large, where one race or ethnic group has or seeks total control over another. Whether it's Jim Jones's Guyana cult or the Suicide Cult in Japan or the Nazis at Auschwitz, total domination to the point of mass murder or collective death is the ultimate purpose. In totalistic institutions, where the dynamic hasn't escalated to mass murder or genocide, the controlling group oppresses the victim group, exploiting it for the sake of power and profit. But the sadistic murderer is ever lurking just beneath the cool visage of the controlling boss. And only a spark of insubordination can bring him forth in rage-filled violence.

In Mississippi this happened sporadically before the civil rights movement and regularly during it. The shootings, bombings, jailings, and beatings were all reactions to black self-assertion. John Perkins had systematically done things to enable the black people he worked with to come out from under white domination. And by late 1969 anger and hatred toward this uppity black preacher and all his race-mixing cronies were festering in the heart of many a white citizen walking the streets and working the store counters of downtown Mendenhall. All that was needed was a provocative racial incident to light the fuse that would detonate the keg of dynamite. And that incident came two days before

Christmas, as John and Doug Huemmer, one of the young white volunteers who worked with Voice of Calvary, walked into a mom-and-pop variety store up on Main Street.

Doug had come to Mississippi from Glendale, California, where he had grown up. Glendale Presbyterian was one of the churches that had developed an ongoing relationship with John, giving him regu-

Doug Huemmer with children of Voice of Calvary.

lar speaking engagements and contributions. While Doug's parents were members and had given him a Christian example, he had absorbed more of social ethics than belief. Coming of age in the sixties, his persona displayed that era's common mixture of activist and hippie. And a decided irreverence for hallowed American institutions, including those of evangelical Christianity, was an inevitable part of his generational nonconformity. He was a lanky youth with long sandy hair, glasses, and a scraggly beard. He often wore a fringed buckskin vest and drove around town in his red and cream-colored VW van.

Shy and soft-spoken, with an off-the-wall sense of humor, Doug had come to Mississippi because of his passion for black civil rights. Voice of Calvary's evangelism was beside the point. In the early seventies he would marry and later be divorced from Artis Fletcher's sister Ernestine. Doug's radicalism and his hippie appearance were just the kind of trigger that would fire off many white Southerners. And he loved to do it too. He hated the white supremacists, and they returned the sentiment with interest, seeing him as one of those dangerous "commie agitators" who invade the South to cause trouble by "stirring up the niggers."

On December 23, 1969, John helped Doug get ready to fly back home for the holidays. They stopped to get some Mississippi cane syrup to take to his family. As they went inside the little variety store on Main Street, they heard a disagreement turning rapidly into an argument between a black youth, Garland Wilks, and the white grocer. Garland had asked the man to accept his check, and when the grocer refused, Garland had not politely assented and humbly left, as racial etiquette dictated. He had been drinking and the alcohol had unbridled his nerve and clouded his discretion.

The obsequious bowing and scraping that whites required eventually got to most blacks, and particularly for a young man, the temptation to rear up and talk back might get the best of him on occasion, especially while under the influence. But the man behind the counter and other whites in the store were steaming with outrage at this young man's lack of proper manners. John was well aware of the trouble Garland was getting himself into and he and Doug moved quickly to the rescue by hustling him out of the store and cramming him into the backseat of their Volkswagen bug. Unbeknownst to John and Doug, the grocer had already called the police, and as the VW crossed the tracks, a squad car moved behind them and began to flash its light for them to pull over.

The police officer, in an ugly mood, arrested Garland for being "drunk and disorderly" and took him up to the police station at the big courthouse on the crest of Main Street. John then went to tell Garland's grandmother what had happened to her grandson, and Doug went on to Voice of Calvary, where the kids were rehearsing a Christmas pageant. When John arrived at VOC, he learned that Roy Berry, another black youth, had been arrested by the police, beaten, and jailed on a charge of asking a white woman for a date.

Such accusations have long been used as excuses to beat up, torture, and lynch black men in the South. They have also been used when southern white authorities have felt their total control over blacks might be slipping. These accusations gave them an excuse to terrorize the black community back into complete outward submission. Now it seems that rage was breaking out among the custodians of white dominion in Mendenhall as they were feeling a loss of control over the local blacks. This smart California preacher had been snatching "their niggers" out from under them and giving them wrong ideas about who they were and now the forces of law and order were going to teach these boys a lesson.

John and Doug wanted to go to the courthouse to see what they were doing to Garland, but John knew that their going alone would be risky. So they piled the youngsters who had been at the rehearsal into three cars and drove up Main Street. John didn't think the police would be so extreme as to arrest all of them. On arrival at the courthouse parking lot, they found that the police still had Garland sitting in the squad car. But a confrontation of sorts developed between some of the young people and the police chief as they expressed anger at what the police had done to Roy Berry and demanded to see him. The chief told Roy's cousin she could go over to the jail nearby and see Roy for herself but he probably didn't expect the whole crowd of kids to go with her. But that is exactly what they did, overwhelming the jailer, Jimmy Griffiths, who reacted on a gut level, arresting and throwing most of them in jail, including John and Doug.

The white authorities were not pursuing any thought-out plan. Everything they did was in reaction to what the blacks did. As the blacks challenged them, they reacted more, and the seriousness of the situation escalated. These young African Americans had a whole different sense of themselves than their parents had had. For a decade the Freedom Schools, VOC's leadership development program, and the integration and voting rights campaigns had all served as consciousness-raising experiences for the youth of Mendenhall. Challenging arbitrary white authority, demanding their rights, and refusing to be docile were behaviors that grew naturally out of the new life blacks in the South had been creating for themselves, a life that promised to realize their full humanity. When the enforcers of white people's law found themselves facing black resistance, the whites reacted by trying to shut down the resistance with more repression.

So when the young people went to the jail and demanded to see Roy Berry, Griffiths and the police retorted by arresting them along with John and Doug and throwing them all into jail together. This left white law enforcement in an embarrassing spot because they were now faced with a whole crowd of hollering kids and no real charge to place against them. They didn't really want the minors in jail. They did want to hold John and Doug, the adult men they deemed responsible for what was really the "crime" of black insubordination, and they tried to get the kids to leave but they refused to go without the two men. Meanwhile some of the youngsters, who had managed to remain outside as the jailhouse door slammed shut, went back across the tracks to spread word of what had happened.

It was not long afterward that Vera Mae stood anxiously outside the jail with a whole crowd of people, including Nathan Rubin and other men in Simpson County who were fighting for civil rights. Four Perkins children were inside with John, and Vera Mae could hear a lot of commotion going on in there. A good many of the people standing outside the jail with Vera Mae had children inside. The women were worried and becoming agitated enough to rush the jailhouse. Vera Mae felt tears of anguish streaming down her face.

After bringing John, Doug, and the young people into the jail, the police had herded everybody upstairs. Joanie thought the place looked like a dungeon. The light was thin and gray, and everything—walls, floors, and steps—were cold, hard concrete. As they ascended to the top of the spiral staircase, Joanie could see three tiny rooms and three jail cells. A terror-stricken Roy Berry was lying on a cot in one of the cells, his face all beat up and swollen. As they all crowded into the hallway and around the open rooms, John went over and talked to Roy, while Joanie and the others watched and listened.

Joanie shuddered as she glanced at Lloyd "Goon" Jones, the big, scowling highway patrolman, who stood with one high-booted foot up on a cot, monitoring the movements and conversation of the group. The local police had radioed the highway patrol for backup, as they customarily did in Mississippi when there was racial trouble. As Jones stood there, he struck an authoritarian posture. His highway patrolman's uniform had an intimidating military style that any banana republic dictator might have appreciated, and with his goggle sunglasses and ample girth, he perfectly fit the image of the southern cop. The police also brought Garland Wilks upstairs, spraying him in the face with mace. Since he was drunk and disorderly, they felt justified in taking this measure.

Meanwhile the people who were gathered outside were becoming ever more aroused as they heard the children's cries of dismay emanating from the jailhouse. The Williams brothers, bad youths of black Mendenhall, ranging in age from their twenties down to their early teens, were armed and ready to lead an assault on the jail. The police, for their part, did not really want such a confrontation. They didn't want to provoke an insurrection, since their purpose was always to control the blacks. Before they made any move to calm the crowd down, however, John began speaking to the people through the bars of the window.

This whole train of events as it had progressed filled John with a sense that this was the time when they all had to take a stand. Since the warm rays of faith had flooded him at his conversion back in Pasadena, he had felt God's life animating his best moments. And it was that divine life that made a deep spring of compassion well up inside him, a compassion for his people as they stood there hurt and confused and waiting anxiously in the night outside the jail.

All the evangelism, discipling, and developing that he had been doing to set the people free were culminating in this moment. He began to speak to them and he spoke with a warm passion and deep conviction as he admonished them not to give way to anger, hatred, and violence. He told them that they must not become like their oppressors, victims to their most destructive emotions. At the same time, he knew that events had propelled them to take their stand now.

And spontaneously the idea of a boycott of white Mendenhall businesses took possession of his mind. As he called for the boycott, he told the people not to pick up the Christmas gifts they had put on layaway. This would cost the retail stores dearly, because poor people, including the whole black community, took advantage of layaway so they could have the maximum time to accumulate money enough to make their purchases. Not picking the gifts up tomorrow, the day before Christmas, would of course cost the people their down payments.

John conceived the boycott as a means of wresting justice from the white power structure. He told the people it was not only to protest police brutality and harassment. It was to get equal treatment, and that meant good jobs, not just the menial ones. None of these downtown businesses would employ blacks, who had always been restricted to domestic work and unskilled day labor, jobs even illiterate white folks considered beneath them. Since the civil rights movement had begun in earnest in the mid-sixties, John and the Mendenhall black community had been protesting conditions and trying to get something done about them. John thought about how hard they had worked and how meager had been the tangible gains.

Now this incident was providing the opportunity to get some real leverage on the white power structure. John reminded the people of the miserable conditions—unpaved streets with no lighting, inadequate drainage, no sewers, no garbage collection—down across the tracks. The boycott would be a forceful demand that public authorities stop neglecting these obvious needs of the black community, that they take real, concrete steps to end the existence of two Mendenhalls, separate and unequal.

John spoke for a long time and with deep intensity. It was a moment of high drama as the words of this black Bible teacher rang out through the jailhouse window, inspiring the people to stand up and resist oppression. He recognized that he was drawing a line, issuing an ultimatum to the guardians of the old order right under their noses. And as he did so, he kept reiterating that if someone had to give all to gain social and economic justice, then he was willing to be that person and take that risk. Jesus said, "Greater love has no one than this, that he lay down his life for his friends," and John was willing to follow his Lord that far if he had to. The law officers never tried to stop John from speaking, probably because they did not want to exacerbate the crowd's anger.

Spencer was sixteen at the time, incarcerated along with his father. As he listened intently to his daddy's words, warm feelings of pride surged through his body. Of course he didn't want to see his father get hurt or killed but he knew these words had to be spoken, and the boycott had to happen. He knew what courage it took to take this stand and say these things.

After John finished speaking, the police decided to separate him and Doug from the children. They wanted to get the children out of the jail to calm and disperse the crowd. But when they removed the two men and placed them in an adjoining cell, they treated them roughly, pushing them around, and they broke Doug's glasses. Joanie heard the thuds through the wall and she screamed so that Vera Mae and the others could hear her outside the window. "They're beating up Daddy!"

The police now were anxious to calm people down and reassure them. They wanted the crowd to believe that they were only interested in punishing real troublemakers. With no idea of the yawning gulf between the way they saw themselves and the way the blacks saw them, they commonly deceived themselves into believing they could persuade responsible blacks of their good intentions. What they were ever blind to was the fact that even the most self-effacing Uncle Tom hated and distrusted them as his bitter enemy.

Having the children in jail had been an exasperating encumbrance to the police. So they now moved to get them out and they did so with all the poise and restraint of gangland thugs. As the children were being shoved out the jailhouse door, some of the older ones, like Sarah and Eva Quinn, protested that they didn't want to go without John and Doug. They knew that the police might feel less hesitant about beating up the two men if the children were gone and there was no crowd outside. They had already assaulted Roy Berry and had inflicted an untold number of past atrocities on blacks. But despite their protests, the children found themselves suddenly back outside the jail surrounded by momentarily grateful adults and hugged by their parents.

The crowd dispersed but the people felt no real relief. The cops still had John and Doug, and it had gotten to the point, as black and white Mendenhall faced one another down, that some terrible things were likely to happen. Vera Mae was deeply worried as she drove her children home. They were holding her husband in jail, and she didn't know what they would do to him.

The boycott began the next day.

12

SACRIFICE

Vera Mae worked feverishly to solidify support for the boycott throughout Mendenhall's black community and in the surrounding area. As had been true throughout the length and breadth of the civil rights movement, the churches served as communication and transmission centers. They were the places for publicizing and rallying all organized action. Long before the movement, the black church had been the place for issuing proclamations and giving public circulation to letters and other documents written to the community. Announcements from the church podium remained the most important form of public communication, especially since there were still few telephones and much illiteracy in the black rural South.

So Vera Mae composed an official-sounding letter announcing the boycott and made mimeograph copies to distribute among black churches in Simpson County, where she knew it would be read to the people at Sunday morning service. Working with Nathan Rubin during the voting rights campaign, she and John had established a cooperating network of twenty-eight churches. She had always been the complement to her husband's broad visions with her ability to organize and put all the nuts and bolts into a program to make it run smoothly. Now with John in jail—she didn't know for how long—and with the police acting unpredictably and often violently, she moved quickly and efficiently to bring about 100 percent support of the boycott.

On the morning of the day before Christmas, she was standing at the bottom of the Main Street hill, the entrance to Mendenhall's shopping district, handing out leaflets. "Don't buy in Mendenhall. They're holding my husband in jail," she cried. Rev. Curry Brown, John's old friend from the Fishermen's Gospel Crusade in California, was visiting and he and a group of the young people accompanied Vera Mae, helping to announce the boycott. That day, holding their hastily drawn signs, they began to picket the Mendenhall stores.

The police, for their part, wanted to strike some kind of bargain with John. They would drop whatever charges they were going to make against him and Doug if he would call off the boycott. In fact they would have to manufacture charges, since neither John nor Doug had done anything illegal. No matter to the police. The real purpose of police in the Deep South, when they arrested, jailed, and assaulted people engaged in civil rights activity, was to harass and intimidate them in order to maintain white control. It was all a power game, and the police had the means of force, which they did not hesitate to use.

Legal niceties like informing people what they were charged with meant nothing to them. The actual charges against John and Doug were largely irrelevant; they could be fudged. To the police, who stood for white authority in general, the real crime was upsetting the established order by working for desegregation and black power. But since the federal government now legally stood against southern white supremacy, the police had to always be trumping up some phony charge to level against civil rights activists.

Typically, white segregationist strategy was to enlist whatever residual accommodationist sentiment might exist within the black community in hope of getting a significant number to abandon direct action, in this case the boycott. It was, after all, a risky venture, since it would hit whites economically, and that might provoke painful reprisals against blacks. Working these potential fears, white authorities tried to persuade blacks that they would give them jobs and help them to progress in piecemeal ways. Thus the whites would be doling out favors and getting the blacks to accept paternalism in place of power. This approach, which white leaders liked to call "cooperation," always left the whites firmly in control. Holding out such "cooperation" as the safe alternative to the boycott's bold confrontation, they hoped to peel off enough people from its base of support to cause its collapse.

As John continued to sit in jail while his wife and the others picketed uptown, keeping the blacks out of the stores, the police were sending in a steady stream of friends and neighbors to see John, and, they hoped, persuade him to call off the boycott. Even Mr. Buckley came to see him. But John was able to win over all but a very few. He talked about how nothing else had caused any real change in the underlying conditions keeping black Mendenhall dirt-poor and powerless.

The boycott was the economic lever they needed to bring genuine progress to the entire black community. Together with the organizing efforts of Vera Mae and Nathan Rubin, John's powers of persuasion worked to sustain the boycott. And by the time he and Doug walked out of jail after the stores had closed on Christmas Eve, the "selective buying campaign" was set firmly in place. Mendenhall's blacks would carpool and ride up to Jackson or to nearby Magee to do their shopping.

With John now out of jail, he and Rubin worked with Lawrence Ross of the Lawyers' Committee for Civil Rights Under the Law to formalize their boycott and protest of police brutality and injustice with a concrete list of demands. The Lawyers' Committee had been formed and funded to go into the Deep South back in 1963, the last year of the Kennedy Administration, when JFK had introduced the bill to integrate public accommodations. The continuing presence of these civil rights lawyers in Mississippi would be of vital help to John Perkins and others who were placing their bodies in harm's way to end white supremacy.

Titled "Demands of the Black Community" and dated December 23, 1969, the document they produced contained a preamble, a list of fifteen broadscale demands, and a coda. The preamble stated that the boycott was being waged "primarily to secure employment in the business establishments in our town." And it noted that because the black population comprised 30 percent of the buying public, they should also have 30 percent of the uptown jobs. The demands also called for black employment on the police force and as deputy sheriffs, as well as in jobs in the public sector, including the school board and the draft board.

The list of demands, which also expressed a willingness to negotiate, was like the collective bargaining proposal of a new labor union seeking management's recognition and changes in the work environment. Back in the thirties, the New Dealers had passed the National Labor Relations Act. It had guaranteed organized labor the right to bargain collectively with corporate management. It remained for the CIO and AFL unions, armed with this right, to organize the industries. Organization sometimes involved risky tactics, and even bloody battles, when some companies hired goon squads to go after strikers.

Similarly, blacks in Mendenhall, as in boycotts that went on throughout the South, were armed with newly enacted national legislation that gave their actions and their demands legitimacy. Just as the corporations were no longer supposed to be the private preserve of the capitalists, so the public and commercial life of the South was no longer to be the fief of the white overlord. Mendenhall's black community was seeking the same kind of inclusion—the equivalent of better jobs, wages, and working conditions—that industrial workers had sought and won. Of course blacks had to start on a more basic level, the right to have a full range of jobs open to them. And so they demanded full inclusion in public and private sector employment. They demanded that every business with more than three employees include blacks among them. And they demanded that at least the minimum wage be paid all black workers, including domestics, and "premium pay for over-time."

The analogy with labor is valid inasmuch as it pertains to seeking a redistribution of power and wealth through collective action. But blacks, particularly in places like rural Mississippi, were trying to overcome a much more thoroughgoing and ruthless system of domination than laborers had to contend with. If one institution stood out as the chief agent of oppression, it was the system of justice, or as regards blacks, institutionalized injustice. So the demands enjoined the police to stop brutalizing and murdering black people and the courts to obey the Constitution and the Supreme Court. They listed the rights of the accused, regularly ignored by Mississippi's police and courts whenever a black was the one being accused. And they called for a biracial human relations committee to oversee the administration of the law and fire any law officer guilty of misconduct.

In the South, blacks had always been the ones acted on. Never had they been the ones doing the acting—never the authorities or decision makers or administrators. John, Vera Mae, Nathan Rubin, and everyone else involved in the boycott knew that a redistribution of power was what they were after. They knew that if they could lay claim to their legitimate right of inclusion in the power structure, they would gain a measure of control over their own lives, something they had never enjoyed in Mississippi. So the fifteenth and last demand read:

"We demand our freedom. We demand the power to determine the destiny of our community. Black people will not be free until we are able to determine our own destiny."

Other demands covered the other important areas of civil rights: equality of public services within the black community and desegregation of the schools. And keeping the specific event leading to the boycott in mind, they demanded that all charges against John Perkins and Doug Huemmer be dropped. Finally they stated that the boycott, or "selective buying," would continue until the "employment situation" was changed. Then other specific items in the list could be negotiated. Hence they saw equal employment opportunity as the key to opening up the whole system to black participation and power.

With the boycott well organized and proceeding with close to full support of the black community, John, Vera Mae, Nathan Rubin, and Jesse Newsome began to lead daily marches uptown to picket the stores and dramatize the demands. The boycott was publicized throughout the county and much of the state, and people came from far away to offer their support. They joined the marchers, and before long hundreds of people were marching.

They paraded up one side of Main Street, around the courthouse, down the other side to the base of the hill, back across the street, and up and around again all day long. Many people carried placards telling people not to buy in Mendenhall stores and demanding black civil rights. "Do right, white man, do right," they chanted over and over again as they marched in front of the stores. During the holiday season the marchers were out every day, but after the first of the year, with work responsibilities pulling at the people, the leaders decided to restrict public demonstrations to Saturdays.

As in Montgomery fifteen years earlier, the boycott held together well and it launched an economic missile that inflicted severe damage on Mendenhall stores. Whites reacted in sullen bitterness, feeling even less inclination to love their black neighbors or even regard them as human beings. But Mendenhall's business and political leadership tried hard to detach influential blacks from the boycott. They offered healthy wads of bribe money, a great temptation to black people who were so poor they couldn't afford most basic necessities. Yet few broke ranks and abandoned the boycott, and many who remained stalwart in their support of selective buying paid for their stand with the loss of a job.

Whites did manage to secure the cooperation of one black preacher who was actually an NAACP leader. But when he tried to use his influence to talk people out of the boycott, John, Vera Mae, and Rubin were able to stop him by getting Aaron Henry to come to Mendenhall and march with them. Henry was by this time well-known and respected in civil rights circles around the country. The head of Mississippi's NAACP, he came to Mendenhall to join the marchers and was able to pressure the anti-boycott preacher, who was also his subordinate, to link arms with him and John at the head of the Saturday uptown parade. But afterwards the preacher went back to trying to undermine the boycott. The few black people whom the whites were able to tear away had little if any negative effect on black solidarity.

The boycott and the marches up and down Main Street generated a great deal of antagonism among whites, and Klansmen cruised the demonstrations and made life-threatening phone calls to the Perkinses. The Deacons established a presence in Mendenhall to protect the marchers and they were the main reason that violence and bloodshed didn't occur there during the weeks of the boycott. Whites who might have caused such trouble were restrained by the presence of these armed black guardian angels.

In fact the very purpose of the boycott, if it succeeded, would make the existence of the Deacons unnecessary, for blacks were seeking to pry open all the bastions of white privilege and domination, most notably the police and sheriff's departments, and ultimately the highway patrol, to their participation. When blacks finally did become law officers in Mississippi, the police and sheriffs' departments and highway patrol would cease to be identified with the maintenance of white supremacy. Hence they would stop acting as stormtroopers, the hired thugs of a racist order, and for the first time they would begin to protect and serve the black population.

This monumental change would occur during the 1970s, and it was events like the Mendenhall boycott, in which blacks stood up and applied economic pressure to the white commercial establishment, that would be instrumental in bringing it about. Not only did blacks have to be willing to risk their lives and property, but they had to develop an internal cohesion and an economic and psychological independence from white paternalism. John Perkins understood these essentials of gaining black freedom and progress in the South and that

is why white power brokers hated him and called him a "smart nigger." A "smart nigger," in their parlance, was a black who was showing other blacks how to be independent of whites. Whites would violently resist any would-be liberator who dared interfere with their
addictive need for absolute power and total control of black people.

All during the 1960s, the period of confrontation in Mississippi
between violent white supremacists and a determined black civil rights
movement, John Perkins had been quietly laying the spiritual, economic, and educational groundwork of black independence. His evangelistic work in the schools, his leadership development, and his tutoring program and adult education had worked together to raise his
people's self-image. The cooperative movement began to teach them
the principles of capital accumulation, investment, and development.

With a deepened sense that they were beloved children of a God
who believes in them and wants to bless them and with a sense that
they could build better lives for themselves, they were acquiring new
knowledge, skills, and hope. By the first year of the new decade, they
were spiritually, mentally, and emotionally equipped to challenge the
white power structure.

White supremacists had a gut-level recognition that they were losing control of the blacks and they nursed an anger that threatened at
any moment to burst forth in murderous frenzy. Mendenhall itself, however, had become something of a haven for black civil rights insurgents
by this time. National civil rights legislation now protected the very
forms of direct action that John and Vera Mae Perkins and Nathan Rubin
had organized there. Mississippi's civil rights leaders, like Aaron Henry
and Charles Evers, and the civil rights lawyers were often on the scene,
and the Deacons were there too with their protective resources. Mendenhall had become a fishbowl of the civil rights movement by 1970.
Goings-on there were all too visible for uniformed or street-clothes Klan
types to have much room to maneuver. So when the police, acting as
the shock troops of white supremacy, decided to go on the offensive,
they had to lure their prey away from Mendenhall.

It was around dusk on the seventh of February, a midwinter chill in
the air and the deciduous trees at the edges of Highway 49 bleak in
their skeletal dormancy. Two vans of black college students headed up
the road for Jackson. They had spent about an hour that Saturday

marching for civil rights around the Mendenhall town square, they had met with the leadership of the movement in the back of the cooperative store, and now they were on their way back to Tougaloo College. Two of Voice of Calvary's white volunteers, Louise Fox and Doug Huemmer, were driving them.

The students' excitement was still bubbling after the day's activities and they kept up the rhythmic chant, "Do right, white man, do right." The refrain of the Mendenhall marches punctuated the young people's enthusiastic freedom choruses. They were enjoying the positive energy that came from standing up together for their rights and they paid little mind to the highway patrol car that had been tailing the two vans from the time they left town. Going to Jackson from Simpson County you traverse Rankin County. It was after they entered Rankin County that the highway patrol car made its move. Doug was driving the lead van, and the patrolman passed Louise and got behind Doug, flashing his blue light to pull him over.

The Civil Rights Act of 1968 had legislated protection from arrest for all acts related to civil rights demonstrations. In addition to protecting against harassment of demonstrators by police, the act gave federal rather than state courts jurisdiction over crimes allegedly committed in proximity to demonstrations. But if participants in the Mendenhall civil rights movement were caught and indicted for crimes they supposedly committed outside Simpson County, they could be prosecuted in state courts, the legal arm of white supremacy.

Stopping one of the vans, the police and highway patrol cooperating in this effort hoped to get the Mendenhall marchers for "offenses committed" in another county and unrelated to the federally protected exercise of their civil rights in Mendenhall. They knew they'd have a freer hand to mete out the traditional penalties for black self-assertion in Brandon, in Rankin County, away from all the civil rights clamor. Bending the law in typical Mississippi fashion, they also figured that in Rankin County they could make it look like whatever charges they were making had no connection with any civil rights activities.

Jonathan Edwards, the Rankin County sheriff, had made himself a Simon Legree of law enforcement. His beating up a black citizen who had been trying to register to vote led to a federal case, *U.S. v. Edwards*, in 1964. The Justice Department had sought an injunction to protect his interference with the federally protected right to vote. The court denied the injunction, referring to the incident as an "isolated occurrence." Over the next six years Edwards lost none of his racist venom. During the Saturday marches in Mendenhall, he had had his men, including his son, Jonathan Edwards III, doing surveillance, photographing participants, and checking their car licenses. They had monitored all traffic in and out of Mendenhall during the demonstrations and had thus learned who was who in the present civil rights agitation.

The initial pretext of a traffic violation didn't last long after Highway Patrolman Douglas O. Baldwin stopped Doug. He ordered Doug out of the van and eyeing the students, he radioed immediately for backup, saying he had "some niggers and a white" and that they were armed. When about five squad cars quickly arrived, the patrolmen piled out, crouched and weapons drawn, as if they were apprehending a dangerous band of terrorists. They spread-eagled all nineteen students against the van and patted them down.

Doug became the special prize of one Officer Frank Thames, a man with a personal mission against the civil rights movement. The summer before he had warned this race-mixing, hippie "Moscow man" he had better go back to California or he would kill him. Doug personified most of the things that made Thames and other upholders of the established order crazy, and now Thames was about to show this outside agitator a little Mississippi hospitality. He cuffed Doug and shoved him into the back of Baldwin's squad car, kicking and punching him and slapping him in the face. Then he unlocked one cuff, grabbed Doug's arm, and pulled him over the seat, yanking at the hated long hair and pummeling him in the stomach and crotch.

Eventually the highway patrol stuffed all nineteen students into the line of squad cars and hauled them off to the Rankin County jail to be booked on a variety of the usual charges: interfering with the duties of a law officer, resisting arrest, carrying a concealed weapon. The weapons in this case were a single brick and some broken tiles, which were left over from VOC's construction projects and littered the floor of the van. They would also later charge that Doug's van had concealed a pistol and some bent forks, items that were probably planted by the police.

Meanwhile Louise Fox had stopped her van in sight of Doug's so she could see what the highway patrolman was going to do. As she watched Patrolman Baldwin, later joined by his reinforcements, manhandling

Doug and the students, roughly patting them down, and pushing them into the squad cars, she knew she had to contact John in Mendenhall as soon as possible. And this is exactly what the police wanted her to do.

Working closely with Highway Patrol Inspector Lloyd "Goon" Jones, Edwards had baited a trap he hoped would get John out of Mendenhall and into *his* territory, Rankin County. The movement in Mendenhall threatened to bring real power to blacks, and the police, as enforcement arm of the white power structure, were determined to shut it down. And now they were acting to get the leader away from his protective support system. Responding to the urgency in Louise's voice, John felt concerned for the students' safety. He had to get to Brandon right away.

He was in his yard with two men, Curry Brown and Joe Paul Buckley, when the call from Louise came in. Joe Paul was an old farmer in his sixties, one of the rare people who had actually been able to make something from sharecropping. He and his children and grandchildren had become actively involved with Voice of Calvary. Despite his economic dependence on the whites, he had not shied away from involvement with the civil rights movement and he had come in solidly behind the boycott. That night he made the trip out of the protected VOC compound on up to Brandon with John in his VW bug. Darkness had just come on as they started for Rankin County, and John was thinking about the nineteen students in jail up there with Doug. He felt responsible for them. He had encouraged their enthusiastic involvement in the Mendenhall movement, bringing them down from the Tougaloo campus more than once.

The Rankin County justice complex was an imposing structure, about the size of the one in Simpson County, but differing architecturally, in that it displayed the efficient, impersonal lines of a modern building. When John, Curry, and Joe Paul arrived, a highway patrolman was there to guide them to a parking space. John told him they had come to see the sheriff, and the officer said he would go get him, and that was the last routine transaction they would experience in Brandon. The three men got out of the car.

As they did so, John took a thirty-two special from his pocket and placed it under the front seat. He customarily carried a pistol and there was a rifle in plain sight in the car. He had been carrying these weapons since the voting rights campaign, when he had begun to get death threats by phone and by word of mouth. With the boycott going on, the phoned murder threats, the drive-bys, and the Klan types hanging around town had increased again. Charles Evers had warned blacks publicly that they needed to protect themselves, and the Deacons had been patrolling Mendenhall regularly. So John and the others always carried guns with them. But acting as law-abiding citizens having come here to Brandon to post bond for the Tougaloo students, they of course left their guns in the car.

As they got out and stood there talking, a phalanx of twelve patrolmen suddenly came rushing out the door at them. The three men were immediately surrounded, arrested, searched, and propelled into the building. As the horror of what was happening jolted his body, John suddenly realized they had been set up. He had been focused on getting Doug and the students out and had not considered the possibility of an ambush. And now they had been captured by a brutal county sheriff who had been working with "Goon" Jones to create an incident they could use to crush the Mendenhall civil rights movement.

And so the reign of terror came down on John, Curry, and many of the students and it lasted many hours, through much of the night. Edwards began by identifying John to the others as "the smart nigger." Then he crowed that this was a "whole new ballgame" now that he had John and his friends on charges in Rankin County. He followed this declaration with a series of blows to John's body, which were a cue to the deputies and patrolmen present to begin venting their own simmering rage on their captives. As they battered, bludgeoned, and bloodied the heads of John and Curry, their rage grew into a wild, uncontrollable fury.

The police didn't beat up Joe Paul Buckley. When they were starting in on John and Curry, Joe Paul got scared to death and he yelled out, "I've got heart trouble," and they left him pretty much alone. Perhaps it was because he was an older man. Perhaps it was the more deferential manner in him that had come from a lifetime of sharecropping on white men's plantations. At any rate he was not the "smart nigger," nor was he a brash Californian come here to "agitate." And despite his associations, the lawmen didn't want his death on their hands. That would bring in the FBI and possible federal prosecution, something they were more than anxious to avoid.

These policemen, transmuting the law into their own acts of violent retribution, became the hideous monsters that racism creates.

White supremacy had been a hothouse for the growth of a murderous, institutionalized sadism. In this part of the South, whites—many of them from backgrounds of poverty and abuse, many of them victims of authoritarian parents—had license to displace all the negativity of their lives onto blacks. The scapegoating of blacks was so ingrained in southern culture that whenever one or more of them stepped out of line, they became lightning rods to absorb whatever bitterness and anger whites had accumulated and internalized in the course of their lives. Among the whites most likely to act out scapegoating were the police, the ones who had the society's license to do so.

They had moonshine there in the Brandon jailhouse with them. Edwards would later deny that they were drinking, but John noticed the paper cups of clear liquid many of them were holding as he was being pummeled into unconsciousness. It was customary for a lynch mob to get liquored up. Alcohol is the common fuel of antisocial behavior and as it acts to release whatever restraining conscience might still be there, it enables people to give way to their dominant emotion.

And so as the beating went on into the night, the level of violence against John, Curry, Doug, and some of the students escalated. One young man's teeth were knocked out. And Edwards, Thames, and some of the other cops used hard leather blackjacks to pound their captives. The police mayhem took on the mocking, humiliating quality that so often characterizes such rites of victimization. They shaved and then poured moonshine over Doug's head, thus getting rid of the long hippie locks they so detested.

John and Curry received the brunt of the beating. As the leader of a movement for black power, Voice of Calvary's founder was the inevitable target for much of the lawmen's furor. They battered his head with their clubs, and as he was escaping into unconsciousness, they roused him and shoved a copy of the "Demands of the Black Community" into his face, ordering him to read it. John tried to comply and he tried to do as they said later on when they ordered him to mop up his own blood from the floor. They had gotten interested in getting the blood off the floor when the radio dispatcher warned them that the FBI was coming. They also forced John to stagger into the rest room and wash his face and clean up so they could hide evidence of their brutality.

One wonders how they thought just washing the blood off would conceal the battering, but nothing the police did that night was very rational. As it turned out, it was a false alarm, unfortunately for John and the other captives. Now the police, buoyed by this reminder that no one would restrain their behavior, escalated their intensity. The storm of rage fed on itself as they went on a torturous rampage, shoving a bent fork up John's nostrils and down his throat.

The beating was so long and intense that John's body defenses began to take over, and he went into a state of shock. He lost consciousness during much of the later time they were beating him, and his body went numb. But woozy as he was, John could see the crazed expressions on the faces of his assailants and he could see their deranged behavior for what it was, a disease, a monkey on their backs. They held him captive physically but they themselves were captive of something that had completely taken them over. The wolfman myths took on a weird reality in the rabid mania of these men sworn to uphold the law. Here they were hell-bent on controlling him and every other black person in Mississippi but they had totally lost all control of themselves. Transformed as they were into raving lunatics, John could not hate them. He strangely found himself beginning to pity them.

When the deputies and highway patrolmen finally finished mauling him, they put John in a cell with the Tougaloo students. Through the remainder of the night, the students cared for him, soaking their shirts in cold water and applying the wet cloth to his throbbing head. He was badly bruised and bloody and breathing irregularly, and the young people there with him thought he was going to die before morning.

Meanwhile Louise Fox, who had found out that John and the others were being held, called Vera Mae. After Louise told her of the men's fate, Vera Mae spent a sleepless night, sick with worry. Early Sunday morning, she rose and drove to Brandon with the other two wives, not knowing what she was going to see and fearing the worst. When they let her in to see her husband, she found his head beaten and swollen out of shape and full of deep lacerations. His eyes were protruding as a result of the swelling, and he was in great pain. He whispered to his wife to get him out of there before they killed him.

Nathan Rubin was able to contact people he knew in Rankin County who could put up money and property for the bond. They managed to raise enough to get John, Doug, and the students out before the end of the day, but the police were demanding five thousand dollars bail for Curry. Having been a leader of the boycott, Curry had attracted the white merchants' attention as well as that of the police, and during one of the marches, a white store owner had come up and punched him. The police, always on the lookout for a chance to get a "nigger," had seen the incident and hauled Curry in and booked him. So they had pegged him as one of the lead troublemakers and had been more than anxious to hurt him in Brandon.

Curry was a strong-willed man and had tried to hold up his head and resist his attackers. He had grown up in California and had never had to submit to the kind of control southern blacks were used to. The police, conscious of his role in the boycott and his arrest in Mendenhall, had had it in for him to begin with, and now his passive resistance turned their rage white hot, and they beat him even harder and longer than they might have otherwise done. Because of his resistance, added to all the other things that made him a special target of their wrath, they slapped the big bail fee on him, and it was to be another day before Rubin could raise enough to get him out. Curry finally walked out of the Brandon jail on Monday, hurt as badly as John, his head split open and swollen to almost twice its normal size.

John was dazed and throbbing with pain when they got him out of jail, and it would take him many months to recover from his injuries. He, Curry, Doug, and the students who had been beaten went to see Dr. Robert Smith, a black physician, who cleaned, stitched, and dressed their wounds. He drained about a cup of blood and fluid from John's inflamed, swollen head. The way the cops had beaten so hard and long on John's and Curry's heads, it seemed they were trying literally to bash their brains in. The whole white supremacy myth was predicated on blacks being dumb beasts of burden, incapable of an original thought, happy in their ignorance, and always ready to do the Man's bidding. Leaders like John were independent *thinkers*, whose *ideas* were working to undermine the system and set blacks free to grow and exercise their own gifts and develop their personhood.

Playing the role of a black Prometheus, John had been giving knowledge, power, and an independent, healthy identity to a victim people. It was the head, the brain of the "smart nigger," that made him such a threat, and so the enforcers of white supremacy had tried to crush his skull. Curry Brown, the bold, assertive minister from the freewheeling West Coast, was also full of dangerous, *wrongheaded* ideas of his own self-worth, and so they had sought to rearrange his brains too. All during the beatings they kept raving about teaching these smart niggers a lesson. Their desperate frenzy was an attempt to beat out the creative self-assertion that the black men displayed and reduce them to the dumb, unthreatening pawns they wanted all blacks to be.

All systems based around one group's total control of another operate in much the same way: all power to the keepers and mindless submission to the inmates. In Kesey's *One Flew over the Cuckoo's Nest,* when Mac McMurphy threatens to give a life, a consciousness, humanity to the drugged-out patients, the doctors and nurses grab and subdue him, finally performing a lobotomy on him, thereby reducing him to mindless submission.

While they had seriously injured John, they had yet failed to subdue him. The beating would alter his consciousness, but not in the way the white supremacists would have wanted. The change in his thinking had actually begun while they were battering him. He had begun to see how much they were the prisoners of their own racism. It was one of those lucid, rational moments that strangely surface in the midst of acute trauma. In life-threatening circumstances, there is something in us that can come out and stand as if outside the body, outside the situation, and evaluate it objectively. And it was this part of John that had seen into the souls of his tormentors. In the months to come he would have more time to ponder his insight.

As traumatic as they were, the beatings lasted only one horrible night. The aftermath of this whole collective episode—the Mendenhall arrests and jailings, the boycott, the ambush and beatings in Brandon—would drag on for many months to come. John would go through two court cases, one coming out of the Mendenhall Christmastime incidents and the other from the Brandon arrests. The effects of the beatings and the stress of these cases would take their toll on his health and extend the time he had to spend in recuperation.

13

REDEMPTION

The first of the cases concocted by county prosecutors against John Perkins was the one coming out of the train of events that had precipitated the jailing of John, Doug, and the children. They had no real case against John, who had simply been trying to keep Garland Wilks out of trouble and then, once they had jailed Garland, to see about getting him out. But the police, touchy from a decade of black challenge to their arbitrary ways, had been on a campaign to intimidate an increasingly assertive black community. That is why Roy Berry had been accused of lusting after a white woman, jailed, and beaten. And that is why the police had snatched Garland Wilks from John's car, jailed him, and sprayed him with mace. The unwritten axiom of southern law as regarded the races was that an arrested black was always guilty.

Government in the segregated South was of men rather than of law when it came to judging and controlling African Americans. It was set up to humiliate them and keep them down. The initial level of judgment for criminal offenses lacked even the pretense of fairness. On February 16, 1970, just nine days after the beating, John had to appear before a justice of the peace. These justices of the peace were not people trained in the law. Since the state did not even require a high school diploma to hold this position prior to 1975, they were not even educated men, just old boys enforcing the rules of an old game.

John was never charged with violation of any law. The justice of the peace simply went over his actions of December 23, 1969, and imposed a penalty, three hundred dollars fine and three months in jail. He was given this fine and sentence because he had disturbed the established order and thus activated its rituals of self-defense. Of course John's lawyers would not permit such a summary judgment to stand. They had the right to a "new trial" before a jury, and so they made this motion. The State was then compelled to find a formal charge to bring against John.

Thus challenged, they resorted to their customary practice in prosecuting blacks. The district attorney, working with the police, manufactured a charge and the evidence to support it. Twisting Jimmy Griffiths's blundering, punitive actions around so as to make John out to be the wrongdoer, they charged him with contributing to the delinquency of a minor. According to the prosecution, Rev. John M. Perkins had persuaded one Georgia Quinn, eleven years old and the youngest of the Quinn sisters, to enter and remain in jail while Griffiths had been trying to release the children.

In essence, the State was saying that John, working against the good graces of the jailer, had been responsible for Georgia and the others being in jail with him. They painted him as the one who had instigated the jailing of the children to create the emotional confrontation that led to the boycott. Georgia Quinn testified that John had not talked her into going to jail, and the defense also marshaled testimony that Griffiths had not been the conciliatory character he had depicted himself as, having slammed the steel door on the children and sprayed mace through the slot. But not surprisingly the train of defense eyewitnesses failed to persuade the all-white jury that Griffiths had been misleading them.

It was long experience in Jim Crow courtrooms that had convinced African Americans that they could not get a fair trial. The courts provided the legal sanction for institutionalized scapegoating. Police commonly arrested blacks they were out to get and once they arrested a black, guilt was presumed. The designated criminal was usually a man, and the crime he was charged with depended not on the facts, but on the weight of the lesson they were trying to teach him. The menu of regular items included disorderly conduct, resisting arrest, carrying a concealed weapon, and indecent exposure (urinating outdoors). But if they were really laying for him because he had been violating racial proscriptions, they would charge him with something more serious.

While it was still a misdemeanor, contributing to the delinquency of a minor was considered a more serious charge than the customary ones, though it was probably less than what they would have liked to level against John. In the bad old days he likely would have been lynched or he would have died in prison from natural or unnatural causes. This is not to minimize the horrors of the Brandon episode, but he had been freed while still hanging on to his life, and once out of Edwards's torture chamber, he could avail himself of formidable defenses.

A decade and a half of civil rights activity had made it more difficult for the white power structure to carry out its traditional draconian penalties for black self-assertion. A looming federal presence coupled with that of militant black organizations, a battery of civil rights lawyers, and an aroused black public all worked to dull the means of repression. And these things worked to keep Edwards and his cronies from actually killing John. But the punitive court system was still very much in place, its purpose to accuse, judge, and condemn blacks in order to retain white supremacy. So the police and the DA had found something to charge John with and then proceeded to conjure up the witnesses and the evidence.

As ridiculous as Griffiths's account of himself as a good guy trying to free the kids might sound, the jury took it as gospel because it was the word of white authority against a black man. The white jury took little time to rubber stamp the State's case. John's attorney, Constance Slaughter, a young black woman, the first to argue a case in Mendenhall, would file an appeal. Slaughter was twenty-three and just out of law school at Ole Miss, where she had been the first black female student. She had graduated in January of 1970, and the Perkins case was her first actual court case.

Larry Ross and Frank Parker of the Lawyers' Committee for Civil Rights Under the Law had gotten her on the case. At the time, she was the only black person in Mississippi on the Committee. Inevitably nervous in her pioneering role, she had forgotten at the beginning of the trial to stand up before the judge when addressing him. Judge Joe McFarland Jr., a personable older man if still a stalwart representative of the white establishment, called a recess and took her into his chambers. He spoke with some warmth to her, asking her about her personal life. This gave her more confidence, and she went on to perform skillfully in examining witnesses and making numerous pertinent objections to irregular courtroom procedures, all of which Judge McFarland overruled.

During the trial, Slaughter observed Griffiths, who besides being the State's chief witness was also the bailiff, standing in the jury box talking with a member of the jury, a clear procedural violation. She immediately objected and moved for a mistrial. Judge McFarland overruled her because the conversation had not been about the trial. She appealed this ruling and she included other trial irregularities in her appeal. She also filed suit against the State of Mississippi for having denied John a jury of his peers.

Courtroom procedures were tedious, and John spent a long time on the witness stand, with the prosecutor going to great lengths to assail his character. With legal proceedings in Mendenhall beginning such a short time after the mayhem in Brandon, John's body was still very much in the throes of reaction to acute stress. The police thrashing had been so severe that every organ of his body had been traumatized. And there had been no real time to bed down and heal. The Mendenhall trial would be followed by another related to the Brandon events. If there had been no charges to deal with and no trials to slog through, it still would have taken many months for him to recover from the trauma inflicted on him. The pressure had been escalating since the Garland Wilks incident before Christmas.

It felt like all his labors of the past decade had built up to this prolonged confrontation with the white power structure, a confrontation that threatened to tear John and his movement apart. The police had inflicted bodily harm almost to the point of killing him, and now it seemed to be the time for the courts to take over and assault his character. John knew who he was and he knew that God was in him and in the work he was doing. But the relentless hammering of the State's accusations hurt and discouraged him. He wondered what all the work would come to, whether it was really possible to change the way things were in Mississippi. Maybe he had been swimming against too strong a tide and now he was being engulfed by it.

During a recess in the Mendenhall trial, John was mulling over these thoughts and sinking into despondency when an old black woman suddenly appeared before him as he turned around after getting a drink at the water fountain. She was a woman like Aunt Babe or Aunt Coot, the kind of rock-solid nurturing mother who had given an oppressed people the courage to endure and go on. She was the kind of backbone of the black community fabled in *The Autobiography of Miss Jane Pittman*. The

Auntie Janes who were often present in downtrodden peasant cultures gave identity, continuity, and courage to their people. And this Auntie Jane stood there, with wrinkled countenance and feet firmly planted, looking intently at John, her eyes glowing.

"Stand up, son. Stand up," she said quietly. And suddenly the muddle in John's mind cleared and he felt energized. A rush of warm pride bubbled through his exhausted body. All at once he had a deep awareness that he was standing up for everybody, all the black people in Mendenhall and all the black people in Mississippi and all the black people in the South. He was a present witness to the age-old stand of oppressed peoples against their oppressors, victims against perpetrators, freedom fighters against tyrants. He straightened his spine and strode back into the courtroom.

In the difficult months to come, when he and his lawyers were embroiled in the battle that would become the two *Perkins v. Mississippi* cases, he would never again become so downhearted. He would retain a stalwart sense of his purpose. But the grinding courtroom ordeal, the continuous stress of having to be ever legally defending himself to keep out of jail, where he surely would have been in danger of his life, wore him down.

The Mississippi Supreme Court heard the Perkins appeal and on February 15, 1971, they reversed and remanded the case to the circuit court, citing the lower court's error in having a "courtroom deputy" who was also a material witness for the prosecution. In their unanimous opinion the six judges stated the circuit court had erred in not granting a mistrial because a material witness who was also a bailiff of necessity had close contact with jury members and hence the "opportunity for actual and improper influence which can and should be avoided." And in rebuttal to Judge McFarland, they stated that ". . . there are many ways a jury could be influenced without the witness actually discussing the case." Having a bailiff who was also a material witness furthermore gave the "appearance of unfairness," which could undermine "public confidence in jury trials . . . [and] threaten one of our sacred legal institutions."

A year after Brandon, John could take heart from this legal victory, a rare event for a black man in the Deep South. It would give him leverage to bargain with the court. He ended up pleading guilty to a lesser charge, disturbing the peace, and dropping the suit over the all-white jury issue, with the State agreeing not to prosecute him on the lesser charge. This was about the best outcome that could be expected for such a case in Mississippi in 1971.

But within a few months after the first trial, while his lawyers were appealing his conviction and the Brandon case was brewing, John's health began to break down. He had always felt happiest and most completely integrated when he was hard at work, immersed in a project, or many projects. If working felt natural to him, inactivity felt strange and uncomfortable. After the Brandon affair, he took only the most necessary time to recuperate. He was meeting and strategizing with his lawyers the week after it happened. The Mendenhall court case began in less than two weeks.

And besides the ongoing stress of all this legal embroilment, he quickly resumed his many roles at Voice of Calvary. He went back to work with Father McKnight's organization, and he was traveling around visiting cooperatives in the different parts of Mississippi as well as speaking to church and parachurch groups out of state. In short, his docket was crammed full. The work would not have hurt him if it had not been accompanied by the physical and mental stress caused by the beating and the court cases.

One steamy Saturday afternoon in July he had just finished work and was about to go out and watch Voice of Calvary's team play ball, when he was suddenly overcome with a bone weariness. He was so exhausted that all he could do was go to bed and sleep. And he slept well into the evening. When he woke up he was not at all refreshed. He was still feeling exhausted and unsteady. He slept much of Sunday. On Monday he was scheduled to drive up to Mound Bayou, an all black town in the Delta, to visit a co-op. He decided to make the trip, but Monday night, at the home of some friends, he was again overcome with exhaustion and he had chest pains. Checking himself into the black-run Tufts Medical Center there in Mound Bayou, he was diagnosed with an irregular heartbeat and acute hypertension. He was forced to spend three weeks in treatment there and after he went back to Mendenhall, he continued to have symptoms, so he had to be readmitted for another few weeks.

During the time in recovery from his heart ailment, John was forced to lie or sit in one place, well away from his work environment and the plethora of concerns that had constantly absorbed all his attention. He was driven down into himself and into reflection about what had happened to him and to the work he had begun in Mendenhall just over ten years before. What had he accomplished?

He knew that the human development he had been doing in its spiritual, economic, and educational aspects was a good thing. But as blacks in Mendenhall had begun to progress, whites had reacted with bitter, toxic hatred. The sickness of an embedded, stagnant racism engulfed the people of Mississippi like the dank air of summer. And John found himself beginning to give way to despair that real positive change would ever occur. It was hard not to let the events of the past months embitter him. A fierce anger burned down inside, the anger he had felt when the white farmer paid him fifteen cents for a day's work and the anger that had burned much hotter when the white cop gunned down Clyde. Whenever blacks exercised their will to power and personhood, there was the ubiquitous white tyrant to beat them down.

The stern warrior in John would never let him quit but he felt a strong desire to abandon all hope of peaceful cooperation and integration with the whites. He could feel himself resonating with the strident, bitter nationalism of Stokely Carmichael and Rap Brown. He had read the Algerian doctor Fantz Fanon's revolutionary work *The Wretched of the Earth* and he identified with all the colonized, brutalized peoples of the world and their primal need to rise up and free themselves, "by any means necessary," as Malcolm X had put it.

He knew that if he went with these powerful feelings, he would move to cut himself and his community completely off from whites and seek to go it alone. The Black Muslims were doing it, spurning involvement with whites, who would always be the racist enemy in their eyes, and turning wholly to their own resources. They were disciplining themselves, with a strong ethic of work, family, self-discipline, and sexual restraint and they were getting results. They were gaining wealth, literacy, and independence from the incorrigible white oppressor.

But what of the dream? What of Dr. King's vision of reconciliation between black and white? What of peacemaking and real cooperation? As John lay in bed in Mound Bayou, his spirit still longed to actualize this hope. He thought about the increasing number of white people who loved what he had been doing and were giving him support. Wayne Leitch, a white man, had mentored him and been a father to him. Mr. Hayden had believed in him and given him every chance to advance at Shopping Bag, and the Haydens had given money in support of his work in Mississippi.

There were the white evangelicals in California who backed him from the beginning, and other white Christians around the country were hearing about his work and getting in touch with him, inviting him to speak at their churches and sending contributions. John thought of the white volunteers who came to Mississippi and risked their lives: the radical and hippie types like Doug Huemmer, the northern Jewish youths whose heritage gave them a natural identity with oppressed peoples, and the earnest young men and women from Brethren and Quaker backgrounds whose traditions had breathed a love of equality into them.

Yes, John had to acknowledge, a diverse assortment of white people had been there to help him and become friends with him since before he had become a Christian. Even a few whites in Mississippi had tried to reach out. John often pondered the tragic case of Dr. Odenwald. Robert Odenwald had been the minister at the First Baptist Church of Mendenhall. The Southern Baptists are the biggest denomination in the South, and their churches dominate southern cities, towns, and hamlets. So Odenwald, as pastor of First Baptist, inevitably held a prominent position among the gentry of Mendenhall.

Evangelical Christianity forms the cultural backdrop of the South, and both the black and white churches and folk traditions are awash in its forms. Yet, as with everything else, an iron curtain separated white Christians from black Christians. As a minister, Perkins was always much more evangelist than pastor, and his vision was always broad and inclusive. He was ever looking for ways to bring people of different backgrounds together under the banner of Christ, the Christ of Paul's Ephesian letter, the one who has broken down the wall of separation between Jew and Gentile.

One day John ventured up to Dr. Odenwald's church office to see him about a Mendenhall community matter. In the back of his mind he harbored a desire to establish some common ground between them. John knew, even if the white pastor did not, that they shared the same evangelical faith and even spoke the same language. And as he began to convey his passion for youth evangelism and leadership development, Odenwald began to lower his racial guard and warm to this black preacher's words. John was able to reach around the barrier of racial caste to connect with the man's essential faith. As the two men shared their heartfelt concerns, the deep cleavage racism had caused between them momentarily receded.

Odenwald had been thrilled to discover that John's orthodox evangelical beliefs in God's inerrant Word and all the fundamentals of the faith exactly paralleled his own, and they were fellow laborers in the same vineyard. For a time the two men were able to enjoy a friendship and a warm sense of Christian brotherhood as they shared their mutual love of spreading the gospel. The white pastor experienced a change of consciousness, an opening up toward a people whose travail had too long been ignored by the good Southern Baptists who dutifully gave their tithes and sat attentively in the pews of his uptown church. And he began, ever so haltingly, to try to awaken their charitable Christian consciences.

But the task of overcoming the monster racism proved too great for him. With a new awareness that Christian love meant loving black people, just as Jesus had called haughty Jews of his time to love the despised Samaritans, he came to the somber recognition that his people would not hear this truth. And with the knowledge that racial reconciliation was at the heart of the gospel, he could no longer go on as a man of God in the poisoned racial atmosphere of the Deep South. Dr. Odenwald committed suicide, and John Perkins went to his funeral, the only black man in attendance.

John thought often about Dr. Odenwald. He remembered how exuberant they both had become as they had shared their faith together. What a breakthrough that had been, and then the old demon of racism had intervened and claimed another life. But John was not one to give up on the good fight. In Brandon he had begun to see the disease for what it was, something that had hold of the whites, like a cancerous parasite living off their souls. And now convalescing there in the sheltered retreat of a black hospital in an all-black community, he began to see that the only way for blacks to be freed of the shackles of racism was for the whites to be freed of the same shackles. The two races were handcuffed and leg-ironed together. As Dr. King had said, they were going to have to learn to live together as brothers, or they would perish together as fools. John began to wonder if his focus on freedom and advancement for blacks, with white supporters helping out, was too limiting. Maybe the mission of evangelism and development among blacks in Mississippi needed to be broadened. Maybe blacks were not the only people in dire need.

As these thoughts gelled in his mind over the next six months or so, John resumed work in Mendenhall and his travel and speaking to white audiences outside the South. His mind-set was shifting more toward a conscious effort to promote racial reconciliation. In February of 1971, just a year after Brandon, he was speaking in this vein to a group of Christians at the University of Michigan when he felt a terrific pain in his stomach that doubled him over: bleeding ulcers. He ended up back in Mound Bayou where a surgeon removed most of his stomach. Again there was a long convalescence. Joanne Roberts, a white internist who was also a committed Catholic, treated him with warmth during his convalescence. She was also the doctor who had treated his heart condition and high blood pressure. Speaking frankly to him as a friend, she told John that if he did not change his overly stressful pattern of living, he would not live a lot longer. John knew she was right and he began thinking about making some changes that would take much of the workload off his shoulders.

During this time of painfully taking stock of himself, of reevaluating his life and his mission in Mississippi, John began to think about giving over the day-to-day running of Voice of Calvary to the younger generation he had discipled who were just now starting to come of age. Dolphus had come back and taken over the outreach programs while John had been trying to recover from Brandon. Artis was pastoring a church in Maryland but his heart was in Mendenhall and he was back every summer. John thought he would come back and take the helm of Voice of Calvary Church. That would leave John free to travel and get blacks and whites involved together in evangelism and development in communities of need. He could open an office in Jackson.

John had thought for some time that Mississippi's largest city was the natural place to expand the work he had begun in Mendenhall. A Jackson office could sponsor development projects there, and Jackson had an airport that could conveniently service John's increasing travel needs. The work in Mendenhall had been getting publicity through the new "radical" evangelical publications *Post-American* (later renamed *Sojourners*) and *The Other Side* and through mainstream ones like *Christianity Today*. John was becoming known to broadbased parachurch organizations like InterVarsity Christian Fellowship, which provided an intelligent evangelical voice on the college campuses, and the Billy Graham Evangelistic Association, which had always supported integration. And many of the white evangelicals he had known since his California days had wealthy, influential Christian contacts who were becoming interested in providing support for John's work and new forums where he could spread his ideas. He was beginning to get invitations to speak and lead development conferences and workshops at seminaries, colleges, and churches around the country. With this broadening focus, John was envisioning a Jackson office that would be something of a promotional arm for his work and a base for his missionary travel.

Whether this new locale and this more peripatetic work style would slow John down any, indeed whether anything besides his health would slow him down, was highly questionable. John had always thrived on having a lot to do. He kept regular hours, going to bed in the early evening and rising before dawn to read his Bible and pray, wanting to line himself up with the heart of God. Travel never exhausted him. He was able to take periodic catnaps and recharge himself. So it had not been the volume of work that caused John the lethal stress that attacked his heart and his stomach. It was the intense racial confrontation that had been going on in Mississippi since 1964 and the sharp focus that had been on him for over a year as leader of the Mendenhall boycott.

Everybody knew him in Mendenhall. Many had expectations of him, and many in the white community felt bitterness and even hatred toward him. What's more, the Klan types had put a price on his head. John's removal of himself and his family to the state capital, where he was not a public figure and leader of a civil rights campaign, would take him out from under the pressure of this environment and give him more of a cloak of anonymity. He could relax more there and refocus and reorder his life. And so in 1971, as John was recuperating from his surgery, Vera Mae was out looking for a house near downtown Jackson.

The case that grew out of the Brandon episode worked its way through the courts during 1970 and '71, with a final judgment coming down from the U.S. Court of Appeals in June of 1972. The police had leveled an assortment of charges against John, Curry, Doug, and Joe Paul as well as at the Tougaloo students and the two other civil rights workers who accompanied them. Among the complaints filed were the usual resisting arrest and concealment of a deadly weapon.

Doug was charged with reckless driving, the offense that supposedly caused Patrolman Baldwin to pull the van over in the first place. They charged Doug with carrying a concealed weapon, which they said was a pistol but did not name in the complaint. Each of the students was listed as carrying a concealed brick. The students were also charged with resisting Doug's arrest and interfering with the duty of a law officer. John and Curry were charged with inciting a riot, resisting arrest, and possession of a concealed weapon. None of the charges had any evidence to support them, only the muddled and often contradictory testimony of the different police officers.

The strategy of the civil rights lawyers was to petition for removal of these cases from state to federal jurisdiction under a provision of the 1968 Civil Rights Act. They argued that the law applied in this instance because the arrests had been part of a concerted attempt by the sheriff's department of Rankin County and the Mississippi Highway Patrol to punish the defendants' civil rights activity with harassment and intimidation. But since the federal courts, at the district and the appeals court level, were under control of Mississippi judges, removal was no easy matter.

Both the district court and a three-judge panel of the U.S. Court of Appeals, Fifth Circuit heard the case and held against removal, affirming the police officers' "probable cause" for the arrests and denying that the defendants could not get a fair trial on the state level. Their decisions had nothing to do with the facts, as the jurists were not really weighing the evidence and passing reasoned, impartial judgment, but playing out their accustomed role of giving legal sanction to racial business as usual.

John's lawyers had one last avenue of appeal. They petitioned for a hearing *en banc,* meaning before all fifteen judges of the Court of Appeals. These judges were by and large products of the racist system. And Judge James Plemon Coleman, the former Mississippi attorney general and governor, who had spoken for the panel, now wrote the terse opinion of the court. Speaking for himself and ten other judges, he upheld the essential position of the police.

In the case of the arrests on Highway 49, he went along with the fiction that Doug's "reckless driving" had given the police probable cause to stop the van and that he and the others were armed and hostile. In fact there wasn't a shred of evidence of any resistance to arrest and interference with law officers. The "arms" consisted of one brick, some broken tiles, and silverware (knives and forks), the latter not mentioned in the official charges. In reality Coleman's opinion gave tacit high court approval to the practice of capturing and falsely charging law-abiding civil rights demonstrators in another county to punish them for engaging in civil rights activity. In this way the courts acted in complicity with the violent, repressive behavior of the white supremacists.

Judge Coleman's construction of the trip to Brandon by John and his two companions was also an exercise in selectively reporting the facts and twisting them to make the behavior of the three men look so aggressive and injudicious as to provoke their arrests and jailings, and maybe even the beatings. He made it look as if the men were about to conduct some kind of armed assault on the Rankin County sheriff's headquarters when they were apprehended by the police. Approaching a jail facility "armed to the teeth" late at night "after visiting hours" was such a provocative act, as Coleman described it, that in his estimation it provoked the arrests.

With regard to the beatings, Coleman cited Edwards's sworn statement that Perkins had taken a swing at him as the reason for the police response, with the caveat that he did not condone any excesses that might have occurred. In another reference he said ". . . the three voluntary nocturnal jailhouse visitors . . . were not arrested on Highway 49 but . . . got into a fight at the jail and evidently came off the worst of the encounter." Ignoring the obvious brutality and serious harm inflicted by the police, he indirectly blamed the victims, suggesting their indiscretions had provoked the whole thing. The official description of what happened in the Brandon jail was a "fight" or a "scuffle" and not a savage battering inflicted on innocent people. As the court turned a blind eye to the real behavior of the police, it upheld the ancient and painstakingly constructed fabric of lies that perpetuated victimization of African Americans in the South.

But a bright ray of light did shine through in the Perkins case. John R. Brown, the chief judge of the court, joined by three others, wrote a ringing dissent of one hundred twenty-five pages, bringing forth all the salient facts of the case and thereby letting the truth come out. At the outset he set the case on its appropriate moral grounds. He compared Rev. John Perkins to Mordecai pleading at the gate for his people in the biblical Book of Esther. Haman, the Hitler of his time, was chief minister of the king of Persia, where the Jews were captive. He had decreed their extermination. Esther was a wife of King Xerxes, and Mordecai, her cousin, was at the city's gate, in sackcloth and ashes, crying out in anguish for the plight of his people. His cries influenced

Esther to go to the king at the risk of her life, and the king ultimately heard Mordecai and spared the Jews.

Saying that John Perkins was a modern Mordecai and that the court should let him through the gates, Brown cut through all the legal obfuscations to the heart of the matter. And that of course was the continuing use of law enforcement in Mississippi to brutally punish African Americans claiming the human rights guaranteed them by the United States Constitution.

Brown followed this declaration by a detailed recounting of the events that led up to the case. By simply spelling out the facts, beginning with the Mendenhall boycott, Brown showed how Sheriff Edwards and Highway Patrol Inspector Jones had carefully monitored the goings-on in Simpson County and then set up the arrests in Rankin County. He included pages of self-contradictory police testimony that cut the ground out from under their charges. And he refuted each of the charges against John, Curry, Doug, and the Tougaloo students by citing the complete lack of any evidence to support them.

Among the more salient charges were the ones against the two black leaders, John and Curry. The "inciting to riot" charge was so ridiculous that its only mention was in the appendix Judge Brown included, which detailed the original charges filed against all twenty-four defendants. Coleman, while he equivocated about who started the "fight," avoided mentioning the riot charge. But Brown brought it up in the context of John's, Curry's, and the students' accounts of what went on in the jail that night.

The idea that they could, in this southern "bastille," with scores of armed police holding them, "organize," "encourage," or "promote" a riot was absurd. The concealed weapons charges, which Coleman had paid much attention to, were also easy to refute. Because John's life had been threatened, and, as he testified in the trial, thousands of dollars had been offered as a reward for killing him, he was entitled by Mississippi law to carry weapons, even a concealed one, for his protection. Coleman knew this but he was arguing that John's approaching the jail at night with what he grandiloquently called "an arsenal of weapons" inevitably provoked the police.

Brown presented the "thoroughly developed and undisputed facts" in hope that an impartial reviewer of the case would conclude ". . . the State criminal proceedings [were] merely ill-disguised attempts to punish conduct protected under Federal law." And after his detailed review of the events and the testimony of the case, he concluded that *Perkins v. Mississippi* was a classic instance for removing a case to federal jurisdiction.

In making his final statement, Judge Brown noted the contrived and mechanical way in which the State had kept the case from being removed. Any arrest, he said, that is "geographically and temporally remote" from the civil rights activities, regardless of "how plainly and exclusively motivated by the antecedent exercise of the Federal right to protest racial segregation, will automatically insulate the subsequent spurious criminal prosecution against a quick and painless death by removal to a Federal court, thereby encouraging the repetition of incidents like the present one."

So another John Brown had struck a blow for racial justice. But the majority opinion left John Perkins with no alternative but to bargain with the state court for his freedom. As with the Mendenhall case, his ace in the hole was a suit he had filed against the state, this one for police brutality. And again it was the ripeness of the times that was on John's side. The full weight of federal authority was strongly disposed toward black civil rights, particularly in the Deep South, and guardians of Mississippi did not want to have its appalling law enforcement practices as regarded blacks once again exposed and condemned on a national level, perhaps by the Supreme Court. Nor did they want to risk federal enforcement officials again being sent into the state. And Judge Brown, in his dissent, had laid the groundwork for just such a scenario. The final outcome of the case saw John drop his suit in exchange for the state dropping all charges against him and the others.

Were there any positive implications of *Perkins v. Mississippi?* Did John's travail in Brandon and then in the courts help blacks in the state to gain anything? In fact the progress of civil rights was a matter of small victories advancing the people and the culture of the South inch by inch until real changes began to occur and equality came into sight. John liked to consider his own case one of the significant inches on the yardstick. The black people of Mendenhall saw a black man who had radically and frontally challenged the system stay out of prison, and a young black attorney had argued his cases. Those were encouraging things to see. It was hard to get a clear-cut civil rights victory in the Mississippi courts. But a changing national climate of opinion and increasing numbers of people in the South like Judge Brown, who were unwilling to sanction continuing injustice, would before long swamp the old order.

By the time the Court of Appeals was deciding not to grant removal in June of 1972 and John's attorneys were seeking to work out an accommodation with the State, John had already moved to Jackson and begun to establish Voice of Calvary's presence there. His two-year clash with the white power structure marked the conclusion of the civil rights period in his work. He could look back on tangible gains. He had mobilized his community and inspired them to actively fight for equality. They might not be a lot wealthier, but a definite shift in the power relations was occurring. White store owners in Mendenhall had begun to hire a few blacks by the summer of 1970, and the number would gradually grow with time. The boycott had hurt the white community economically, as John had planned it to, and they had tried to break it by offering money and other bribes to the blacks. The beginning of hiring and the bribery eventually had their effect, and the boycott petered out before summer.

Full school integration also came to Mississippi in 1970. And despite diehard racial hatred the two separate societies were beginning to merge. But as John had observed, the confrontations of the civil rights movement, while necessary, had generated a bitterness, an enmity that separated the races inwardly more than ever, even as integration and black advancement was steadily going forth. It was also observable outside the South in the northern cities in the wake of the assassination of Dr. King and the ghetto uprisings of the late sixties. Even as blacks were making tangible gains as a whole in the seventies, John could see racial animosities on the rise.

He saw this lingering and intensifying racial hatred and distrust as a spiritual problem. As a Christian organization, Voice of Calvary was not just about evangelism and development for African Americans. It was about love of one's neighbor, and that was a mutual proposition, black for white as well as white for black. The Brandon experience had jolted this truth to the center of John's awareness. He had grown up with contempt for the kind of people who had beaten him. And it was all he could do not to let those feelings, intensified by the beatings, crystallize into a full-blown, established hatred that would cause him to give up on any hope that black and white Christians could work together in loving fellowship.

What stopped him from going in this direction was his strong conviction that it was God's will for him to let go of his bitter resentment and love and forgive his enemies. As he made this decision and he felt the poison of bitterness begin to recede in him, he began to feel better, his old positive spirit returned, and he knew he was doing the right thing.

He was left with the problem of how black people could flourish in the poisonous climate of racism. John thought it was not enough for white church communities to send some of their wealth and a few volunteers to help blacks. Blacks too must reach out to whites. They must take the initiative wherever possible. John would begin this painful process at Voice of Calvary in 1971, as the Jackson expansion was starting to take place. He brought a large number of black and white volunteers to Mississippi that summer, but the results were not what he had anticipated.

The summer of 1971 saw Voice of Calvary's first attempt to implement John's augmented vision and become a model of black and white racial reconciliation. Jack MacArthur's Calvary Bible Church in Burbank had discontinued their monthly contribution to their namesake Mississippi mission in about 1969. White evangelical churches were ever uncomfortable with the civil rights movement, preferring to support verbal evangelism without addressing injustice in the structures of society. But Jack MacArthur's son, John, was building his own congregation, Grace Community Church, in the San Fernando Valley and he had continued to maintain an informal tie with John Perkins's work in Mississippi. He made a number of trips to Mendenhall and Jackson in the late sixties and early seventies and was in Mendenhall the day Martin Luther King was killed. It was the younger MacArthur's church that sent the first contingent of young white evangelicals to work in John's inaugural summer volunteer program.

Before this summer, white Christian volunteers had usually come from the peace churches. These "plain folk" of the Quaker and Mennonite traditions had the broad social concerns of missionaries working among the impoverished. Louise Fox and Chris Erb, for example, were young Quaker women from Pennsylvania. The Friends are a communion with a strong heritage of social awareness. Quakers had been among the first Christian abolitionists in North America and they were the only denomination to embrace the antislavery cause officially. In the 1960s, often through the auspices of the American Friends Service Committee, they were active supporters of black civil rights as well as the movement against the draft and the Vietnam War.

The fundamentalism of the people in John MacArthur's church had none of the social activism that permeated the peace churches. In fact, fundamentalists, with their inveterate nineteenth-century individualism, were suspicious of most social reform. The children of the rural fundamentalists, who had separated themselves from theological and social liberalism in the mainline Protestant churches, had carried the middle-class personal success ethic into the sub-urbs—places like the San Fernando Valley, where they gathered in churches like MacArthur's Grace Community Church. Nevertheless their pastor had raised their consciousness about the Mississippi mission, and a contingent of idealistic young men and women journeyed to Mendenhall during that summer.

The black young people who came to Mendenhall in the summer of '71 were from Michigan, many from big urban ghettos like Detroit and Flint. They were full of the black nationalist militancy so characteristic of the time. During the "long hot summers" in the cities of the late sixties, Detroit had had one of the worst racial conflagrations. John had met these black Christian students in Ann Arbor the previous winter, during the trip when his ulcers flared up. Noting that they had just missed the civil rights movement that their older brothers, sisters, and cousins might have been involved in, he could feel their longing to do their own thing to improve the condition of their race. And John wanted very much to accommodate their need.

The mix of white suburbanites from Southern California with blacks from Michigan was not a fortuitous one. The whites were of the same background and belief system as the ones whom Dolphus had encountered at Los Angeles Baptist College, and while they were probably more sensitive than the ones who cheered Martin Luther King's assassination, they were not at all prepared to deal with youthful black anger and militancy. Neither group of people had lived closely among people of the other group. The white students came from quiet suburban neighborhoods, which likely had not yet received even the first trickle of middle-class blacks. The culture and habits of street-smart urban black youth were totally foreign to them.

Many a confrontation and not much Christian harmony occurred between the two culturally disparate groups that summer at Voice of Calvary. The black youths had a heightened consciousness of institutionalized racism and imbedded poverty in black America. Instead of realizing the dream of racial reconciliation Dr. King had spoken of eight years before in the March on Washington, they had seen him killed by an assassin and racial antagonisms persist and even deepen as the violent sixties gave way to the seventies. So for these black young people, the presence of white suburban youths often triggered their pent-up racial resentment. John and Vera Mae found themselves breaking up verbal fights and some heated encounters that almost got physical.

The Jackson ministry was in its early stages, and John ended up trying to keep the peace by placing most of the black students there, while he based the whites in Mendenhall. The Perkins family had just moved into a house in Jackson but John and Vera Mae had a trailer in Mendenhall they lived in much of that summer in order to be on hand to supervise the newly enlarged volunteer program there. VOC made use of the black and white students in various construction and educational programs, but John, Vera Mae, and the others were not able to break down the thick barriers between the races.

By the end of the summer John could see that a common Christian commitment was not enough to breach the deep American racial chasm that these two groups of young volunteers so symbolized. Bringing in white groups and black groups from the outside, each of which had their own cultural baggage and hidden agendas, was not a good way to heal racial conflict. For one thing, neither group of volunteers had much identity with the indigenous Mississippi people. So the whites tried to make themselves feel like the work they did at VOC was in a good cause, even though their lives and their souls didn't really touch those of the people they were working with. And the black students were often too full of their cause and their nationalism to really see the people around them.

John had felt a flush of optimism when he first made plans for the two groups of young people to come to Mississippi, and now he was disappointed. He knew how strong and resistant to change the racial problem was and he knew that it was going to take more than just summer volunteer programs to make any kind of dent in it. As he thought

196

about the sad experience of the summer of 1971, he began to see that outsiders coming into Mississippi, whether black or white, could not, in a short time, develop a relationship with the people who lived there. If people had a commitment deep enough to pull up roots and actually move into these run-down neighborhoods and live among the people in need, that might spark real racial reconciliation. John had made such a move in 1960. Were there white people out there in the suburbs who would join him?

14

Evangelical Social Action

From the time he started Voice of Calvary, John was traveling and speaking in white assemblies about his vision of evangelism and development in black Mississippi. But his heart and soul involvement in the civil rights movement affected the support he received, causing some to fall away. Evangelicals as a whole were biased against mixing what they saw as politics with religion, especially politics that was identified with liberalism, as civil rights was. Jack MacArthur's Burbank congregation discontinued their regularly monthly allotment as events in Mendenhall built toward the boycott, even as the younger MacArthur was making regular trips to Mendenhall. But John's strong preaching was causing others to take notice, apparently for the first time, of the dire needs in black America.

John had received his training from fundamentalists, and it was in fundamentalist churches and ministries that his work first had become known. Through organizations like Jack MacArthur's syndicated *Voice of Calvary* radio program and influential congregations like Vernon McGee's Church of the Open Door in Los Angeles, word of a Negro brother who was doing evangelism among his people in Mississippi spread. And John found himself receiving invitations to preach at some of these fundamentalist churches and schools.

During the sixties, fundamentalist churches, schools, and missions, which had largely withdrawn from a threatening liberal world and hence all social action, were beginning cautiously to get involved in social issues. Fundamentalism had begun as a militant movement within the evangelical churches during the first decade of this century to defend the supernatural basis of Christianity. Twelve booklets, called *The Fundamentals,* were published from 1910 to 1915 and distributed throughout the country. The writers were an American and European cadre of Bible scholars committed to spirited defense of Protestant orthodoxy. Among the doctrines they defended were the verbal inerrancy of Scripture, the virgin birth, miracles, bodily resurrection, and the substitutionary atonement of Christ. Liberals, with a modern bias toward naturalism, challenged the literal interpretation of the Bible, preferring to view supernatural events as metaphor or allegory.

Fundamentalism had become the militant arm of evangelicalism, upholding the faith against the incursions of secular modernity. Fundamentalist clergy penned the apologies and thundered in their pulpits against all things liberal. This prolonged conflict between Protestant orthodoxy and liberalism took in more than matters religious. It was a contest of two different and basically incompatible sets of ideas. Conservative American Protestants revered not only Scripture, but also classical economics and rugged individualism. Their Bible was firmly rooted in the camp meetings and white clapboard churches of nineteenth-century America. And that world had celebrated the entrepreneurial virtues of Rev. Horatio Alger's heroes and the moralistic economics of Brown president, Rev. Francis Wayland, which baptized the free market.

But as urban industrialism produced deep class divisions by the end of the century, the liberals who took up the social gospel challenged these old shibboleths and identified with the progressive clamor for reform. They believed that government and collective action were necessary to correct the urban squalor created by corporate excess, the spoiled fruit of an unregulated capitalism. But the labor legislation and welfare statism they championed remained anathema to evangelical traditionalists, who insisted that all public blessings flow from unrestricted private enterprise.

As the war of words escalated, splitting the churches and polarizing Protestant America, liberals absorbed social action as their special province, and fundamentalists, in reaction, moved away from it. Their reaction became so pervasive as to stifle even private social work. This development reversed a continuous involvement in social matters that had characterized evangelicals throughout the nineteenth century.

Their public conscience had created a large number of urban rescue missions, industrial schools, and homes for a variety of disadvantaged populations. In the 1890s, Reuben A. Torrey, one of the authors of *The Fundamentals,* had served as president of the International Christian Workers Association, which engaged in a broad variety of social service activities. Booker T. Washington, in an address to the Christian Workers convention in 1892, commended his audience for their earnest attention to people's material as well as spiritual needs. But such holistic concerns among conservative Protestants would die off by the 1920s, as the nation retreated from reform, and fundamentalism, having gained Prohibition, now beat its own hasty retreat from public life.

The fundamentalist-modernist controversy, the culture war of the first third of the century, split many denominations into broadly antagonistic camps. By midcentury, American Protestantism was firmly divided along one great fault line, with liberal social action on one side and a highly personalized evangelical faith on the other. The liberal churches expanded their influence through ecumenism, joining in the Federal, then National, then World Council of Churches. Their politics tilted ever leftward, and church leaders commonly endorsed welfare statism and the struggles of oppressed peoples for liberation from colonialists or indigenous right wing (but never left wing) dictators.

The fundamentalists represented only a segment of orthodox Protestantism, but it was *their* animus against modernism and the social gospel that permeated the evangelical churches and cut them off from the broader society. This turn inward would begin to break down as the generation who came of age in the Great Depression and fought the Second World War began to come to prominence. In 1947 Carl F. H. Henry, a Baptist theologian, published *The Uneasy Conscience of Modern Fundamentalism.* Henry issued a prophetic call to a ghettoized fundamentalism to get involved in the great public issues of the day.

While he saw social morality in largely personal and familial terms, he wanted the church to speak out for racial equality and he wanted evangelicals to care for the disadvantaged. In publications over the next quarter century Henry would lay out the case for evangelicals to apply their biblical perspective to social issues. Idealistic Christian young people would be seduced by secular ideologies and reject an irrelevant religion, he maintained, if evangelicalism did not address issues like poverty and racism.

When evangelicalism reemerged as a public faith during the post-war era, it was a group of people around Carl Henry who led the way. He and Harold Ockenga, pastor of Boston's venerable Park Street Church, and the fiery young evangelist Billy Graham, became leaders of the National Association of Evangelicals (NAE), founded during the war to counter the National Council of Churches. In 1956 they began publication of *Christianity Today* to offset the liberals' *Christian Century* and *Christianity and Crisis*. While Henry was calling for evangelicals to take action to make American society more equitable, he avoided mention of any specific steps to be taken. His generalized social concern was not potent enough to stir much action, and the powerful individualistic bias that so defined the evangelical mind swamped any nascent movement on behalf of the dispossessed. With the notable exception of World Vision, the weight of evangelical opinion in post-war America supported the social and political status quo.

Spurred by Cold War anticommunism, traditional evangelical individualism now took on the dimensions of a patriotic crusade for the American way of life. Evangelical spokesmen shunned most forms of government intervention and regulation as steps toward godless communism. Identifying their faith with private enterprise, they would go on to embrace Barry Goldwater's laissez-faire economics and states' rights opposition to civil rights legislation. In unity with their southern brethren on the white citizens councils, most nonsouthern evangelicals supported Goldwater for President in 1964, the year of "Freedom Summer."

While mainstream evangelicals, such as those clustered around *Christianity Today,* spoke out in favor of racial equality, they backed away from supporting the federal legislation and the black civil rights movement that would bring equality about. Fundamentalists, with many of their number in southern churches and colleges, were even further to the right and often openly or covertly segregationist. Such was the racial bias of the evangelical world as John Perkins carried his message to the faculty and students at a fundamentalist school in Cleveland, Ohio.

Fred Alexander was one of the teachers who heard John speak of the needs of black people in Mississippi and he felt deep conviction. How, he wondered, could Bible-believing Christians be so blind and deaf to the Negro cry for justice? He became convinced not only that the fundamentalist churches had been on the wrong side of the civil rights movement, but that they had actually been aiding the forces of oppression. His eyes were opened and he was seized with a desire to speak out prophetically against the self-serving complacency of fundamentalists on the racial issue.

In August of 1965, two years after Martin Luther King had proclaimed his dream of racial reconciliation during the March on Washington, Fred Alexander, together with his son John, published the first issue of *Freedom Now*. In an opening editorial Fred declared his belief that ". . . fear, ignorance, prejudice, and apathy have placed fundamental churches among the most segregated groups in America." He went on to confess that he too had been ". . . fearful, ignorant, prejudiced, and especially apathetic until the last few years. . . ." On the next page, John Alexander laid out the platform of *Freedom Now*.

Civil rights alone would not bring freedom to the Negro, he said. They needed the gospel of Jesus Christ to bring them spiritual freedom. With this statement he established the orthodox credentials necessary for any credibility with his evangelical readership. But then he went on to say that the gospel ". . . touches every phase of an individual's life, not just the religious phase." The gospel that sets people free spiritually also has an interest in their political, social, and economic freedom. In words that echoed the message he had heard from John Perkins, the younger Alexander declared *Freedom Now* an advocate for "the whole gospel."

The Alexanders' little bimonthly journal became a forum for black evangelicals and their white allies to advance the black cause among a religious population long insensitive to racial issues. The early editions were largely couched in terms of personal piety, emphasizing white fundamentalists' neglect of evangelism among America's black population. But they also hammered away at the civil rights issue, citing nineteenth-century evangelical support for the antislavery and other human rights causes. The recurrent theme was that fundamentalist Christians had defaulted to the liberals on civil rights and that liberals were lacking the crucial emphasis on conversion. Only personal conversion, the heart of the evangelical faith message, could transform bitter segregationists and angry black militants into loving brothers and sisters.

The third issue featured the young Perkins family—John, Vera Mae, Spencer, Joanie, Philip, and baby Derek—on the cover. At thirty-five, with closely cropped hair, John looks intently out from the picture, and you can almost feel his determination. His brief featured article,

"Oneness of Believers," blamed divisiveness among Christians for their ineffectiveness in the world. In a broad statement, he warned a Bible-believing readership that if they did not find ways to live up to their beliefs and heal racial strife, their pious words would fail to ". . . impress this generation as a Gospel for the whole world." Though he was focused at this time on the concerns of blacks in Mississippi, John was already speaking to the centrality of the reconciliation message as he spoke and wrote publicly for evangelicals of both races.

The Alexanders thus waded into the racial conflagration of the sixties, laboring to arouse the dormant consciences of their fund-amentalist brethren. They used biblical exegesis to explain in a lengthy series of articles that the curse of Ham has nothing to do with Africans. They pointed out the hypocrisy of fundamentalists who verbally sup-ported evangelism among blacks but who strenuously resisted the idea of an integrated church or having anything to do with blacks them-selves. A lead article in the summer of 1966 was devoted to Martin Luther King. It was a mild statement that distinguished the right-eousness of King's cause from the limitations of his liberal theology. It refuted the common right wing notion that King was a commu-nist, but at the same time admitted his association with people who had been communists or fellow travelers. Sensitive to the fundamen-talist readership, the purpose was to gently nudge them toward greater tolerance of civil rights activism.

The article stirred up an inferno of anger, drawing many heated and often unsigned letters breathing fire and hatred toward Martin "Lucifer" King. When King was killed in April of 1968, the Alexan-ders revised the May/June issue as a memorial to him. Their lead edi-torial began: "The time for polite discussion is past. Our cities have begun to burn. Martin Luther King has been murdered. Last night seven people were killed here in Chicago. In Washington machine guns were placed around the White House." They followed with a blast at fun-damentalists and their churches for burying Christian love beneath a thick-skinned legalism that cloaked their racial bigotry. Fundamen-talists' doctrinaire refusal to support nonviolent movements for black social justice along with their irrational hatred of Dr. King had helped create the climate for his assassination and the violence that followed.

The hatred and resistance the Alexanders drew from many in their con-stituency in response to their advocacy of the black freedom movement horrified them and drove them toward closer identification with blacks and other oppressed peoples. A community of young evangelical activists was now beginning to come together and make stronger efforts to explore and combat the racism they saw poisoning American institutions. And *Freedom Now* became an early outlet for the developing ideas of a number of the most visible black evangelicals. One was Tom Skinner, a "preacher's kid" from Harlem who had rebelled, as many PKs do, and become a notorious gang leader. In the sixties he was converted and he began using his formidable energies to build an evangelistic associa-

VOL. I, NO. 3   DECEMBER, 1965

MR. & MRS. JOHN M. PERKINS
and children (left to right): Deborah, Joan, Phillip, Spencer

Freedom Now, which first appeared in 1965, marked the rebirth of support for black civil rights and social action among American evangelicals. This issue featured the Perkins family.

tion, which focused on blacks and their distinct concerns. Another was Howard Jones, an associate with the Billy Graham evangelistic team. The southern-bred Graham was one of the first well-known white evangelicals to actively recruit and work with blacks.

In an interview printed in the Martin Luther King memorial edition of *Freedom Now,* Jones criticized whites for not supporting nonviolent black leaders like King, Whitney Young, Roy Wilkins, and A. Philip Randolph. Because they turned a deaf ear to these moderates, they were now faced with "violent black power advocates like Rap Brown and Stokely Carmichael."

Another eloquent black evangelical was William Pannell, a graduate of a white Bible college who was on the staff of Youth for Christ, an outreach of mainstream evangelicalism developed during the Second World War. Pannell's early writing was personal and evangelistic, but he would later develop into a major voice calling the evangelical churches to account in the realm of racial relations. A fourth and frequent voice enlightening insulated whites to the culture, religion, and immediate concerns of black people was that of John Perkins.

The Alexanders and their collaborators' engagement with the black movement for social justice sensitized them to the plight of other oppressed and suffering people throughout the world. In the fall of 1969 they officially broadened the focus of their magazine, renaming it *The Other Side*. In its pages John Alexander and other young evangelicals would take on the pacifistic, communitarian animus of the counterculture, while trying to avoid its self-indulgent bohemianism. The new expanded journal highlighted public issues like crime, prisons, poverty, Third World missions, the environment, and the women's movement.

In 1971 in the Chicago area, a group of evangelical divinity students walked out of their seminary, as many young radical Christians were doing at the time. They moved in together and began to share a common life and they started an underground-style tabloid, which they provocatively named *Post-American*. Jim Wallis, who would soon become the leading voice of a new radical evangelicalism, spoke out boldly against the "Christian Americanism" so zealously advanced by his elders in the faith. Wallis spoke in strains that echoed the secular radicals who had founded Students for a Democratic Society (SDS) a decade earlier. Wallis's impassioned declaration in the first *Post-American* recalled the original SDS of the 1962 *Port Huron Statement*. There Tom Hayden and Carl Oglesby had inveighed against militarism, materialism, and the power elite, calling for a more humane society and a "participatory democracy" that would include the many who had been marginalized.

Wallis was strongly influenced by the early populistic SDS and sounded many of the same themes. But he went on to place the struggle against war and for social justice in Christian terms. The gospel, he said, is "the entrance of Jesus Christ into history," and as such it implies a revolutionary transformation of the individual and the social order. But the American church has become the weak-kneed captive of American culture and institutions. It has failed to challenge a prevailing materialism, a bellicose and self-serving nationalism, and the habituated racism of the society-at-large. Wallis cited the inadequacy of both conservative and liberal formulations of faith, the one for sanctifying oppressive policies and practices of the status quo, the other for watering down the historic Christian faith and denying the need for personal transformation. He called for a radical alternative that was "distinctly post-American" and dedicated to creating a new society consistent with the love of one's neighbor that animates the gospel.

The Other Side and *Post-American* became rallying points for a movement of young evangelicals who wanted their churches to stand with the poor and outcast rather than with the comfortable and complacent.

Around Thanksgiving time in 1973 a diverse group of evangelicals committed to social action came together in the blustery cold of Chicago and hammered out a public document. They christened their work "A Declaration of Evangelical Social Concern." It began with a confession that as evangelicals they had cheapened God's love by lack of adequate attention to the material well-being of the needy. And it went on to catalogue the various forms of evangelical complicity with social evil. Beginning with the church's sanction of racist attitudes and practices, the document continued by calling evangelical Christians to a repentance that must move against all forms of social injustice. Idolatry of wealth and nation in rampant American materialism and militarism were to be condemned. And a partnership of men and women in life, rather than the usual male domination, was to be encouraged.

There were fifty-three signers including a broad spectrum of socially conscious evangelicals ranging from the conservative Carl Henry to the radical Jim Wallis and John Alexander. The liberal middle included Reformed ethicist Lewis Smedes, Senator Mark Hatfield of Oregon, social scientists Richard Pierard and David Moberg, and feminists Sharon Gallagher and Nancy Hardesty. And there were a number of black signers including William Pannell, John Perkins, and the young activist scholar, Ron Potter. The signatories to "A Declaration of Evangelical Social Concern" represented the full emergence of a social evangelicalism among a small but highly articulate group of people.

The example of John Perkins was especially important to radicals like Jim Wallis and others in his community, such as Joe Roos and Wes Michaelson, who also signed the Declaration. Having met John at the Chicago conference, they kept in close contact with him. He became a contributing editor to *Post-American,* telling Voice of Calvary's story and describing his experience doing holistic ministry and community development among the poor. Wallis and the young men and women around him were fired by the idea of living among the poor and taking on their felt needs. In early 1976 they renamed their community and their magazine *Sojourners* and they moved to Washington, D.C., where they located in an inner-city black and Latino neighborhood.

Perkins served as a mentor to the Sojourners Community, as his work provided them with a model for Christian community development, particularly as Voice of Calvary expanded to the urban neighborhoods of Jackson. In the nation's capitol, their magazine would grow into a major forum for their style of social evangelicalism, expounding a gospel of peace, social service, and advocacy for the world's underclasses.

While the various shades of social activism never captured a very large segment of greater evangelicalism, they did create important linkages that would eventually generate a formidable movement. The rise of a diverse, loosely connected body of social evangelicals had immediately favorable consequences for the work of John Perkins. In Jackson, in the early seventies, John was juggling a growing number of ongoing projects. At the same time as he was building new Jackson ministries, he was transitioning the Mendenhall programs to independence under the leadership of Dolphus and Artis, and he was on the road speaking nationwide. In the seventies, as a younger generation of evangelical intellectuals in colleges and seminaries around the country became more socially conscious, John Perkins became an increasingly popular speaker on campuses.

Wheaton College, often thought of as the best of the evangelical liberal arts institutions, was one of the first to have him as a speaker. Wheaton is one of a number of small Christian colleges founded in the Midwest before the Civil War. As with its sister, Oberlin, the train of antebellum democratic reformism ran through Wheaton, with the antislavery movement as engine. Jonathan Blanchard,

Wheaton's founder, was a fervent abolitionist. But unlike Oberlin and most of the other colleges founded by evangelicals, which secularized as they encountered modernity, Wheaton remained staunchly evangelical.

Following the common path of twentieth-century evangelicalism, Wheaton lost the reformist passion of its early years. But sensitivity to African American causes remained, and Billy Graham, Wheaton's most illustrious alumnus of the World War II generation, became the first mass evangelist to integrate his platform. In the early seventies, Wheaton's tough fundamentalist president, Hudson Armading, was impressed with John Perkins's work in Mississippi. He liked John's practical, hands-on approach to evangelism and development among blacks. More than mere civil rights oratory, John was preaching justice in a way that made it possible to get involved with him. It was two Wheaton students who went as volunteers to Mendenhall to help Voice of Calvary start its Genesis One elementary school.

As he was transitioning between Mendenhall and Jackson, John received invitations to speak at a number of other colleges, most with some Christian, usually evangelical orientation, a few secular. A notable secular institution was the University of Pittsburgh, where a friend John had made in the social work department brought him in as a speaker. And at the other end of Pennsylvania, in suburban Philadelphia, he spoke at the prestigious Swarthmore College. Swarthmore is a Quaker school, and Chris Erb, one of the young women who was working in Mendenhall during the boycott, was a Swarthmore graduate. Also the United Brethren in Christ, another of the historic peace churches, had colleges in Pennsylvania and Ohio that often brought him on campus to teach his style of ministry.

He also spoke at Gordon College, a broadly based evangelical school coupled with Gordon Conwell Theological Seminary in Hamilton, Massachusetts, a seaside village just north of Boston. Evangelicals in the liberal Bay State were relatively small in number, but they retained a strong social conscience. A few historic churches like Park Street Congregational had remained stalwart bastions of evangelical orthodoxy from the early nineteenth century when the Unitarian movement was bathing Boston in urbane liberalism. And in recent years Park Street, under Ockenga's leadership, had become a pioneer of renewed social conscience among evangelicals. Twelfth Baptist, another Boston evangelical congregation, was black by the sixties and piloted by the prophetic orator Michael Haynes. These and a few other churches gave substance to Boston's evangelicalism and supported Gordon College, enhancing the quiet little campus's social awareness.

At the same time that he was becoming familiar to the academic communities at Wheaton, Gordon, and other colleges, John was traveling regularly back to the Pasadena area, where he became close friends with faculty members at Fuller Theological Seminary. Founded in 1947 by radio evangelist Charles E. Fuller and Dr. Ockenga, with Carl Henry as its first professor of systematic theology, Fuller had become the chief proponent of the new evangelical social activism. By the seventies this West Coast seminary would house a solid collection of socially enlightened scholars, among them theologian William Pannell and Reformed social ethics professor Lewis Smedes.

Paul Jewett, the Fuller systematic theologian who wrote *Man as Male and Female,* which criticized traditional evangelical male dominion, was a warm enthusiast for John Perkins's work. But Jewett told John he didn't think it would be profitable for him to spend time trying to convert white evangelicals to his development philosophy. He thought whites wouldn't listen to a self-made black preacher and that John should expend his efforts among whites in pure fund-raising. Jewett knew whereof he spoke, as racial prejudice and insensitivity ran deep in evangelical circles. John too was aware of this but he felt a strong sense of calling to teach his ideas in white congregations and colleges.

As one originally trained by white evangelicals, John had come to Mississippi with an overall respect for their biblical knowledge and their expressions of faith. He had been focused on doing evangelism and countering emotionalism, illiteracy, and lack of sound biblical teaching among black Christians. And in that endeavor, the emphasis on Bible study and evangelism he had learned from white evangelicals like Wayne Leitch, Vernon McGee, and Jack MacArthur had provided a solid place to stand. But events of the past decade had opened John's eyes to the tremendous gaps between the professed beliefs and the practices of white American Christians.

Experience with their churches in other parts of the country as well as in the South had shown him a shallow religion of personal security and middle-class success, a religion that blinded people to the gospel's ringing demand for justice. John had seen that whites were as needy as blacks, but where black impoverishment was largely material, the white churches suffered no less an impoverishment of the spirit. Now he wanted to immerse white evangelicals in a theology of development that would awaken them to the biblical commandment to care for the poor and oppressed in their midst.

15

REACHING OUT

$\int$omething that helped John in this reorientation of his message as well as in the expansion of Voice of Calvary's ministries in the early seventies was a change in the sources of his funding. At the outset, much of VOC's support had come from white suburban churches. But as white churches and individuals squeamish about civil rights dropped away, other people and agencies with a stronger commitment to the cause of black advancement replaced them.

When VOC first started in Mendenhall, John received much of his support from a few white churches and a number of small black congregations in various parts of the country. A few wealthy whites had been involved, like John McGill and Dave Peacock in California, but funding for day-to-day operations had come in good part from the ten- and fifteen-dollar contributions from people in these black churches. By the time the Jackson ministries were starting up, the main sources of support were shifting to wealthy whites with a commitment to black development, some of whom headed foundations.

One of the first was a man John met through his networking around the Burbank church. One of Jack MacArthur's secretaries, a woman named Betty Wagner, had inherited some money and become one of VOC's regular supporters. She introduced John to a Mr. Bauersox, a wealthy older man who would die in the seventies as the Jackson operations were expanding. His sizable estate was divided among eight different ministries, Voice of Calvary being one of them. This infusion of money helped launch the expansion, with the lion's share going to

People's Development Incorporated (PDI), a corporation John chartered in 1974 to repair, restore, and rebuild dilapidated housing in the run-down black neighborhoods near the Jackson inner city. PDI would turn out to be one of the most enduring and successful operations VOC maintained in Jackson.

Another wealthy donor, and in some respects a model of the kind of people who would be mainstays in the future, was a North Carolina–bred businessman named Curt Lamb. John had met Lamb back in 1963 through his son-in-law, Richard Williams, who taught at a little Christian school in Dallas, Texas, where John was speaking at a banquet. This was the period, early on in his work, that he was speaking to thousands of black children a week in Mississippi and increasing numbers of white school children and their teachers outside the state. Williams was impressed by John's message and spoke enthusiastically about him to his father-in-law.

Lamb was a businessman and part-time investment banker who had started as a cookie salesman. While he was plying this trade back in Charlotte, a black man had befriended him and nurtured him in Christian faith. This personal experience with a black Christian gave him sensitivity to causes like John's. Lamb began to donate generously to the Mendenhall work, and when the MacArthur church curtailed its support, he was pleased to fill the gap. He provided the bulk of support for the summer program in its first year and he would thereafter contribute between five and six thousand dollars a year, a good deal larger figure a generation ago than it is today.

It was ironic but hardly surprising that this wealthy southerner supplanted the California church as a prime giver. In the South whites lived closer to blacks and were generally more involved with them. Lamb's beneficence drew on his personal experience; it was not an abstraction as it was with many outside the South, where suburban whites rarely interacted with blacks. Also wealthy southerners enjoyed some social insulation from the racial issues that so inflamed middle- and working-class white people. Their wealth afforded them the opportunity to remain above the racial fray and, if they were so inclined, pursue philanthropy.

Besides Lamb, Voice of Calvary drew support from a number of other philanthropic southerners, including the Stuart Irby Foundation. Irby was a local Jackson businessman whose father had started an electrical cable company, which built the steel posts for high tension wires. They had begun with REA contracts in the thirties and by the seventies they were working as far afield as Saudi Arabia. The Stuart Irby Foundation gave a number of grants to Voice of Calvary. Another local Jackson man, Victor Smith, who had struck it rich in Texas oil, became a close friend of John Perkins and a regular donor to Voice of Calvary's growing ministries.

As John traveled more and his work became more broadly known, he was also able to draw grants from large mainline denominations and from an expanding array of secular foundations. While the Jackson office was gearing up, Voice of Calvary in Mendenhall was building the large, multipurpose R. A. Buckley Gymnasium and they were starting a cooperative health care clinic. A major grant from the Campaign for Human Development, the Catholic charitable outreach, and others from the Episcopal, Presbyterian, and Christian Reformed churches were of crucial help in funding these and other projects.

Aided by a number of trips to New York to visit foundations, John became increasingly adept in the science of grantsmanship. From the beginning he had recognized the necessity of gaining a large and diverse network of contributors. During the years in Mendenhall, he had gathered a list of nine hundred who actively supported him. Many were white church people who wanted to support evangelism among poor blacks in the South, much as they might support a foreign mission. By the early seventies, John was emphasizing development and aiming for closer involvement with white contributors.

For whites from more affluent circumstances who supported it, Voice of Calvary in Mendenhall and Jackson would become much more than a mission. In the seventies John's vision of racial reconciliation and cooperation began to transform these ministries into sites where affluent whites could bring their skills and work directly with African Americans—both VOC's workers and local people in need. Convinced that evangelicals needed to be jolted out of their middle-class complacency, he went into their colleges and churches and called for "relocation" to communities of need, as God had relocated himself to earth among people in the incarnation of Christ.

Orthodox Christian doctrine holds that in Jesus the Word of God took on human flesh. The significance of this belief for John was that God did not relate to humanity from afar, but moved into the hurting community. He lived right here on earth among suffering, needy people, taking on himself the common lot of humanity. Only in this way could he exercise genuine compassion for people; only thus could he really affirm and empower them.

More and more during the seventies John moved into the role of prophet among white suburban evangelicals. With the sources of outside funding shifting to foundations and commitments of wealthy individuals, his work was not so dependent on church largesse as it had been early on. This development had a freeing effect on him psychologically, which gave him all the greater independence to speak his mind. Increasing numbers of evangelicals were ready to hear him, particularly younger ones who had grown up amid the social movements of the sixties. Like any good evangelical, John carried his Bible and drew his message from it but he would go deeper than the personalized pieties of suburban Sunday sermons. He would illustrate broad, underlying principles in the Old and New Testaments that addressed the church as a community of believers called to bring justice to the poor and oppressed.

This prophetic message was wholly unlike anything twentieth century American evangelicals were accustomed to. And had he been the standard liberal Social Gospeler, even one with the verbal power and eloquent turn of phrase of a Martin Luther King, he would not have gained much of a hearing among them. But John knew how to make contact with his evangelical audience. Having worked closely with white fundamentalists, he understood their mentality and style—an intensely personal style based in recounting one's walk of faith with God. White evangelical audiences would continue to be accessible to John Perkins, first because he rooted everything he said firmly in Scripture, and second because he personalized his delivery, much as their pastors and evangelists did.

When he taught, he always began with a biblical passage, and one that he found most illustrative of his message was the encounter of Jesus with the woman at the well in Samaria. Comparing the Samaritans with inner-city blacks in our own society, John noted the Jews' hatred and scrupulous avoidance of them. But Jesus, he emphasized, flouted custom and not only traveled through Samaria, but approached a fallen woman there.

John drew more than one important principle from this account. Jesus didn't intrude on her from a place of superiority, saying something like, "I have a wonderful plan for your life," as a modern evangelical might do. He "affirmed her dignity," said John, by asking her to minister to his bodily need in giving him a drink. Jesus opened communication around their mutual "felt need" for water. Having done so, he could then approach her about deeper things. John used this to illustrate his point that white suburban Christians need to get personally involved in the lives of the black poor, not minister to them from above and afar.

He didn't just explain the passage and make the modern application, as a liberal, social-action preacher might do. He wove these things together with his personal testimony. Establishing his common ground with his audience, he talked about his own quest for middle-class success and respectability in a California suburb. It was easy and natural, he said, to fall into the cult of individual upward mobility, since that is what our American culture endorses. John confessed he had felt good about his own successful escape from the community of need in Mississippi. But he had been stopped dead in his tracks when he saw the sad young men in the San Bernardino youth camps and realized how poorly their lives in the Deep South had prepared them for the scramble in California. And so he had decided to go back home and address the felt needs of these young men where they were first being generated.

John talked about how the white folks in Bible-believing Mississippi churches had turned coldly away from their own Samaria. He spoke about how he had defied racial etiquette to venture into Dr. Odenwald's office and talk Bible with him and that this Baptist pastor had recognized their bond in common faith. John told how the white clergyman realized the need to speak to his congregation about reaching out in love to the people down on the other side of the railroad tracks whose children were going without shoes and warm winter clothing and how these good fundamental Christians had cold-shouldered their pastor's pleas to love their black neighbors. He told of how their refusal to open their hearts broke Dr. Odenwald's heart and drove him to a despair that caused him to take his own life.

"The purpose of the gospel of Jesus Christ," John emphasized, "is to burn through racial and cultural barriers," barriers between Jew and Samaritan, and in our own day, between white and black Americans. And yet in America, in Mississippi, where evangelical Christianity was the norm, the evangelist would put up a sign saying, "Revival tonight. Everybody welcome." "And I knew," John said, "that if I went there, it would start a riot." John's white audiences laughed when he made this statement, but it was a poignant laughter that disarmed them, drawing them closer to him. Then he would drive home his point that white American evangelicals, in their avoidance of their black neighbors, were akin to the ancient Jews who avoided the Samaritans. John did not mince words about the failure of the suburban churches to assume their responsibility to the poor.

Laying out the biblical pattern, he built his case for the church's duty to care for the poor and oppressed, describing God's requirements of ancient Israel. He spoke of how God had made the Jews a nation in slavery and then freed them so they would have a natural sensitivity to others who were oppressed. He spoke of God's requirement to leave grain in the field and to make other provision for the poor and of God's ordaining the sabbath and the sabbatical year for universal rest from labor and enjoyment of the fruits of his creation. John emphasized God's requirement in the Mosaic law of periodic Jubilee years of feasting and release from accumulated debt, but with the exception of a few godly people like Boaz in the Book of Ruth, the Jews failed to follow these divine laws of redistribution and care for the poor. Because they had worshiped wealth and they had oppressed and neglected the poor, God allowed a train of judgments to come on them.

John drew the familiar connection between Israel, the Old Testament people of God, and Jesus and the church in the New Covenant. The church, he said, is the continuing presence of Christ on earth, "a people called out of the world to be the prophetic voice of God to champion the poor and oppressed of society." The early church had developed the parish system to meet the needs of local communities in response to that ideal but like Israel before it, the church eventually turned into an institution that served the interests of the rich and well-placed. The modern American church has done likewise, said John, adapting to the prevailing culture. It has moved out of the cities, as they have become habitations of the poor and needy, and into suburbia, which caters to harried middle-class commuters on a frantic "search for personal happiness and meaning." John saw much of the organized American church relegating itself to the superficial role of "artificial joymaker" for individuals seeking their own spiritual comfort.

If the church would reclaim its mission as "Christ's life in the community" it could become "an agent for real change" and social transformation. To do so, John stressed that the church needs to again locate as a parish church in neighborhoods of need, discovering and addressing those needs. With his Mendenhall experience as touchstone, he laid out a fuller conception of evangelism than these conservative Christians had heard before.

Evangelism, according to John, is sharing what God is doing in your life. This is the preliminary work to be done by Christians in a community. John began evangelizing Mendenhall by teaching in Vera Mae's Oak Ridge Missionary Baptist Church. The tent meetings they held were a more visible means of evangelizing. In Mendenhall, John said, they had pretty much evangelized the whole town in a few months.

But the day-to-day work of the church was not supposed to be in evangelism, which is done in the community, but in equipping already evangelized people to do ministry. John thought the evangelical church had made its life superficial by focusing so much on evangelism and so little on discipling, or "leadership development," as Jesus had done. The latter meant showing Christians how to address other people's immediate life needs. The verbal evangelism of the tent revival was a good start, but this alone did not give people a sense of "how we identified with their issues."

When Vera Mae organized a day care center so that single mothers could go to work, the women saw a genuine concern for their lives and they began to come around and get involved. This helped the ministries expand. Building the gym, the cooperative store, and all the other projects and social ministries that Voice of Calvary started up were natural extensions of evangelism. "God's love is fleshed out in our bodies," John said. And the people themselves, as they got involved, staffed the ministries and expanded the church, which grew naturally out of their life and work together. Social action then became an integral part of the evangelistic process. And this concern for the whole of people's lives in turn led right into economic development and the ongoing battle for justice.

Moving in and getting involved in the lives and felt needs of an indigenous people does not mean doling out money or goods to them. John agreed heartily with his conservative white audiences that welfare saps the initiative and vitality of the people who receive it. But he firmly maintained that the way to end welfare dependency is not simply to cut off government aid, but to develop enterprises, like the co-ops, which empower people to make positive changes in their own lives.

217

It is not merely the projects and enterprises for economic development that make the changes happen. Christians must see people as individuals each with his or her own need. Jesus saw the material and spiritual needs of the Samaritan woman and he addressed them and affirmed her dignity as a person. Likewise, working among the poor in Mississippi meant seeing and working with each one as an individual with unique personal needs and thus affirming each person's dignity. When you affirm people's dignity, you instill new confidence in them, which helps them develop their own resources.

Doing development among the black poor inevitably led to concerns about justice, which John saw in terms of "who owns what." He liked to quote Psalm 24:1: "The earth is the LORD's, and the fulness thereof" (KJV). Because God has created everything, and everything is his, that means he is concerned about how people relate to his whole creation. The world is not ours, but God's, and in our capitalistic economy, John said, "we practice ownership too tightly." He reminded his middle-class listeners that people are only stewards, and the Owner will eventually require us to account for how we used his creation. Nevertheless, it is good, he said, for people to own property, since it gives them dignity and a strengthening self-reliance. Biblical justice, as prophets like Amos spoke of it, called for property to be dispersed and not concentrated among a few great landowners.

For blacks in the South before the civil rights movement, ownership of property was not common. Obtaining justice meant opening up opportunity for all people and redistributing the wealth among the poor. Working for the full range of civil rights was necessary to enhance the possibility of black ownership and the empowerment it conferred. John was careful to clarify that redistributing the wealth by simply taking it from the rich and giving it to the poor would be ineffectual, since the rich would only have it again in a little while as the poor went and bought Cadillacs and alligator shoes with their new unearned income. On the other hand, a more just and equitable redistribution occurs as the poor learn the skills needed for owning and managing property, as they develop their resources, and as they build the enterprises that develop their community.

John wanted white people in the colleges, seminaries, and suburban churches where he spoke to help bring about this kind of redistribution. It was not merely funding that he was after. Foundations and wealthy individuals were providing seed money for development. He wanted people who felt a calling to actually bring their talents, skills, and experience into black communities and pass them on to the people living there.

It was not just a matter of white helping black. John knew that black Christians in the impoverished towns and hamlets of Mississippi and in the urban ghettoes in and outside the South could deepen the faith of the whites who joined them. Coping with the daily burden of living in such places strengthened the character of those who looked to their spiritual resources. The poor have much to teach those whose lives have been more insulated. In forming communities based on loving service and reconciliation across lines of race and class, the faith of whites could deepen in ways not often possible in the fragmented, individualistic life of the suburbs. John preached restoration of the parish church, as whites with the calling to do so relocate in rural and urban communities of need and join the people there to develop their faith and their lives together.

He believed this concept of a local parish church, practicing racial and class reconciliation and community development, was the truly effective one with the potential to transform society. In the early seventies he was beginning to convey his vision of the church to college students, seminarians, and white evangelicals in churches across the country. This vision had grown out of his own commitment, toil, and blood, and as he conveyed it to his listeners, his vivid language bespoke the sacrifices he had made to have it. His speech had a warmth, a depth, and an intensity that forged immediate bonds of friendship with his audiences. Some of the young, idealistic Christians who were born too late to have marched for civil rights began to see how they also might have something to do with healing the deep wounds of racism.

Glendale is an older southern California suburb nestled in the sometime verdant foothills of the San Gabriel Valley, not far from Pasadena. In the fifties and sixties it was a quiet enclave of stately, tree-lined drives hiding neatly landscaped Spanish-style homes. Harold Philip Spees, whose friends all called him "H," moved there with his parents when he was in the sixth grade. They had been living in Canoga Park, in one of the mass-produced tract neighborhoods of the booming San Fernando Valley. Glendale was a definite move up for his dad, but it was no big deal to H, who missed his buddies in the valley. The new neighborhood didn't have any kids his age, and he soon concluded Glendale was a boring place, populated mostly with retired people and their ridiculously clipped poodles.

The year the Spees family moved there was 1963, the year JFK was shot. H remembered the announcement coming through the PA speaker in his sixth-grade classroom that November afternoon, what a shock it was, and how he wept as news of the president's death in Parkland Hospital in Dallas quickly followed. H remembered how moved he had been when Kennedy had challenged young America, saying, ". . . ask not what your country can do for you. Ask what you can do for your country," not quite three years earlier. Like so many youngsters of that sanguine time, H thought he could do just about anything he put his mind and shoulder to. He was excited by the space program and the astronauts. He was also listening when the president threw his support behind Martin Luther King and the civil rights movement. The March on Washington had happened just a few months before Kennedy's assassination, and King's "I have a dream" rang in H's memory, as it did in that of the whole younger generation.

There were no blacks in Glendale during H's childhood. The few who could have afforded to move there were quietly excluded by restrictive covenants, before the Supreme Court ruling put that practice into gradual eclipse. H had his first real contact with a black person during his high school years, when he became active in Key Club. An outgoing, personable youth and something of a politician, H ran successfully for regional office. Going to large club gatherings, he made a number of friends in the youth service organization. One was Gerald Salter, a young black man from Pittsburgh, who had been elected Key Club governor. Gerald became this sheltered white suburbanite's first informal tutor in the subject of racial relations. Once when the two were together, Gerald had cut his finger. He held a Band-Aid next to his ebony skin and asked H what color it was. "Flesh color," came the automatic response. "Not my flesh!" was Gerald's rejoinder.

During the years of the fundamentalist controversy in the early part of this century, Southern California sprouted a number of theologically conservative Presbyterian churches, including the congregations in Hollywood and Glendale. H had grown up Episcopalian, but in the sixties he found his church in a debilitating mood of doubt, debating such questions as, "Does God exist?" Looking for a climate more nourishing to his nascent faith, he was drawn to the stirring sermons of Bruce Thieleman at Glendale Presbyterian. Thieleman was one of the new breed of evangelical clergy sensitized to racial issues and preaching a strong social message.

One Sunday when H was there, Thieleman preached a sermon called "Nerve Enough for Nineveh." The subject was Jonah and his dogged resistance to God's command that he go into the Assyrian capital and prophesy to its inhabitants their need to repent to escape the wrath to come. It was the racial prejudice of a Jew toward the Assyrians, said Thieleman, that made Jonah so set against going to Nineveh. He then drove home the application, saying that safely ensconced there in prosperous Glendale they would all be unlikely to go and minister to black people in Watts.

Here now was a white suburban pastor sounding a theme similar to what John Perkins was saying when he talked about the church's need to go over into Samaria. The message bore deeply into H's conscience as he listened. That year, 1971, John Perkins came to Thieleman's church, followed by Artis Fletcher, who was attending seminary nearby, and they both spoke dramatically of the work in Mendenhall and the need for white volunteers to come and help them. H was convinced that he had to go to Mississippi, so he joined a team of volunteers including his girlfriend, nursing student Terry Ash, who were going to Mendenhall for the summer.

The summer of '72 was just a year after VOC's fiasco involving militant black students from Michigan and conservative white evangelicals from California. The summer volunteer programs were still in an early, liquid phase of trial and error. H and the other five white volunteers stayed on the second floor of the house that had been the Perkins family's home. The Perkinses were now living in Jackson and John and Vera Mae came to Mendenhall every week and stayed in their trailer. The six volunteers included three men and three women, all of whom were in various stages of higher education. Living in the prefab house, which still lacked insulation and sheet rock over the frame, they suffered through the dense blanket of Mississippi heat and the culture shock of staying in the quarters amidst all those poor black folk.

H and the others read Dietrich Bonhoeffer's *Life Together* and they all tried to think that what they were doing was a great step of faith, but the realities of their surroundings and the demands of what they were doing stressed them all and drove H toward personal crisis. He would lie on his bed sweltering as he tried to get to sleep and he would think about how hard it was to be there. It was hard for him to see Aunt Sally across the street boiling and washing clothes by hand and the ragged people, many without teeth. The sights and smells offended his middle-class sensibilities. He wasn't used to being around such poverty, and it made him uncomfortable. He didn't want to go into those dark and dirty shacks. And he felt deeply ashamed that he should feel this way.

The work, however, provided some sense of meaning and cama-raderie, and there was always a great deal of it to do. John simply brought these young white volunteers alongside him, Dolphus, Herbert, and the other VOC staff, and they all worked together on tutoring and con-struction during the days and then teaching in vacation Bible school in the evenings. For John, working round the clock was just the natural way to live, and long, hard hours of work put him in stride with his purpose. But for these young Californians, John's daily schedule was grueling and it took some getting used to. There was an endless amount of construction work to do, since they were building the Buckley Gym that summer. They had a team of bricklayers at work, and H and the others carried cement blocks for them and helped put up the walls.

The physical labor helped relieve the tensions and difficulties H and the others experienced as they tried to relate to the people in the com-munity. Working in the tutoring program had become a daily exercise in frustration for H. The children he worked with had had such inad-equate training and were so deficient in fundamental skills that he despaired of ever getting them up to grade level. Also, Joanie and Spencer Perkins, who were his peers, quickly made him aware of a prejudice he didn't know he had. Their own racial sensitivities honed to a razor's edge in the tribulations of integration, they quickly called him on his subtle paternalism.

H began to see how naturally he had associated spirituality with education and the cultural trappings of the white upper-middle class. He began to measure his life against the lives of people like John and Vera Mae, Herbert Jones, and Mr. Buckley and he felt its superficial-ity. He admired these gritty people who had simply nailed their shoes to the floor and said, "We're not leaving until God uses us to change our community."

During the steamy dog days of August, H hit bottom, feeling a deep sense of his own spiritual inadequacy. Lying on his sweaty bed in the unfinished Perkins house, he realized he lacked the faith and commitment of the black people he was spending the summer with, and crying out to God, he received back a deep impression. It was as if God were saying: "When you accepted me as your Savior, you accepted everything I had to give you and I'm glad to give it. Now you have come to a point in life where you feel inadequate at all these different levels. You now have the privilege to receive me as Lord, which means you have the opportunity to give back to me all that you have, all that you are, and all that you aspire to be in all of its inadequacy. I will take that from you and I will return it back to you. I will make up the difference, so that you will be sufficient."

In Mendenhall H had quickly arrived at what he knew was the end of his spiritual tether. He had come into a cultural situation where he felt alien and incompetent in his efforts to make contact with the people. Here the education and the individual success ethic he had grown up with had actually become a barrier and he found himself unable to rely effectively on his own resources. So he cried to God for help, and God met him where he was and caused him to see that he could not even begin to do this work in his own power.

The experience H had, which he would think of as a second conversion, paralleled that of John Perkins when John had felt the power of God working inside him in his own conversion. As John had felt, now H would feel a life ablaze in Christ. He began to feel that it was not he doing the work among black Mississippians, a work that had once seemed beyond his capability. In surrendering to God, he got his own need to perform and achieve out of the way and he allowed God to work in him, much as John had done before. The immediate effect was a deep sense of relief and then a growing sense of meaning, mission, and empowerment from God.

When he went back to California, he intended to finish college. One of the projects he had worked on with John that summer was a chronicle of the Mendenhall community building experience. With John speaking and H writing, they had produced a piece called "Thirteen Years in Mississippi," which would become the germ of John's first two books, Let Justice Roll Down and A Quiet Revolution. Wanting to improve his writing skills to continue this work with John, H transferred to

U.C.L.A. as an English major in the fall of '72. Terry had finished her nurse's training, and they got married during that year. The experience in Mendenhall had given them a whole new idea of practical Christianity that ignited their spirits.

H's crisis the previous August turned him toward living a more intentional Christian life, rather than trying to fit his faith into the common mold of American middle-class individualism. And when the summer of 1973 came, he and Terry returned to Mississippi eager to become a part of Voice of Calvary's community. There were plenty of new projects at Voice of Calvary that summer. They were starting up the new health care facility in Mendenhall, and the Jackson work was in its formative stage. H and Terry spent the summer working in tutoring, health care, construction, and a pile of other things. At the end of the summer, John asked H and Terry to stay on, and they eagerly accepted, though it meant H would leave college without graduating. But no matter. He knew this exciting thing going on in Mississippi was his calling and now was the time for him to get on with it.

16

JACKSON

A s you drive east into downtown Jackson on Capitol Street, just
before you come to the cluster of state office buildings, your line
of vision is impeded by a great, dirty-yellow brick building sprawled
across a city block of land. The derelict structure used to be the King
Edward Hotel and it mournfully displays the big steel sign, minus the
neon, that attests to that fact. Before desegregation, it was the inn for
anyone of the right color coming to Mississippi's state capitol on public or private business. But as the order of white supremacy gave way
in the civil rights era, the King Edward closed its doors.

They say several options for selling the old hotel and adapting it to
another purpose were considered. But as if it were the intransigent old
order itself, none of them worked out, and the vacant hulk continued
its decaying presence there, refusing to accommodate change. Its rooms
became so filled with bird droppings that the air grew toxic and the
uninhabitable relic of the closed society broods over a changing city
in a silent wait for demolition.

Just a few minutes' drive away, at 1655 St. Charles Street, something
new was happening in the early seventies, something being birthed out
of the changes that the King Edward's Mississippi could never accept.

When Dr. Roberts told John he needed to reduce the stress in his
life if he wanted to live much longer, he took her advice to heart. It
was contrary to John's nature not to have a dozen or more projects
going at once but he did move out of Mendenhall during his long recu-
perative period. Vera Mae found the family a house in Presidential

Hills, a quiet black neighborhood on the outskirts of Jackson. John was still living there and commuting down to Mendenhall when H came on with Voice of Calvary in the fall of 1973. That was when John began to focus on building a separate Jackson office, and H and Terry were the ones who would pioneer the work with him.

They began with the purchase of a rambling two-story house at 1655 St. Charles Street. It was in an older residential part of Jackson a few miles from the downtown area. The neighborhood had once been one of the nicer ones in town but it was getting shabbier as white flight drained away its residual prosperity. Stretched across a broad driveway behind the house was a wooden structure that had once been a barn for dairy cows. Fixing up the house and this outbuilding so they could serve as Voice of Calvary's new general headquarters would be the first order of business in Jackson.

H and Terry returned to California for a time to raise their support. While they were there, they learned that the Glendale YMCA was remodeling and discarding its old furniture. Beaten up as the tables, chairs, and couches were, they still looked good to the young missionary couple. So they piled the furniture into a truck and carted it back to Mississippi. H and Terry were the first residents of the house on St. Charles Street, and the Y's cast-off furniture was their first living room set.

In the early days of the Jackson ministry, John, Vera Mae, H, and Terry commuted down to Mendenhall almost daily. H acted as John's personal secretary, handling his voluminous correspondence. Then John gave him the position of volunteer coordinator, and H found himself with the responsibility of training and supervising the hundreds of different volunteers that VOC funneled through its Mendenhall ministries. In 1973 they were in the midst of starting up the community health center in Mendenhall, and H found himself with a mountain of paperwork from that project.

Being chief assistant to a man in perpetual motion, working with the volunteers, and getting the run-down St. Charles house into shape taxed H's energies to the hilt. John was always focused on finishing one task and moving on to another. Patience was never his long suit. He assumed anyone working with him would be as big a workhorse as he had always been. H was not afraid of a good day's labor and he felt strongly committed to what he was doing but he was twenty-one, fresh out of college, and just beginning to work into his complicated job.

Tempers eventually flared up as H had trouble matching the speed John was demanding. One day, standing there with paintbrush in hand in front of the old dairy barn, H confronted John, and John reacted by saying, "Then why don't you just leave?"

"Well you can leave," H retorted, "but God has called me here, and I'm going to stay." H showed a will as strong and stubborn as John's. The older man then fell silent, and the two went on working together. For his part John accepted H as a peer and not as a youth and so he respected the young Californian but he also demanded a lot from him. The two men were able to work through their differences this time and other times in the future when they would not see eye to eye. And as they would challenge, confront, or "raise sand" with one another, as they say in Mississippi, their relationship deepened.

H and Terry Spees and their first three children, 1977.

John was a personable man—warmly responsive, smiling and laughing readily—but he was never an easy boss. Hard-driving and task-oriented, he was wholly the executive personality and so he paid little attention to cultivating or smoothing over relationships. To work with John, his colleagues had to share his vision, his passion for the work of development. He demanded total commitment but he also valued a person's independent judgment. Not needing his ego massaged, he didn't have to surround himself with yes men. On the contrary he valued a conflict of opinion, and when someone like H differed with him on policy or even called him on his relational shortcomings, John would try to get past his initial hostility and open himself to the other's point of view. Challenging him was good, if you had something to say, and the leaders at VOC often held meetings full of lively debate long into the night to hammer out policy.

The civil rights movement had absorbed much of Voice of Calvary's energies during the late sixties. Though John and the others couldn't have foreseen it, the crescendo of activity culminating in the Mendenhall boycott and the violence in the Brandon jail would mark the movement's thunderous conclusion for them. White supremacists knew that their order was dying, and so their resistance had become all the more desperate. But the inexorable pressure of the federal government in cooperation with local civil rights leadership worked to grind down the opposition, and on April 3, 1970, the Mississippi state legislature capitulated, repealing the laws against integration. The end of legal segregation released the barrier to complete integration of the schools and other public facilities, and the seventies would see the opportunities blacks had long fought for gradually opening up to them. John could now fully concentrate Voice of Calvary's resources on the mammoth tasks of overall community development and racial healing.

One of the most visible and devastating results of entrenched poverty in the black South was the absence of adequate health care facilities. Good, affordable medical and dental care were all the more important in a place where people commonly suffered from chronic poor health due to the lack of a nutritious diet. Hungry, tired people crammed together in drafty little shacks lacked the bodily resistance to stave off a wide range of debilitating diseases. In 1969 a killer tornado coming in the wake of the giant hurricane Camille had caused devastation throughout Simpson County, and Voice of Calvary had plunged its resources into the relief work that followed.

Mounting a well-coordinated effort through their organization and their local co-ops, VOC received national publicity in *Jet,* one of the mass circulation magazines of African America. Federal officials came

to investigate conditions following the storms, and their interest produced a grant to study health conditions in the affected geographic
area. Vera Mae drove the country roads of Simpson County and interviewed people in their homes, compiling statistics on the state of their
health. What the federal survey revealed was what everyone already
knew: the tremendous need and the total inadequacy of health care
delivery among the rural poor.

As the survey called attention to the need for decent medical care
in the area, Voice of Calvary committed itself to starting a community
health center. Ever since John first walked the streets of the quarters,
talking with the people and seeing how many children were sick much
of the time, how many pregnant women went without any prenatal
care, and how many of the old folks had no teeth and needed glasses,
he had dreamed of a community health center. In 1971 Dolphus Weary
finished his master's degree in Christian education in California. Now
married to Rosie Camper, he returned to work full-time as the executive director of VOC in Mendenhall. Among his many other duties he
assumed leadership of the health care project. In 1973 the Wearys, the
Speeses, and the Perkinses were expending much of their time and
effort in starting up the health center. John focused on it in his fund-
raising speaking tours. After they got the facility built, Terry Spees
came on as nurse and commuted there every day from Jackson.

During the first two years it was hard to get a permanent doctor.
Christian physicians would come to Mendenhall temporarily as mission work but they had other commitments and didn't feel the calling
to stay. A number of factors contributed to making it hard to get a
physician to relocate in Mendenhall. Medicine is among the most lucrative and high-status professions in American society, and a doctor working among the poor in Mendenhall would have to sacrifice much that
our commercial society values. The charitably motivated people who
might have been willing to come on permanently there felt more drawn
to Third World missions.

American evangelical religion has supported that tendency by advocating evangelism and care for the wretched of the earth in foreign missions while commonly overlooking people at home in similar dire need.
They fail to appreciate the degree of domestic want because they continue to buy into American exceptionalism, the persistent myth that
the United States is an open society where people invariably have the

opportunity to move upward by their own efforts. This idea, which evangelicals have often made an article of patriotism, leads to blaming the American poor for their poverty, ignoring the formidable obstacles posed by iniquitous social structures.

Despite the difficulties in obtaining a permanent doctor, no one at Voice of Calvary was about to abandon the commitment to health care. They went ahead with planning for and outfitting the clinic with good, up-to-date equipment. John publicized the need for an X-ray machine, and people around the country responded with donations. They purchased one for thirteen thousand dollars.

Prayer had always been the animating force behind whatever John accomplished, whether in child evangelism, civil rights work, or in any phase of development. He, Vera Mae, Mr. Buckley, Jesse Newsome, and the others had held many an all-night prayer vigil as Voice of Calvary expanded and adapted to meet the needs of the moment. Health care, providing new resources never before seen in rural black Mississippi, taxed them once again beyond what they had and sent them to their knees. From the time he had returned to Mississippi, John had lived on the edge, relying on God to show the way and provide the

John Perkins and H Spees. The early years of VOC Jackson.

resources, and it had worked. VOC had grown and thrived. Now expansion into health care was another test of God's provision.

The greatest test of their collective faith in the health care project came in April 1974 when heavy spring rains, a common seasonal event in Mississippi, caused the creek that borders the low-lying quarters to burst its bed, pouring muddy water indiscriminately through the streets and buildings. It was a complete disaster, with houses being lifted off their slab foundations and floated down the streets, many damaged beyond repair. The neighborhood by this time had become interspersed with attractive contemporary houses, the fruit of John's attention to housing in cooperation with the FHA. But the new homes were little more immune to damage than the weathered shacks. Many of them too were flooded and dislodged by the rampaging creek waters.

One of these new homes belonged to Dolphus and Rosie Weary. Living most of their lives in the squalid housing of the black South, they had been thrilled to have a solid, spacious new home with modern appliances. Yet they hardly had a chance to get used to it when grimy floodwaters poured in, discoloring the walls and floors and depositing a thin layer of silt and a dank smell throughout the house.

Floods like this one were not uncommon in Mendenhall's black community, given the fact that it lies in a floodplain. The Army Corps of Engineers had researched the situation, but because of the inhabitants' lack of influence and the area's lack of economic value, nothing had been done to divert the creek or devise any other form of flood control. Hence anything built on this side of the tracks was ever at risk of being flooded out. The health clinic, with its new X-ray machine, was the most outstanding casualty of the flood. As water lapped over it, the unit suffered $8,500 in damage. And many people, having precious little to begin with, were now homeless, their few possessions waterlogged or washed away.

As in the jailing crisis that precipitated the boycott, the crisis of the flood became another occasion for Voice of Calvary to act as vital unifier of the black community. On April 12, as the floodwaters were swallowing much of the VOC compound, Dolphus put in a call to Jackson. John, Vera Mae, H, and Terry hurried to Mendenhall. John knew he had to get the people together, encourage them, and motivate them to go to work. For him a disaster like this was not a cause for lamentation, but a time to seek God's direction and redouble his and the community's efforts. Arriving in Mendenhall, he waded into the two little churches where cold, wet, despairing people were huddled together. Gathering the whole community in one big meeting, he led them in prayer and then got them down to work.

From the days of union building at the foundry, John had always felt at his best when he was motivating and organizing people to do something big. His mind characteristically moved quickly into gear, churning out ideas for meeting the crisis at hand, assigning tasks, enlisting support. But this time he found himself providing mainly the initial inspiration and impetus for coping with the devastation of the flood. The VOC leadership quickly formed a Community Disaster Committee with Dolphus in charge. It was only proper for the younger man to be in that position now that he was executive director in Mendenhall. Long ago John had recognized Dolphus's leadership potential and had brought him along, encouraging him to go to college and then on for a master's degree in Christian education. Recently John had presided at a ceremony at VOC's church in Mendenhall, where Dolphus had been ordained along with Herbert Jones and H Spees. Artis Fletcher, who was just completing his graduate study in California, would soon be coming back to pastor the Mendenhall church.

John felt gratified that his years of leadership development work were paying off. But he also felt a sadness welling up in him, as he thought he was now no longer needed in Mendenhall, the place where he had poured out his life's blood. For a moment he thought about taking the handsome offer a church in New Jersey had made him. But no, he was not a pastor, and there was still so much to do in Jackson. Plunging headlong into that work would bring him back to his emotional center. Work, the work of building an organization, the work of building a movement, that was what gave John his sense of purpose. You didn't work for salvation; that was by grace. But it was your work for God that gave meaning to your life.

Dolphus, together with the others on the Disaster Committee, worked out mass feeding and shelter programs that were so efficiently executed that when the Red Cross got to Mendenhall, there wasn't much for them to do. For many years now, John had been training the people to identify felt needs and minister to them, and in the midst of the flood crisis they knew what to do. An unexpected dividend that came from the black community's well-executed response to the crisis was that the mayor of Mendenhall, Ray Layton, was made chairman of county disaster relief. The mayor felt grateful to the people on the low side of the tracks and likely he experienced a new respect for their competence. This positive publicity, about how Mendenhall had effectively grappled with its flood, set the stage for improved relations uptown.

Meanwhile, with the new clinic inundated, the X-ray equipment damaged, and the doctor about to leave, VOC was back at square one in health care. Morale was sagging, and as the cleanup and rebuilding proceeded, Dolphus and the VOC staff held prayer meetings to discern God's will and find new spiritual energy to persevere in the work. The sentiment began to build to place the health center in an uptown location that would give it the high ground to make it safe from future flooding.

White Mendenhall had previously shut black enterprise out of the town's business district, and Dolphus had always thought a health care center that serves the black community should be located in its midst. But winds of change were starting to blow. A former medical clinic adjacent to the courthouse at the top of Main Street was vacant, and its owner wanted to keep the building dedicated to its original purpose. John and H labored over the application for site approval they would send to the National Health Service Corps, the federal office that provided funding for medical clinics in poverty locations.

As they worked and prayed for the recovery of their medical enterprise, things began to come together. The uptown clinic began to materialize, and Dr. Eugene McCarty, a young pediatrician from Colorado, responded to VOC's extensive advertising for a physician. Moving to Mendenhall with his wife, Dr. McCarty became the pioneer of this new venture in interracial contact. In the direct shadow of the courthouse where John had battled Mississippi injustice, the integrated clinic started up in early 1975. It had served both races in its earlier form, but black patients had had to enter through a separate entrance, sit apart from white patients, and wait to be seen after the whites. The new Voice of Calvary clinic had one entrance and waiting room and one list of patients for both races. So the degrading forms of racial etiquette died away, though lingering resentments would smolder just beneath the surface. With the exception of the mayor, no whites attended the dedication ceremony for the new clinic, though many whites would receive treatment there.

John praised the McCartys' decision to relocate in a community of need, but the peculiar pressures of being pioneers in integrated health care took their toll. As Voice of Calvary developed in its new Jackson location, a strong support system for interracial living would eventually take root. But Mendenhall, in the years just after the boycott, was another story. Whites joining VOC from other parts of the country had to deal with real culture shock in rural Mississippi. Being an integral part of the organization that John Perkins had developed while trying somehow to fit in with the white community became a constant source of tension for the McCartys. As a white man living in the black community and working for a black-run uptown enterprise, Dr. McCarty inevitably had to endure the stigma of white Mendenhall as a race mixer.

Dr. McCarty made an initial commitment of two years to the clinic, and during that time he threw his substantial energies into making the little clinic a comprehensive health care facility. At the end of two years, however, the McCartys decided to leave Mississippi. It was a big disappointment, especially to John, Dolphus, and the black community. But southern racial barriers proved too formidable for the McCartys.

VOC's best recourse was the National Health Service Corps, and John set H to the task of obtaining a Christian doctor from them. The staff at VOC prayed hard, and H worked hard on the application. In early 1976 a black physician from New York, Dennis Adams, came with his wife, Judi, to take over the directorship of the Mendenhall health facility.

Signing the contract to buy the uptown health center in Mendenall.
Seated left to right: **Irv Houston (Voice of Calvary worker), Janie Rotenberry (who built the original clinic with her husband), and John.**
Standing, left to right: **Dolphus Weary and Dr. Gene McCarty.**

Though he was black, it was no easy adjustment for Dr. Adams, with his northern background, to come to Mendenhall. But his race made it easier for him than it had been for Dr. McCarty to be director of an integrated health clinic a stone's throw from the Simpson County courthouse.

Meanwhile John and H were busy developing VOC's ministries to address felt needs in Jackson. As evangelicals, John and Vera Mae had always placed Bible study, prayer, worship, and evangelism at the center of their ministry. Unlike liberals who did church-based social action, they regarded these spiritual functions as the essential ground of what they were doing. Without these strong spiritual underpinnings, they knew their mission would disintegrate amid the pressures of life around them. It was not merely the tense atmosphere that surrounded black development in tandem with whites in Mississippi. It was the endless train of difficulties the world subjects everyone to as they try to make it.

The ongoing problems of child care, schooling, jobs, bills, illness, and the inevitable emergencies of day-to-day life—all complicated a hundredfold by living in a poverty setting—would have splintered and destroyed Voice of Calvary had it not been for its strong spiritual foundation. John and Vera Mae had long since learned that the development of spirituality through discipleship of all the people involved was at the core of their work, the basis of its meaning, its cohesion, and its durability.

While still hammering and painting the house on St. Charles into shape in 1973 and '74, John and H began using it as an all-purpose center for the changing and growing business of Voice of Calvary in Jackson. When they and their families came together, they began worshiping, praying, and studying the Bible together right away. They called their meeting house on St. Charles Street the Center for Continuous Christian Community, which quickly became the Four C Center.

The basis for community was the spiritual connection of the Spees and Perkins families around their common faith and work. Voice of Calvary Fellowship—the church that would take shape in the front room of the Four C Center initially with just the Perkins family, H, and Terry—was the natural outgrowth of their common life. The process of church planting had been similar in Mendenhall. The church there, which eventually would be called Mendenhall Bible Church, grew organically out of the spiritual and economic development John was doing in cooperation with the elders supporting him and the young men and women he was discipling. John's unique holistic orientation made his work entirely different from that of the black churches in the area, and so it had become necessary to found his own church to provide a spiritual hub for holding together and nourishing the many spokes of ministry. This was true also in the Jackson setting, but development of the church fellowship there came slowly at first because they all had to spend so much time in Mendenhall.

When they were commuting to Mendenhall, they attended the church there, but gradually as the Four C Center began to develop, they added neighborhood people and students from the nearby Jackson State campus, and they began worshiping regularly together. John had become active with InterVarsity Christian Fellowship, an association of evangelical students with chapters on college campuses throughout North America. InterVarsity was one of the interdenominational organizations most open to the animus of the 1973 Declaration of Evangelical Social Concern.

John became an IV staff member at Jackson State, a chaplainlike position that enabled him and H to meet formally with students on campus. Jackson State was the most prominent black campus in the state, drawing students from all over Mississippi. Young men and women on the campus often recognized John.

"Reverend Perkins. You remember me?"

"Help me."

"I was in your Bible class down in Prentiss."

John had itinerated his way through schools all over the south central part of the state and had done child evangelism with thousands of children every week for a decade. And now many of the kids had reached college age, and here was their old Bible teacher in campus ministry. Many students were active in Jackson State's InterVarsity chapter and many came over to the Four C Center for services. Some even got involved with Voice of Calvary.

This was the period when the older Perkins children—Spencer, Joanie, Philip, and Derek—were going to college, Spencer to L.A. Baptist and the others to Jackson State. With children of this age, John became all the more sensitive to the specific needs of collegians as they moved into vocations and assumed the responsibilities of adulthood. He, H, and Herbert, who joined the Jackson office, funneled the students into different aspects of VOC's rapidly developing ministries.

One place where many young men got practical vocational experience along with mentoring and warm camaraderie was in PDI. John started People's Development Incorporated in 1974 as a means to grapple with area residents' substantial housing needs. The neighborhood around the Four C Center had been about 80 percent white in 1970, when federally mandated open housing began in Mississippi. Then blacks started to move in, which brought on panicky white flight, and the neighborhood began to change. The hasty white movement out created a big buyers' market for homes in the area, but few blacks had the money to take advantage of it. Banks routinely denied blacks loans due to their low income, coupled with ingrain prejudice toward black homeowners as poor financial risks. So real estate investment companies ended up buying many of the houses and turning them into rentals. As more houses became rentals, the once middle-class neighborhood declined.

John had always believed that ownership was what made the difference between self-respect and the motivation to succeed on the one hand and demoralizing dependency on the other. In order to bring entrepreneurship to the black community he had poured his energy into building cooperatives and a cooperative bank, the Southern Cooperative Development Fund, which was fast becoming the premier black financial institution in the South. And home ownership went right along with business ownership. John remembered how proud he had been of the spacious house he and Vera Mae bought in Monrovia as their family ascended to middle-class status. Here in Jackson, John wanted to help local black residents get the training and skills to own their own businesses and to compete with others in the employment market. He also wanted to make it possible for more of them to own their own homes.

This ongoing commitment to help neighborhood people become homeowners caused him to charter PDI. It would be some time, however, before conditions and availability of loans would improve enough in Jackson so that a sizable number of blacks could purchase their own homes. In the meantime, PDI bought and renovated many homes in the area, initially becoming a benevolent landlord, concerned for the needs of its tenants. By 1977 PDI had some seventeen houses, some of which were used for ministry, and others that were rented out for ten to fifteen dollars a month less than other landlords were charging. PDI also did repairs on the homes of local area residents free of charge, thus helping to shore up the neighborhood against further deterioration. John's ultimate goal was to sell the houses they bought and renovated to residents at low prices, thus helping blacks in Jackson to become homeowners.

John's approach, as it had always been with people, was to go one house, one block at a time. VOC could not afford to do it any other way, and the painstaking, incremental nature of the work kept VOC's housing ministry people-centered. Close personal relationships developed around the positive experience of building and repairing together. Everybody got involved: John, H, Herbert, black students from Jackson State, and assorted white volunteer crews. The second house they bought, on Wacaster Street, taxed H's infant construction skills to the limit. Future occupants could stare up at moon craters in the ceiling, the visible remnant of his early efforts at laying Sheetrock. But it wasn't long before VOC could boast a well-disciplined construction crew under the skilled leadership of Herbert Jones, who had made his mistakes years before in Mendenhall and now had the expertise to mentor others.

PDI proved to be one of the soundest ministries of Voice of Calvary. As houses in the area around the Four C Center came available, PDI bought them for eight to fourteen thousand dollars and sold them for about twenty after the building crew had renovated them. As the crew became more skilled, the renovations and remodelings would become more extensive. In the late seventies and early eighties, black and white people relocating in Jackson to work with VOC were the main purchasers of these houses, not yet the indigenous people. Because the immediate neighborhood around VOC had been white, there were no initial indigenous blacks. Most of them lived in the miles of slums that encircled the outer perimeter of VOC's neighborhood, sprawling all around Jackson State University. PDI's early success would give it the means and the skills to eventually go there and rebuild whole streets of narrow, dingy row houses, thus bringing real progress to people long mired in urban squalor.

It was in PDI that John's attention to black economic development in Mississippi over many years really began to pay off. The Southern Cooperative Development Fund, which he had played a major role in building, became the bank that would finance this grassroots urban renewal program. SCDF had acquired a good deal of capital, having become a prospering money broker to the outside world. Financing at low interest rates, the cooperative bank gave PDI the means to expand rapidly as a realty company.

With the help of the Bauersox bequest and money from other wealthy donors and foundations, PDI was able to put down sizable

**Before-and-after views of row houses in Jackson, renovated
by People's Development Incorporated.**

chunks of cash for run-down houses that sold for as little as eight to
twelve thousand dollars. They would resell the renovated houses for
sixteen thousand, and plow the profit into reinvestment.

Thus a solid, profitmaking partnership evolved to finance the
housing end of VOC–sponsored community development. If a house

sold for twenty thousand dollars, PDI would carry four thousand of it, thus gaining that much equity in the house. Typically the buyer, usually a VOC staff family, would make no down payment but would pick up the closing costs, which were under a thousand dollars. They would end up with a one-hundred-fifty-dollar monthly mortgage payment.

John's strategy was to seed the neighborhood with his community-minded Christians, placing three to four families on each block, and in this endeavor he was quite successful. By the early eighties, they would have some thirty-five houses and more than a hundred people on the staff of VOC owning a material stake in the community. Black and white families together were pumping their commitment and their skills into the neighborhood, and it began to show, as white flight slowed and the look of the area improved.

VOC staff members had various kinds of financial arrangements to support themselves and their families. Some preferred to live like missionaries, raising much of their support from the donations of Christians across the country who took an interest in the kind of work Voice of Calvary was doing. Others depended on VOC for their entire salary, and as PDI became a money-making enterprise, and John's speaking tours brought in donations and grants, they were able to pay staff workers quite liveable wages.

When the Jackson ministries were getting up and running in the mid-seventies the poverty level for an average family was set nationally at four thousand dollars. Using that figure as a reference point, VOC doubled it, and salaried workers usually got between eight and nine thousand dollars a year. With Mississippi's relatively low cost of living, that amount went further than it did in most other parts of the country. People who raised support beyond the standard salary put the excess into VOC's common fund to help sustain the ministries. In this way all staff families lived at the same income level.

In the early years of the Jackson ministries, much of the staff, blacks and whites from evangelical church backgrounds, came from other parts of the country and sometimes from outside the country. Later on, concerted efforts were made to indigenize the staff. Jean Thomas, a Haitian seminarian, was one of the early people to come from abroad to work in PDI and the other Jackson ministries, learning John Perkins's approach to development.

Haiti is a land of stark contrasts, where Caribbean cruise ships disgorge affluent American vacationers in the capital, Port-au-Prince, amid some of the most wretchedly poor people on earth. But this black former French colony also has a thriving evangelical movement, whose pioneer, Claude Noel, had discipled young Jean Thomas. In that land, ruined by parasitic dictatorship, it was impossible to practice evangelism without trying to do something about the desperate material condition of the people. And so Jean came and spent some years working with Voice of Calvary and studying John Perkins's principles and practices so he could adapt them to the situation in Haiti.

Another young man who trained in community development along with Jean Thomas was Ed McKinley. With a background the opposite of Jean's, Ed came from H's hometown of Glendale, California. He had been acquainted with H as a child and heard him speak about Voice of Calvary at a Christian event when he was in college. In the same class as H's younger brother at the elite Stanford University, Ed was part of a large evangelical college fellowship. It was while he was in college that he began to feel the weight of his privileged status and a gnawing sense of duty toward the dispossessed. After graduation he worked for a time in a large firm in a public policy specialty but he quickly tired of corporate gamesmanship and in 1976 he went to Jackson to use his skills in service to the black poor.

While he was working with Voice of Calvary, McKinley wrote an article for *The Other Side* addressing the racial problem as he was grappling with it out of his white elite background. He could see a subtle and often not so subtle arrogance of status that gave him and other whites a paternalistic attitude toward blacks. An underlying sense of superiority bred into racial majority culture caused whites to take charge whenever they got involved with blacks. And at the same time they resisted the direction of blacks placed in authority over them. As Ed was working into his staff position at VOC, the young Californian had found to his surprise that he too had this superiority complex. But he had courage enough to address the problem frontally, admitting his racial arrogance and declaring his need to "submit to black leadership."

As a Christian in the white American elite, Ed likened himself to the disciples of Jesus who wanted to be in his inner circle. Jesus had responded to their status hunger by telling them that the one who would be first among them must be everyone's servant. He told them that in the Kingdom of God the last would be first and the first would be last, and he demonstrated this imperative to be lowly and serve by washing his disciples' feet.

In calling attention to white arrogance and relating it to the general human love of distinction and telling his fellow whites that they needed to submit to black leadership, Ed McKinley was identifying the key insight whites needed to gain if they were seriously interested in racial reconciliation. They needed to learn how to serve humbly and they needed to become a part of the process of nurturing black leadership. From the days of discipling Artis and Dolphus when they were teens in Mendenhall, John Perkins had been about the task of developing black leaders who could in turn develop their communities. And this was the work Ed McKinley was joining as he gave of himself to Voice of Calvary.

It was hard to give up the socially patterned role of the white decision maker. Ed found himself struggling with it, as did the other whites who came to Jackson and seriously tried to become a part of the VOC community. Blacks, hurt by white paternalism, were more painfully aware of and sensitive to the issue than the whites. They experienced anger when whites fell into their habits of taking over and not really listening to them. This continuing spectre of America's racial past would have to be faced honestly, repentantly, and with forgiveness if real reconciliation of the races was to occur and genuine Christian community built. That would eventually happen at Voice of Calvary as the issue came to a head in the eighties. But the earlier years of the Jackson work saw the foundation laid for racial reconciliation in the building of Voice of Calvary Fellowship, one of the first biracial churches in the South.

John was ever eager to engage other people, to stimulate them with his ideas, and in turn be stimulated by theirs. An animated conversationalist, he was enthusiastic about whatever he was doing. His mind was constantly generating and distilling ideas, and thinking people—writers, teachers, seminarians, or homespun philosophers like Mr. Buckley—loved to chew the fat with him, sounding him out about everything in general. John loved to be on the road: teaching community development from the Bible and laying out his projects and his goals before any sort of gathering of people, whether a small meeting of wealthy donors or a chapel full of boisterous college students.

He was especially in his element when he was milking a book of the Bible for its application to present-day social justice issues.

From the days with Wayne Leitch, he was most at home in the Scripture. He carried it with him and took it out several times a day to read as reference and guidebook for his thought and action. Because he was so familiar with the Bible and had so worked it into the contours of his life, he could preach from it with power and conviction. So he was strong in the pulpit, and during the first decade or so, he served as VOC's main preacher. But John never saw himself as a pastor.

Pastors needed the patience and empathy to spend long hours with people, encouraging, consoling, making peace among them. And John knew he didn't have that kind of time and emotional energy to spend on people's personal concerns. He was too focused on the work of organizing and development, his mind astir with ideas and with finding the means to bring them to life. He could inspire, animate, and make something go and he could bring people together. But another's careful attentions were needed for a pastor's day-to-day work of counsel, visitation, and church administration.

Since John's concept of addressing the people's felt needs implied a cohesive church at the center, churches would grow out of the ministries in Mendenhall and Jackson. As the churches developed, people with the gift of pastoring emerged out of the indigenous community and also came from elsewhere in the country to join Voice of Calvary. Herbert, Dolphus, and Artis were the pastoral figures who developed within the context of John's formative work in Mendenhall.

From the time he joined John and Vera Mae's evangelistic ministry back in 1962, Herbert remained a dedicated Christian servant. He did pretty nearly every kind of work that had to be done, including some of the most strenuous and dirty construction jobs that everybody else would go out of their way to avoid. In 1971, when they were putting up the Buckley Gym, it was Herbert who powersawed cement blocks with goggles masking his eyes to keep out the dust that was flying all over him. Herbert's real gift, his first love, was the care of children and youth. Like a great Father Christmas, he could be walking down a street in Mendenhall or later in Jackson, and children would come bursting out of their houses to be with him.

While the Perkins children were growing up, Herbert was their big brother, patiently showing them how to do things, all the while laughing and joking with them. He was something of a buffer between them and their parents, who were so serious-minded, expecting a great deal of work and total commitment from their children. Later, when the older ones were in their teens, Herbert taught them to drive. During one of Spencer's early outings behind the wheel, he lost control and ran the car across a neighbor's yard, bouncing off a tree and ending up in a ditch. "You done good," said Herbert, and the big man roared, shaking with laughter. The nervous, chagrined teenager found himself relaxing and giggling alongside his instructor.

So Herbert became a pastor to the youth and to the little children. When he was living in the Perkins home and working in ministry in Mendenhall, Vera Mae spent time showing him how to put his exuberance and natural affinity for children to practical, systematic use in teaching and guiding them. It was in Jackson that Herbert's gifts with youth and children would bloom brightest, and in 1978 VOC opened the Herbert Jones Youth Center there.

Dolphus was another big brother and pastor to many of the youth of Mendenhall, including the Perkins children. After he returned to Mississippi in 1971, he spent much of his time working with the young people. He and Chris Erb worked hard to develop a comprehensive tutoring program that did more than address the educational deficiencies of the children. In countless, painstaking ways, from simply seeing to it that they maintained proper hygiene and had enough to eat, to teaching them black history, Dolphus, Chris, and others whom they trained affirmed the children's dignity as persons.

But not until 1974, when Artis finished his graduate study in Los Angeles and returned to Mississippi, did Voice of Calvary have a pastor primarily devoted to the building and nourishment of the church. John and his original body of elders had started up Voice of Calvary's church back in 1964, initially naming it the Berean Bible Church. But prior to Artis's return, it served mainly as a place for the people absorbed in all the development ministries to worship. When Artis became full-time pastor, the church was able to develop as the chief means of spiritual nurture to the community.

During his early years as pastor, Artis was often preoccupied, working with Dolphus to develop the ministries. But as the Mendenhall ministry transitioned successfully to independence by the eighties, Artis focused more and more on the church and he began networking with other pastors in the area. His outreach efforts bore fruit as many of Voice of Calvary's ministries became available to other churches along with training programs, which Artis inaugurated for their pastors.

John could not have forged the kind of bonds Artis would with neighboring pastors. He had come up amid the stresses of the civil rights movement, and many of his closest associates in the sixties had been the worldly men and women who were its leaders. The black clergy who had risked their lives along with him had become his friends and frequent companions. But to the more traditional leadership in the black churches, John Perkins remained a controversial figure and he didn't have a lot to do with them. But Artis, with a self-knowledge of his destination from the days when he was preaching to the cows, had been away getting his education during the most searing years of the movement.

Now back in the community, equipped with formal training and a good deal of church experience, Artis as pastor of Voice of Calvary Church was in a better position than John had been to reach out and really engage with other pastors and churches. For John this was exactly as it should be: a youth he had mentored going elsewhere to get education and experience but now bringing his newfound skills back to the community as a powerful resource for development. When he thought about how both Artis and Dolphus had come back to Mendenhall to take the helm of the ministries he had started, he felt deeply gratified.

17

COMMUNITY BUILDING

With John, H, and Herbert recruiting people into the Jackson ministries, the embryonic church in Jackson, Voice of Calvary Fellowship, needed the attentions of a full-time pastor. Since the enterprise in the state capital was a new one, there had been insufficient time to nurture an indigenous pastor, so John was open to finding one from outside. In 1975 a young white man, Phil Reed, came to Jackson for a four-month stint as a volunteer. The Jackson church was in its earliest days of having Sunday services when this seminary student from Earlham School of Religion in Richmond, Indiana, came to Jackson.

His idea of what he wanted to do with his life and the nature of his Christian commitment were only vaguely defined, despite his enrollment in seminary. Earlham was a liberal seminary that didn't require any confession of faith from its students, and like many of the young men and women attending such institutions in the sixties and seventies, Phil saw Christianity more in terms of social work than personal faith experience.

He had gone to seminary more as seeker than believer. He was trying to find his way out of a personal morass that had started in high school when he had begun burying his anxieties beneath a haze of alcohol. Phil's father had been an active Christian, with roots in the holiness-oriented Church of God, Anderson, Indiana, and he had been a stabilizer in his son's life. But as Phil was about to graduate Indiana University and begin to figure out what he was going to do with his life, his father was dying of cancer. It made a deep impression on the son as his dying father sat up in his hospital bed, surrounded by pastor and church elders, singing "Leaning on the Everlasting Arms," but when he quietly succumbed later that day, Phil felt empty and rud-derless. He continued with his education, taking a master's in math at Miami University of Ohio. Math was something he was good at, and maybe staying in school he could get a better handle on his life.

But while mathematical equations held out the surety of answers, they were not the answers to the questions that he could never quite shove out of his mind. Gnawing at the root of his being was the question of faith, the faith that had given his father a certain serenity and the courage to face death. Phil knew he lacked any of that peace or courage and he knew on a gut level that faith did matter. And so despite his lack of belief, his sense of the rightness of Christianity propelled him into Earlham School of Religion. He went almost out of a sense of duty, but at the same time, he was looking for meaning in life and a chance to serve, and sem-inary seemed like the logical place to find those things.

The skeptical temperament of Earlham's liberalism made it easy for Phil to slip-slide around the question of personal faith commit-ment. He could treat religion as social work and avoid making his soul vulnerable to God. This was his frame of mind when John Perkins came to Earlham College for a long weekend of lecturing, preaching, and firing up the undergraduates. Phil attended the meet-ings and found himself getting excited about what this southern black preacher was saying. And so he signed on for four months of work at Voice of Calvary in Jackson. Maybe this would give him some of the answers to the questions that had been disquieting his conscience for so many years.

Phil was a gentle, self-effacing person, the kind who took every-thing in and seldom made waves. As a student, when life bruised him, he would try to drink away the pain. By the time he was in seminary, though, he had been able to pretty much get past the alcohol problem. In Jackson he could reorient his caring nature in a positive direction, working with children. During 1974 and 1975, Herbert was out of state at Maryland Bible Institute, honing his pastoral skills with formal train-ing. So that left an opening for someone to start up a youth group, and Phil, though newly arrived, volunteered.

He put out a call for kids interested in gathering for games, crafts, and Bible study, and to his surprise thirty-five showed up the first day. It was a good thing Phil had the VOC community supporting and working closely with him, because as a single man with a heart for children but no experience he often felt a bit overwhelmed. Vera Mae gave him a lot of help, showing him how to teach with Child Evangelism's flannel graphs, and then Herbert joined him when he returned from Bible college.

In those early days of the Jackson ministry, everybody worked in everything, and Phil, who was the only volunteer for much of the fall of 1975, found himself working on housing renovation alongside H and Herbert. During these times, Phil talked theology with the other men. At Earlham the professors had taught him to de-supernaturalize much of Scripture and intellectualize the faith, rather than seeking God's grace to live it. But here in Jackson it was different. John and the others loved and lived by the Bible, quoting it often, and they held prayer meetings at six o'clock every morning. Phil wondered what made them run spiritually, what gave them such strong commitment to their mission. He asked H if he believed in a literal bodily resurrection, and H surprised him by saying, yes, he did.

One December morning, just before he was scheduled to return to seminary, Phil came to the morning prayer meeting all excited. He had stayed up late the night before talking with Herbert and a young black college student named Walter Montgomery. Herbert had asked him what his beliefs were. Phil had echoed some of the theology he had learned at seminary. Then Herbert looked him in the eye and said, "You just need to know Jesus." He said it so directly and so lovingly that Phil felt disarmed. They prayed together for him to receive Christ personally, and something astounding happened.

Phil heard God say to him in an audible voice, *"You have to start over."* Not the kind of person who went around hearing voices, he was awed and transformed by this experience. Suddenly he had a faith basis for the work he was doing. Suddenly God was tangibly present in his life, to motivate and empower him.

When Phil first came to Jackson in the fall of 1975, he heard John speak about the levels of personal commitment. Whenever John felt strong conviction about something that he was speaking publicly about, his manner would turn forceful and penetrating. The audience could hear the volume and intensity of his voice go up and they would automatically sit up and take notice. It was never a negative or scolding voice that John used, but an energizing call to arms. His listeners paid attention to what he was saying and seriously considered how it might apply to their life. As Phil heard John speak on commitment, he heard him say that limited commitment was no commitment at all.

The following summer, when Phil returned to VOC, he heard John call for people who would make a lifetime commitment to the ministry. Phil had now graduated from seminary and more important, he had experienced a growth in personal faith, faith implanted at Voice of Calvary. Now he felt ready and he wanted to make the full commitment John had been asking for.

It was in December of that same year, 1976, that they asked Phil to be pastor. John had first broached the subject with him. He said, "We need a pastor. I'm too hard on people, too impatient with people, and I don't like the pastoral mission." But John thought he saw something in Phil that he didn't find in himself. Others at VOC—H, Terry, Joanie, Spencer, Herbert, and Ed McKinley—all of them saw something in Phil that confirmed John's insight.

They weren't looking for a spellbinder or a great administrator. They wanted someone who would love and extend a hand to the drug addict, the ex-convict, the down-and-out, and homeless. And people on VOC's staff thought Phil was the right one to become pastor of a church in a neighborhood drowning in need. As a white man in a black ministry and a black environment and as a newcomer to Christian faith, he felt completely unequal to the task. The others sensed this too and they felt all right with it because they saw in Phil a servant's spirit. He was aware of his limitations and was eager to learn, eager to help, eager to ask for help. In the first year, a black co-pastor, Romas McClain, was appointed to share the burden with Phil. But Romas decided later that year to leave for seminary, so that left Phil with the full pastoral responsibility.

Since the tumultuous days in Mendenhall, John had nursed the vision of a renewed parish church, a church that does not build and enhance itself as an institution, but one that acts as faithful and resourceful servant within the community of need. As he had evolved the ministries and enterprises—child care, housing, tutoring, cooperatives—he had done so in response to felt needs in the community. In Mendenhall the ministries in effect birthed the church. With hindsight John thought it should ideally be the other way around, with the church planted as spiritual hub, spinning off and nourishing the various ministries in response to the felt needs of the community.

The early Christian movement in the Mediterranean world, Asia Minor, and Europe had developed the parish church as a means of ministering to the spiritual and material needs of all the people within a given geographic location. In a pluralistic, heterogeneous society like the modern United States, a parish church could not for the most part become spiritually involved with whole neighborhood populations. But in the black

Phil Reed (*right*) and his wife, Marcia (*center*), and their children, Kristen (*bottom*), Erin (*middle*), and Matthew (*top*).

rural South and in the inner city, where material needs were great, a church like Voice of Calvary Fellowship could serve the community by extending a loving hand to hurting people. It could also serve as the linchpin of the ministries, giving them and their staffs a spiritual home, a center. That is what John had in mind when he, Vera Mae, H, and Terry first set up the church in Jackson and later when he chose Phil Reed to be its full-time pastor.

As Phil moved into his vocation at Voice of Calvary, he became the primary vehicle for extending the vision of the church as spiritual home for neighborhood people and for the staff. VOC Fellowship evolved a group form of leadership, a pastoral team, initially including H and Herbert and then recruiting others. But building and nurturing a parish church was Phil's distinct calling; he was the one who had focused his concern at the neighborhood level since he first came as a volunteer. Together with Marcia, another former volunteer, who became his wife in 1978, Phil concentrated on developing youth leaders in the church, much as John and Vera Mae had done in Mendenhall. Phil and Marcia burrowed into the community and became a warmly available resource to every kind of hurting and destitute person.

Over the years to come they would open their home to bottoming-out drug addicts, young men coming out of prison, homeless, and other desperate people. Some of these individuals they would be able to help onto the road of recovery and a living faith. Others, more set in their misery, felt threatened by hope and change and they proved more resistant. But whoever stayed with the Reeds received a warm dose of compassion and likely were changed in some way by the experience.

Marcia and Phil would rear their three children in this caring environment so that for them the poor were not an abstract statistic, but their neighbors down the street whose kids came over to borrow the "S" from their dog-eared set of encyclopedias. As they extended themselves as a family to the neighborhood, so they also extended the resources of the church. Voice of Calvary Fellowship restored the function of the parish church, doing every kind of crisis intervention with families and singles, while at the same time evangelizing, instructing, tutoring, and providing recreation for children and youth across the community.

As Phil and others in VOC worked to develop the church in Jackson, John was carrying this conception of the church across the country and abroad. During the seventies he began to network with others who were simultaneously developing the concept of a servant parish church. This was probably the most valid and lasting idea to come out of the meteoric Christian community movement of the 1970s. *Sojourners* magazine became a forum for its discussion as Jim Wallis and his fellow communitarians in Washington entertained regular columns by contributing editor John Perkins, among others.

Both John and Episcopal clergyman Graham Pulkingham, another contributing editor, emphasized the accountability of people to one another in the community of serving Christians. John often reiterated his conviction that American society has distorted God's relationship to his people with the false icon of individualistic success. He wanted people to find their own gifts and get the best higher education or vocational training possible but he told his often youthful Christian audiences that the God of the Bible is not some kind of genie to aid an individual's movement upward. In the biblical model, God helps an individual realize his or her gifts in order to use them in service to a community. And that person becomes a servant accountable within that parish community, rather than roving around as a self-styled Lone Ranger.

The mid- to latter seventies were a formative period in the development of Voice of Calvary's Jackson ministries. It was in Jackson that the idea born in Mendenhall really matured and took root and began to reproduce itself. Mr. Buckley said that in Mendenhall, John planted a seed, and now Jackson was becoming the seedbed. As Voice of Calvary burgeoned in its urban setting, John traveled, publicizing its work and its vision and he kindled the interest of many talented like-minded Christians. Always wanting to get the input of others, John made it possible to become involved with VOC at many different levels. With this intention to draw on others' expertise in the many fields related to Voice of Calvary's mission, John created the Board of Servants in 1976.

He called this advisory body a board of servants, rather than directors, because he wanted to turn traditional, pyramid-shaped, corporate government upside down. This was in line with the concept of serving the community and empowering the poor. Service at the level of the people rather than policy directives from above fit with the model that Jesus gave the church in the Gospels. The size of Voice of Calvary's Board of Servants was open-ended, in keeping with John's desire to draw on as many different points of view as possible. Always the pragmatic problem solver, John liked to get a broad cross section of opinion in a variety of fields of expertise.

So he combined people in a number of disciplines and from a broad spectrum of political and economic opinion. Indeed, he swam against the polarizing currents of the time by having liberals together in cooperative dialogue with conservatives. What unified them was evangelical faith and a love of John's unique style of ministry. Liberals liked the focus on the needs of the disadvantaged, while conservatives liked the empowerment of people to do for themselves without dependency on government, and both groups believed in the intelligent evangelism and discipleship programs VOC carried on.

One of the most potent and prophetic voices on the Board of Servants was that of Harlem-bred evangelist Tom Skinner. In the early years of his ministry, in the sixties, he was popular in white evangelical circles, as he appeared to be a Billy Graham for the black community. But when he started to speak out on social issues, much of the mainstream white support fell away, as it had with John Perkins during the civil rights movement. The locus of his energy would gravitate to the black college campuses and increasingly the black churches, though he would remain close to socially committed white evangelicals.

Skinner had come to Mendenhall in the sixties and had quickly become a close friend and advisor to the Perkins family. John's work fired Tom's own passion for black indigenous development. His membership on the Board of Servants brought his prodigious managerial talents and evangelistic gifts into close contact with the ministries of Voice of Calvary. And as the Jackson seedbed began to flower in the late seventies, Skinner was one of the key people who helped pollinate the nation with John Perkins's concept of Christian community development.

Another strong voice on the Board of Servants was that of Al Whittaker, a former high-level executive with the Mennen Corporation. Whittaker was on the verge of a well-heeled retirement on a bucolic New Jersey estate when his Christian conscience got the better of him. For some years he had worked abroad developing Mennen's international operations in Europe, Africa, and Asia. During their travels he and his wife, Marian, had made contact with Christian missionaries who gave them on-site exposure to some of the most rancid poverty in the world. Marian wondered out loud more than once how long her husband was going to continue making rich people richer. Her gentle prodding led him to leave the corporate world in his mid-fifties and start the Institute for International Development, a company that provides resources for people in the poorest nations to start small businesses.

Whittaker's experience as a Christian doing basic economic development in poverty areas was the kind of thing John was always looking for. The headquarters of Whittaker's Institute was in Washington, D.C., and the two busy men arranged a get-acquainted meeting at the Dulles Airport one day when John had a layover there. Somehow Whittaker conveyed the impression that he wasn't especially interested in domestic development projects, and the conversation ended coolly. Later, when he became aware of his miscommunication, Whittaker called John to let him know that he was indeed deeply interested in the work in Mississippi.

This call caused the relationship to gel, and Whittaker began making regular visits to Jackson. As a board member he could offer a rare expertise on the process of building viable enterprises in impoverished communities. As John brought people like Al Whittaker into Voice of Calvary, he was further enriching the seedbed, molding a technology of Christian development that would be applicable in diverse environments.

During the latter seventies, through the Jackson office of VOC and his constant speaking tours, John was in the process of building an international constituency for Christian community development. This outward orientation was already driving him when he spoke at Inter-Varsity's Urbana '76 convention. It was at that conference that he and H first came in contact with a black Virginian named Lemuel Tucker. An impressive speaker, Tucker was one of the young, socially conscious evangelicals increasingly making themselves heard in the seventies. He would become a leader in the National Black Evangelical Association (NBEA), which had split from the NAE in 1964 because a white-dominated evangelicalism failed to adequately address black issues.

A graduate of William and Mary College with a major in psychology and four years of football to his credit, he was due to receive a master of divinity from Westminster Theological Seminary in 1977. Lem's parents had struggled to gain solid middle-class status, and when Lem graduated, they thought a Philadelphia church's respectable fourteen-thousand-dollar-a-year offer was a splendid first position for their son. They were more than a little disconcerted when instead he accepted a post as head of leadership development at Voice of Calvary for half that figure.

But Lem had been captured by John Perkins's magnetism and his linkage of evangelism with development. While still at the Philadelphia seminary, Lem hosted a conference on justice, featuring John as speaker. As they spoke and taught together, John felt a strong kindred spirit in Lem and he decided then to offer him the position in Jackson. Lem was a penetrating Bible student who saw the people of God in terms of Old Testament prophetic justice.

He believed deeply in the need for haves to relocate and give of themselves in the communities of have-nots. And as an educated, prospering black Christian, he felt a responsibility, as the self-made John Perkins had, to go back into the place of his people's most dire need. Exodus guided his commitment, as he thought of God's calling of Moses out of Pharoah's court and then back out of exile to identify with and lead his own downtrodden people. The many creative enterprises John had married to evangelism in Voice of Calvary fired Lem's enthusiasm as he got ready to relocate to Mississippi.

John had an idea that Lem was the one with the breadth of skill and leadership ability to eventually succeed him, though the personality of the twenty-five-year-old was a sharp contrast to that of John.

Quiet, even a little shy, and studious, Lem was a visionary like John but he was also a good detail man with a strong interest in administration. John had always had an intuitive sense of what would succeed and what wouldn't, but his ambassadorial leadership led him to focus more on the direction of the overall mission than the ways and means of each project.

For that purpose he had always depended on Vera Mae, who focused in on the budgets, the nuts and bolts, the minutiae necessary to make a success of each operation. Whenever John told Vera Mae of a new idea, she would shoot it down, and they would argue about it, and this process of justifying every project to his wife made John consider all its ramifications.

Lem, on the other hand, combined qualities of both John and Vera Mae. In a polished academic style, he could communicate a vision of development in the black community, supporting his assertions

Dedication of the Voice of Calvary Family Health Center in Jackson. Mississippi Governor William Winter is third from left, then John, Jackson Mayor Dale Danks, and Voice of Calvary Ministries director Lem Tucker.

255

The Voice of Calvary Fellowship, mid–1980s.

with charts, graphs, and statistics. His ruminative, introverted temperament and close attention to administrative and budgetary detail made him an effective planner. John's charismatic, venturesome personality, that thrived at the crest of the movement's progress, brought ideas and people together and made things happen. But it was the painstaking operations management Lem was capable of that could keep Voice of Calvary effective, thriving, and expanding its services in the years to come.

Not much more than a year after his arrival at Voice of Calvary, Lem took over as executive director in Jackson. As he transitioned into a role similar to the one Dolphus had taken on in Mendenhall, planning and overseeing the expanding operations of the ministries, John felt freer to do more traveling and teaching.

By the late seventies John had distilled the essence of his work in Mendenhall and Jackson to what he called the "Three Rs" of community development. They stood for: *relocation* of people to serve within the community of need; *reconciliation* of people across racial lines and all other lines of antagonism; and *redistribution* of skills and resources, which would come from educated, affluent people joining together with the poor in their communities. John would use these principles as an organizing motif, expounding them to a broadening Christian public in sermons, speeches, books, and articles.

By 1978 John was making the Jackson locale of Voice of Calvary a teaching center of the Three Rs for an international audience of mission-minded Christian laypeople and professionals. He was convincing many of the people he spoke to that the VOC model could be applied elsewhere to bring healing across lines of social division as well as hope to those who were being thrust aside in a rapidly changing world economy. In June of 1977, just before Lem arrived, John had proposed the establishment of an international study center to be located in Jackson. With its opening the following year, VOC Jackson would become host to an increasingly cosmopolitan group of Christians.

Such growth and broadening of ministry necessitated some redefining of Voice of Calvary's mission, structure, and operations. One thing that needed to be worked out, for example, was the question of what was to be the relationship of the Jackson office to Mendenhall and to any other local Mississippi operation that might develop in the future. The late seventies and early eighties would prove to be a time of transition and growing pains for Voice of Calvary—and for John Perkins.

18

TRANSITION IN MENDENHALL

When John opened the Jackson office, he was thinking of it as a publicizing arm for the ministries in Mendenhall, showcasing them as a means to spread his concept of holistic ministry. He did not at first think of Jackson as a whole new venue for doing ministry. But that is inevitably what it became, given John's love of doing evangelism and development in whatever locale he found himself. And because he saw the Mendenhall work as a model of Christian community development, he wanted to replicate it elsewhere, beginning with Jackson.

The Mississippi capital, with its urban conditions, was a lot bigger, more diverse, and more complex than Mendenhall and it inevitably absorbed more and more energy and resources. Making Dolphus executive director of Voice of Calvary, Mendenhall, in 1971 had given John less immediate responsibility there and set the stage for him to focus on what he was doing in Jackson. Then Artis returned to Mendenhall, and the Jackson ministries and the Jackson church developed quickly, and John's orbit of activity gravitated more and more around Jackson and his travels.

He had always thought that as indigenous leadership took over, Mendenhall should become self-sustaining and not have to rely on his generating the funds to make it go. And with the Jackson ministries expanding, John's fund-raising was being funneled more into them and less into Mendenhall. This was creating some stress and resentment at the original VOC site, as the leadership there began to think of themselves as the poorer relatives. Mendenhall's ministries were also expanding rapidly in the seventies, and they too had a pressing need for funds.

John thought that Dolphus and Artis would begin to do their own fund-raising and thereby make Mendenhall a thriving operation, wholly independent from Jackson. Independence would be empowering, giving them a sense of their own competence as they came fully into their own as leaders. John resolved inwardly on this course of action, but with his time taken up in travel and the Jackson projects, he neglected to have the detailed planning sessions with Dolphus and Artis that were necessary to smoothly transition Mendenhall to separate status. His focus was more on achieving the goal of separation than on working out all the details for accomplishing it.

For Mendenhall the late seventies was a period of consolidation of existing ministries and expansion into new ones. From its prominent uptown location, the Voice of Calvary Health Center was now in position to move rapidly to fill a void, providing medical services to Simpson County's black and white poor. And in 1977 VOC's staff were busy starting up a school and expanding a church-based discount retailing operation.

Dr. Adams worked solidly into his position as director of the health center, becoming an elder in Voice of Calvary Church and an integral member of the community. At the clinic he had the full-time assistance of three women, a pediatric nurse practitioner, a nurse, and a nurse's aide. The VOC Health Center became south central Mississippi's headquarters for the federally funded WIC (Women, Infants, and Children) program to teach nutrition to poor mothers and help provide them with adequate food. It also developed its own Community Health Education Program (CHEP) for teaching nutrition and health education in the schools and churches and other community settings. Along with this community-minded approach to medicine went a spiritual openness. Seeing the patients as whole persons and not merely bodies, Dr. Adams and his staff often counseled and prayed with them. Health care meant caring for the whole person at the VOC Health Center, instead of attending merely to immediate physical needs.

Since his days at Piney Woods, Dolphus had been sensitive to the acute need for decent quality education for blacks in Mississippi. The state ranked a perpetual last in expenditure for education and in student performance on standardized tests. Only five grades of schooling were compulsory, and Mississippi had no kindergarten requirement. Of course black educational needs were habitually the most neglected. Many of the whites had put their financial resources into the private academies that had been set up to avoid integration. Along with church-based preschools, the academies filled the deficit in early childhood education for the racial elite. But black children, shut out of the white churches and most private education, rarely received the enrichment of preschools or kindergarten. With these things in mind, Dolphus, in 1976, marshaled Voice of Calvary's resources to start a little preschool in the building that had housed the original health clinic.

Dolphus Weary, director of the Mendenhall Mininstries, early 1980s.

The first students of the Genesis One school in Mendenhall. Dolphus Weary is on the right.

The following year greater opportunity came as two young Wheaton graduates with training in education relocated in Mendenhall and committed themselves to developing a viable kindergarten. With Dolphus and Voice of Calvary's blessing they named it Genesis One. Here was John's proselytizing of Christian community development in the evangelical academy bearing fruit. The two Wheaton evangelicals, Debbie Hale and Steve Hayes, were living out John's Three Rs: They came to Mississippi, lived in the community of need, and offered their skills to further the reclamation work going on down across the tracks in black Mendenhall.

The kindergarten was the seed that would flower into a full-blown elementary school in the eighties. Dr. Adams's wife, Judi, would become the moving force behind the formidable tasks of research and development to bring quality private education to black Mississippians. As chief administrator she successfully developed the school's endowment to fund its expansion to a full elementary school with more than 130 children by 1990. With the help of white donors and volunteers who were mostly Southern, VOC renovated the abandoned cinder block building that had housed Mendenhall's original black high school. Modern kitchen and playground facilities were added, and Genesis One became a tangible means of black elevation, an embodiment of a new interracial cooperation in the Deep South.

It was also Voice of Calvary's Mendenhall ministries that had begun the enterprise that would eventually grow into a chain of large, cooperatively owned thrift stores based in Jackson.

The original thrift store occupied an old funeral home in the midst of the black community. Above the large front windows its big sign displayed the familiar Coca Cola logo next to the words, CHRISTIAN THRIFT STORE. But it was more than a store selling secondhand goods; it was an outreach of the church into the struggling lives of the people. Among the most visible felt needs was the means of day-to-day subsistence: adequate food, clothing, and the items necessary for running a household. In the early years of Voice of Calvary, donors to the ministry often gave used clothing, food, and durable goods. It was VOC Church that ran the giveaways and rummage sales, and eventually, in 1976, it was the church that established the thrift store.

VOC formed the thrift store as a cooperative, and while it served the community as a whole, this co-op's membership was limited to people in

Artis Fletcher, pastor of Mendenhall Bible Church, with his wife, Carolyn, and three daughters, early 1980s.

the church. The reason for this restriction was that the church was providing the staff and services needed to run the store. So the church owned and operated the thrift enterprise, which in turn served the community by providing a full range of goods for prices poor people could afford. They could get a virtually new pair of shoes for a dollar, and there was a whole rack of clothing items that sold for a dime apiece. And despite its big discounts, the thrift store still made profits because the items were all donated, and with VOC church people running it, overhead was low.

The thrift store put a compassionate face on supplying people in poverty with their necessities. If a person was sick and out of work or just didn't have the money, he or she could get things on credit, and the store would help that person find a feasible way to pay off the debt. The church also used money from the store's profits to provide relief to people who were destitute. There are many stories that illustrate VOC's exercise of compassion to the impoverished through the ministry of the thrift store.

When a store worker caught a woman we'll call Jane stealing, VOC was alerted to her desperate situation. If the incident had occurred uptown, she would surely have been arrested, booked, and likely jailed. But VOC was concerned about the conditions this woman was living in that were driving her to steal. When Artis paid a pastoral call at her home, he found things in a deplorable state. Her husband was unable to work because of a debilitating chronic diarrhea, probably caused and certainly aggravated by the family's poverty. His illness caused them to sink deeper into economic misery. With the gas and water shut off and the house grimy and ice cold, the children froze in their tattered, skimpy clothing.

VOC moved into Jane's life with both feet, not only paying the utility bills and getting food and warm clothing to her family, but also getting warmly involved with them on a personal level. VOC introduced the family to the health center and home Bible study and gave them credit in the store. Dolphus, who remembered how poverty can cause its victims to isolate themselves in shame, visited Jane's family and encouraged them to stay involved. Here was social work at its best. VOC made contact with the most needy through its thrift enterprise and then acted as servant church to the most desperate people in Mendenhall.

The thrift store was so successful that the Mendenhall leadership in tandem with John and the Board of Servants made the decision to build a new and larger one. The new store had such great bargains that it drew about 20 percent of its clientele from the white community. With this biracial appeal in mind the leadership decided to place the new, enlarged store just below the tracks at the edge of black Mendenhall. Construction started in earnest on a big new warehouse-style discount store to be called Thrifty Mart. This project was the biggest venture VOC had yet undertaken.

In May of 1978 Artis spoke at the ribbon-cutting dedication, summarizing the essence of what VOC's thrift store business meant to the community. His words bespoke the economic-mindedness John had instilled in him in his teens as the two had walked the streets of Mendenhall together. Saying that Christian faith works in the community and not just behind the church doors, Artis stressed the need to develop businesses and jobs as well as to make good quality, low-priced merchandise available to the people in the black community. It was vital, he said, for blacks to be able to spend their money within their own community, nurturing black-owned businesses there.

The new modern thrift store, built within sight of the uptown shopping district, would draw almost half its clientele from white Mendenhall, thus reversing the ancient practice of blacks spending all their money in white-owned businesses. Less than a decade after the boycott, it was heartening to see black and white customers shopping alongside one another in VOC's bright new discount store.

With the health care, schooling, and the thrift store operations in place, Mendenhall's church and ministries were blossoming under the leadership of Artis and Dolphus. Nineteen hundred seventy-eight, the year the new thrift store opened, turned out to be the year of transition. During the summer John was evaluating leadership development and observing the new younger generation, his elder children among them, as they were maturing into leaders. He concluded that the Voice of Calvary organization had become a womb that inhibited their personal initiative, and they needed the seasoning that would come from having to chart their own course.

For John, self-reliance had, of necessity, been a crucial life value since his childhood. Some of it was a trait of the risk-taking, entrepreneurial Perkins family. But most of it was rooted in his own experience of being shoved out of the nest at such an early age. At any rate he made up his mind to encourage Spencer and Joanie to go to work in a business in the outside world and he decided that now was the time for Voice of Calvary's Mendenhall ministries to become independent.

Without discussing the matter with the Board of Servants, John sent a memo to Artis and Dolphus sketching out his plan to make Mendenhall a separate organization, raising its own support. The time he gave them to complete the transition was a mere three months. John's memo exploded like a bomb in the Mendenhall office. Both Artis and Dolphus felt as if the floor had been blown out from under them. Dolphus recognized that Mendenhall was evolving into a separate organization but he wanted a weaning process with some start-up time to establish their own support base. Instead, John was cutting them off precipitously, and the abruptness of his action made it feel harsh and uncaring to these two men who had been like sons to him.

Mendenhall Ministries' Thriftco, early 1980s.

John did feel a fathering kinship with Artis and Dolphus but for him it was natural for fathers to push their sons into taking responsibility for their own lives. He didn't know how to do it in any kinder and gentler way. Being cut off was indeed what had happened to him as a child and as a youth. And it had happened on three traumatic occasions that had cut their deep impressions into him and influenced the way he would make some of his decisions as an adult.

The first time he had been cut off was before he could reason through what was happening to him. A little boy wanted a real daddy, and his daddy had come home and picked him up and loved him, and the next day the same daddy was whipping him away when he tried to follow him. And then Jap was gone out of his life again, having cut his son off.

And twelve years later Clyde, the big brother he was so proud of, the father figure who took care of him and all the other Perkins children, was shot down crazily, and he choked out his last words with his head on his teenage brother's lap, and the youth was again cut off. Then a year later, when the family sent him to California, he was cut off a third time, but now for reasons that he understood would insure his survival.

Each cutting-off experience served to turn John inward to his own resources. He had learned to stifle his emotional pain and his natural longing for relationship and to focus on outer material goals. Conversion had opened his awareness of a divine Father who loves him and had revolutionized the kinds of goals he worked for, but the lessons of self-reliance, of striving for tangible gains more than cultivating personal relationships, were implanted in him. They were a survival mechanism, a means of overcoming and winning the prize. So for John, the process of being cut off was intimately related to becoming strong, becoming a man. It was something parents and parent figures did to foster independence in the young, and it was something he felt impelled to do with Artis and Dolphus and then with his own children.

In truth he believed that the leaders he had trained in Mendenhall had the mettle to rise to the occasion, as he had risen to it. But what he was not counting on was the bitterness his action engendered and the rift that would grow between him and them. Dolphus was deeply hurt because he had been cut out of the decision-making process. The action was taken and he had to deal on his own with the momentous consequences. There was no good reason not to include him and Artis in that process. John had reflexively reenacted what had happened to

265

him. Transitioning new leadership would continue to be a stress point for John. His own early trauma had given him the tendency to let go too abruptly and unilaterally.

The Board of Servants met and tried to smooth things over but they essentially left John's plan of separation in effect, and Dolphus and Artis had to scramble to obtain support for Mendenhall's ministries. The ministries were in fact doing quite well, especially the thrift store, which was making enough profit to cover its monthly loan payments to the Southern Cooperative Development Fund. And both leaders had established contacts locally and across the nation who could be tapped for help.

Dolphus thought, however, that the crisis in Mendenhall could have easily been avoided by developing a three-to-five-year plan of transition with a gradual lessening of support from Jackson. During such a transition period, Voice of Calvary could have publicized Mendenhall's becoming a separate organization, The Mendenhall Ministries, with a new generation of indigenous leaders and its own support needs. Thus the transition would have been accomplished much more smoothly and without the bitter feelings.

19

Growth and Pollination

The seed John had planted in rural Mississippi had grown, prospered, and flowered richly and he would leave its continued cultivation to others as he turned his attention toward much broader fields of work. In June of 1977, speaking at a staff lunch in the Four C Center, he first mentioned the idea of starting an international study center to teach his Three Rs of Christian community development right there in Jackson. The wheels were set in motion, and with the help of a grant from a Tennessee foundation, VOC purchased an imposing, three-story house, with gables and dormers, and set their expert hammers and saws to work on it. The renovation was accomplished quickly, and the house opened as the John M. Perkins International Study Center in early 1978.

Lem Tucker shared John's love of teaching and desire to proselytize to Christian community development on as broad a plane as possible. It was his minute attentions to acquiring funding and qualified people to staff the center that made it thrive over the next decade. One of the first things Lem and John did was to recruit Tim Robertson to serve as director. Tim was a man in his early twenties, just graduating from Conservative Baptist Seminary in Denver. In the seventies Denver Seminary was one of the places where professors like Vernon Grounds were making evangelical theology more prophetic and influencing students like Tim to go, live, and work among disadvantaged people.

Working closely with Lem Tucker, Tim formalized the concepts and practices John had been living and working out over eighteen years into a body of knowledge that could be imparted through an academic program. He recruited faculty and networked with colleges like Wheaton, Calvin, and George Fox to develop a strong set of courses that would complement theirs, giving missions students vital, hands-on training and field experience. The original program was conceived as a year-long commitment for twelve students, but as the center evolved, it developed a broad variety of offerings including weekend workshops and weeklong seminars to accommodate the wide-ranging needs of pastors, missionaries, and students from places as different as Chicago and Kenya.

One of the most popular formats was the winter term session, given between the fall and spring college semesters. Students came to Jackson from evangelical colleges around the country and from the local Christian schools—Belhaven, Tougaloo College, and Reformed Seminary—to take courses for credit. Another format was the three-month internship program, which combined course work with fieldwork in Voice of Calvary's ministries. The International Study Center also coordinated the summer volunteer programs, combining work with study. The mixture of academics with real-life involvement, theory with practice, became a fundamental aspect of VOC's training, and anyone who came to anything longer than a weekend workshop got some experience working in the trenches.

Taken as a whole, the program had the comprehensive quality of a well organized undergraduate major or a seminary concentration in domestic missions. The International Study Center catalogue listed eighteen courses in three general areas of study: Community Development, Black Experience, and History and Vision of VOC. The Community Development area included courses exploring what God designed the church to be, the church's role as community developer, the principles, process, and goals of church-based community development, and the application of community development principles to situations in the poor nations of the world.

Paul Fowler, a professor at nearby Reformed Seminary, laid out the broad theological basis for holistic ministry in the course he designed and called "On Being the Church." Paul had been a friend of John and VOC since the civil rights period and he now sat on the Board of Servants. His purpose in this course, which set the tone and framework of the overall program, was to impart the need for churches to locate in poor communities and get constructively involved in the lives of the people who live there. A subsequent course explored the biblical linkage between evangelism and social action, the artificial splitting of the two in the modern evangelical church, and the necessity for their creative resynthesis.

The International Study Center closely linked theoretical with practical knowledge, as students received a theological and historical treatment of community development taught in tandem with subjects like the economics of cooperatives. The curriculum's coverage of concrete tasks—analyzing needs, planning, budgeting, proposal writing, and fund-raising—closely reflected the intense practicality of John Perkins. Like the man, the program was concerned not merely with producing people who think a certain way, but people who know how to put ideas into concrete action. For John Perkins and for those he discipled, the content of the Bible and of Christianity was thoroughly pragmatic. It was not whether an idea was acceptable within the traditional discourse of evangelicalism that mattered so much as whether it contributed to improving the lives of people in need.

Racial reconciliation provided what Dr. King had called the "soul force" behind community development, and the International Study Center gave emphasis to the middle "R" in a course applying a biblical perspective to contemporary racial relations in society and the churches. The general area they called Black Experience included black history and black church history. Taught by people like Lem Tucker, these courses effectively broadened white students' knowledge of the African American experience. At the same time, they raised consciousness and expanded blacks' awareness of their own cultural development. Sitting together under such instruction inevitably provoked interchange between black and white, and sometimes tensions between the races increased. Studying, working, and living together at Voice of Calvary generated racial interaction and friction, which became a basis for dialogue and ultimately reconciliation between black and white.

Other related studies focused on the varieties of cross-cultural ministry in America and development of indigenous leadership. Indigenization had always been John's goal, as he expanded the means of black advancement in Mendenhall. He remembered what it was like to grow up under a southern white paternalism that strangled black initiative. And so he had always concentrated on developing leaders with the education and skills to grow black-owned businesses, which would bring greater independence and prosperity to the community.

Mendenhall, now in the throes of transition, was the prototype for successful indigenized development. As a member of the International Study Center faculty, Dolphus regularly led student volunteers in study and fieldwork at the Mendenhall ministry site.

By the late seventies clusters of socially conscious evangelicals in colleges and seminaries, in the parachurch organizations, and at evangelical publications were looking to Voice of Calvary as a model to emulate. Out of the ongoing experience at Mendenhall and then Jackson, John had been honing his practical theology of Christian community development. The felt need concept, indigenous leadership development, and the Three Rs were elements in a strategy for development that John had worked out as he labored to relate principles he discerned in the Bible to the real lives of poor black people in Mississippi. And the eight courses listed under Community Development in the study center catalogue taught the content of those principles and practices.

The distinct experience and evangel of Voice of Calvary were reserved for the third series of courses, History and Vision of VOC. The four offerings in that category began with the history of Voice of Calvary from John's return to Mississippi in 1960. Next the biblical concepts at the root of the VOC experience were explored. The third course in this series, Insights from John Perkins, gave students the opportunity to personally get to know John and his way of thinking. Here was a forum for John to expound philosophically, much as he did on Christian college campuses. The many complex facets of the community building process could easily overwhelm the neophyte. John had a unique ability to synthesize the meaning and significance of the overall enterprise and inspire people with its vision. Students were also exposed to his infectious energy.

The program's final course continued this personalizing process by giving students the chance to discuss their individual experiences at VOC and how they might apply them elsewhere. The underlying purpose of this whole third segment of the curriculum was to make the elements of Christian community development real and operative in the lives of the student participants.

Most people who attended the International Study Center over the next decade would not get the full program, but one or another abbreviated version. What might be called "Basic Perkins" included an explication of the Three Rs in relation to biblical sources, such as Nehemiah's returning to a despoiled Jersusalem and rebuilding the wall or Jesus addressing the felt need of the Samaritan woman or Israel proclaiming cancellation of debts every seventh year at the time of Jubilee. From the biblical accounts and concepts came the principles of present-day community development. Moving from principle to practice, the economics, human relations, and other nuts and bolts of community development were discussed in greater or less detail depending on the length of the particular program. And finally, in good evangelical style, the whole message and body of knowledge were personalized with application to each individual's life and ministry.

The center gathered the broad content of what they had learned in two decades of work, integrated it with relevant material being taught in the evangelical academy, and disseminated it to missionary-minded men and women from around the country and from foreign countries like Haiti, Kenya, Uganda, and Australia. The seeds in the seedbed now in full flower began pollinating all over. The work of John Perkins that grew into Christian community development had been born in Mendenhall and grew to maturity in Jackson. Flourishing in the eighties, the International Study Center foreshadowed the seminary programs in urban ministries, which would serve a community development movement that was burgeoning by the nineties.

In the same period when the International Study Center was opening, VOC purchased a derelict lumberyard in one of Jackson's many impoverished black neighborhoods. John was always looking for ways to infuse capital and build businesses and create jobs in the black community. Utilizing Al Whittaker's expertise in starting small businesses in poor communities, he planned a co-op to sell new and recycled merchandise, similar to the operation in Mendenhall. Unlike the one in Mendenhall, however, this store would not be church-based. Memberships would be open to everyone at a cost of five dollars a share. People could buy more than one share and get a greater portion of the yearly dividend, but they still had only one vote, thus preserving the egalitarian basis of the cooperative concept.

Thriftco, the new Jackson co-op, would eventually become the most profitable of the ministries in Mississippi, absorbing the Mendenhall store and opening a number of branch operations around the state. But during its first few years, the store was not at all profitable and was

Ribbon cutting at the opening of Thriftco in Jackson, 1979. Second from left is Vera Mae, then John; Dr. Cooley, dean and economist at Jackson State; James Davis, president of Mutual Savings (Jackson's only black-owned bank); Jean Thomas; and Mutual Savings vice president Al Benson.

mainly a worrisome liability to John and then to Lem. It continually operated at a loss, and John had to raise money through the ministry to keep Thriftco afloat. One of the many factors that contributed to its unprofitability was the difficulty of getting a manager with a strong entrepreneurial bent who would make this work a full-time passion.

Between 1979 and 1985 Thriftco went through nine managers. During its time of troubles Ineva Pittmann, one of the indigenous citizens who served on its board, labored mightily and with a modicum of success to keep the store going but she was not the trained manager they needed to organize it efficiently and make it grow. As John was getting ready to leave the Jackson ministry to a new generation of leaders in the early eighties, Spencer inherited management of the troubled merchandising venture.

Growing up a Perkins, Spencer took in enough of the family's economic-mindedness to get his degree in business administration. During the mid-seventies he had felt the need to do something on his own apart from ministry, and he and brother Philip ran their own auto parts

272

business. At that time a firm sense of what he wanted to do with his life had not yet gelled and spending some time away from the pressures of being John and Vera Mae Perkins's eldest child gave him some breathing room. John had always encouraged individual initiative but there had also been great pressure to perform within the ministries.

Within a couple of years, Spencer was selling real estate and moving back within the sphere of the VOC community. In 1979 Bill Berry, one of John's friends who headed a Christian advertising firm in Chicago, agreed to hire Spencer and Joanie to further develop their business skills. It was after Spencer had worked and trained for a while in Chicago and returned to Mississippi that he was tapped to manage Thriftco, which was by this time running a serious deficit.

Spencer had a creative mind that needed space for reflection and quiet contemplation to be productive. But if Thriftco was to be turned around, it would take decisive troubleshooting and relentless managerial oversight, and Spencer's talents simply didn't thrive amid that kind of stress. Lem, John, Al Whittaker, and other board members met and brainstormed to come up with the reorganization plan that would bring solvency and prosperity and eventually they tinkered enough with the store for it to succeed.

In 1982, the year John left the Jackson ministries, money was raised and borrowed and invested to thoroughly remodel Thriftco. The warehouse, previously in a separate building, was now joined to a mammoth, modernized discount department store. The new store was attractive and had the capacity to do a much greater volume of business than previously. On the financial side, Thriftco was changed from a cooperative to a nonprofit business, more along the lines of Goodwill Industries. With this status, donors could give money and merchandise directly to the store and didn't have to channel their giving through Voice of Calvary. In the mid-eighties, Lem hired a Nigerian, Babs Salu, as manager. He was the shrewd entrepreneur they had long sought.

It was back in 1979, when Thriftco and the International Study Center were in their earliest stages, that John actually began the transitioning process to new leadership. For nineteen years, as he had developed Voice of Calvary in Mendenhall and then in Jackson, John had gravitated more and more toward a primarily itinerant role. The younger four children, Deborah, Wayne, Priscilla, and Betty, never knew a time that he wasn't traveling some thirty-two weeks out of the year. Having effectively fused evangelism with economic development among the poor, he became the world-traveling apostle of holistic ministry. It was others, indigenous leaders in collaboration with people who had relocated, who did the day-to-day problem solving and community building.

In 1979 Lem had worked about a year in Jackson as head of leadership development, but the ministries in Jackson and Mendenhall were expanding so fast that John saw the need for an executive director, so he created the position and filled it with Lem. The young Virginian took over the responsibilities of ministry coordination, staff development, and supervision while John kept his hand on new projects and the purchase of property. As much the organizer as John had been, Lem had a more closely attentive, patient quality with people. John was ever focused on the work and the goal, and the people who learned from him generally had to be self-starters who learned as they worked alongside him, just as he had learned alongside his uncles as a boy. Lem would stay in closer touch, instructing and correcting a new worker, and he possessed a rare ability to develop people's hidden talents.

The new director's very personal mentoring paid dividends later in the development of people. In the eighties Lem trained Melvin Anderson in budgeting and operations management. Melvin was one of the young men John had discipled in Mendenhall who moved to Jackson in the seventies and was rapidly coming into leadership. A capable manager with PDI, he didn't think he could give the fastidious attention to detail necessary in planning VOC's budgets. But Lem saw greater possibilities in Melvin and spent hours painstakingly training him and thereby drawing out more of his potential.

Nineteen hundred seventy-nine became a pivotal year of changing leadership in Jackson. Mostly it was a matter of certain key people's change of job description or their cycling into another venue of ministry, as did Lem and H, who moved to New Hebron to open a second rural health center. Voice of Calvary also went through its most devastating loss to date that year with the death of the beloved Herbert Jones. Herbert and Phil Reed had worked hard to get the Herbert R. Jones Christian Youth Center opened in Jackson just the year before. It provided a nourishing environment where neighborhood kids could congregate, as opposed to the streets and the seedy little bars known as clubs. Recreation and craft activities were available and the young people received Bible lessons and discipleship training from VOC staff.

Herbert, whose love of children epitomized VOC's focus on the young, was to have headed the youth center but he died at thirty-nine of pneumonia and heart failure. The burden of a progressive overweight condition that had begun just after he was discharged from the army had finally overtaxed his heart and claimed him. His funeral in Mendenhall was a major event in rural Mississippi that year. Hundreds and hundreds of people came from many miles around to mourn the gentle giant and give him a spirited send-off. Herbert's casket was so big that the pallbearers couldn't fit it through the door of the Buckley Gym, so they had to have the service at the funeral home. A band played gospel songs, and people ate and talked and milled around all day. It looked like summer revival time.

H and Terry had a special interest in health care, and when the opportunity came to develop a facility in John Perkins's hometown, they decided to move there. This was in the transition year of 1979. Having specialized in new project development since he, Terry, John, and Vera Mae had started the Jackson ministries, H thought their leaving Jackson would give the new leaders there a better chance to become primary decision makers. A whole crop of them were joining VOC in the late seventies and early eighties. Among the white relocators were Phil Eide and Jim Taylor, who lent their substantial housing development skills to PDI. Tim Robertson was settling in, designing courses at the International Study Center. In the early eighties, Lem married his sweetheart, Eleanor, a broadcast journalist who had been an anchorperson in Norfolk. She put her lucrative career on hold to join Lem and become Voice of Calvary's director of publicity.

In the early seventies, as they started health care in Mendenhall, H had learned the process of applying to the National Health Service for money and doctors. Over time he became expert in obtaining grants for rural health care development and he recruited personnel to set up health centers in three rural Mississippi counties. In 1978 two people in New Hebron—the white pharmacist and John's old friend Isaac Newsome of Oak Ridge Missionary Baptist Church—had contacted VOC, asking for help in setting up a health clinic. H and John had spun off a ministry from VOC, which they called the South Central Mississippi Rural Health Association. The reason for separate incorporation was to distance some of the government money from Voice of Calvary, thus protecting the parent organization from liability. New Hebron had started an embryonic clinic in 1974 and under the new umbrella corporation, they would obtain the funds and personnel needed to upgrade that clinic.

As H began recruiting physicians and dentists for New Hebron, he began to have second thoughts about the way he was proceeding. John's unshakeable ideal had always been Christian community development, and H feared that in sending medical and dental personnel to New Hebron who may not share that vision he would end up compromising the clinic there. That was when he started thinking about relocating himself.

For some time Terry resisted the idea of moving to New Hebron. After all, she and H had been the Jackson pioneers. They had seen Voice of Calvary Fellowship expand from just them and the Perkinses praying in the front room of the Four C Center to a thriving congregation, now meeting in the Masonic Hall on Lynch Street. They had played key roles in building the ministries and the VOC community into a sturdy family-support system. Their own first children had been foster children with special needs, and VOC had been a nurturing environment for them. These considerations made it hard for Terry to pick up suddenly and move forty-five miles south into Mississippi's rural hinterland. But they both prayed earnestly about it, and one morning about a year after the initial call from New Hebron, Terry sat up in bed and said, "It's time to go."

When they moved into New Hebron, H and Terry worked to develop the health center and a VOC-style fellowship around it. Wisely they avoided making their community of Christians into a full-scale church. Coming into this hamlet and starting their own church would have drawn the antagonism of the existing black churches, which would have seen them as competition and maybe scorned them as some kind of a cult. Sensitive to the ongoing life of the indigenous community, H wanted to serve as a support and a resource to existing churches. So he and Terry and the people who joined them in the expanding health care ministry attended the local churches. With twenty-four people eventually involved in the ministry, the whites went to white and black churches on alternate Sundays, and blacks went only to the local black churches, since they were not welcome in the white ones.

As a means of holding and disbursing the federal money they were eligible for, they formed a separate nonprofit corporation called Rural

Services Incorporated (RSI). The federal salary levels they qualified for were two to three times higher than the ones Voice of Calvary had paid them. So they covenanted among themselves to use only the wages equivalent to what they would be getting from VOC. The rest of the money, which they put into RSI, was used to purchase a tent and then a farm and houses. They hired people and began to develop ministries similar to those in Mendenhall and Jackson, but on a smaller scale. H served as chief administrator of the health center, and Charles Hatten, a local black high school teacher with a strong background in agriculture, became the head of the farm.

The deep significance of what they were doing in New Hebron was not lost on H. The health center was across the street from the old Carolyn Theater, and as he looked out the front window he could see the little alleyway where the "colored" entrance had been and where Clyde Perkins had been shot down some thirty-three years before. In fact they had carried John's dying big brother across to the pharmacy, which had stood on the very spot where the health center was now. And now the first white man John had discipled was bringing health care services and economic development to New Hebron. RSI and the expanded clinic would become important vehicles for black and white reconciliation in that rural outpost of Southern traditionalism.

To start up the corporation that would run the clinic, H first had to compose its board of directors. In accordance with federal guidelines and area demographics, he was supposed to recruit six blacks and five whites, with a black chairman. Of course this neck of the woods had never seen anything like that level of formal interracial association. Knowing it would be easier to organize the black side of the board, H went to John's old Christian friends like Isaac and Jesse Newsome and Eugene Walker, and they handpicked the best people for him. They also advised him of people in the white community who might be willing to serve on a black-dominated board. Traveling the narrow piney roads in his Toyota on his way to see those whites, he wondered, "What's a nice white boy like me doing trying to pull off something like this?"

He could feel the tension as he spread out the census map, which indicated the target areas and the required racial composition, before these prospective white recruits. As he sat explaining the plan in the small frame house of one white dirt farmer, his wife in the background hollered, "You mean there are gonna be darkies on that board?"

Mississippi Governor William Winter talks with Ralph Wolf, an early Voice of Calvary supporter, at the dedication of the health center in New Hebron, 1979.

Nervously, H replied, "Yes, ma'am, there are gonna be black people on that board."

The man said, "Let me see the list of board members you got there." H showed him the list and there was a pause.

Then the man said, "Those are some good nigras." And as he looked up at H, he had an expression of deep humility. He said, "I'd be honored to serve on that board."

This was the kind of response that caused H to draw deep satisfaction from what he was doing. The white farmer went on to serve on the board, cooperating with black board members and treating them with respect. These were the little milestones of racial reconciliation in Mississippi. In 1980, when they held a grand opening celebration for the augmented clinic, John Perkins was on hand and so was Governor William Winter, a progressive by Mississippi standards. Locals gathered in a big tent to hear the governor make a speech and give John an award as outstanding public citizen. A white banker took H aside and told him, "You'll never know the impact you've had on this town, bringing black folk and white folk together." Racial progress still had a ways to go, but things had indeed changed in the decade since Brandon.

278

In the late eighties, after H and Terry had left New Hebron, the black and white co-directors grew at odds, and the clinic fell apart. But RSI continued to expand and prosper, particularly the farm, which marketed its vegetables through Thriftco. Charles Hatten, fearing widespread hunger as the old rural culture was dying off, wanted to redevelop truck farming among Mississippi's poor classes. The acknowledged leader of Christian community development in New Hebron, Hatten would also bring the health center's black directors back together and reorganize the clinic in the nineties.

With Artis and Dolphus having taken the helm of what was now called The Mendenhall Ministries, with Lem effectively piloting Voice of Calvary, and with the New Hebron work succeeding, John once again felt that he had worked himself out of a job. In 1981 the Board of Servants acknowledged his status by making him minister-at-large and Lem president of Voice of Calvary. For many years John had spent much of his time out of town spreading the word and raising money, but with his formal connection to the Jackson ministries now ending, he found himself with that familiar itch to move on. John wanted to give the new leaders a chance to make their own decisions and he had begun to think moving out of Mississippi would be the best way to do that. As he and Vera Mae talked about leaving, they thought about their strong connection with California. They had warm memories of that mobile place where they had started their life together and they still had close friends and family there. So by 1982 they found themselves again facing west and planning a move back to Pasadena.

With these plans being set in motion, the transition time again became a testing ground for John. This was the period that Thriftco was in financial trouble, and they were developing a new health clinic in Jackson, this one without federal funding. In the throes of expansion, Voice of Calvary Ministries was grappling with problems of cash flow and debt. Lem was coming into his own at the helm, but VOC was still dependent on the tremendous amount of support John could generate in his speaking tours.

Thriftco's problems, as they developed in the early eighties, were especially painful for John. He had thought it would become a profit-making venture much earlier and he had never thought it would accrue so much debt. With the building not large enough to draw a clientele sufficient to pay its overhead, they had done the remodeling and expansion, thus acquiring more debt. As a director of the Southern Cooperative Development Fund, John was able to get a loan of two hundred thousand dollars to fund the investment, but it would take time before Thriftco had sufficient receipts to make the monthly payment on the loan. So John had to go on the road and raise the money to make up the difference.

He felt sorely divided during this crisis, coming as it did when he was getting ready to move to California. On the one hand he was the one who had made the commitment and he felt constrained to see it through at least to solvency. But at the same time he was moving out, and it seemed that the new leaders should deal with this problem. The pressure he felt to come through with the support came in conflict with his desire to let his successors assume the main responsibility. His impatience came to the fore and he began to blame others for not adequately shouldering their tasks.

As happened during the transition in Mendenhall, the Board of Servants failed to play the strong, mediatory role that may have better facilitated the transition. Instead, as they had earlier, they supported John's tendency to let go too precipitously. Again the rationale was that having to work under financial pressure would make the new leadership stronger. The crisis came to a head with John out of town and Lem overburdened and working round the clock.

It was to be H, and not the soft-spoken Virginian, who would call John back to Jackson. From the time when John had just about told him to leave, and he had countered that God had called him to Mississippi, H had never been one to avoid confrontation with his mentor. Once, reacting to Dr. McCarty's leaving Mendenhall, John had dumped his pain in a sermon, making negative comments about whites' commitment to relocation and unfairly predicting that H too would leave. Deeply hurt, H drove to the airport, as John was catching a plane, and again forcefully confronted him. John came to love the younger man's courage in calling him on hurtful things he had done and practicing the hard, honest communication necessary for reconciliation to get beneath the surface.

The meeting that took place with H, Lem, and the staff in Jackson had a jolting effect on John. When H told him how he had hurt people with negative comments and how he was abandoning the new leaders in their hour of need, John listened in silence. After the meeting, H went back to New Hebron, where John was also staying as he visited the ministry. The next morning the telephone rang at H's house, and as H picked up the receiver, he heard John at the other end.

"I don't know if I'm gonna make it," he kept repeating in a breaking, anguished voice.

H jumped in his car and sped over to the dentist's house where John was staying. He found him on the floor, sobbing, his body shaking.

"I don't want to hurt anyone," John kept saying over and over. The two men sat together for some time and talked it through, John letting out his burden of grief and H helping him bear it.

Mr. Buckley had once said, "When I pray for Perkins I always pray that Perkins would see hisself." The old farmer understood the seductive effect of public praise and honor. And so did the man he had been a father to. In the personal crisis he went through, John had been open enough to see himself, and the experience broke him down.

John's childhood and youth experience of being cut off from relationships abruptly and then having to make it on his own again guided his actions. He grieved deeply for having hurt the people he had discipled, but his own learning had never included a gentle weaning process. At this point John could recognize this as his weakness, and in the future he would avoid building big organizations with large budgets that would become too dependent on him.

Paradoxically John's weakness was also a source of health for the ministries he started. For John never became the controlling old patriarch that many charismatic leaders become. He knew that the empire builders, the ones who hold on too tightly, controlling things personally, do so at the cost of others' maturation. Growing up black in Mississippi in the Perkins family had given him an enduring hatred of paternalism and dependency. So he had worked to develop leadership and build the organization simultaneously, and then he got out and let the new leaders take over. His scrupulous training for independence and then letting others take the reins of control would enable Christian community development to become a generative movement, growing and spreading to other places.

Part of the transition in John and Vera Mae's life as their time in Jackson drew to a close was the coming of age of their eight children. In 1982, when they returned to Pasadena, Spencer was twenty-eight, and Betty, the youngest, was sixteen. Growing up had been a rich but tumultuous experience for the Perkins children. John and Vera Mae had instilled rigorous standards of conduct in each of them. They were

The Perkins family in 1980. *Foreground:* **John and Vera Mae.**
Back row, left to right: **Betty, Priscilla, Wayne, Deborah, Derek,**
Philip, Joanie, Spencer.

up several times a week for five A.M. Bible studies, and there were always
plenty of verses to memorize and all kinds of work to do. Inevitably
the older children got the sharpest discipline and the most responsibility. When Spencer was seventeen and John was about to go under
the surgeon's knife, John had sent his son a note, saying that if he didn't
make it, to help mama put the kids through school.

All eight of the Perkins children had been under pressure to serve
as righteous, high-minded examples to the community. But the intense
experiences of integration and the civil rights movement had left smoldering embers of anger in the four oldest ones. For years Joanie carried the sting of anger over the police beatings of her father. Philip and
Derek got some of their aggressions out on the gridiron at Jackson
State. And they released tensions that had long been building up in
them as they partied and ran wild for a while as college students.
Spencer had first overcome by starring on the courts of high school
and then college basketball. And like Derek and Philip, he and Joanie
also let off steam during their college years. Both of them were asked
to leave white evangelical institutions they were attending for breaking the *in loco parentis* rules.

During these days of youthful rebellion, the young Perkins men resisted the constraints of missionary life. They zoomed around Jackson on motorcycles, distancing themselves from parental demands at Voice of Calvary. Pushing away the stern weight of authority would give them the space to choose whom and what they wanted to become.

By the late seventies Spencer, Joanie, and Derek had come back to the ministries. Joanie, with more of the executive personality than the others, became chief of staff and chief of youth ministries. Derek divided his time between college classes and VOC. Philip married Eva Quinn in 1977 and eventually left VOC to go into trucking. Wayne learned the printing trade. And Deborah, adept in business, would put her accounting skills to work at Habitat for Humanity. Priscilla, with the help of the Whittakers, was receiving a quality high school education at Stoneybrook, a Christian girls' school in New York. Betty too would attend a private academy after she finished junior high.

As Voice of Calvary was internationalizing its mission, John made a trip to Kenya in 1980, taking Spencer and Derek with him. The thirty-two-day experience altered the consciousness of the two young men, injecting them with a fresh sense of pride in their African heritage. Unlike America, Kenya still had a vital village culture with a strong spirit of family, clan, and community. When the villagers were doing a large common labor, similar to a house raising or corn husking in an earlier, rural America, they would chant the Swahili words, "Harambee nyio," or "Let's get together and push." Their ebullient spirit of cooperation inspired Spencer and Derek, who decided to bring it back to Mississippi. When they returned to Jackson, they enthusiastically conveyed the spirit of "harambee" to Joanie, who in turn became the organizing force behind the Harambee Christian School of Business.

As John and Vera Mae were nearing departure for the West Coast, Joanie, Spencer, Derek, and Priscilla, along with a coterie of VOC volunteers, were putting together an afternoon program to teach spiritual, academic, and vocational skills to neighborhood young people. The Harambee curriculum ranged from Bible and black history, to reading, math, cooking, sewing, and computer. But more than its school program, Harambee was a living movement. Flowing through it and giving it cohesion was an exuberant blend of African American self-expression and the revival enthusiasms of evangelical faith. Children and teachers gave voice to this warm spirit in the rhythm of songs and recitations they wrote and performed together.

Spencer wrote a creed that gave definition to the movement and that Harambee students memorized.

> We are what we make of ourselves. We will no longer fit into the mold that has been prepared for us. We will strive for a completeness in Christ that will compel us to stand against the social and economic injustices of our time. We will identify and understand our heritage, thus affirming our family. We will broaden our educational and technical skills. We will learn to use the economic system to free our people from the poverty cycle. We will never discourage but always encourage our sisters and brothers. Then we will join hands and move together to change our society. Harambee! Harambee! Let's get together and push.

Harambee Christian School of Business and the movement it embodied would flourish at VOC for about seven years, expanding to 160 students by 1988. That year, as Joanie gave up directing the program so she could finish college and attend law school, it would go into decline in Jackson. But Harambee's unique style of Christian education for the young would become a source of enrichment in the broader movement of Christian community development. During the next decade, Derek, Priscilla, and Betty Perkins would bring new vitality to their parents' work as they expanded Harambee in Pasadena.

Journeying back to the West Coast in the winter of 1982, both John and Vera Mae found themselves in a pause from their ever hectic, event-filled lives. They knew they would continue to be involved in the Mississippi work on one level or another. Most of their grown children were still there, involved in the ministries, completing their education, or trying to run a successful business.

Over the years, as John had continued to travel and proselytize, his work had spawned a growing subgroup of evangelicals. Evangelical culture as a whole was middle-class suburban and absorbed in personal rather than social concerns. But among minorities, intellectuals, missionaries, and young people in parachurch organizations like InterVarsity, interest in holistic evangelism was burgeoning by the eighties, placing

John in ever-greater demand as a speaker. His Three Rs concept was having a slow, building effect, as small but growing numbers of white evangelicals were starting to reach out to the minority poor in the inner cities.

Ever since the early days in Mendenhall, John had felt impelled to travel and speak, spreading the word of what they were doing in Mississippi. Initially the travels had a lot to do with raising the money that was necessary for them to survive. And fund-raising would continue to be part of their rationale. Over the years, however, people of wealth—investment bankers, media moguls, entrepreneurs, philanthropists with foundations—had become his friends. And their continuous underlying support had made travel for fund-raising less necessary. But as John's mental creativity organized and drew on his experience, he had become a unique resource and guide for others interested in the field he had pioneered.

So the traveling and teaching on the road had spiraled, and John had become used to pulling heavy suitcases loaded with books, brochures, and a few rumpled changes of clothes on and off planes. He was always rushing to and from airports. He adapted well to the rigors of constant air travel. He kept trim, and his body fit comfortably into cramped coach space, and he was able to refresh himself by catnapping. Even at home, John never slept for long periods. The chronic condition that had taken two-thirds of his stomach pained him especially at night, and he rarely slept more than three or four hours at a time.

He was used to rising well before dawn, and poring over a passage in his well-marked Bible, drawing out new substance and committing himself to God for guidance. His Bible was his constant companion, as he carried it near him and referred to it concerning whatever issues or current projects he was considering. He would commonly take it out and meditate over it in flight, though in his easy, friendly way he could be distracted into conversation with whoever might be around him. With an inveterate interest in people and whatever they might be involved in, he liked to draw others out. He kept up with public issues and conversed easily about a broad range of them.

The family was used to John being away much of the time, though it deprived especially the younger children of his mentoring. Back in Mendenhall, when his travel schedule had been lighter, he had coached his older sons and neighborhood boys in league softball. But as he got busier and traveled more, his family got less of him. John's itinerating served to detach him from the concerns of everyday family life and the life of the ministries he presided over. So he had come to rely more and more on others to keep them going and do the daily trouble-shooting, while he provided general direction, broad vision, and vital fund-raising.

As the children grew older and became more self-sufficient, Vera Mae often accompanied her husband on his trips. But while the children were growing up, she had had to shoulder most of the burden. And she was ever immersed in work, dealing with all the nitty-gritty details that afforded John the luxury of putting them on a back burner. In Mendenhall she had taught and fed all the community's children and wiped their noses and taken care of their endless little and big emergencies. At the same time she had shouldered all the tasks and periodic crises of rearing her own eight children. In the sixties, during the civil rights struggle and the bruising stresses of early integration, she had had to submerge her own emotional needs and be there for her children and for the community's children. As confrontation had escalated and the police harassed her, stopping her every time she drove her children across the tracks, she had had to stifle, cope, survive.

From childhood, Vera Mae had known how to make do with little to no help. Like John she had learned to bury her personal pain in hard work. Satisfaction if not salvation itself was in a job well done. In her intensely competitive nature and dogged determination she was every bit John's match. And she was bound and determined that her children, and all Voice of Calvary's children, were going to win and have their own. But it was hard having to always be so strong. John had been on the road when she had gone into labor with Priscilla and she had had to get sixteen-year-old Dolphus out of school to drive her to the hospital.

Some four years later, in the Brandon aftermath, with John about to go into surgery, she was driving up to the Delta hospital with little Betty sitting next to her chattering away. She liked Betty's chatter; it lightened her heart a little, but she couldn't answer her little girl because a lump of pain in her throat made it hard to talk.

"Mama, are you angry, or are you just thinkin'?"

"Just thinkin'."

Quietly, stoically, she had carried the daily burden, but there were times like this one that things seemed so hard that she thought she would break. "My Lord knows the way through the wilderness," she kept on singing to herself, her eyes wet. "He'll give me strength for today and tomorrow."

Sometimes she resented John's flying off everywhere and coming back spouting off about a hundred projects he had going all at once. But she had a forgiving nature and she and John could be open and honest and fight with one another up front. Sometimes the volunteers would witness their frank, voluminous exchanges and would be shocked. But their candid and sometimes rough informality kept them going, accepting, and loving each other. John would wryly say, "Vera Mae and I have had only one fight in our marriage, and it's still goin' on."

PART 3
THE MOVEMENT
1982-1997

20

Northwest Pasadena

In 1965 as LBJ was powering the Voting Rights Act through Congress, Pat Moynihan published his controversial report on the black family. Moynihan, then assistant secretary of labor, was one of the bright young Irishmen who had accompanied JFK to Washington in the flush of hopeful activism that had begun the sixties. Liberal in the tradition of FDR, as non-southern Democrats were then, he wrote his originally confidential policy paper to stir the government to action amid worsening conditions in the black urban ghettos. But he used words like "tangle of pathology," as he characterized the black family as victim of three hundred years of oppression, and the report drew the harshest fire from the very constituency he had set out to help.

To many civil rights leaders, and particularly to emerging black nationalists and black power advocates, Moynihan's diagnosis felt insulting and demeaning. Much of the African American intelligentsia accused him of "blaming the victim for the crime." They feared his report would shift policy planners away from concrete housing and jobs programs and toward some paternalistic, fruitless resolve to improve black family stability. With militants pillorying him as racist, Moynihan sadly withdrew to the temporary cloister of the academy, feeling wholly misunderstood. His purpose, he maintained, had been to make the case for maximum government action against the massive unemployment that was splintering black family life in cities throughout America. But the hornets' nest he had stirred up deterred further investigations of ghetto pathology for more than a decade.

By the 1980s, as teenage pregnancy and single motherhood were exploding in much worsened urban settings, the issue of the black family began to reemerge as part of a broader American problem of familial and cultural decay. The intervening years had seen the jobs and housing programs of the Great Society come and go. And they had seen the fastening of welfare dependency on the fatherless families that were now normative among the underclass that populated the ghettos. Conservatives blamed federally administered welfare—Aid to Families with Dependent Children—with its single-parent eligibility requirement for creating and sustaining the underclass. And likely the incentive of government support did contribute to the proliferation of teenage pregnancy. As government maintained these young women and their children, it helped to perpetuate single motherhood, dependency, and poverty. But the welfare mess was more the chronic symptom than the underlying cause of inner city misery.

The diminished black family that Moynihan had called attention to in the sixties actually belied a healthier black family of which he had made no mention. His seeming dismissal of the multitude of strong, successful African American families was probably one of the things that raised the hackles of his critics. In fact black families had held together against withering odds throughout slavery and Jim Crow in the South and in the swelling urban slums of the North and West. As with the walled-in Jews of antisemitic Old Europe, so with African Americans before civil rights: All lived together in the ghetto. So lawyer, doctor, shopkeeper, and teacher were there along with washerwoman, ditch digger, and others of very humble means. In the days of entrenched institutional discrimination, all the layers of black society touched on one another, and the influence of the accomplished, responsible, and enterprising was there to create modest wealth, stable families, and healthy community life.

The civil rights movement was highly successful in creating a black, suburban middle class. Open housing and affirmative action brought the gospel of individual success to African America, and the ones who could compete, the natural leadership, fled the inner cities en masse. Black flight followed white flight and this evacuation of the black middle classes devastated the old urban neighborhoods. Departure of the most stable, productive segment came on the heels of a suburban migration of industry that had been going on since the early postwar years.

By the seventies, businesses of all sizes were fleeing at an ever-increasing pace, taking capital, employment, and prosperity with them, and the economy of the inner cities sank below subsistence. Public institutions—schools, hospitals, libraries, parks—corroded, and social life decayed, as streets became meaner and more derelict. By the time Ronald Reagan took office in 1981, steadily deteriorating conditions in the inner city had devoured opportunity, creating a largely immobile lower caste, an underclass made up primarily of African Americans and the growing population of Latinos.

An economic and cultural vacuum now existed in the urban environment that made it the natural hothouse for all the antisocial behaviors that had been growing in America since the sixties. Amid entrenched joblessness, poverty, and family breakdown, addictions, drug-dealing gangs, and criminal life now proliferated. The black urban churches that had nurtured and stabilized families earlier in the century were now in a much weakened state, their economic base evaporated and their most productive constituency migrated out. The churches that remained with their greatly diminished resources could not cope with the spiraling problems of drugs, crime, and vice. Many withdrew into Sunday pietism, bolting their doors against the harsh culture and random violence of the streets.

While enduring the deep disadvantages of the ghetto that drove so many black men into hustling and women into prostitution, the black family in the first half of this century had drawn stability and nourishment from traditions the roots of which were in Christianity. By the eighties those influences that had induced people to restrain their creature lusts, defer gratification, and accept the responsibilities of home and family had eroded throughout American culture. The hucksterism always endemic to our public life, yet previously held in check by ethics and morals based in religion, now became the dominant cultural influence. Ubiquitous mass media now enshrined a self-indulgent consumerism as the purpose of life, and this cult of immediate gratification drew people into excessive behaviors that tore apart much of the remaining social fabric.

Loss of the old canons of sensual restraint had particularly devastating effects in the inner city, where there was so little left to cushion life. With no significant mediating influence of family or church, and an enticing media ever laying out its sexual smorgasbord, teenage pregnancy, single motherhood, and fatherlessness climbed to new heights. Boys without fathers turned feral, forming into territorial packs that roamed and dealt drugs and consumed drugs with one another. Murder, mayhem, and theft became the customary way of life for these angry, alienated young men who lacked the conscience that could come only from sustained contact with responsible, involved fathers, uncles, and grandfathers.

Education was the natural way out of underclass life, and many of the cities had public two- and four-year colleges in and around them where young men and women could pick up the new technical skills that could give them jobs and respectability. But lack of parents, particularly fathers, who could encourage and restrain their children and model a work ethic, left adolescent boys and girls easy prey to all the destructive influences swirling around them.

Each element of the decomposition of life in the inner city reinforced the others. With family life atrophied and pop culture purveying unrestrained sex, young girls longing for personal contact, meaning, and love became child mothers. Boys grew up sullen, without mentoring fathers to show them how to master a skill or resist the gangs. Without the countervailing force of strong fathers, a toxic street culture that disparaged study and learning and all forms of legitimate work and self-discipline kept the young men addicted, uneducated, and unemployed. The centrifugal forces of the streets sucked the young into their vortex, further dismembering family life and social stability. All around were the criminal inducements that landed people in prison or violent premature death. The only hope was for strong influences to somehow break in, come alongside the people, and offer them the means to extricate themselves from this sinking morass.

When John and Vera Mae returned to the San Gabriel Valley in early 1982, they found a Pasadena awash in the same problems now festering throughout urban America. The most severely blighted neighborhoods, which quartered chiefly blacks and Latinos, were in the Northwest, not far from the Rose Bowl. This part of the city had become a sinkhole of violent crime, drug trafficking, and jobless despair.

John had toyed with the idea of retiring from the immediate responsibilities of running a local ministry to the less troublesome occupations of itinerant teaching and writing, but as they were staying with their old friend Kevin Lake, one of the doctors who had helped them start health care in Mendenhall, John and Vera Mae began to feel drawn to the deep needs of northwest Pasadena. When an opportunity came to buy a house at the corner of Howard Street and Navarro Avenue, a flash point of the highest crime area in the city, they took it, and just eight months after their return to California, they found themselves back in the thick of neighborhood ministry.

Greater Pasadena is a more cohesive environment than much of the rest of sprawling Southern California, and the different levels of society live in fairly close proximity there. Early in the century, the San Gabriel foothills had been a millionaire's paradise. As you drive just away from the central city, the terrain turns green and the streets tree-lined. Lovely neighborhoods with rolling lawns showcase Spanish hacienda homes interspersed among the styles of American eclectic. Much wealth still encircles the city, remaining committed to its resilient economy. The smaller cities nearby—Monrovia, Altadena, La Canada, Arcadia, and wealthy San Marino with its famed Huntington Library—cluster in proximity to Pasadena's downtown hub. For Pasadena then, the exodus to the suburbs that had so sapped the wealth of other urban locales was muted. The communities of the San Gabriel Valley boasted a strong civic spirit, and there were wealthy Christians there who were ready to help bring renewal to the festering neighborhoods of the Northwest.

Lake Avenue Congregational Church was one of the solid old institutions that maintained a benevolent presence in northwest Pasadena. Its name came from the New England denomination originally brought to America by the Puritans. Congregationalism had been one of the Calvinistic creeds that had built the socially minded evangelical consensus of the nineteenth century. When modern liberals jettisoned its modified Reformed theology, embracing a more naturalized humanism, a few Congregational churches chose to hold out and stand by their oldtime religion. One of these was doughty old Park Street Church in Boston, which drew local support from Gordon Conwell Theological Seminary. Lake Avenue, Park Street's western counterpart in Pasadena, fed on the new progressive evangelicalism being generated at nearby Fuller Seminary.

While risky, the Perkinses' move into Pasadena's worst neighborhood was a far cry from the pioneering mission they set out on in 1960. Their present endeavor had the support of many leaders in the growing social action wing of American evangelicalism. Lake Avenue Congregational became the Perkinses' home church, and John often spoke at Fuller, where his good friends Bill Pannell, Paul Jewett, and Lewis Smedes, among others, were bathing their students in the holistic gospel. And just down the road in Monrovia was World Vision, the most visible institution of the evangelical church's expanded social ministry. John had become a board member in 1978, and now that he was beginning a ministry in Pasadena, the relationship between him and World Vision grew closer.

While it was mainly known for its development-based evangelism in the poorest regions of the globe, World Vision retained a strong interest in helping America's impoverished. With John's help during the eighties, they would expand their domestic operations into a large separate office.

As John was getting ready to move into northwest Pasadena in 1982, a local electrical contractor named Steve Lazarian was named to World Vision's board. John and he had met back in 1960 at the local Christian businessmen's fellowship, just as the Perkins family was preparing to move back to Mississippi. About eight years older than John, Steve was a native of Pasadena, having grown up in the northwest when it was a thriving community of upwardly mobile blacks and white ethnics.

Working together on World Vision's board cemented a relationship between Steve Lazarian and John Perkins that would become a powerful alliance for empowerment of the poor in northwest Pasadena. The World Vision board was a forum that brought together a number of creative minds interested in development. Roberta Hestenes, a Fuller professor with a gift for breaking down the wall between classroom and street, worked closely with John and Steve on World Vision's board. Hestenes later became president of Eastern College in Philadelphia, where Ron Sider and Tony Campolo were elaborating evangelical social action.

Lazarian was also a member of Lake Avenue Congregational Church, and Paul Cedar, the senior minister, commissioned him and three other men to be the church's liaison to John's mission. The others were Roland Hinz, a magazine publisher who would become one of John's closest friends; Mark Bassett, a professor at California Institute of Technology; and George Terzian, head basketball coach at Pasadena City College.

In October 1982 John and Vera Mae began to set up shop at Howard and Navarro. They saw bottles, bricks, and garbage strewn through the street, and the drug houses were all around them. They began by gathering their friends together for regular prayer and strategizing during a six-month period and holding what John called "listening conferences" in the neighborhood.

The listening conferences were John's way of tapping into the community's felt needs. He knew that success depended on how effectively they could respond to immediate neighborhood pain. And they heard many, many tales of woe as they gathered with neighbors in their backyards. Diagonally across from John and Vera Mae's house at Howard and Navarro, in front of a little variety store, cars stopped all day and the drug deals were going down. Throughout urban Southern California, Bloods and Crips and Hispanic gangs were dealing in cocaine and speed and strong marijuana, and like the Chicago gangs of the Prohibition era, they vied for territory, killing one another as a matter of course.

These modern gangs of the black and Latino underclasses were composed largely of adolescents, some as young as fourteen, thirteen, twelve, even eleven years old. And killing was fast becoming the accepted rite of passage for boys in packs to become "men." Gunfire often punctuated the night sounds as the listening meetings were taking place, and one night a fourteen-year-old boy was shot and killed in the street out front.

They met with the people in a mood of urgency and determination and they got city officials—the mayor, police chief, and council members—to attend. John's plan was to galvanize a movement of the local residents, drawing support from city services, to bring grassroots change. As in Mendenhall a generation earlier, he wanted to find the needs and develop the people's own resources to meet them. The big difference with Mendenhall was that here affluent, influential whites and city authorities did not stand in their way. Here, as John began to organize, he found a reservoir of friendly support in the larger community.

They met together in several backyards in several neighborhoods in northwest Pasadena and they talked in depth about the violent crime and the despair that they saw and felt all around them. The older people said how they were afraid to walk down the street at night. They talked about the growing problem of homelessness. Entire families of homeless people were now sleeping in cars and in public places. In each of the neighborhoods, the people came out and voiced their concerns. The listening conferences provided a powerful means for the people to vent their griefs and anxieties. At last they had a place to bring the accumulated pains and grievances of their lives in hope that something might be done to change things.

The message of the meetings that came through loud and clear was the need to do something about the children and youth at risk: the

John with two Harambee boys.

latchkey kids running through the streets, the teenage mothers, the teenage boys in gangs. It was Vera Mae who knew how to make contact with the children. She began, as she and John had in Pasadena so many years before, with child evangelism. Standing out on the corner of the street in front of their house, she greeted the school bus as it stopped there, the children flooding out the door. "I'm going to start a Bible class," she said, "and I want you all to come."

"Who are you?" said one boy acting as spokesman for the rest. "I don't wanna come to your Bible class," he added smartly.

"Okay, you don't have to come to my Bible class. We're gonna have pajama parties and go to the beach and go to Disneyland. But if you don't wanna come, don't come to my Bible class."

"Oh, I'll come. Who are you?"

"Do you have a grandma?" asked Vera Mae.

"No, I don't know my grandma."

"Okay, I'll be your grandma," she said.

Vera Mae became "Grandma Perkins" to each of the scores of children who came to her classes. And she introduced the children to "Grandpa Perkins." She held the first Child Evangelism classes in temporary quarters they patched hastily together in the garage of their house. The songs, prayers, missionary stories, and brightly illustrated Bible lessons on the flannel graph formed the structure of the Good News Club as Child Evangelism Fellowship had designed it.

As Grandma Perkins taught the children and gave them their little treats, she created a cheery, loving atmosphere that was wholly absent from the rest of the children's lives. The after-school hour became the highlight of their week, and before long a sea of children were inundating the little makeshift classroom. Vera Mae was not some magical

Mary Poppins. The weight of relentless stress and responsibility some-times frayed her nerves, but the children always remained her special delight, and the Good News Club hours brought her enthusiasm bub-bling to the surface.

Child evangelism would once again become the germ of a much expanded ministry. In Pasadena's inner city the Perkinses' work focused on the needs of young people and their splintered families. Out of the listening conferences in the neighborhoods and the early discussions that John held with his family and friends came two organizations: the Harambee Christian Family Center and the John M. Perkins Founda-tion for Reconciliation and Development. Harambee was to be the base for an expanding array of neighborhood youth ministries, and the foun-dation would have its eye on the world. Harambee would relate to the city of Pasadena, though it would draw volunteers internationally, as had the ministries in Mississippi.

The foundation reflected John's abiding passion to disseminate his ideas and practices to communities everywhere. He and those who supported him believed that the Three Rs, as they had developed in Mississippi and were being taught at the International Study Center, had universal applicability. The Perkins Foundation would become an important catalyst for the development of the new urban ministries programs, which would spread through the most advanced evangeli-cal institutions to counter the economic, social, and cultural decay that was impoverishing life in late twentieth-century American cities.

Another need that came out strongly at the listening conferences, one that became the special concern of Steve Lazarian, was the grow-ing problem of disfranchised families—cold and hungry parents and children living in tents and cars and under bridges. Steve had done a great deal of buying, selling, building, and restoring of homes and office buildings in the Pasadena area. He drew on John's experience with PDI, and the two worked with local churches and parachurch organizations, like Focus on the Family and the Council of Churches, which had interest in helping homeless families.

Initially they supported a little makeshift rescue mission that was put together by the pastor of a Foursquare church, but it had only the most meager facilities, and the pastor had to let people shower in his home. Before long it became evident that a whole new or substantially reno-vated facility was needed to meet the needs of a number of families. After much care and consideration, Steve funded the purchase and renovation of a large, historic house at 669 North Los Robles. Originally they planned to expand it, altering its appearance appreciably. But the Pasadena Historical Society insisted they retain the building's original architecture. With the facilities to service five families with fifteen to twenty children, they ended up with a smaller but more care-giving operation.

The house was turned into a nonprofit corporation called the Door of Hope. It provided a spectrum of services, giving material and spiritual succor to down-and-out families, with the goal of getting them into their own quarters and regular employment. As one of its founders, John continued to serve on its board of directors. This ministry cooperated with the Harambee Center as the two addressed differing facets of the general urban crisis.

Almost as soon as John and Vera Mae began the Harambee Center, they needed more room to expand its operations. With help from local businessmen like Roland Hinz and Norm Nason, a real estate developer from the Bay Area, John would obtain the means to eventually expand into four additional houses on Navarro. But Harambee's permeation of the neighborhood with its nurturing presence did not happen smoothly or overnight. A tough war of nerves went on for some years against the drug dealers and gangs who had claimed so much of northwest Pasadena as their territory. The three houses immediately adjacent to the corner one were drug houses, and the dealers, like a bunkered enemy in house-to-house warfare, had to be flushed out.

One of the most effective means of taking back the streets was the direct approach, the street rally. Unlike other inner-city activists, John did not concentrate on arousing the neighborhood against the drug dealers. He took a more positive approach, presenting the spiritual alternative. John was operating in an American tradition of open-air revivals that dated back to George Whitefield's booming exhortations in the 1740s. He and Vera Mae set up about twenty-five chairs on their corner lawn, and John began to preach. Bringing the mayor, city council, and the police into dialogue in the listening conferences paid immediate dividends. They were able to obtain the city's permission to block off the street and gather a crowd.

At their evangelistic rallies, as in all genuine revivals, quite a few remarkable conversions occurred. Drug dealers, addicts, and prostitutes, people who felt hopeless, desperate, and miserable, found themselves coming forward and asking for salvation. When a brother who lived right there on the block told them that God loved them and would help them get clean if only they would let him, they could feel the depth of his sincerity. The plain-speaking country preacher from Mississippi who lived on the corner was able to reach down deep and touch their pain. He wasn't some holier-than-thou churchman coming in from the outside, but a neighbor reaching out to help them in their ongoing battle for survival. Mothers could see tangible evidence of that care in the faces of the kids in Vera Mae's Good News Club.

The evangelistic rallies did not transform the neighborhood instantaneously. Drug deals continued to go down in front of the store at the corner, and armed gang members cruised the streets, but John and Vera Mae had planted a flag of hope at the opposite corner, and people were beginning to respond. One young prostitute, strung out on drugs yet moved by John's message, came into the house and talked late into the night with him and Vera Mae. They gave her warm support and helped kindle the spark of faith she needed, and she was able to let go of the life she was living. Years later she came up to John at a fund-raising event and reintroduced herself. She was a well-groomed executive, and John grinned broadly in delighted surprise as she spoke of her personal transformation.

As John and Vera Mae expanded their rallies, Mr. Davis who lived down the street, made his big yard available. Local black pastor Tyrone Cushman joined John in preaching. Around fifteen years John's junior, Cushman had grown up in Detroit and had formal training in the Church of God, Anderson, Indiana. His polished preaching style and urban manner complemented John's more informal, southern idiom. John was eager to involve local churches in his work and he was gratified when Pastor Cushman, Pastor Caldwell, of the Good News Church of Christ Holiness, and a Latino evangelistic association helped lead the rallies. Back when he had started his ministry in Mendenhall, the black clergy had felt threatened by this upstart, who did things differently, and had shunned him. In the more urban Jackson setting he had been able to network better with area churches. The Pasadena work would profit from his many years of organizing experience and bear the richest fruit in interchurch cooperation.

With his toehold at the corner of the street and help from the white businessmen who had joined him, John first purchased the house adjacent to his and then the fourth house in on the block. The third remained the lair of the drug dealers, who at one time had occupied each of the four houses, and they were not about to surrender their territory without a fight. Their resistance began in earnest as they broke out all the front windows of the second house while the Perkinses were out of town. When they had them repaired, the drug dealers came back and broke them a second time. Then John went to the chief of police and the city council to enlist their support in his campaign to take back Navarro Avenue. He had been in such turf wars before, and the challenge only strengthened his determination. Here in Pasadena, with the local government and police squarely behind him, he felt power he had not had twenty-three years ago in Mississippi.

The second house became the center of battle. On two occasions the drug dealers firebombed it. Harambee volunteers were in the process of renovating the house, and a young white volunteer by the name of Bill Kings was living alone there. Kings was a self-styled evangelist who tramped around the country publicizing the gospel and working in different ministries in exchange for room and board. When the second firebomb hit the roof, he scrambled up there and quickly doused the spreading flames. After this second firebombing John and the police met and strategized. They developed a plan that would flush the dealers out of the third house.

Each day Vera Mae went to pick up two detectives, who would crouch down in the car as she drove them to her home, pulling into her garage on Howard. The detectives went through the Perkins home and through the side door of the second house where they set up photography equipment. For ten successive nights they camped there, spying into the drug lair and photographing the evidence. At about nine o'clock on a morning shortly afterward, John and Vera Mae were suddenly interrupted by the loud, rhythmic vibrations of a police helicopter. Rushing out front, they saw patrolmen emptying out of squad cars and moving on the third house. How sweet it was to feel warm relief and not terror or bitter animosity at this sight. This was the beginning of the end for the drug ring, as the dealers were arrested and jailed and later tried and sent to prison. The seemingly intractable third house was now officially vacant.

The police cut the electrical lines to it, and the city turned off the water. But still, in its derelict state, it continued to shelter local miscreants, who would break in, use, deal, party, and crash there. And it

The Harambee Christian Family Center, Pasadena, late 1980s.

got even filthier as they continued to use its bathroom with the plumbing facilities cut off. John wanted to buy the house, but with his heavy out-of-town speaking schedule, he didn't find time to get together with the landlord. Then as he was embarking on one trip, a mix-up occurred, and he found himself at LAX when he was supposed to be at Burbank Airport. Missing his plane, he decided to go back home and when he got there, he found a realtor driving a "For Sale" sign into the ground. "Don't bother with that sign. I'll buy it," he said. Roy Rogers, an investment banker who sat on the Perkins Foundation Board, helped out, so they didn't even have to take a bank loan on this house. It was theirs, and now they had a row of four on Navarro.

21

MENTORING

The war against the drug dealers and the purchase of the four houses did not climax until the mid-eighties. All during that time Harambee Christian Family Center was growing in size and scope. In 1983, when they had obtained the second house, Eva Meyers came out from Mississippi to help Vera Mae expand the Good News Club into an afternoon tutoring program. One of the young Brethren volunteers, Eva had developed a strong interest in Child Evangelism. Vera Mae had directed her to go to Missouri for the three-month intensive training. After she had done so, Eva trained a local black woman to take over leadership of Voice of Calvary's Child Evangelism program. Having thus indigenized Child Evangelism at Voice of Calvary, she was ready to help the Perkinses expand Harambee. She moved into the second house, and they added a large family room across the back, which became a multipurpose center and the meeting place for Harambee's rapidly growing tutoring and Child Evangelism programs.

Because John was on the road so much, with Vera Mae now often accompanying him, it was necessary to bring people into the organization and train them rapidly so they could carry on in John and Vera Mae's absence. Eventually four of their grown children—Derek, Deborah, Priscilla, and Betty—would be working with them in Pasadena. But for now they had to rely largely on others. John had learned to delegate day-to-day decision making and had always placed high value on training for independence. He considered the lack of his

The Perkins family and Harambee staff, 1986. *Front row:* John Wayne Perkins, Eva Meyers, Addie James. *Second row:* Betty Perkins, Vera Mae, John, Priscilla Perkins, Deborah Perkins. *Back row:* Roger Haith, John Williams.

presence on site as a positive thing. Locally and in transit he was always on the lookout for individuals he could bring on board to do a variety of different jobs.

One street-smart young man, James Shepherd, was converted in one of the evangelistic rallies. When John became aware of a need for someone to act as his liaison to the local churches while he was out of town, he set about training James to do the job. He got him business cards to make it official. Serving in this capacity had a powerful effect on James's sense of what he could do with his life. He was able to parlay his experience as John's assistant into a subsequent position with the YMCA, which he would hold for a good many years before a change of administration ended it.

Between 1983 and 1987 the underpinnings of Harambee Christian Family Center were put in place and a whole cadre of young men and women came on staff, were trained, and learned to work with the children and youth and to supervise the volunteers. They were black, white, and Latino. Many were local people, and many others were from places around the country. The volunteers likewise came from a broad number of locations, some from African countries like Kenya and South Africa. The Bruderhof, a community in the Mennonite plain folk tradition in Schenectady, New York, became actively involved with John's work. They gave money and handmade furniture from their wood shop and they sent a good many volunteers to Pasadena. Like the Pennsylvania Brethren who had come to Voice of Calvary, the Bruderhof's volunteers were modest, diligent workers whose disciplined habits fit well with the strenuous, unadorned Perkins lifestyle.

As they ministered to young people's needs in Child Evangelism and after-school tutoring programs, Harambee also began to address the complex subject of vocation. Skills training and job finding, along with getting a good education, were ordinary social functions that had all but disappeared from the environment of the urban underclass. In the mid-eighties, Kent Bailey—a young man who lived in the neighborhood, had come to the listening meetings, and had become a volunteer—now became a paid staff worker. He and a white woman from one

Staff and supporters of Harambee. *Front row:* **Stan Lazarian, John, Vera Mae, Betty, Priscilla.** *Back row:* **Derek Perkins, Rev. Rosey Grier (former N. Y. Giant), Cedric Cebalos (L. A. Laker), Johnny Mountain (T.V. personality).**

of Pasadena's large corporations came together to teach business skills to young people on Saturday mornings. Out of their Harambee Business Club came a silk-screened T-shirt enterprise and a little studio that made and marketed tapes from John's many recorded teachings.

Harambee took a variety of approaches to get people into productive work. They set up computer training as part of the tutoring program. The Business Club had people in different trades like carpentry and plumbing come and speak and do demonstrations of their work. And they got teenagers into internships in various businesses around the city. Here John's networking with the different churches in the area was especially useful. Many Christian business people were eager to provide internships and eventual employment to young people Harambee was discipling. One was Stan Lazarian, Steve's son, who managed operations at the Electrical Service and Supply Company his father had founded. Chairing Harambee's board of directors for many years, Stan made vocational training and employment his special province. He hired interns every summer and helped Harambee develop a program to place and fund internships in Pasadena-area companies.

Stan also became a key figure in ServNet, an umbrella cooperative that John obtained funding for in the late eighties to foster black entrepreneurship. ServNet grouped together a number of local tradesmen in fields from carpet cleaning to carpentry. With Stan's supervision and money from a foundation, they rented and remodeled an old Pasadena theater building to house their offices. ServNet was supposed to market together the variety of skills represented by the tradesmen. But somehow ServNet never gelled, and the men went their separate ways to ply their trades independently or to work for someone else.

The disintegration of ServNet, following an investment of over ten thousand dollars, was a bitter disappointment to both John and Stan. Both thought the ServNet tradesmen could have worked harder at marketing and coordination, but Stan was cognizant of the tremendous number of hurdles in the path of such a business. The interface with city, county, and federal government in permits, taxes, and other paperwork was complex and required a lot of painstaking attention. Stan thought that had they employed someone with contracting experience on a day-to-day basis, such a person could have mentored the men, raising their confidence in the overall mission. One ongoing problem they had to face was competition from the "underground economy."

John Williams with Harambee students, mid–1980s.

Many of the people who do small jobs in carpentry, electrical work, carpet cleaning, or window washing in places like northwest Pasadena do it informally for cash, and therefore for a good deal less money than ServNet could afford to charge.

The creation of small business ventures was never more than a sidelight of Harambee. The heart of the Perkins mission in northwest Pasadena, as it had been in Mississippi, lay in the instruction and nurture of young people. Vera Mae's Good News Club was the germ out of which all the children and youth programs developed. The after-school programs began as tutoring and branched into athletics, campouts, summer day camp, Wednesday night Bible study, and sleep-overs. Beginning about the time they got the second house and Eva Meyers came to Pasadena, the neighborhood children would come to Harambee to do their homework with the adults there to help them.

Derek Perkins, who became the key person in expanding and deepening the programs, was there with Eva in the first years of the Pasadena ministry. Then he returned for a time to Mississippi to join the Antioch Community, a biracial communal household that Spencer, Joanie, and others in the Harambee movement were forming in Jackson.

During the period of Derek's absence, John Williams, an energetic former car salesman, relocated from New Jersey to Pasadena. He began at Harambee as a volunteer and worked up to leadership. In his early twenties, Williams had been inspired as he heard John Perkins speak in his church, a black Pentecostal congregation just outside Philadelphia. During the mid-eighties Williams and Eva Meyers worked together to solidify and expand the after-school programs. Eventually both people would cycle out of Harambee, Williams into the legal profession, as Derek returned to Pasadena and moved into the youth director's role.

Mentoring teenage and preteen boys was Derek's special talent and love. In Mississippi his contribution to the Harambee movement had been Harambee House, a residence he started for black teenage boys at-risk for crime and prison. As a child in Mendenhall, Derek had grown up in the leadership development program, close to Dolphus Weary, who was his model. In Jackson he had been one of the participants in Herbert Jones's loving youth work. The Perkins family was in relatively comfortable circumstances during most of the Jackson years, and Derek had pushed ministry away for a time while he and Philip were playing football and coming of age at Jackson State. But as he matured, Derek began to feel the weight of his father's example, and it became a natural course of action for him to move into the worst part of Jackson to open his refuge.

He didn't do it alone. John and Vera Mae had drilled into each of their children the perils of being a "Lone Ranger." So Derek had started his house as a part of VOC and the Harambee movement. When he moved into the VOC renovated house, Mike Bailey, a young white man, moved with him. He also got help and counsel from Phil and Marcia Reed, who took needy people into their own home as part of their pastoral work at Voice of Calvary Fellowship. So with the people and ministries of VOC in support, Derek and Mike began to take in boys whose harried parents lacked the spiritual, emotional, and material resources to give them what they needed.

They developed a core of four residents, and a group of others joined them for Bible study and an array of VOC activities, including the courses of the Harambee Christian School of Business. When Mike left, a Minnesotan named Don Stroehn replaced him. So the boys got hands-on supervision from committed adults who took an abiding interest in their success. And they got the example of black and white leaders working together. Derek and his collaborators didn't save everyone. Some fell into drug addiction and other besetting problems. But they had notable successes, like Billy Ray, who became a skilled carpenter, and Clyde, who became a leader in the Jackson youth ministry.

Harambee House formed the paradigm for the work Derek would do in Pasadena. As he developed the youth ministries there, the closeness and intensity of the Jackson residence formed his baseline, and so he was never satisfied with the superficialities of typical school and church youth work. A skilled painter, he poured his passionate artist's temperament into his work in the people medium. He had married schoolteacher Karyn Farrar before coming back to Pasadena. But people called him a man's man, and he retained a special love for the in-depth mentoring of boys. Raised in the community his father had created, he never bought into American individualistic success, preferring the close personal relationships and mutual aid of a more tribal order. And he gave himself wholeheartedly to raising up a clan of strong young Christians whose healthy rites of passage could offset the destructive tribalism of the gangs.

In the late eighties, after the Harambee Christian Family Center had become four neat, white houses adorned with brown trim and bright flowers, the drug dealers made a bid to retake their old territory. They scrawled "J.P." on a wall near the center with a line through the letters. John and Vera Mae had moved into a fifth house, just across Howard, but John was gone most of the time, and now it was up to Derek to defend the turf. The dealers and gang bangers were in the street in front of the house, and there were killings in the neighborhood. One day the dealers were standing in Vera Mae's way as she was coming home. She steeled herself to walk through them and as she did so, she experienced such tension that when she got into the house she collapsed in tears. Derek held her up as she said again and again, "I know I'm doing God's will."

Bryan Robinson, who had come out from inner-city Philadelphia, was there to back Derek up. Derek had come to depend on Bryan as an invaluable right hand in working with the boys. And Bryan was there with him as he went into the street and confronted the drug dealers. The dealers threatened but they backed off. Scary and painful though it was, Derek felt himself standing up, the way his father had in Mississippi. He remembered John's telling him that courage was not being fearless, but acting in the face of fear. The drug dealers began to find that Harambee's expanding presence and implacable opposition made this neighborhood a less friendly place to do business. By the early nineties there were still some individual deals going down, but the big dealers were gone and the violence had largely abated.

Derek Perkins at the 1994 Christmas program at Harambee.

Bryan Robinson, teaching guitar to a Harambee student.

As Harambee grew its roots deep into the neighborhood, its staff got more and more involved in the lives of the people. They developed linkages with the public schools, supporting and networking with embattled teachers and overseeing the kids' homework. Their involvement in the lives of the young people and with their families gave them great leverage and credibility, so they could become effective instruments of discipline in the broadest sense of that term. If a child was having some kind of problem at school or in the home, Harambee staff would be apprised of it and they could address it.

Sometimes a child having behavioral problems in school or in the afternoon program might have to forego a camp-out or a field trip, or even the program itself for awhile. But penalizing misbehavior is only the simplest and most negative corrective. The instilling of personal discipline in the positive sense, as in discipling, became Harambee's special gift. This process of what John had always called leadership development had been refined for over a generation in Mendenhall and Jackson. And now a second generation of Perkinses, Derek, Priscilla, Deborah, and Betty, themselves discipled in the Mississippi ministries, were applying it and further refining it in Pasadena.

A gathering in Harambee's amphitheater, summer 1994.

Student in the computer lab at Harambee Christian Family Center.

Boys and girls in the program have many activities together—tutoring, Bible studies, field trips, camp-outs and the like. But the discipling process, as it was developed in Mississippi and adapted to Pasadena, has benefited from intense woman-to-girl and man-to-boy mentoring. Years of experience taught the Perkinses and the people they trained in leadership development that the girls won't show their deepest selves around the boys, nor would the boys around the girls. So much of the interpersonal contact that touched the core of the young people's personhood was carried on in spheres separated by gender.

Derek and Bryan worked to develop the boys, with thirty or more in the overall program. They worked more closely and intensely with an inner core of fifteen. On the girls' side, Betty, the youngest of the Perkins children, as she finished school and came into adulthood in Pasadena, took charge of the discipling program, modeling and teaching a strong and assertive—yet caring and modest—version of womanhood to the teenage girls in her program.

313

These discipling programs have become especially vital and effective because Derek, Betty, and the staff people around them get involved in the young people's lives and have embedded their mentoring in their natural day-to-day contact. They see the children nearly every day, not only in the center, but around the neighborhood. And they have developed an easy, personal relationship, going into one another's houses and sitting around on their couches and talking together and raiding each other's refrigerators. This free flow through the neighborhood houses naturally involves the parents, usually the mothers, and Harambee staff often eat dinner at their homes, and the mothers sometimes accompany their children when they eat at staff homes.

Serious issues come up in the natural course of conversation between staff and kids: problems at school with gang kids who are threatening them or family problems or nearly anything. And the staff people suffer through these crises together with the kids. Derek likes to strategize with the boys about the best way to deal with gang members who might be threatening them. When one of the Harambee kids got caught with a knife and was suspended from school he said he didn't know how he could defend himself without a weapon. Derek showed him how to play on the big gang kids' egos. "When you see one, say: 'I know you're tougher than me. I'm not no tough guy. I'm just a little guy. But you tough.' Hearing he's tougher is all he wants to hear," said Derek. When the kids put such ideas into practice, the gang bangers, feeling their prowess properly acknowledged, nod, smile, and move on.

Another youth had spoken up when a gang kid had made some negative remark about Jesus. When the Harambee boy spoke knowledgeably about Christian faith, the gang kid felt put down and he got angry and threatened to shoot him. Derek said, "When you see the guy next time, you need to go up to him, look him in the eyes, say, 'Only reason I had an argument with you is 'cause I'm crazy 'bout Jesus. I'm kind of a freak like that.'" He followed Derek's advice, and the gang kid said, "Aw man, that's cool." The skills Derek and Bryan teach the boys at Harambee are lifesaving, sometimes literally and immediately so, with the nightmare of guns and killing now common and spreading among young boys in the cities.

Getting around the kids for long bull sessions in prolonged Bible studies and sleep-overs on Wednesday nights gives them a chance to air all these kinds of issues. Deep, hands-on mentoring takes place as Derek and Bryan and other staff and kids huddle together at Derek's or one of the other staff houses until late at night. Some of the boys in the group are Latino, and Rudy Carasco, a Harambee board member who has some of the sleep-overs at his house, has been a strong role model to them. In the long Wednesday night sessions and in other informal gathering times they discuss openly black, white, and Latino stereotypes and other racial issues. They talk about problems, like the high rate of black young men dropping out of school and ending up in prison. And Derek tells them they need to work harder and expect more of themselves. "And it ain't no different for the Mexicans either," he says.

Talking to the group at large, he inspires them to rise above mediocrity to a life of real commitment: "Your whole future is set up for you," he warns. "You're gonna be a janitor somewhere in some cubbyhole, drinkin' beer, sittin' on the porch. You gotta do somethin' for other people." The kids listen because they know that Derek, Bryan, Rudy, and the others love them. Derek asks the Mexican kids what they've got against the black kids and the blacks what they've got against the Latinos.

They dispel the stereotypes and they look inside themselves to see if they are doing things that confirm them. In a group with one Latino and the rest black, Derek, after airing the black kids' complaints about the Mexicans, turns to the Mexican kid and says, "What have you got against black boys?" And he responds, "They'll fight you all the time." Derek turns to the black kids and says, "Is he right? Think about at school. Who are the main fighters?" In this kind of open, confrontive dialogue, he gets the boys to pause and think about the destructive roles being thrust on them through peer pressure and the violent culture of the streets.

As might be expected with the boys, and as was true in Mississippi, some of the discipling is worked out in athletic competition, commonly on the basketball court. A high-quality, full-length basketball court was installed behind Harambee's houses in the late eighties. At Harambee, as at Voice of Calvary, while they play the games hard, winning is not what athletics are about, but the building of discipline, integrity, and self-respect. As Derek officiates with Bryan or Rudy, the games become a metaphor for life. They call technical fouls, and kids get angry and frustrated. One boy will yell at a teammate, and Derek or his partner may stop the game and say: "Now look what you just said. How you gonna get the best results from him if you doggin' him like that?"

315

The boys learn to stay in there and concentrate on the game and the goal and not take their frustrations out on others. At game's end, they go over the boys' behavior toward one another more than they discuss their moves. The game, whether basketball, football, or soccer, becomes a grid for experiential learning and character building. Gradually they knit together a high-spirited, cohesive group, a strong yet accessible counterculture, resisting the surrounding violence, yet reaching out warmly to others caught in it.

Derek and the other Harambee staff work at building healthy rites of passage into the discipling program to mold the youths into productive, compassionate people. They consciously counter the destructive rites of drugs, promiscuous sex, violence, and killing that surround them. When a boy reaches twelve, they give him a more adult-sounding name, as in changing Ricky to Rick. And they initiate him into Harambee's smaller, more intimate "main group."

They take him with a group of boys on work trips to poor places like the barrios of Baja, California. If a new initiate works as hard as Derek, then Derek and the staff declare him a man. His initiation is into a way of life that stresses giving rather than getting. Extending themselves to others in this way, rather than always being the needy ones on the receiving end, works to strengthen their sense of who they are and what they can do. John had taught these values to his own children and to the others whom he had discipled in Mississippi, and Derek continues the process.

Besides building virtuous character these work expeditions together with the camp-outs, sleep-overs, and games all serve to increase closeness, bonding, and camaraderie. Derek, Bryan, Rudy, and other staff members are affectionate and openly encouraging to the boys—often giving a hug, a pat on the back, a "good job," or "way to go."

John, in his early mentoring, had not been so openly affirming. In the environment he had grown up in, the common wisdom was that you don't want to give somebody a swelled head so you don't praise him to his face. But it was okay to praise him to others. He had reared his own children this way but as he got older and softer, and as he observed the positive effects of Derek, Betty, and the other staff's encouragement of the young people, he became more affirming and openly affectionate with the Harambee children. It was not uncommon for a child to get a warm smile, kiss, hug, or a loving remark from Grandpa Perkins.

Despite the premium African American men have put on being cool, tough, and unemotional in the stress of a hostile, racist environment, John always had a capacity for emotional transparency. He could cry openly and he would do so not in sorrow for himself, but for others. Derek imbibed this model of emotional transparency, and it became a powerful means of bonding with the boys at Harambee.

In one instance, Derek was reprimanding a boy who had been "feeling on" one of the girls. As he talked with the boy, conveying his disappointment, their faces a foot from each other, a sense of anguish came over Derek, and he began "crying at him." The boy became so ashamed of what he had done and so moved by Derek's deep concern about him that he immediately decided to reform himself. Days later, when some of the girls were "runnin' after [him], messin' with [him]," he pleaded for Derek's help, saying: "I changed. I don't do that no more. Tell them to leave me alone."

As the Harambee young people bond with one another and with the staff, a sense of mutual accountability evolves, and a sense of responsibility to the group keeps them away from drugs, sex, gangs, and the innumerable little acts of antisocial behavior that are constantly going on all around them. This kind of accountability had worked for Derek during his wild late teen years in Mississippi, helping him to stop smoking "weed" and come back into a close, mutual relationship with the youth and staff at Voice of Calvary. An intimate peer community had developed at VOC, and it developed again at Harambee. This deepening sense of a common life where people can openly share themselves and their concerns with one another causes Harambee to develop an esprit and a strong identity. At the Pasadena public schools the young people are known and respected as "Harambee kids," spirited clean livers. And some of the tough kids, hungering after caring, friendship, and a better life, are drawn to the four white houses at Howard and Navarro.

Of course the younger a child comes to Harambee the fewer old, bad habits they have to break, and the greater the formative role Harambee can play in molding the child's character. This is the method behind Vera Mae's Good News Clubs, which are places, not only for Bible teaching, but for a whole range of early modeling and training in politeness, civility, and human decency.

Older children and adults are not neglected at Harambee. Harambee has become a place where adults in the community can begin to reclaim their lives. While focusing on the nurture of the young, John has always been aware of the needs of adults. They developed adult education and skills training programs in Mississippi and then again in Pasadena, including training in basic skills and computer literacy. With the prevalence of crime and incarceration among black males, an abiding concern for John and his coworkers has been for men coming out of prison. They have desired to lower the rate of recidivism by helping these men find meaningful work and involvement.

As John was acquiring the houses on Navarro, one of the people he met was a middle-aged, maternal woman named Gladys Jackson. Gladys had a heart for the men coming out of prison and she wanted to obtain one of the houses on Navarro to use as a halfway residence. With the help of John, the Perkins Foundation, donors, and allotments from a county program, she was able to set up and maintain such a facility in the sixth house in from the corner. Having Harambee, with its expansive youth programs, as neighbor made the surrounding environment a good one for these men to turn their lives around. John brought them into the five A.M. Bible studies he regularly conducted when he was in town, and Derek brings them on as helpers in the youth programs.

One former prisoner, call him Walter, got deeply involved with Derek and Bryan in their work with the children. Walter had met John and been tangentially involved with Harambee before getting into trouble and having to do time. While in prison, he wrote John a letter expressing his pain and shame over what had happened to him, and John had written him back, affirming his love for him and his desire that he come back to the neighborhood. When Walter got out and returned to the neighborhood, Derek had him coaching basketball and working in the tutoring program. Walter felt a deep spiritual nourishment from the process of working with the children. He identified with the boys he helped and felt as if he were getting a second go at his own childhood.

As an outgrowth of John's holistic approach, Harambee is sensitive to whatever felt needs exist in the neighborhood. In greater Pasadena, with its plentiful church and parachurch resources, John wanted to focus on developing a rich and close network of Christian bodies that could attend to the whole range of human need. In the nineties, in the aftermath of the Rodney King case and the ensuing L.A. riots, he and other Christian leaders in Pasadena moved to create just such a network.

22

INTERNATIONALIZING

When John was converted in Pasadena in the fifties, the strongest influences on him were the Child Evangelism missionaries. From them he imbibed a love of restoring people's souls that became his essential purpose in life. In Mississippi, when he was back among his people, he worked to help the community grow in new, more fruitful soil. He understood and nourished their felt needs through evangelism, nutrition, education, housing, economic enterprise, youth leadership development, and civil rights. His intense involvement in developing the community, in Mendenhall and again in Jackson and again in Pasadena, tempts one to see John primarily as organizer and community builder. And while these things are integral aspects of his work, they were not at its center. At heart he is and always has been a missionary evangelist.

Despite being raised in the midst of the Perkins clan, John, without mother or father, had felt like an orphan. And his sense of aloneness had only deepened when Clyde was killed and he made his solo journey to California. But when he experienced conversion, he felt a loving God taking him into his family and he was overwhelmed with gratitude for his new sense of belonging. As a result he felt compelled to carry the good news that had brought meaning and purpose to his life as far and wide as he could. He wanted other people who were growing up cast off, poor, and lonely to experience, as he had, the love and rehabilitation of God. And so from the earliest possible date John was traveling and proselytizing to an ever-expanding audience.

Itinerant evangelism thus became John's primary calling. He was spreading word of what he was doing in Mississippi and preaching his holistic gospel on the road during much of his time as early as the mid-sixties. As he became better known, his ideas refined in the mill of experience, he was in ever greater demand and traveling all the more. His family lived the life of missionary families, Vera Mae with the responsibility overload of a missionary wife, the Perkins children with the distinct stresses of "MKs." They were always working and having to live up to an impossible standard and getting little bonding time with Daddy. But they were given the discipline of a strong work ethic and the inspiration of a high calling. These things would give depth to their lives as adults.

The white evangelicals who had discipled and were supporting John were from missionary-minded traditions. They did not think all the religions of the world were equivalent and they did not reduce evangelism among the poor to social work. They believed that people need Jesus, and John believes this too. When John started out as a domestic missionary evangelist, his work and style closely resembled that of his white counterparts. They valued him because he was a natural for evangelizing southern blacks. But as his work developed, he cast evangelism in an economic and social mold, and this began to set him apart.

John's holistic approach was especially relevant to the lives of downtrodden peoples. World Vision was the missionary organization that understood the need for development to be integrated with evangelism among the impoverished. As the staff at World Vision became aware of the work John was doing, they wanted to get him involved in their missions.

John first came to World Vision's attention at InterVarsity's 1975 Urbana Conference when he met one of their missionaries, an East Indian named Sam Kamaleson. Impressed by John's natural sensitivity to the plight of the world's poor, Kamaleson was struck by how Voice of Calvary's development work paralleled that of World Vision. Bob Pierce, its founder, had begun as a Youth for Christ evangelist in Korea, the Philippines, and Japan just after the Second World War. When he encountered the tremendous physical needs of the children he was working with, he was moved to create a means of responding to them, and World Vision was born in 1950. Out of this work grew a new emphasis on helping people to economic viability as a compassionate arm of missionary evangelism.

What Kamaleson saw in John's work was not merely the common ground his community development practices shared with World Vision. He saw in John and heard in his presentation something deeper. There was a special anointing on this black Mississippian who had gone back home and was giving his people the tools to lift themselves into dignity. He saw John's ability to touch something deep in people and give them hope and he wondered if his concepts would be transferable to peasants in India or Aborigines in Australia. When John came on the board of directors at World Vision, he not only participated in the evaluation of their programs and policies, but he also began to make trips with their missionaries into the field.

As John's work had matured in Mississippi and the International Study Center was opened, he found himself going abroad more and dialoguing with people of foreign cultures. He taught among indigenous peoples in formerly colonized countries, often under World Vision's sponsorship, sometimes on his own or in coordination with other organizations like Evangelicals for Social Action or the Oxford Center for Mission Studies in England.

The interactive process of public speaking and teaching was always energizing to John. When he got aroused about an issue, his voice would intensify and the words would come faster and hit harder. John's favorite speaking format was Bible teaching and as he taught, he would open his Bible and draw his Three Rs from it, applying them in different contexts. His outgoing personality helped him make positive contact with people in diverse cultures. As he conversed with the people, he would be looking for ways to adapt his ideas to address their specific issues. He was an inveterate problem solver, and the missionary fields abroad presented a bewildering variety of problems that ever fascinated and engaged John's pondering mind.

One of the earlier and more significant trips John made was to Kenya in 1980 along with Spencer and Derek. A young missionary, late of African Inland Mission, was instrumental in arousing John's interest in the former colony of British East Africa. In line with John's concept, he had encouraged educated young Kenyans to go back into their villages and start businesses. His innovative approaches had not set well with his superiors, however, and he found himself back in the United States with time on his hands to go to Mississippi and be with the

Perkins family. This young missionary had tapped a potent entrepreneurial spirit in the Kenyans, and his descriptions of their faith and openness to development piqued John's desire to go there.

Wedged among Ethiopia, Uganda, Tanzania, and Somalia on the Indian Ocean, Kenya had wrested *uhuru* (independence) from Britain in 1963 under the leadership of Jomo Kenyatta. The Kenyans were warmly receptive to John and his sons, with both nationalities having a strong impact on each other. It was there that Spencer and Derek first observed the communitarian spirit of harambee, which they brought back to Jackson and then to Pasadena. They spent thirty-two days in Kenya, as John spoke in churches around the country and they stayed in the villages and talked faith and economics with the tribespeople.

While Kenya's urban life was influenced by the economic elite and international corporations, Kenya's rural village economy was quite decentralized, with the government providing only basic infrastructure, roads, and education. Businesses were small, localized, and portable, with very little overhead. At the traditional outdoor marketplaces, merchants go early in the morning and spread out their wares, dismantling their displays and carting them home again at night.

In the villages of Kenya, John found great receptiveness to the idea of developing economic cooperatives. Capitalism was there in its simplest form without big banks, store chains, and the costly complications of the corporate world to stifle the small entrepreneur. With the economy so basic, there was an absence of western gadgets and gimmickry to generate demand, as the small enterprises arose in response to a multitude of genuinely felt needs.

Cooperatives were useful in Kenya for the same reason they had been in Mississippi, to raise the capital and give an agrarian people experience in running their own businesses and making profits. John talked the ins and outs of cooperative development with Kenyan villagers as he observed a number of their cooperative retailing operations. One cooperative store he saw flourishing was a little print shop that turned out books and pamphlets. It survived in rural Kenya, as it likely would not have in a more developed economy, because it didn't have to compete with big printing chains and their economies of scale.

The formative state of the rural Kenyan economy and the people's eager openness stimulated John's native inventiveness. Once he was watching farmers laboriously making fodder for their animals by turning a wheel. The wheel brought a blade in contact with upright corn-stalks. Even though there was a handle, it was difficult to turn, and the task was slow and cumbersome. John got the idea of connecting an upright steel beam to the top of the wheel to give it weight and leverage. The Kenyan farmers proceeded to make this device, and it made their work easier and more efficient. Seven years later, on a return trip to Kenya, John noticed the fodder cutting wheels were now running on electricity, but each one still had its steel beam.

On another occasion he noticed that village farmers were skimming off the cream from the top of their cows' milk and feeding it to the hogs or using it for cooking grease. If they used butter at all, they bought it at a store in a population center like Nairobi or Mombasa, since they didn't know how to make it themselves. John took a milk can, removed the handle, cut a hole in the bottom, and made a butter churn. Then he showed the farmers how to make butter, just as he had learned to do it himself as a child on the plantation in Mississippi.

For John, Spencer, and Derek the Kenyans were heroic and inspiring. Early in the century British settlers had created a caste hierarchy with Europeans at the top, then Arabs and Asians, and finally Africans at the bottom. The settlers had gradually taken over most tribal land, forcing Africans into the cities where they exploited them as the lowest class of laborers. But decades of being alienated from their land had ultimately provoked the Kikuyu tribe to retreat to the forests and organize a terrorist movement to throw the whites out of Africa.

These were the people the whites called the Mau Maus. They accused Kenyatta, the longtime leader of Kikuyu nationalism, of plotting against the government by creating the Mau Mau movement. They jailed him for eight years, and during that time the nationalist movement spread. It was inspiring to hear how the many Kenyan tribes had put aside their differences to "pull together"—harambee—in a nationalist movement that finally overcame the British Empire. With the revolution's success, indigenous people became free to reclaim their land and build an economy serviceable to their own needs. Touring the country, John could feel the immensity of possibilities around him.

One of the most moving experiences he, Spencer, and Derek had was to sit and listen to one of the old revolutionary leaders tell his story. They spent a morning with him in his home, and he told them how he had grown up on a plantation where his father had been a butler. Once, when his father had dropped a tray, the young boy saw his white boss take him out back and beat him. The boy's anger burned, and years later after he had grown up, he heard Kenyatta speak and he decided to join the nationalist movement.

In their forest outposts the Kikuyu nationalists held elaborate oathing rites to bind themselves in loyalty to one another and to the revolution. The old colonel spoke of gathering with other revolutionary leaders as they opened the veins in their arms, letting their blood run together into a bucket, drinking from it, and vowing their permanent loyalty to the movement and the secrecy of their transactions on pain of death. As happens in uprisings of oppressed indigenous peoples, the Mau Mau movement was often excessive, with Africans killing other Africans they deemed collaborators more often than they killed Europeans. But the Kikuyu were also dexterous in forest warfare, and crack British troops could not overcome them.

This old revolutionary colonel became a convert to Christianity after the revolution. He told John and his sons, "I fought to free my people the first time, and then I came back to free them a second time." His story and the story of the Kenyan revolutionary struggle stayed with all three Perkins men. They admired the fierce determination of these Africans who had stood up to the British Empire and won. The experience recalled their own recent struggle against a white caste system in the American South. They identified with the Kenyans and they felt a surge of pride in their African heritage. The spirit they caught in Kenya would kindle their own harambee movement when they got back to Jackson.

In Kenya John had found an indigenous people with self-respect and cohesion, committed to the process of economic development. When he first went to Australia in 1983, he encountered a much less promising situation among the largely demoralized Aborigines. Sam Kamaleson had asked him to be one of the facilitators at a conference involving worldwide church leadership and representatives of the Aborigines and other concerned Australians. He thought the common ground between African Americans and Aborigines, both in terms of their blackness and their cultural and economic marginalization, would add much to John's credibility as a speaker.

Traveling around Australia John found the Aborigines to be among the most needy people in the world. As Australia developed its freewheeling urban capitalism, the indigenous population was shunted aside, just as Indians had been in the development of the United States. In the 1960s the Australian federal government took responsibility for the condition of the Aborigines, appropriating a large and continuous cash allotment to provide fully for their needs. As he gained exposure to it, John came to think this system was so all-encompassing that it reinforced the very poverty and helplessness it aimed to relieve.

He knew from his own experience that government aid could have salutary effects. In poverty-wracked Mississippi he had seen federal programs for the financing of homes and for rural electrification that improved conditions among his people. Public aid in the form of cheap loans and programs to spur development could help the poor toward employment, a modicum of autonomy, and prosperity. Selective welfare was often necessary as a safety net. But complete government provision, he thought, undermined people's will to solve their own problems. John observed rampant alcoholism and self-destructive behaviors among the Aborigines and attributed these problems to the demoralization that occurs in a system that abrogates personal initiative. He favored bringing capital and training into the community along with evangelism, thus stirring hope and competence among the people.

Sam Kamaleson saw qualities in John that gave him unique effectiveness in addressing the needs of marginalized peoples like the Australian Aborigines. Three factors undergirded John's appeal: his African American identity, his ability to simplify and articulate the concepts of development making them accessible to everyone, and his unique way of wrapping these concepts in a biblical vision that captured people's hearts. In the 1983 conference John dialogued with Aboriginal leaders, including the only Aboriginal senator, who made a strong profession of Christian faith at one of John's teaching sessions.

Many of the people who came to this and later conferences where John was teaching were people of mixed descent who were generally more educated and integrated within white Australian culture. They were often more interested in Christianity and development than were the pure-blood Aborigines. The traditional Aboriginal religion was centered around totemism and ancestor worship. Many indigenous peoples around the world, including a number of the North American Indian tribes, have practiced totemism. It is a faith based on close clan identification with a particular animal or plant, which forms a totem that imparts spiritual strength to the community. Together with veneration of ancestors, totemism gives the clans cohesion and continuity, but these practices hinder their receptiveness to Christianity and contribute to their isolation from the larger society. On the other hand, John's strong emphasis on building and strengthening community life gave his holistic gospel resonance among many of the Aborigines he spoke to.

The first trip to Australia stoked enthusiasm for his message among church leaders and led to a return invitation. A few months later, in early 1984 during the Australian summer, he came for two weeks to teach at a large Christian gathering held at a soccer field campsite near the town of Port Augusta. The atmosphere was similar to a camp meeting, with people staying in tents and motor homes, cooking their own food as well as participating in communal meals, going to morning worship together, and listening to John's teachings. In this jamboree-like setting John spoke daily to eight or nine hundred people. After teaching in the mornings, he had lunch with the people, and in the informal afternoons forty to fifty young people gathered around him and they talked faith and development.

Many of the Aborigines responded to John enthusiastically and this led World Vision to sponsor a third trip in which John spoke in population centers across the Australian continent. On this trip he held press conferences and presented his philosophy of community development with the purpose of stimulating hope in the broader Australian society. A pall of resignation had hung about the country for years concerning the plight of the Aborigines. The welfare programs had been launched largely because the government had become convinced that these indigenous people were incapable of improving their own economic state.

Vera Mae accompanied her husband on the third trip along with philanthropist Howard Ahmanson. Scion of a prominent Los Angeles banking family, Howard had been attracted to the unique Perkins mix of evangelical theology, self-help, and social action. He had attended Voice of Calvary's 1982 Jubilee gathering in Jackson and was now becoming personally involved in John's development projects. Prior to their arrival in Australia, they had stopped in India, where John had spoken in Poona and Bangelor before flying on to Melbourne. Seeing the wretchedness of Indian poverty, Vera Mae remarked on how grateful she felt for what they did have even in the poor places in America.

After arriving in Australia and resting for a day in Melbourne, John met with his World Vision sponsors and they held a press conference. The media's interest in John stemmed from his being black and his having done successful development among his own people in the United States. As he spoke to the press, he did not pretend to have in-depth knowledge of Aboriginal issues. Instead he talked about the African American experience, presenting it as a model that could be adapted to fit Australian needs. In that context he described how helping people become more productive and self-sufficient gives them hope and changes their whole outlook.

On this trip John spoke mainly in cities along the east coast—Melbourne, Sydney, Brisbane, and Townsville—where much of the country's population live. The Aborigines and people of mixed descent he spoke to in those urban areas were among the ones more assimilated into white Australia. But he also made forays into the Aboriginal reserve in the outback, where he could experience culture and conditions directly. On a later trip in 1987 he spent a good deal of time in Alice Springs, a reserve community at the center of the Australian continent.

John learned that church missionaries had originally played a key role in the reserve settlements, bringing literacy to Aborigines, planting orchards, and starting up enterprises like furniture factories. But as is common in developing nations, people who acquired education and skills often abandoned their ancestral communities and moved to the cities in search of opportunity. A secularizing process also occurred as government bureaucracy moved in and eclipsed church influence. John observed that while the missionaries had taught skills and self-reliance, the white government workers who replaced them did everything for the Aborigines. They not only doled out the money, but they also became the administrators and teachers and plumbers and electricians, and the native people were reduced to idleness. They had the government allotment, so they did not starve, but their dependency and lack of meaningful work demoralized them.

John's 1987 tour in Australia, which lasted fifty-two days, was one of his longest trips abroad. Vera Mae didn't go this time, but Derek did. And he absorbed a powerful experience that would fire him up to return to Pasadena and begin his clan-building among the youth at Harambee. They went to all the major cities on Aus-

John Perkins with Aborigines in Australia.

tralia's heavily populated east coast, from Darwin to Melbourne. And John spent a great deal of time teaching development in the outback in places like Alice Springs. Along with evangelism and spiritual training his purpose was to teach the principles of cooperative small business development. People expressed interest in the cooperative idea, and when he returned to Australia a fifth time in 1991, he was pleased to find a scattering of small craft and retail co-ops around the country.

This shorter trip down under in 1991 became an occasion for his eldest son to participate with him in speaking at Australian colleges. Spencer and his wife, Nancy, had accompanied John and Vera Mae earlier that year on a trip to South Africa.

Spencer and Nancy had met at Voice of Calvary when Nancy served as a volunteer. She came from a Mennonite family and had grown up in the rolling farm country of southern Pennsylvania's Lancaster County. Their interracial love incarnated the theme of reconciliation as Spencer and Nancy became leaders of Antioch Community, the biracial communal household they had formed in the early eighties.

The South African trip had been one of John's few disappointing engagements overseas. Though apartheid was breaking down by this time, its grim effects were everywhere and deeply disconcerting to outsiders sensitive to racial oppression. Seeing the great disparities of wealth—wretched black poverty just down the road from great white opulence—John, Vera Mae, Spencer, and Nancy all felt the pain of the chasm apartheid had created.

John's church presentations went well because there was a strong minority of black and white Christians who supported reconciliation and interracial engagement. At one big evangelical church in Johannesburg he spoke to a thousand people on a Sunday morning. About 10 percent of them were black, and for South Africa that was indeed racial progress. But while individual churches received him well, he kept running into deep factionalization among South African Christians, blacks as well as whites, which severely compromised the church's power to lead in the process of racial healing.

Most of the evangelical churches were racially segregated and staunchly resistant to change. The liberal Anglican and Methodist com-

**John talks with urban missiologist Ray Bakke
in Johannesburg, South Africa.**

munions, which were working against apartheid, consequently shunned involvement in evangelical events. Evangelical intelligentsia, coming out of Dutch Reformed backgrounds, were strongly supportive of racial reconciliation, but the deep fissure between evangelical and liberal churches cut these more conservative Protestants off from their intellectual counterparts among the Anglicans and Methodists.

Hence John and his party of progressive evangelicals enjoyed little success when they tried to rally people of diverse religious backgrounds together in events like a March for Jesus. The marchers were to gather in an amphitheater that seated five thousand, but as they filed in at the march's end only about a thousand people scattered through the stands. A major black leader who had marched with them did not feel comfortable enough to sit on the platform with John, caught as he was between hostile factions.

The deep and persistent divisions among South Africans and resistance to reconciliation among both black and white Christians made it impossible for John to act as a unifying force. He thought about how when David had overthrown King Saul's tyranny, he had gathered together all the poor, the outcast, and people in debt to help him do so. But here in South Africa most of the churches were hardly doing likewise, immured as they were in stubborn division and mutual hostility. John, Vera Mae, Spencer, and Nancy found themselves leaving South Africa feeling frustrated and discouraged. The state of the evangelical church there resembled that of Mississippi in the sixties.

Later in the same year, when Spencer spent two weeks teaching with his father in Australia, they found a much more positive situation, with Christians united in support of Aboriginal advancement and receptive to the reconciliation message. Yet while John's ideas were becoming popular in Australia, he saw monumental problems of Aboriginal disadvantage harboring little prospect of rapid change. Still he believed the principles of development he had worked out in Mendenhall were strongly applicable here.

He urged assimilated Aboriginal Christians along with sympathetic whites in his audiences to relocate in communities in the reserve. And he urged them to start businesses there and do discipleship training and leadership development. He knew that relocating people with skills and developing an indigenous leadership among the Aborigines would give them the best chance for real progress. To aid this process John tried to get Aborigines to come to Jackson for training, but with little success. He found they were so tied to their clans that the sense of isolation and loneliness they experienced when away from home kept them from coming. Here a little American-style individualism might have been helpful.

As John made his trips down under, he also was invited to New Zealand on three different occasions, initially in 1986 by the Anglican Dean of the Chapel at Auckland, who also happened to be chairman of World Vision's board. His purpose in coming to New Zealand had somewhat more to do with racial reconciliation than development. The indigenous people had long since made peace with and integrated their lives and institutions with those of their British colonizers and they had moved successfully toward a status of full equality. But racial tensions were increasing, as native New Zealanders strove to reassert their separate non-European status. They were partaking of a growing movement of indigenous peoples the world over to assert their cultural independence from the West.

When the British colonized these large islands in the South Pacific in the eighteenth and early nineteenth centuries, there

A *hui* (tribal gathering) at a Maori *marae* (community center) in New Zealand. Spencer and Vera Mae are fifth and sixth from the left.

331

were a number of indigenous Polynesian tribes whom they called the Maori living there. The British were able to take advantage of inter-tribal warfare and their own superior technology to establish them-selves in New Zealand. The Maoris were fierce warriors who commonly slaughtered one another and they annihilated more than one group of colonizers. But Europeans came in ever greater numbers in the early nineteenth century, and they warred intermittently with the Maori, purchased and occupied their land, and eventually made an ambigu-ous peace in the 1840 Treaty of Waitangi. The treaty gave sovereignty to the British Crown but permitted Maori to possess land as British sub-jects. In Maori tribal custom land tenure was communal, while Euro-peans (Pakehas) held it individually; and so the Maori were at a dis-advantage in countering the flood of Pakeha claims to land ownership.

The remainder of the nineteenth century was marked by Pakeha purchase and occupation of most of the land that encompassed New Zealand's north and south islands. This Europeanization of land, sim-ilar to what had gone on in the United States and Australia, did not occur without a good deal of Maori resistance. Like most indigenous peoples, the Maoris' tribalism hurt their ability to resist the European onslaught. In 1858, with the goal of providing unity and government to keep their remaining lands from falling into Pakeha hands, three tribes came together and chose a king.

Most of the tribes did not support the "King Movement," and loss of land continued. War occurred from 1860 to 1865. The immediate result of war was the Pakeha government's takeover of millions more acres of the native population's land. But reversal began as peace was made and Maoris received manhood suffrage and four seats in Parlia-ment in 1867. Through the acquisition of political power they began to gradually acquire a firmer position for their people and culture.

One thing that helped the Maoris ultimately to make peace with the Pakehas and obtain equal standing was their Christianization. In the early years of the nineteenth century missionaries were able to make strong inroads into this population. Many converted, abandoning their accustomed practices of slavery, cannibalism, and polygamy. Chris-tianity gave the Maori common cultural ground with Pakehas and the basis for eventual dialogue and cooperation.

In New Zealand the Maori influence was much stronger than that of the Aborigines in Australia. The islands were much smaller than the

Australian continent, and the Maori culture much more sophisticated and pervasive. So when John visited New Zealand as the guest of a Maori queen in 1988, he had a strong sense of an intact, well-functioning nation and culture among these indigenous people. He saw none of the degradation, alienation, or isolation from the society-at-large that he saw in Aboriginal Australia. A strong Maori presence in Parliament, the result of proportional representation, made government policy bend in their direction, and they were able to regain some of the land formerly taken from them.

The queen who invited John to come and share his philosophy of reconciliation and development was the reigning monarch over the three tribes that had begun the King Movement in the previous century. Like most of the Maori, these tribes were Christian, with the highest proportion being Anglican. The occasion was the queen's twenty-ninth annual coronation celebration. It was marked by a *hui*, or peaceful gathering. It was very much a communal event, held in one of the *marae,* or open areas with meeting houses that were interspersed throughout New Zealand where Maori were able to carry on their public events. The *hui* lasted four days, and something close to two hundred people stayed the whole time in the meeting house, which was like a big gymnasium with padding on the floor for bedding down. So John had a captive audience to instruct in his Three Rs.

One reason the Maori were so receptive to John was the previous contact they had made with him during his 1986 visit. On that occasion, as representative of World Vision, he had addressed a number of MPs and department heads in a room in the Parliament building. This kind of exposure aroused in a core of New Zealanders interest in his ideas, and the following year he greeted seventy-five of them, chiefly Maoris, at the Destiny Conference in Atlanta. Destiny was a short-lived black-led movement that split off from InterVarsity to attend specifically to the interests of African Americans. The Maori who had heard John in New Zealand and had come to Atlanta were attracted by the nascent movement's support for indigenous peoples worldwide.

In his travels to foreign countries John's purpose was mainly one of motivation and encouragement. He roused people's awareness of the material and nonmaterial resources they had and he encouraged them to tap into those resources, organize, and develop them. His encouragement also came as he acted as ambassador for reconciliation. His own story made him a spokesman and living symbol of the reconciliation message and a powerful catalyst for change. This was a role he relished and played with singular effectiveness on two occasions in Ireland, first in the Protestant North and then in the Catholic South.

In 1988 the leadership of the Presbyterian Church, the largest religious body in Northern Ireland, invited him to speak in four major population centers. In Northern Ireland ancient issues of territorial nationalism, economics, and culture have played themselves out on a bloody field of religion. Irish nationalists, who want separation from the United Kingdom and union with the Irish Republic to the south, are of the Roman Catholic minority. The Protestant majority, in all its denominational forms, represents the country's historical tie with Great Britain. For many centuries the English occupied and oppressed Catholic Ireland. At the same time Scotch Irish Protestants, who migrated to Northern Ireland in the Puritan epoch, eclipsed its Catholic population and forged its identity as part of Great Britain.

**John and Vera Mae at Oxford with Chris Sugden
of the Oxford Center for Mission Studies.**

A superficial appraisal would find Northern Ireland today a deeply religious place, since the great majority identify closely with a religious label. But the religion has a lot in common with the white Protestantism John had experienced in Mississippi during the civil rights movement. It is largely a badge of ethnic nationalism cloaking the ancient antagonism between Protestants loyal to Great Britain and Catholics with ties to the Irish Republic. Recognizing the contradiction between this spirit of hatred and the reconciling spirit of Christ, the northern Irish Presbyterian leader extended John the invitation.

Because organized religion is such a prominent factor in Irish public life, John's speaking appearances became major events, which drew broad media coverage. He spoke in some of the country's largest auditoriums and he was interviewed on radio and television. The schedule he followed was virtually identical in each locale, meeting with pastors from mid-morning through the noon hour and then speaking to groups of students. As had been common over the course of John's career, he made his biggest impression on the youth. With his itinerary moving toward its conclusion in Belfast, he became more and more aware of the walls of religious antagonism the young people were growing up behind. From his discussions with Protestant students, every indication was that they would not take the initiative and reach out to their Catholic peers. John searched for a way to counter this resistance. He knew that if his presence and his testimony were going to have any lasting impact, he had to get through to the younger generation and challenge them to break down those walls.

The last occasion when he spoke to students was in Belfast. The auditorium was packed with Protestant youth, pastors, and church people. As John was concluding his message, he wanted to say something that would drive home the centrality to Christianity of the concept of reconciliation. He wanted to make it plain and personal, and so he said, "The purpose of the gospel is to reconcile people to God and to each other across racial, economic, and cultural barriers, and if your love for Christ doesn't cause you to reach out and embrace a Catholic, you don't even understand the purpose of the gospel." As soon as he got the words out of his mouth, the whole body of students rose clapping and cheering. His bold challenge had touched their idealistic young spirits. John stood there engulfed in the thunderous ovation his words were receiving. The students' powerful response deeply moved him. And at the same time he noticed that most of the pastors were remaining in their seats.

Four years later John returned as main speaker for the convention of the Presbyterian General Assembly. But this time the venue was in the south, in Dublin, a historic occasion. It took place in a convention center that had once been a place where cattle were traded. Every night it was packed with people, and there were thousands of Catholics there along with the Presbyterians. John spoke daily, retelling his story, explaining his ideas, and laying emphasis on reconciliation. And every day he was on radio, once for an hour and a half with a Catholic priest who was the most popular talk show host in the country. Religious news is deemed as important as any other news in Ireland and is always well covered. The American black preacher's story and his appearance as keynoter in a Presbyterian convention in the heart of Catholic Ireland were more than newsworthy.

In the trips he made for World Vision, John played an inspirational role, gathering people together and motivating them to reconcile across lines of division and work for development of the disadvantaged. Closer to home in the Caribbean, he could get more integrally involved in economic and human development. In 1977, at the invitation of Claude Noel, the Haitian who headed the Evangelical Association of the Caribbean, John first went to Haiti. The occasion was the annual retreat of the board of directors of the Southern Cooperative Development Fund. Their practice was to meet in a place in need of the kind of projects they were funding, and Haiti, the poorest country in the Western Hemisphere, was most appropriate. Noel wanted them to see some of the development projects that were already in progress.

As a result of John's visiting Haiti, Voice of Calvary became involved in Haitian development, largely through the training and support of Jean Thomas, the seminary student who came to Mississippi in 1977, shortly after John visited Haiti.

When Thomas returned to Haiti, he had been away from his country for fourteen years and he had to thoroughly refamiliarize himself with rural Haitian needs to be of any use there. Like Dolphus Weary, he might have said, "I ain't comin' back," when he left his long-suffering homeland, and who could blame him? Haitians, brutalized by two generations of Duvalier tyranny, were pouring into the United States. But when Thomas went to work at Voice of Calvary, becoming John Perkins's assistant and learning the process of community development, he began to see the necessity of relocation.

336

John taught that relocating among the people in need is the essential incarnational act that affirms the inherent dignity of the people. It celebrates others' worth, he said, when you go and live where they live, feel what they feel, suffer what they suffer. He liked to talk about how the prophet Ezekiel went among his people and sat with them and agonized with them. And the gospels say that in Christ's incarnation God became one of us, "pitched his tent with us," so he was able to show his love to us and bear our burdens. This was the teaching that Jean Thomas was constantly exposed to at Voice of Calvary, and the mentoring he received from John Perkins gave him the motivation to go back to rural Haiti and live among the people.

In 1978 Claude Noel and Voice of Calvary cooperated in organizing a pastors' conference in Port-au-Prince. The large American contingent, led by John and Jean Thomas, chartered a plane out of New Orleans to the Haitian capital and stayed for a week in the dormitories of a boarding school where the conference was held. John taught at the conference and he spoke in several churches. The week's events sowed the seeds for Christian community development in Haiti. Businesspeople, missionaries, doctors, and others attending the conference came alive with enthusiasm. Voice of Calvary started a special development fund for Haiti, with Thomas as chief administrator and fundraiser. And the Netherlands later issued a grant of two hundred thousand dollars in support of Christian community development in Haiti.

In 1981 Jean Thomas's brother Paul began the work of development in six rural Haitian communities. One of those six hamlets, Fond des Bancs, became the target community for VOC's Haiti Christian Development Fund. It was where Jean Thomas would relocate when he returned to Haiti. As he reacquainted himself with the felt needs of the people, he was able to spark vital development, drawing on the resources based in Jackson. John Perkins, H Spees, Phil Reed, and others went on-site, helped, and encouraged Thomas as he set about launching a series of projects that would develop the basic infrastructure and the agricultural economy of Fond des Bancs. Together with the people, they built roads and they reforested the land with fast-growing hardwood trees that would protect the soil from erosion and produce wood for fuel. They found a way to pipe in pure drinking water, the lack of which had caused disease and death among the townspeople and their animals. They also built and stocked two large pig barns to replenish pigs, which they had had to kill because of an epidemic of swine flu. They brought in medical teams to develop a health care facility and help fight the diseases of malnutrition, which have been common among Fond des Bancs's children. When Jean Thomas and Fond des Bancs's families celebrated the opening of a new community school, John Perkins came down to participate in the week-long ceremonies.

Fond des Bancs became a community akin to Mendenhall, serving as a model of Christian community development for Haiti. It was the first, the most direct, and most thoroughgoing transplantation abroad of John Perkins's holistic development concept. Jean Thomas had come to Jackson, where he was mentored, trained, and equipped to return to a community in his native country and apply what he had learned. Voice of Calvary remained closely involved with the work as it germinated in Haiti. Here was the seedbed starting to flower internationally.

23

CHRISTIAN COMMUNITY DEVELOPMENT ASSOCIATION

In the early eighties, as he was expanding the Harambee Center into the former drug houses on Navarro, John found himself in ever greater demand as speaker and teacher in evangelical ministries around the world. His work and his ideas were now familiar to many in evangelical institutions of higher learning. In 1980 when he was still in Mississippi, Wheaton College gave him his first honorary degree, a doctor of laws. Some years before, when he had first become involved with World Vision, Bob Pierce had told him it would be good for some college to give him an honorary doctorate, because it would establish his credentials in the evangelical world and open many doors to him. Wheaton, founded in 1835, was one of the oldest and most respected of the evangelical liberal arts colleges. And receiving such an honor from Billy Graham's alma mater was a clear sign of broad recognition among the evangelical intelligentsia.

It was a richly emotional experience for John as he donned cap and gown, walked in the academic procession, and spoke his philosophy of development to the graduating class. He thought about the inadequate little schoolhouse in Mississippi and his stunted formal education. He thought about Maybelle Armstrong, the strong teacher who had encouraged him to take pride in his heritage and learn all he could. John was now a long way from the cotton fields, the sharecroppers' shacks, and the flimsy one-room schoolhouses of his childhood. The talented black adults he had known in Mississippi, people who would not accept the system's judgment of their inferiority, had molded his consciousness. They were the people he knew would feel most proud and vindicated if they could be there with him now.

Other honors followed in rapid succession. In 1982 Gordon College gave him a doctor of public service degree. In 1983 Huntington College, a United Brethren in Christ school in rural Indiana, awarded him a doctor of humanities. As he collected these accolades, requests from the evangelical lecture circuit grew ever more numerous. One of the most gratifying was the invitation to give the Staley Lectures. Delivered at Christian institutions across the country, the prestigious Staley Lectures made an ideal pulpit for an itinerant speaker like John. Among the other lecturers were evangelist Leighton Ford, preacher Tony Evans, and academics Ron Sider, Tony Campolo, and Bill Pannell.

At about the same time, in the eighties, John's work was becoming known at the national level. In 1983 President Reagan named him to a task force he was appointing to investigate the prevalence of hunger in America, review existent programs of food assistance, and make recommendations. Periodically, over the better part of a year, John sat with twelve other task force members, sharing a smorgasbord of political, business, and humanitarian credentials, and listened to testimony. There was one other African American, Erma Davis, who headed the George Washington Carver Association, a health center in Peoria. They met for a week in Washington at the Department of Agriculture, and then they held hearings in selected cities around the country. Individual task force members also traveled on their own to other cities, thus broadening their information base. John went to Honolulu, where he visited rescue missions and talked with destitute women abandoned by navy boyfriends who had brought them to the island paradise.

The Reagan Task Force on Food Assistance drew on the research of a professional staff, which provided detailed working papers with a plethora of statistics and comprehensive descriptions of federal safety net programs dating back to the 1930s. They scrutinized the effects of everything, including school lunches and breakfasts, commodity price supports for farmers, and administration of the food stamps program. They assessed the range and impact of state, local, and private sector food assistance. One set of papers reviewed the nutritional status of Americans and the impact of the different food assistance programs on the needy populations they were enacted to serve. Studies were included on general topics like the nutritional food intake of low-income groups and the complex, growing problem of homelessness.

During the fall of 1983 the task force conducted hearings in Los Angeles, Kansas City, Peoria, Houston, Jackson, and Boston. John was present at all but the Boston venue. They collected testimony from a wide range of people involved in food assistance, including government office-holders, aid recipients, and charitable organization workers.

Among the people who spoke at the hearings in Jackson were Lem Tucker and II Spees. Both men's statements reflected the orientation to holism and empowerment they had gained working with John. Lem advocated passage of a public law that would comprehensively address job training, housing assistance, health care, economic aid, and food assistance. H stressed the necessity of individual "owner-ship and responsibility to a God-fearing society." Representing the South Central Mississippi Rural Health Association, he laid out the importance of locally based programs as opposed to those run by bureaucracies. He was advocating federal support for the kinds of community development work he had been doing over the past twelve years in Mississippi.

In their evaluation of ongoing programs and recommendations for improvement the task force stressed the "critical role played by private organizations in the nation's food assistance safety net." Ordinarily private charitable programs were more caring and closely attuned to people's needs than were those based in Washington. Among these they mentioned food banks, food pantries, and soup kitchens. One of the task force members, Arizona banker John Diggs, was an originator of Second Harvest, which gleaned farm crops remaining in the fields and organized the urban food banks that distributed them to the poor. The food banks, as they had proliferated in the seventies and eighties, had become a highly successful form of privately based food assistance.

Task force advocacy of federal support for private and local efforts recognized the vitality of the food banks and of community-based associations like Voice of Calvary and The Mendenhall Ministries. In support of such voluntary efforts in the private sector, they recommended cutting federal red tape so as to encourage corporations to give more. They also recommended giving similar tax breaks to smaller, noncorporate food donors, including deductions for farmers who allowed gleanings of their excess crops.

In wanting to enhance private sector involvement in food assistance, the task force did not at the same time seek to diminish federal aid. When Reagan had formed it, Democrats, knowing his conservative predilections, had expected it to exercise a strong bias against the public programs. In fact some of John's friends and associates, who identified with liberal Democratic programs, were urging him to write a dissenting statement. But task force appointees were motivated by compassion, and, like John, more pragmatic than ideological. They would commonly defer to his judgment in evaluating rural public assistance, as with the WIC program. John told them about his own mother's death from pellagra, and he and Erma Davis spoke of WIC's effectiveness in providing nutrition for women and children at their own health care facilities. On this and other issues the task force shared diverse opinions but had no trouble arriving at a consensus.

The document they published supported the ongoing programs of the federal safety net, suggesting a number of measures to increase its efficiency. They recommended simplifying food stamps application procedures and staggering distribution of the stamps throughout the month to keep merchants from raising prices when stamps were distributed. John suggested that seniors be permitted the use of food stamps in restaurants. And the task force criticized states that excluded the homeless from eligibility by requiring a home mailing address. Based on the work of staff researchers, they recommended replacement of generalized poverty line figures with a more accurate means of gauging necessary assistance. Establishing a "market basket of general necessities" and tracking changes in prices would enable the government to adjust payments so that low-income households could maintain a basic standard of living.

The practical, humane suggestions that characterized the task force's 1984 report reflected many of John's opinions. Maintaining the public safety net while enhancing private sector participation and decentralizing administration to more accessible state and local levels were policies in keeping with his philosophy. The report recognized the continuing necessity for government programs but at the same time it articulated a belief that public and private sources of aid, operating closer to the recipients, were more efficient and compassionate. Interlaced throughout the report was the position that encouraging private sector and local associational involvement was coming closer to people's needs and working to decrease their dependency. Actual Reagan administration policy would remain less supportive of the federal safety net than were John Perkins or this task force report. Contrary to the report's recommendations, the Reagan budget would cut food stamp distribution and health services to the poor as well as overall welfare eligibility.

While serving on the Reagan Task Force on Food Assistance, speaking internationally for World Vision, and constantly crisscrossing the country, the radius of John's activities had become worldwide by the eighties. Simultaneously he was trying to wrest houses from drug dealers and build an effective neighborhood ministry in Pasadena. Here he relied on others to do the hands-on work in development and administration. Leaders coming out of the neighborhood and from around the country, along with members of the younger Perkins generation, were rapidly taking over. As the means of supporting the spread of Christian community development as an ever broadening movement, John had created the John M. Perkins Foundation for Reconciliation and Development in 1984. During the eighties he came to rely more and more on the collective wisdom of the foundation's diverse and growing board of directors. The semi-annual board meetings became creative forums of ideas for propagating John's Three Rs.

Over the years of his traveling and speaking, John had established ongoing relationships with others who were involved in Christian community development. The Chicago area had become a seedbed of urban Christian communitarianism, beginning in the mid-sixties when missionary-minded people like Mary Nelson began to move back to the city to live and do development among the poor. Mary was a Lutheran who had initially come to join her brother, a pastor of an inner-city parish. Her subsequent work in the deteriorating West Garfield Park neighborhood, along with Wayne Gordon's in Lawndale, Glen Kehrein and Raleigh Washington's in the Austin neighborhood, and a growing number of other holistic development efforts were bringing spiritual and material transformation within some of Chicago's festering slums. And it was starting to happen in many other urban settings across the nation.

Mendenhall, Jackson, the Three Rs, the International Study Center, and years of spreading the holistic gospel had combined to make John the movement's pivotal unifying figure. As the community associations were starting to proliferate in the eighties, people like Gordon and Nelson in Chicago, Bob Lupton in Atlanta, Kathy Dudley in Dallas, and Lem Tucker in Jackson began to dialogue with John about starting a national body to nourish and spread Christian community development. In 1988 John brought the idea before the Perkins Foundation Board and the process was set in motion. In February of 1989 about fifty people came to a one-day organizational meeting at Chicago's O'Hare Airport. Other preliminary meetings followed with Wayne Gordon and Lawndale Community Church acting as host. Out of these meetings came the first full-blown Thursday-to-Sunday convention as one hundred eighty people met at Lawndale in October.

This amounted to the official launching of Christian Community Development Association. They held small-group, workshop-like meetings during the day where they shared their ideas and experiences around subjects like housing and youth ministry. In the evenings there were general speakers, including Perkins and Gordon. Dolphus Weary spoke that year, and Melvin Anderson, who had headed Voice of Calvary's housing rehab program, also spoke. Melvin's appearance was a poignant one because Lem Tucker had died the past June of a rapidly progressing lymphatic cancer. Suddenly catapulted into leadership due to Lem's illness, Melvin was making valiant efforts to guide VOC through the shock of their loss.

**Perkins family members at the organizational conference
of the Christian Community Development Association, 1989.
Left to right: Deborah, Priscilla, Spencer, John, Vera Mae, Derek.**

On Saturday they held their first business meeting, where they voted unanimously to become a formal association. They chose a board of fourteen directors with Wayne Gordon as president. The Pasadena-based Perkins Foundation, which funded CCDA during its first two years of existence, had set up an office near Fresno, California. But with Gordon in charge and the new association's center of activity gravitating to Chicago, they moved CCDA's headquarters to Lawndale. With Chicago's large number of community development ministries, its central location, and the CCDA home office located there, it was the convenient place to hold CCDA's 1990 and 1991 conventions.

CCDA represented the coming of age of a movement that was knitted together largely through John Perkins's relentless traveling and spreading his community-building gospel. While John's work in Mississippi and his Three Rs of Christian community development had become the movement's chief catalyst, a number of pioneers had also played pivotal roles by making independent decisions to reverse the flight to the suburbs and secure beachheads in the inner city. Mary Nelson's 1965 move had led to the creation of Bethel New Life Ministries, which would become one of the nation's largest efforts in Christian urban redevelopment. In the same year Ray Bakke, a pastor and academic who would tutor scores of evangelicals in urban missiology, had also moved into Chicago's inner city. Bakke and Nelson provided strong resources when Wayne Gordon relocated to Chicago's crumbling north Lawndale neighborhood ten years later in 1975.

A contemporary of Spencer and Joanie Perkins, Gordon was one of the new generation of socially conscious evangelicals represented in *Sojourners* and *The Other Side*. But this young high school coach didn't express his commitment in terms of politics or public policy. His style was intensely personal. His desire was to live and work in the inner city because he had a heart for the people there. His roots were not in the individualized seclusion of suburbia, but the more communal atmosphere of a midwestern small town, Fort Dodge, Iowa, where he had grown up close to black families in the poorer section.

He attended Wheaton College in suburban Chicago, just as John Perkins was becoming known there, and after graduation he moved right into Lawndale, doing substitute teaching and assisting the football coach at the local Farragut High School. This was the neighborhood where he would plant himself, making friends, rearing family, growing a church,

Wayne Gordon moved into the Lawndale neighborhood as an assistant football coach, and later the youth group he started grew into Lawndale Community Church, today a 500-member interracial congregation and the center of people-developing enterprises.

reaching out to the community. He was the only white person on the block but he was there to stay.

When he moved to Lawndale, Gordon was only generally aware of John Perkins, but his approach was remarkably similar to John's, since he was relocating and making the community's needs his own. When he was organizing his first little storefront, he put in a donated washer and dryer because some women had told him they wanted a safe place to get their washing done. As he read John's books in those early years, he found strong validation for his own commitment to live with the people and get to know their concerns. Indeed, he lived in the community for some three years, enduring what seemed an endless string of break-ins, before starting Lawndale Community Church. By this time he had worked into full-time positions coaching and teaching, the only staff member who lived in the neighborhood.

Seeing himself more as coach than pastor, Gordon hadn't intended to start a church. But as he became known in the neighborhood, running his Bible studies and discipling his little group of Christians, the people asked him to start a church and they asked him to be their pastor. So they started a parish-style church, and he became pastor but he would never be ordained, preferring to remain just "Coach." His identity was in athletics and he built and publicized his ministry among evangelicals in organizations like the Fellowship of Christian Athletes. Neighborhood sports and the close mentoring associated with coaching played an integral part in Lawndale leadership development, as they always had in the Perkins ministries.

As did John in Mississippi and then in Pasadena, Wayne Gordon, organizing in Lawndale, listened intently to the people in the community as they articulated their needs. Living among them, he had become acutely aware of the absence of jobs, health care, recreation facilities, and adequate housing. As he witnessed the daily inner-city carnage, he knew that cohesive neighborhood action against crime and drugs was indispensable. Partnering with suburban churches and businesspeople, obtaining grants and getting others with skills and resources to relocate, Lawndale Community Church would eventually address each of these concerns.

Gordon didn't meet John Perkins until 1982 when he went to Jackson to attend Voice of Calvary's Jubilee Celebration. By that time he and his wife, Anne, had become co-owners of a Lawndale apartment building with a medical missionary couple, Art and Linda Jones; the church had created a recreation center, and the beginnings of health care were in the offing. When John came on his first visit to Lawndale that year, he found a community development work in a formative stage that was wholly coherent with what he had done in Mississippi, and he and "Gordie" began a close, collaborative friendship.

By the 1990s Lawndale Community Church had become a center for an ever growing cluster of people-developing enterprises. An expanded medical clinic was caring for four thousand patients per month. Neighborhood residents, including a horde of teenagers on spring break, had expended "sweat equity" to build a modern gym. Housing included a shelter for homeless families, apartments with modest rents, and a Rehab for Ownership program, where prospective owners, together with Lawndale's building crews, put in hundreds of hours to renovate previously derelict housing, which they were then able to purchase. This sort of modern community house-raising was becoming an integral aspect of Christian community development. In 1995 Habitat for Humanity would join CCDA's loose affiliation. Started by Congregationalist attorney Millard Fuller in the seventies, Habitat had since become the largest and best-known builder of housing for poor people's ownership. Now Fuller would place its experience and resources behind CCDA's housing ministries, thus partnering with Christian communities as they developed across the nation.

When John had traveled around Mississippi starting cooperatives, and when he had founded People's Development in inner-city Jackson, his goal had been empowerment of the poor through ownership. Again and again community builders seeking to help the underclass gain a footing would come to recognize the need for them to have something of their own. This meant not only housing but also business enterprise. To reestablish viable community in the cities it would be necessary to bring capital back into the urban wastelands that were created by its migration out. It would take more than monetary investment to bring hope and dignity back to people in all the Lawndales around the country. It would take the personal, spiritual commitment that led some to forsake individual success to relocate among people cast aside in the rush of acquisitive society.

John Perkins's relocation from California affluence back to the poverty and racism he had grown up under became the inspiration for the movement. It was the incarnational event, imitative of God in Christ moving in among a corrupted humanity. An act incomprehensible in terms of American success values, relocation would appeal to certain evangelicals who had become disillusioned with individualistic Americanism during the upheavals of the sixties and were exploring more communal alternatives.

One of these people was Bob Lupton, an Atlanta psychologist who visited Voice of Calvary and caught John's vision in 1976. A preacher's kid and Youth for Christ staff member, Lupton grasped the necessity of relocation to make it possible for genuine reconciliation and redistribution to happen. American parachurch workers commonly lived comfortable middle-class lives, segmented off from the poor, while making evangelism a mainly verbal exercise. Lupton moved against this norm when he and his wife, Peggy, chose to make their home in the derelict Summerhill area, Atlanta's equivalent of Lawndale.

Resettlement meant "reneighboring" with the disadvantaged people who had remained in this area when it emptied out during the decades of suburbanization. In an eloquent little book, *Return Flight,* Lupton describes the physical process and its spiritual implications. He recalls an older America of villages, regional commerce, and voluntary association, where the poor were more a part of community life. America prior to suburbanization had been more of a public-spirited culture, with citizens' groups forming all the time to aid the various disadvantaged populations. The smaller, more functional neighborhoods stimulated greater contact, cohesion, and mutual involvement.

The draining of both urban and small-town neighborhoods occurred as giant mass institutions gradually replaced community life, destroying the integrity of locality and region. Lupton describes the Great Society programs of the sixties as failed attempts by government to stop the cities

Bob Lupton. Bob and his wife, Peggy, chose to make their home in the derelict Summerhill area, Atlanta's equivalent of Lawndale. In 1978 Bob founded FCS Urban Ministries, a coalition of Christian community services.

from "hemorrhaging" as industry and people diffused outward. But government money and bureaucracy couldn't rebuild a viable economy and reconstruct functional neighborhoods. Advantaged people of goodwill had to return to tattered urban neighborhoods and "reweave" them by bringing in their manifold resources and becoming neighbors with the disadvantaged. This is the process Lupton goes on to describe as it occurred in Atlanta's Summerhill community.

During the seventies it was becoming fashionable for young, up-and-coming professionals and businesspeople to move back into cities. In blighted neighborhoods convenient to downtown civic, financial, and commercial centers they could pick up old properties for bargain prices, renovate them to their original beauty, and create a restored upscale neighborhood. But such "gentrification" merely transformed the neighborhood into a pricey one, pushing the poor out. All the same, it demonstrated the possibilities for reclamation of inner-city slums. Relocating Christians like the Luptons, seeking community with the poor rather than their displacement, could use their substantial skills, money, and connectedness to revitalize economy, environment, and, most important, people.

Leaving places of safety and abundance and moving into decayed and dangerous inner-city neighborhoods and becoming friends with the people who live there are powerful ways to show love. When people who had it made were moving in next door, inviting you to dinner, studying the Bible with you, getting you to the doctor, tutoring your kids, helping you learn a new skill and get a good job, and helping you buy a house and fix it up, all that could make you think others really cared about you. And it could give you reason to hope and believe you're worth something. Among hopeless people who had let their lives sink into crime, vice, and drugs, hope's restoration was like a miracle. The people who relocated replanted that hope, which became the basis for community building.

Suburban whites whose Christian conscience pushed them to move in among the inner-city poor would only constitute a minority of the relocators. It was among black Christians who had made it and moved to better locales that John Perkins's odyssey became an especially powerful model. Recounting "the Lawndale miracle" in his book, *Real Hope in Chicago,* Wayne Gordon emphasizes the contribution of people like Richard Townsell. An African American who had grown up in the 'hood and been a part of Coach's first efforts at leadership development, he and his wife, Stephanie, had attended Northwestern University and were working in Evanston.

Gordon quotes Townsell as saying, "Coach, for you to live in Lawndale makes you a hero. For me to live in Lawndale makes me a fool." But the Townsells did return, and Richard became director of the burgeoning Lawndale Development Corporation. It was John and Vera Mae Perkins, the acknowledged pioneers of the movement, who had provided the example for upwardly mobile African Americans to return to their communities. Their living out the Three Rs offered people like the Townsells a more deeply gratifying alternative to individualistic success.

All over the country, as Christian community development blossomed in the eighties and nineties, many of the leaders were minority-group members who were educated and had the opportunity for material advancement but who chose to go back into the communities of need. Among them were African Americans like Ron Spann and Eddie Edwards, both leading communities that were doing housing and youth development in inner-city Detroit. Spann is an Episcopal priest who established an intentional community and elaborate social ministry around Detroit's Church of the Messiah. Edwards, who had been a successful businessman, was particularly gifted in mentoring and motivating the young. The Joy of Jesus Community, which he heads in Detroit, includes a summer camp where adult mentors pair with youth and remain in contact with them when they return to the city.

Ted Travis is an African American who became one of the leaders in a profusion of Christian community development occurring in the Denver area. A trained vocalist, Travis was working with Young Life, a parachurch organization that evangelizes youth through such activities as tutoring and camping. He met John Perkins, and John worked with him and inspired him to start something up on his own. Travis's Neighborhood Ministries began with activities similar to the ones he had learned with Young Life. He modeled his programs on the Perkins's Pasadena ministry, developing a center for evangelism and kids' clubs called Harambee. This Harambee reflected the special talent of its founder in its elaborate music and voice instruction program. As its ministries expanded, it led naturally into the founding of Jubilee Community Church to provide a revitalized neighborhood with a spiritual anchor.

Because the purpose of Christian community development is to empower indigenous people, the idea is for successful, resourceful people of the same ethnicity as the people in the community to relocate and become strong role models. With John Perkins playing the generative role in the movement, black leadership moved into special prominence. But John was aware that other ethnics such as Latinos struggled under a similar weight of poverty and powerlessness and he wanted to reach out to them. Some of the emerging leaders in the movement began to address Latino issues and constituencies.

In Southern California, Derek Perkins's coworker, Rudy Carasco, reached out to Hispanic youth. And Michael Mata, a Perkins Foundation Board member and former inner-city pastor, became director of the Urban Leadership Institute at Claremont School of Theology. In Chicago, Noel Castellanos started La Villita, a church community in the barrio working in close association with Lawndale. Castellanos has become one of the key leaders in CCDA and a frequent speaker at its conventions.

Despite some Latino involvement, as CCDA proliferated in the nineties, whites and blacks were by far in greatest prominence. Manny Ortiz, a New York–bred Puerto Rican and professor at Westminster Seminary, raised the issue while speaking to a plenary session of two thousand at the 1995 convention. As if inadvertently to dramatize the problem, Ortiz had been shunted to the end of a long series of speakers on the convention's opening night, and by the time he stood up to speak, it was late in the evening and little time remained. With his edge sharpened by this unfortunate situation, he expressed his concern that brown, yellow, and red might be marginalized in an organization dominated by black and white. John heard Ortiz and, taking the podium as chairman later in the convention, supported his position, promising to recruit more Hispanics and Asians, and, if possible, Native Americans, to be on the CCDA Board, so that these groups' specific concerns would be addressed.

To reweave inner-city neighborhoods, relocators of diverse backgrounds bring in their resources and work to empower indigenous residents. The relocators replant the role-modeling leadership lost in the suburban flight of people and capital, but building a self-sustaining community means finding and developing the natural leaders. John understood the importance of this factor in Mississippi and he worked intensively with Artis, Dolphus, and others in establishing Voice of Calvary's leadership development program. Coach Gordon did the same in Lawndale with Richard Townsell and a number of others he had brought along. If a community is to develop, it is crucial for people who have left to get education and work experience, to return.

Bob Lupton likes to distinguish between programs that strengthen the community—development—and those that improve its appearance or aid individuals but often detract from the community's strength. These latter programs he calls betterment. On the most basic level, betterment would include government housing or welfare programs. Such programs should be only temporary stopgaps because they render people dependent on outside support instead of on the power inherent in their own skills and efforts. Government-funded housing provides shelter for the poor, but never self-respect, as the condition of the projects has invariably betrayed. Educational opportunities that give tutoring and scholarships to kids in the neighborhood effectively empower those individuals. But these forms of betterment, if unaccompanied by development, actually undermine the community by inducing educated young men and women to move out and up.

Betterment is a broad term that applies to any program that makes individuals' and families' lives better. And, as such, it is good insofar as it does so. Development, however, goes broader and deeper, because it revitalizes community life, whether in urban neighborhoods or in rural settings like Mendenhall. The overall process of development is a richly cooperative enterprise. Relocators with their resources and energy come alongside indigenous people. The relocators in turn draw support from a number of sources, such as suburban churches, businesspeople, and foundations who partner with them and the community. John Perkins always spent a major share of his time on the road cultivating these resources. The goal, however, is for the community to become as prosperous and self-sustaining as possible. When local business is growing and local people get educated and do not move away and the community becomes integrated with the life and health of a surrounding city or region, effective development is occurring.

When Dolphus and Artis were considering returning to Mississippi, it was because John had given them a heart for development and because he and the others who built Voice of Calvary were building a growing set of enterprises to return to. Similarly when Richard Townsell returned to Lawndale, he became head of a development corporation already begun by Wayne Gordon and the people of Lawndale Community Church.

In the CCDA model, a parish church or its equivalent provides the spiritual impetus and glue of the movement, but the whole neighborhood, not only Christians, gets involved and receives benefits from the development. This concept would be exemplified, as we shall see, in Fresno, California. There community development would begin in one neighborhood and resonate beyond that neighborhood through a broad spectrum of city-wide public and private institutions.

24

CITIES

H and Terry Spees adopted their oldest son out of Mississippi's foster care system. He had swallowed lye and been severely abused as a small child, and the specialized care he needed was unavailable in New Hebron. The Jackson ministry, with its new medical clinic in capable hands, had no real need of H and Terry, and the New Hebron ministries were under the strong leadership of Charles Hatten. So the Speeses began to think about going back to California. In 1984 they left for the West Coast, settling eventually in a mixed-income neighborhood in Fresno. H took a job as a public health administrator and worked on a master's degree in the field, while Terry continued her nursing. They both had their hands full at home as their family expanded to eleven, with three home-grown, four adopted, and two foster children.

The Spees family spent the next eight years living something close to a middle-class lifestyle. But in 1992, when a suburban Los Angeles jury acquitted four white police officers of beating African American Rodney King and the city exploded in the worst riots in its history, Fresno felt the aftershock. As in greater Los Angeles, people in this middle-sized central California city began to come together and talk with a new sense of urgency about the festering war zone at the heart of their community and the sorry state of racial relations in America.

Fresno was a changing agricultural community with an influx of immigrants and migrants; proliferating black, Hispanic, and Asian gangs; and spiraling crime. But it was the riots in L.A. that galvanized

Fresno's leaders into action, as fifteen of them, including a number of prominent clergy, convened at a local country club to brainstorm. At about the same time, church leaders began to meet together in "prayer summits." They went to the top of the tallest buildings and prayed "in the high places" for their city. Out of the brainstorming meeting came the idea for a "cops and clergy ride-along," which would lead to police taking dozens of clergy in their squad cars to the worst crime areas, where they came in firsthand contact with victims and offenders. This experience produced a consensus across the Christian community for the need of radical measures of social action.

H had joined the staff of Youth for Christ and as he moved back into full-time ministry, he and Terry made the decision to relocate to Calaveras Street, the worst crime area of the city. The years with John in Mississippi had given H the tools he needed for the work he was about to undertake in Fresno. As a parachurch worker he wasn't saddled with the responsibilities of a congregation, and this gave him more time for organizing. He became a leader in forming a fellowship of Christians that met weekly in different painful places in the city, like the exercise yard on the roof of the county jail or the closed-down wing of the juvenile hall. And they prayed together and became a wonderful forum for generating community-development ideas. They called themselves the No Name Fellowship, because they didn't want to become an institution but a servant to the city's existent institutions and to the people in the city.

As H in Youth for Christ networked with six other parachurch organizations, churches, and the private and public sectors, he consulted frequently with John Perkins. John had established close ties in Fresno beginning in the early eighties. Bufe Karraker, the pastor of the large Northwest Church and very much a public citizen, had become a close friend, frequently giving John his pulpit on a Sunday morning. In Bufe's congregation, prominent black physician Robert Brown and his wife, Julia, had become early mainstays of John's work.

Church and civic leaders in Pasadena too had come together in the wake of the riots. The new pastor at Lake Avenue Congregational Church, Gordon Kirk, had given John his pulpit the Sunday after, and the church took an offering of twenty-eight thousand dollars for relief in South Central Los Angeles. Later John joined with Pastor Kirk, Tyrone Cushman, and a number of other clergy to charter Neighborhood Christian Partners, a network of thirty Pasadena churches to cooperate in inner-city development projects. As John traveled more frequently to Fresno to speak and confer with leaders there, he was riding the crest of a new spirit of church, business, and public agency partnering that was emerging in many cities in response to the much publicized Los Angeles riots.

H made the immediate focus of his work the inner-city neighborhood he had moved into. Calaveras Street was a part of the area served by Lowell Elementary School. Almost all of the Lowell neighborhood residents lived below the poverty line. Drive-by shootings, carjackings, rapes, and all the other violent offenses were rampant in this part of the city. About the same time H and his family moved to Calaveras Street, a number of other parachurch workers joined him. Gordon Donoho and David Hernandez of Evangelicals for Social Action/Love, Inc. were among the first to relocate. Hernandez told Donoho that in Spanish *calaveras* actually means "skull," a dead, hollow cavity, and the two agreed it was an apt name and they affirmed their commitment to bring Calaveras Street back to life. Steve Morris, an African American with World Impact, also relocated on Calaveras with his family. Bob and Tina Engel and their children came in from suburban Clovis. These were the people who would secure the beachhead that would begin giving hope to their impoverished neighbors.

H suggested to participants in the No Name Fellowship that since schools are the locus of public neighborhood activity, the elementary school district should be what they considered a neighborhood. His idea was to target the Lowell school district and begin the process of rebuilding there. Donoho and Hernandez engineered one of the early projects, a community house-painting. ESA/Love, Inc. got Darrell Edwards, president of Wilshire Paint Company, to partner with them, donating all the paint. Edwards continued to donate the paint for similar restoration projects. Under the leadership of the parachurch ministers the Calaveras residents formed crews that painted some twenty-five houses. People emerged from their tightly secured homes and came together in a painting crew that became a powerful generator of neighborhood solidarity. The parachurch families also led the way as they formed a neighborhood association and located a kids' club on each block.

Lowell's elementary school was more than a convenient way to define *neighborhood*. It was the place where children lived the public side of their lives together with parents, teachers, and school administrators. H's community-development vision, like John's, did not artificially separate public from private, sacred from secular. Because he saw Christianity in terms of servanthood, the issue of church/state separation never became a problem for him. He went in and introduced himself to the principal and asked him what the school needed.

Tutoring programs sponsored by local churches, World Impact, and InterVarsity came as an immediate product of H's contact with the elementary school. H also was able to get clothing, shoes, and coats distributed to children at the school. And when he spoke of Lowell Elementary School's needs at Rotary Club, two prominent businessmen responded by creating a program to partner with a grade, taking the children on field trips, sponsoring a soccer team, and improving classroom facilities.

Lowell became a prototype for church and parachurch partnering with schools. In 1994 the No Name Fellowship organized a city-wide campaign for a school bond issue, which lost initially but won the following year. This kind of support forged warm new ties of friendship between Fresno's schools and the Christian community. Terry Simerly, Lowell's principal, felt the strong support of inner-city ministers living in the neighborhood and mobilizing a combination of public and private resources to help the school.

Such linkage with an elementary school was an early expression of the extensive coalition building that would characterize the Fresno community development movement. H and his fellow workers would do much to link together the characteristically separate spheres of public agencies and the Christian world. For example, when budget cuts forced a major staff reduction at the juvenile hall, ESA/Love, Inc. produced a number of volunteers to aid the overburdened remaining workers. One of the useful things they did was provide people to supervise juveniles on assigned weekend work projects. Eventually this kind of support grew into a program called Serving Public Servants with more than five thousand volunteers helping out in a number of understaffed public service agencies. As a result of this program the public sector grew more friendly to input from Christian sources.

George Aguilar, head of the Department of Neighborhood Housing and Revitalization, attended a Lowell Neighborhood Association meeting in search of solutions that had vexed public housing for thirty years.

There was a chronic shortage of funds and a waiting list of twenty thousand people for public housing. H suggested to Aguilar that his department adopt the elementary school district designation as the basis for code enforcement, sanitation districts, down payment assistance, and the like. H also suggested that Aguilar go to the people in each of the districts and tell them that money would be allocated on a competitive basis to neighborhoods that organize the best and put in the most sweat equity. To H's surprise, Aguilar, a compassionate man who really wanted to make a difference, adopted this idea and issued a brochure spelling it out in detail. H got so excited when he saw it that he called John to tell him about it.

The No Name Fellowship, which has expanded its mailing list to some 350 members, has been a kind of general assembly of Christian community development in Fresno, the main hatchery of ideas and projects. Almost from its inception it has sought to organize and systematize inner-city development. With this in mind, No Name created an umbrella association called City Builders. It is composed of seven parachurch ministries: Youth for Christ, World Impact, InterVarsity, Habitat for Humanity, ESA/Love, Inc., ETC (Entrepreneurial Training Centers), and Unstrung Bow. City Builders partners with a host of private and public agencies, including the Fresno Police Department, whose chief, Ed Winchester, has become an enthusiastic supporter.

In 1995 the coalition-building and community-development programs of City Builders were given a permanent broad base of support, as the No Name Fellowship chartered the Fresno Leadership Foundation, with H as board chairman and Jim Westgate as president. Westgate was an urban missiologist with many years' experience in the trenches who came to Fresno to teach at Mennonite Biblical Seminary. Teaching and practice flowed together, as Westgate, like other academicians in the movement across the country—Ron Potter, Manny Ortiz, Ray Bakke, Tony Campolo, Ron Sider—rolled up his sleeves and plunged his hands in the dirt.

City Builders has turned the Lowell neighborhood into a greenhouse of community-development programs. Area residents expressed their concerns at neighborhood association meetings, and indigenous "block leaders" began to emerge who learned to keep in touch with the needs of individual households and mobilize relevant support.

As has characterized Christian community development since John began in Mendenhall, youth mentoring has become the central focus in Fresno. Mentor Moms was created to bring mature mothers into nurturing relationships with teenage mothers. And the kids' clubs and teen clubs take on much the same function as the children's and youth programs at Voice of Calvary and Harambee. Nurturing adults pour their life into children and teens in tutoring, athletics, field trips, and summer camp. They provide warm support and all kinds of practical training for parents, many of whom are harried and over-whelmed single mothers.

The partnering of City Builders with the Fresno Police Department illustrates some of the best possibilities inherent in the new private/public collaboration. The police have a proactive "weed and seed" program, where they go in and clean out a particularly troublesome place, commonly an apartment complex or strip mall. This means breaking up drug rings and other kinds of criminal activity and bringing in the departments of housing, public health, and social services to take care of related problems in each domain. But buildings thus cleaned out are soon reinfested unless something is done to help the residents. City Builders brings in church people to tutor and teach life skills and give all kinds of nurturing support services to the people. A barber, for example, came and gave haircuts and then began to teach others to cut hair. This collaboration with the police, called Care Fresno, brings a spirit of improvement and systems of mutual aid, which restore the sense of community.

People acquire hope and common life improves in the Lowell neighborhood as the result of City Builders's organizing and betterment programs. Isolation and obsession with security has declined, as more people come out on their porches and work in their yards. Neighbors visit and bond with one another. Parents in the neighborhood association get active in the PTA, and children's school performance rises. But while City Builders and the relocators have accomplished essential restorative work in Lowell, Spees and Westgate feel they need to go deeper.

Good as they are, these programs are mere betterment and not development, because they do not recreate the economic base that makes Lowell a desirable place for more affluent people to settle. H has seen the families on his block acquire a footing and improve their skills and chances of success and then move out of the neighborhood to a more prosperous part of town. And because of that the Spees children have had to part with many of their friends.

To become a desirable, stable neighborhood, and not just a port of entry, Lowell needs real capital investment, and City Builders is about the task of making it happen. In late 1995 they enlisted the Building Industry Association's support for a project to build housing for people at diverse income levels on the fifty or so vacant lots in the area. Presently they are in the process of acquiring the land. Upscale housing and attractive, affordable housing in close proximity bring people with some means back alongside those of more humble station. The plan is to attract capital, jobs, and economically successful role models back to the community, and thus a formerly isolated underclass will be reabsorbed into society's mainstream.

As of 1997 City Builders's initiative with Fresno's developers is in its early stages, but it looks promising. It is drawing broad backing because it represents a reweaving of authentic community, the most effective counterweight to all the forces of urban deterioration. As he speaks to diverse audiences around town and in CCDA, H reiterates City Builders's goal of rebuilding the city, "one person, one family, one block, one neighborhood at a time," as John envisioned for Jackson, Mississippi. Lowell is the prototype; the intention is to repeat it in the sixty-four other elementary school districts that make up Fresno.

The Christian community development movement in Fresno is working out a new paradigm of urban revitalization at the neighborhood level. Before the 1930s, human services were largely the province of neighbors, churches, and local associations. The Great Depression altered that old pattern, creating social dislocations on an unprecedented scale, which drew in the federal government and an alternative paradigm of publicly administered social welfare. But as government grew more remote, bureaucratic, and burdened with deficits, centralized and fragmented social welfare systems became dysfunctional.

Federal bureaucracies are rationalized systems bearing no relationship to local communities of felt needs. The emerging paradigm—partnering and community development—brings a decentralized synthesis, a creative collaboration of public and private sectors and religious associations to do hands-on work in afflicted neighborhoods. H envisions, and Fresno is beginning to experiment with, the spectrum of social service specialties forming teams that locate next to the elementary schools and work with the people as part of each neighborhood.

The natural forum where H could convey what was happening in Fresno to the movement at large was the annual CCDA convention. The November conventions have become the main gathering grounds where people in the movement come in contact with one another and cross-fertilization of ideas takes place. The number of people attending the conventions has grown seismically since the original gathering in 1989, with close to two thousand making their way to Denver in 1995. John Perkins, Wayne Gordon, and Lawndale's new pastor, Carey Casey, loosely presided over the evening keynote sessions, while the days were packed with a full range of workshops, focus groups, and field trips to local community ministries.

Early each morning of the convention hundreds began their day by filtering into the main convention hall to hear John teach a Bible study, usually highlighting one of the Three Rs. He likes to find biblical parallels to reconciliation and community development in both Testaments. Nehemiah returning to rebuild a wasted Jerusalem or the apostle Paul nurturing cross-cultural churches and mentoring young leaders like Timothy are familiar images he might draw on. With frequent reference to his own experience, he draws a sharp contrast between the painstaking character building of a countercultural, community-minded Christianity and the flashy materialism and status seeking of America in our day.

In one teaching, as he recalls the early "militant days," John says, "I would wear the same clothes for six weeks. And the people in the community would ask, 'Brother Perkins, why do you wear those old clothes all the time? They're not in style.' And I told them, 'You gonna let white folks in Paris determine your style in your ghetto?'" Then he tells the CCDA audience, "We substitute charisma for character." And it is the example of character that "reproduces itself." John points to the powerful effects of living a lifestyle that refuses to "deify money." "When I devalued clothes," he said, "*they* devalued clothes." And they learned to live simply, relying on their own resources and relationships rather than large fund-raising programs and organizations.

With homely illustrations like these, John reiterates the human values that have come to characterize the movement as a whole. At conventions and other gatherings he and other leaders address the movement's overall mission, the obstacles in its face, and the best strategies for overcoming them. Simultaneously underlying the work of the CCDA communities is a broad range of technical services crossing many complex disciplines, including medicine and public health, banking and finance, real estate, architecture and housing, child development, gerontology, and the full range of social work specialties. The workshops, commonly conducted by trained professionals within the movement, reflect this ongoing need for the technical information and competence necessary to be effective in a modern life.

On June 16, 1995, Harambee Christian Family Center held a celebration at Lake Avenue Congregational Church for John's sixty-fifth birthday and his and Vera Mae's forty-fourth wedding anniversary. A rainstorm, unusual for that time of year in Southern California, had left Pasadena's evening air clean and crisp. John's cousin Rosie Lee Dixon was there, and a great many friends of the ministry had come to reminisce and wish the Perkinses well. There was a letter from Spencer that H, acting as master of ceremonies, read aloud. Spencer recalled being by his father when he had given a speech through the second story window of the Simpson County jail. To grow up in the Perkins family, said Spencer, was to grow up with a sense of a special calling on your life. "Your legacy," he told his parents, "will continue long after you're gone."

People who saw John and Vera Mae regularly had mixed feelings that clear June night, because the aging missionary couple was about to leave the northwest Pasadena neighborhood they had poured their hearts into for the past thirteen years. John felt the poignancy of the moment, as he told the people how much their enduring friendship meant to a man who had grown up without a mother or father.

They were thinking about eventually landing back in Jackson and some sort of semiretirement but they were hardly moving toward that retirement now. Within the week they would be packing up all their things to drive halfway across the country to camp in an apartment in Dallas, Texas. With its behemoth airport, Dallas is accessible to every spot in the United States, and so it would be a convenient base of operations for the work that would absorb John over the next year and a half. He would be flying out to scores of cities around the country as he and Wayne Gordon conducted CCDA's American Cities Campaign. A plus side of this transiency in Dallas was the chance for John and Vera Mae to grow closer to their son Philip, who lived nearby with his wife Eva and their two sons, John Philip and David.

John and Gordie had begun organizing the year-long campaign by sending out flyers to church contacts in cities where they wanted to go. Both men received some invitations independently and they conducted the campaign in those cities by themselves. The main thrust of their work, however, was the part they did together, Gordie flying out of his base at Chicago's O'Hare Airport, and John out of

John and Vera Mae with longtime Pasadena residents at the farewell party for the Perkinses, Lake Avenue Congregational Church, June 16, 1995.

Dallas, and meeting on site. The American Cities Campaign nourished and expanded CCDA ministries in places like Milwaukee, Kalamazoo, Grand Rapids, Minneapolis, Pittsburgh, Waco, Albuquerque, and Tucson.

CCDA had mushroomed since its inception, but much of the membership had developed in cities where Christian community development had been going on for many years: Chicago, Atlanta, Baltimore, Denver, Jackson, and Detroit. A large number of other cities had incipient organizations but needed some fuel to ignite further growth and support. These were the ones John and Gordie were seeking invitations from, the ones where they had sent the flyers. Their campaign would expand the movement in these cities, as it exposed a broader spectrum of churches, ministries, and businesses to CCDA concepts. It would stimulate the creation of local networks, which would broaden the developing ministries' resource base. One or the other or both leaders were there to present an overview of church-based development in each city, describing the process of networking with suburban churches and with the greater business community. John and Gordie spent time talking with local pastors and businesspeople about the specifics of their city.

Each copiously organized four-day campaign followed a set format similar to that of CCDA's annual conventions. On Thursdays John and Gordie arrived and met with key people and went with them to look at projects and ministries. A reception followed in the evening where the two leaders learned more about the needs of the particular city they were visiting. On Fridays they had breakfast with the city's pastors and lunch with a large gathering of businesspeople, and at night they led a mass rally. Saturdays were given over to workshops, akin to those at the conventions, where people with functioning programs talked about what they do. On Sundays the event concluded as John or Gordie preached at one of the local sponsoring churches.

As they brought the campaign to these new cities, John found a wealth of talent and programs to bring under the CCDA umbrella. The four-day campaigns worked to get existent churches, ministries, and businesses cooperating in depth at the local level. Bringing them into CCDA gives them access to hundreds of like-minded works around the country. Much of the problem in poor areas is their isolation from contact with the resources that can serve to renew them. Hence CCDA, out of its national office in Chicago, in its annual conventions, and especially in these campaigns in individual cities, works to establish fruitful linkages. Week after week during 1995 and '96, John came in contact with exciting programs doing creative things in the cities.

Grand Rapids, Michigan, was one of the middle-sized cities where Christian action to reclaim deteriorating urban neighborhoods was going on in earnest. The home of Calvin College and Seminary together with many Christian Reformed churches and publishing houses, Grand Rapids has elements of an American Geneva. Calvinism's emphasis on social transformation gives its adherents strong incentive to do urban ministry. In the mid-seventies a group of Reformed believers formed the Inner City Christian Fellowship (ICCF) to do housing among the poor.

Like the housing ministries of VOC, Lawndale, or Habitat for Humanity, ICCF helps people achieve home ownership and greater self-sufficiency. What distinguishes them is the painstaking attention they pay to building beautiful homes coherent with their city's rich architectural history. Their abiding interest is to convey a caring respect to the people who will occupy them. ICCF came into affiliation with CCDA during the American Cities Campaign, and at the 1995 convention in Denver their executive director, Jonathan Bradford, presented their concept of housing that enobles people.

In Milwaukee, white flight had deeded over stately old Lutheran church buildings to a number of black congregations. One of these is St. Luke's Emmanuel Baptist Church. Its pastor, R. E. McCrory, has a vision for economic development. This church became a focal point of the American Cities Campaign, and John got to tour a facility that serves as incubator for a cluster of small businesses. An experienced entrepreneur in the congregation mentors neophytes in janitorial services, electronics assembly, and a travel agency, among other enterprises. The idea is for each new business to outgrow the incubator and go off on its own.

Minneapolis is another city where John had a chance to observe real economic development in inner-city neighborhoods. There, Art Erickson, a United Methodist minister, has created Urban Ventures Leadership Foundation, which organized what has become a parish church in a warehouse, similar to Lawndale's facility. They were buying up old commercial buildings afflicted with adult bookstores and other ghetto parasites and refitting them to develop a new commercial district, drawing suburban investment. The new businesses will infuse the community with jobs, job training, and new money. In the Minneapolis campaign, John spoke to some 350 people at the business lunch and he observed the start of a large business park in the refurbished old Sears building that was expected to bring a thousand jobs to the inner city. In keeping with the CCDA model, economic development was occurring as the product of biracial cooperation.

When John went to Pittsburgh, he saw perhaps the largest-scale Christian community development to date. There he met with Wheeler Winstead, developer and founder of Jubilee Housing, which was bringing home ownership and a renewed commercial life back to a gutted-out area. Winstead has indigenized the ministry, giving it over to a local woman who is adding, among other things, a shopping center.

At the same time, Bob Lavelle, banker and realtor, is going to great lengths to reclaim some of Pittsburgh's most blighted urban real estate. Having grown up in the neighborhood, he retained a love of the people there and a desire for them to prosper. He was able to purchase a little savings and loan and through its offices get low-interest loans to help the people get into houses and businesses. John expressed admiration for Lavelle, seeing him as one who could easily have moved out and up but chose to remain and invest his money and talent to reverse decay in an inner-city neighborhood.

In Pittsburgh John also became acquainted with a black pastor, Joseph L. Garlington Sr., who has joined forces with a white associate, James W. Adkins, to form the interracial Covenant Church of Pittsburgh that is marking out new territory in partnering for development. As happened in Lawndale, the church has acquired a large building, which they are redeveloping as a multipurpose center. The new facility will combine a youth center, gym, swimming pool, and health center. Funding for the many programs it will house is being provided in part by the federal government.

Studying this new joint venturing with the public sector in areas like health care and crime fighting, John thinks it may herald the beginning of a resourceful new development model. At the same time he has wondered aloud to ministry leaders whether government involvement might place new strictures on their spiritual activities.

This church community in Pittsburgh represents one of a growing number where blacks and whites are coming together to do holistic ministry. As he traveled on the American Cities Campaign, John found one of the most inspiring examples of black and white church union in the Twin Cities area. They held the pastors' breakfast in Saint Paul at Open Door Baptist Church, a biracial congregation that formed when Ron Smith, a black pastor, and Dave Johnson, a white pastor, succeeded in uniting their churches. The two pastors now keep track together of parishioners' needs and share the preaching in the combined Sunday worship.

Such biracial congregations could become the fulcrum of the racial reconciliation at the heart of John and CCDA's mission but they are fraught with potential pitfalls that the leaders must confront openly and prayerfully for these churches to survive. The best-known pioneering work in this area is that of Raleigh Washington and Glen Kehrein in Chicago. Kehrein had been part of a Chicago biracial church that disintegrated in the eighties. The problem was in their exclusive focus on action and program at the expense of interpersonal relationships. As a result the church imploded as black and white cultural disparity and misunderstandings flared up, and the leaders did not know how to deal with it.

Kehrein, a veteran church worker who heads Circle Urban Ministries, and Washington, a retired Army colonel, who pastors the Rock of Salvation Church, tell their individual stories and describe their combined ministries in their book, *Breaking Down Walls*. The two Chicago ministers are among the most visible and popular leaders of CCDA.

As CCDA grew geometrically in the nineties, John traveled all the more, helping the communities to grow and network with one another. During the American Cities Campaign, he and Gordie were on the go and into another city and another four-day program almost weekly. The new movement in urban ministry was spreading fast, and John was in ever higher demand as its pioneer and spokesperson. Honorary degrees came regularly now. In 1992 Spring Arbor College in Michigan presented honorary doctors of humanities to both John and Vera Mae. And in 1995 Geneva College in Pennsylvania gave John a doctor of divinity. Both schools were becoming sensitive to development issues, with Geneva making special efforts to enroll students from the inner city and Spring Arbor starting an urban ministries program offering internships in downtown Chicago. As John was traveling, speaking, and networking, knitting the movement together, a younger generation of leaders was putting its stamp on the ministries he had begun.

25

The Healing Process

As architect and chief evangelist of Christian community development, John has always been project- and goal-oriented. Birthing ministries and getting them into motion has required tremendous focus, energy, and concentration on results. Moving from project to project and furthering the work on the road has made it impossible for him to give adequate attention to people's personal needs. In truth John's style of leadership has been the natural outcropping of his gifts—more in generating ideas, organizing, and decision making than in interpersonal matters. But it is those more executive talents that were more necessary in the first generation as the work was gathering its initial force and expanding outward. The skills required in the second generation are the ones that can develop the work more vertically, expanding and deepening the bonds of human relationship.

With the passage of time a more relational emphasis is evolving at each of the three locales where John and Vera Mae have planted ministries. With programs and procedures well in place by the eighties, the new generation of leaders in Mendenhall, Jackson, and Pasadena could afford more time to go deeper with people. They began to experiment with new structures that would give greater priority to the healing of persons and human relationships. Both in Mendenhall and Jackson, the centrality of a pastoral church helped bring this about, and some of the leaders in Jackson, desirous of a closer common life, moved to form an intentional community.

In Mendenhall the initial shock of being suddenly thrust into independence had caused Dolphus and Artis to spend most of their time for the first few years focused on keeping existent ministries going. So Dolphus took over where John had left off, going on the road and speaking around the country to develop new sources of support. Artis, in the first years, had been saddled with all the practical, time-consuming tasks of overseeing Mendenhall's many non-church-based ministries. As a result, he had little time to develop his office of pastor, and the ministries of the church languished. But he and Dolphus had long agreed that the church should be the nourishing spiritual center of an expanding community life, and in 1983 The Mendenhall Ministries was at long last able to yield the time for Artis to get away to a pastors' conference. This was a watershed for him, as it marked his change of focus to full-time pastoring and began the enrichment of his pastoring skills, particularly in the realm of counseling and mentoring.

The years under John's tutelage and then his college and graduate training for the pastorate had given Artis the knowledge and passion to develop a fully functioning church in Mendenhall. And beyond that, he possessed a deep concern for the overall state of the black church in the South. He had long lamented most rural black pastors' lack of formal preparation and their part-time style of ministry. Simultaneously he was aware of how entrenched emotionalism and subliteracy were and how resistant pastors and church people were to changing ancient ways.

When John brought a richer conception of faith and church life to black Mississippi, Simpson County church leaders felt threatened by his activism and his expansive style of ministry. John hadn't had the time or patience to cultivate relationships with these pastors, though he had long recognized the need for local networking. Artis, however, was a low-keyed individual with the tact and motivation to take pains to build local and regional association.

Artis had his own vision to build the Mendenhall Bible Church as a resource center for other churches in the area. With its vacation Bible schools, adult education, leadership development, and now its law office, started in 1982, Voice of Calvary—now The Mendenhall Ministries—had been regionally oriented since its inception. If area pastors were worried in the early years that VOC might wean away their members, they might be all the more concerned now that it is represented by the impressively credentialed full-time pastor of a well-heeled church.

**John and Artis Fletcher
at Harambee, late 1980s.**

Artis was willing to put in the time to get to know the other preachers on a personal basis so that they would trust him as a close friend and value his church as a vital resource. His desire was to bring them into programs to develop their pastoral skills so that they could much better service the needs of their congregations. In what in the mid-eighties would become Mendenhall Bible Church's Pastor's Development Ministry (PDM), Artis was beginning a process to spread holistic development through the rural South by training the pastors who would bring it into their churches.

One of the skills Artis believes pastors need in order to provoke positive change in people's lives is the ability to give good counsel. Rural black pastors may have traditionally not concerned themselves with much more than the weekly church service and Sunday school lesson, but Artis is concerned about the overall lives of the people in his congregation. He knows that encouraging the downhearted, giving direction to the confused, and helping couples in conflict to get back on track are vital aspects of pastoral care. He is also aware that serious emotional disorders, substance abuse, and the like require the intervention of trained professionals.

A well-equipped pastor needs to know how to network with this kind of specialized support. Artis acquired solid training in such counseling and networking from Dr. Willie Richardson's Christian Research and Development Center. The pastor of an inner-city church in Philadelphia, Richardson is the author of a series of books and tapes and founder of this four-year training program in biblical counseling.

From Richardson, Artis received an educational, problem-solving approach to counseling, embedded in a framework of biblical living principles. Counselees are assigned regular homework, which compels them to reflect studiously on their relational issues and the life choices they are making. A crucial aspect of the process is the scriptural concept of self-examination to determine the motives for one's actions. In counseling workshops Artis will paraphrase the words of Jesus: "But the things that come out of the mouth come from the heart, and these make a man unclean. . . ." In laying emphasis on purity of motive, the idea is to get beyond the self-seeking orientation of superficial counsel and behavior change to the personal transformation that comes with real repentance.

In counseling couples, for example, Artis gives the man and woman a series of practical exercises. For example he may give them the following handouts: "Ways a Husband May Express Love to His Wife" and "Ways a Wife May Express Love to Her Husband." From each list of close to a hundred behaviors both parties are assigned to concentrate on doing three or four a week and report how it is going in weekly counseling sessions. This is good, typical behavior therapy, but it becomes a lot more powerful when partners do loving things not just to get something back, but as part of a process of repentance that alters their dispositions so that they actually love giving to one another.

A good many exercises are given to stimulate the process of repentance. One is a checklist to rate self and partner on biblically catalogued vices: envy, malice, deceit, jealousy, laziness, self-pity, impatience, and the like. Counselees read books and watch tapes. Then they record the principles and insights presented, their agreement or disagreement with them, and their reflections on what changes they may need to make in their lives.

Another exercise called a "Self-Confrontation Bible Study" presents a verse and asks the following questions: "What does the Bible say? What does it mean? For me how does it apply? What will I do to change?"

Artis started his own biblical counselor-training program in Mendenhall, which has averaged twelve to twenty pastor trainees during the nineties. Training in counseling functions as part of the broader Pastor's Development Ministry. This program has become a little seminary-without-walls for rural pastors. Among its five staff members is the director, Tim Keys, from Mt. Olive, Mississippi, who joined Artis in PDM in the late eighties.

Another important leader has been Pastor Lloyd C. Blue of Oakland, California. Blue worked with E. V. Hill, pastor of the formidable Mt. Zion Baptist Church in Los Angeles and well-known media teacher. Blue's experience also included a stint with Bill Bright, founder of the giant Campus Crusade for Christ. With this background, Blue brought substantial preaching, teaching, and organizing skills to Mississippi. He brought his own ministry, Church Growth Unlimited, into close collaboration with PDM. By the mid-nineties Blue brought PDM's services into a network of pastors in twelve counties.

PDM, the direct extension of Mendenhall Bible Church, has become the most rapidly expanding of The Mendenhall Ministries. Using its own curriculum, study materials, and training aids it reaches out regionally in a program that places mentor pastors with pastors in local churches. Monthly seminars and a big annual pastors/wives conference are held in Mendenhall. Reformed Theological Seminary, now with campuses in Jackson and Orlando, Florida, has augmented PDM's curriculum with its own Mendenhall satellite curriculum. In other locales, like Jackson and West Point, Mississippi, and Covington, Louisiana, PDM pastoral groups have formed and meet regularly to continue in study and mutual support.

In the winter of 1995 The Mendenhall Ministries' publication reported 134 new pastors reached, twenty-one receiving one-on-one mentoring, and twenty-three enrolled in the quarterly workshops. What was more, pastors in the program were taking the personal risk of moving from part-time to full-time ministry. PDM was fast becoming a major means of nourishment for an expanding radius of African American churches branching out from Mendenhall.

One nearby pastor who made the commitment to move into full-time ministry was Clarence Phillips of Mendenhall's Nazareth Missionary Baptist Church. Phillips was one of the early people to start tutoring, recreational, and free lunch programs in his church. When this pastor had a severe heart attack while at home alone, the close relationships growing in PDM were poignantly highlighted. Phillips had been outside gardening when he had a vision of himself lying face down in the garden dying. He decided not to continue working but to go in the house and phone Mendenhall Bible Church. After he did so, he collapsed in the pain of a severe heart attack. Artis and many of the networking pastors who had become Phillips's friends rallied to his aid during his hospitalization and recovery. PDM was not only developing black rural churches in holistic ministry; it was also bringing pastors and churches that had been largely on their own into close, supportive association.

In 1991 President George Bush greeted Artis Fletcher and Dolphus Weary in a ceremony in Meridian, Mississippi, as The Mendenhall Ministries became one of the Points of Light his administration was honoring for distinctive service. It was a gratifying moment for both men, confirming as it did their stewardship of the work begun by John Perkins more than thirty years before.

Beginning shakily after John's precipitous separation of Mendenhall from VOC, they had successfully placed their own stamp on the organization. No longer were the Ministries engulfing the church. Mendenhall Bible Church had begun to provide a strong umbrella of pastoral care locally, and PDM was now expanding through the region. The new pastoral emphasis brought closer personal contact and cohesion, thus softening and humanizing the heavy project-orientation of John's pioneering days.

Jackson too went through a crisis as it began to transition out of John's leadership in the early eighties. But the crisis there was rooted in issues of power and race. The seeds of conflict were planted as talented, advantaged whites coming in from other parts of the country attained prominence at Voice of Calvary, moving into key leadership positions and eclipsing indigenous African Americans. Ed McKinley's timely admonition to whites working in ministries like VOC was beginning to prove prophetic. He had written in the article for *The Other Side* in the seventies that whites should recognize their habitual paternalism and curb it by "submitting to black leadership."

At Voice of Calvary's original rural site, the racial battle had been fought not within the community, but externally with the southern white power structure. In the circle of John's organizing, strong black leadership had come to the fore during the civil rights movement. At the point of separation in 1979, Mendenhall was a black-run organization, and its further success or failure was wholly in the hands of its black leaders. Jackson had developed differently with leaders of both races, despite John's abiding interest in the nurture of an indigenous black leadership. There the issue of reconciliation had moved center stage, the fruit of John's passion at Brandon when he realized how crucial it is to encourage racial reconciliation. Where Mendenhall had

focused inward, empowering local black folk, Jackson looked outward
to the world. If Mendenhall was a model of black Christian community development, Jackson, as the Perkinses and Speeses had first formed
it, was to be a model of racial reconciliation.

As John had guided Jackson's growth, his two chief interests had
been in black community development and the furtherance of interracial cooperation. With his inveterate focus on getting the job done,
he naturally encouraged whoever surfaced to do it. More often than
not that person proved to be a white male. It was not that those individuals were power hungry; their intentions, more often than not, were
only to serve. But in America, where white male advantage had been
so predominant, and blacks customarily relegated to subordinate and
menial roles, it was inevitable that confident, enterprising white men
would gravitate to the decision-making positions.

By the early eighties Phil Eide from Minnesota and Jim Taylor from
Seattle were leading the housing ministry, and Tim Robertson was heading the International Study Center. Five of the seven elders as well as
the pastor at Voice of Calvary Fellowship were white—this in the midst
of a black community whose residents Voice of Calvary was working
to empower. The contradiction was not lost on African American leaders at Voice of Calvary, and Lem Tucker and Spencer Perkins began to
call people's attention to it. Other prominent blacks in the congregation also spoke out, including Lynn Phillips and Ivory Phillips. The
two were not related. Lynn, the daughter of Rev. Clarence Phillips, was
a medical student, and Ivory was professor of history and chair of the
department at Jackson State.

Spencer had been on the leading edge of integration and he had
endured everything from racial slights and remarks to outright persecution. Having grown up in the Perkins family he had a strong
support system and abiding sense of mission, but those things didn't
render him impervious to the pain. At Voice of Calvary Fellowship
he and other blacks began to openly question whites' motives. The
result was a series of emotion-laden "reconciliation meetings," where
blacks challenged whites' taking charge and doing ministry among
African Americans without ever making efforts to get to know them
on a personal level. How was this so very different from the old
southern white paternalism, doing favors for blacks at a distance
and keeping hold of power?

White power in black organizations had strained racial relations since the days of the civil rights movement. For decades white liberals had been leaders in the NAACP. And white prominence had grown in SNCC before Stokely Carmichael (Kwame Ture) took control and made it an all-black organization. Indeed African Americans from Marcus Garvey to Carmichael to Malcolm X to Spike Lee championed separatism as the only way for African Americans to gain control of their own lives and institutions. At the same time others like Martin Luther King and John Perkins were trying to lay foundations for racial understanding and cooperation. VOC was one of those efforts and yet for all its promise it seemed to be bearing out the separatists' argument that whenever black and white try to work together, white men take over.

The 1983 reconciliation meetings were a bloodletting experience, and in the midst of the heated dialogue, many whites, feeling misunderstood and unwanted, left Voice of Calvary Fellowship. But others like young volunteer Chris Rice struggled inwardly and stuck it out. Chris was the son of parents who had participated in the Mississippi Freedom Summer when he was four years old and then they went to Korea as missionaries. Growing up interracially in a mission made working at Voice of Calvary a natural choice of work for Chris.

Oblivious to racial strain at VOC, Chris was wholly surprised and unnerved when anger erupted among black staff members. He felt unappreciated and resentful and he was beginning to detach inwardly from the church and the movement. Just at this point Donna Wheeler, a white Californian, and Derek Perkins came and asked Chris to join Spencer's small group. The invitation lifted his spirits and he jumped at the chance for reinvolvement. As he went to meetings and listened, he began to understand where these black brothers and sisters were coming from. And he began to realize his mentality had been that of the caseworker, caretaking and uninvolved.

Racial confrontation at Voice of Calvary had rare positive results. The realization dawned that reconciliation of the races and people development in the black community were not going to occur automatically in VOC's programs. It was not enough for whites and blacks to work in ministry and go to church together. For genuine reconciliation to occur, they had to intentionally pursue friendship with one another. This sort of intentionality would also be necessary to bring indigenous blacks into leadership positions. Without such intentionality, whites would fall into their habitual directive roles, and blacks would recede to the background. These insights led to concrete changes both on the personal, relational level and in the approach to development.

The small groups that evolved at Voice of Calvary Fellowship in response to the reconciliation crisis became a means to provoke closer personal contact. Each group formed around the leadership of a church elder. In the wake of the reconciliation meetings, Spencer moved into an elder position, and his and Nancy's small group began to evolve into a center of Voice of Calvary's reconciliation movement. They probed more deeply into the Bible and they sought greater closeness and understanding by telling their life stories to one another at length.

Relationships deepened as people really got to know one another. Delving beneath the common superficiality of church groups, they were pursuing real *koinonia,* the deep bonds of spiritual union. The fruit of their search for stronger commitment to one another became the intentional community they called Antioch, after the New Testament church known for its diverse racial and ethnic makeup. Twelve men and women moved into a big house on six acres in VOC's neighborhood near downtown Jackson.

Antioch would become the leading edge of the racial healing process at Voice of Calvary Fellowship. When they began living together in intentional community, they had no clear sense of how they were going to carry it out. As in many similar movements extending back to the early church, they had been attempting to move their lives into closer proximity with scriptural ideals. Some of the people at church thought they were saying the whole church ought to live this way, and they had to reassure them otherwise. It was more a specific calling they felt as a group to work out the process of reconciliation through their common life.

Among Antioch's founders were Spencer and Nancy Perkins, Joanie Perkins, Chris Rice, Donna Wheeler, and Gloria Lotts. Derek and Karyn Perkins would be leaving soon for Pasadena. Chris and Donna would become the first to marry in the context of community life.

Joanie headed Harambee Christian School of Business until 1988 and then took a leave from VOC Ministries to attend law school. During that transition she met and married Ron Potter, one of the intellectuals active in the National Black Evangelical Association. Joanie and Ron lived for awhile in Philadelphia, where he was teaching, but

The Antioch Community, 1997.

they both felt the pull to community, and in 1995, as she was working into a new position as executive vice president of CCDA, they
moved into Antioch.

Over the first decade of its existence, the Antioch community was
able to attain a stability uncommon among recent attempts at communal living. This is because members strenuously sought to balance
the nourishment of interpersonal relationships and community life
with outreach into the neighborhood and participation in the broader
Christian community development movement.

Life in a house with twelve bedrooms and six bathrooms and anywhere from twelve to twenty people demanded a good deal of logisti-
cal planning. The trick was to wisely delineate which were community matters and which were family and personal ones. If the
community claimed too much prerogative, it would stifle individual
growth. On the other hand, if too much decision making was private
and personal, community life would stagnate or deteriorate as everyone ran in his or her own track.

So the members of Antioch painstakingly worked out the balance
between the two realms. By giving parents and children adjacent rooms

377

and their own bath facilities, families got the privacy they needed. Evening meals are taken in common, while people are on their own for other meals. Adult members put their earnings into a common pot to cover staples and ongoing community expenses and they draw an equal stipend they can use at their discretion.

Major decisions that affect the community are made by consensus. Many communities in the past have had more patriarchal, authoritarian rules, which established order but stifled individual growth. The process of consensus building is messier and more demanding on the whole body of adults, but it empowers individuals and forges more equal, flexible personal ties. The members of Antioch found community life to be like marriage in its need for intimacy, and as with marriage, their commitment to intimate life in community was fraught with all kinds of potential pitfalls, power struggles, and avoidances. To work on their relationships and transact the complex business of the community, they learned to mark out sizable blocks of time to meet together.

Meetings of the adult members have taken a number of forms from recent power lunches at a local restaurant to the current Wednesday morning updates. In these they set aside an entire morning to work on spiritual, relational, and practical community issues. Ron Potter or Spencer leads them in study of the Bible and books like Luther Smith's *Intimacy in Mission*. Discussion becomes deeper as it moves from intellectual to personal matters.

A member may confess a poor attitude about a community concern or in his or her marriage. Everyone feels free to confess, confront, problem solve, and support one another as issues percolate to the surface. After personal matters are aired, discussion moves to the nuts and bolts issues of money and maintenance and the day-to-day running of Antioch's complex household. The meetings work to clarify and heal relationships and oil community life. With members so actively involved in the broader Jackson community, they find the meetings vital to keep their work from squeezing out the quality of their life together.

Antioch's common life works to facilitate its outreach into the neighborhood. Gloria Lotts, one of the community's two single members, runs a child care service and a preschool on the premises. Nurturing a mix of Antioch's children and children from the neighborhood, Gloria spreads the community's service and warm bonds of friendship outward to surrounding families. In the summers she presides over the summer youth program, which brings in young interns to tutor, coach, referee, and supervise anywhere from twenty-five to forty neighborhood children.

The community has been a refuge, a place for mentoring, and a conduit into urban ministry for neighborhood youth. A pregnant single girl whom Antioch took in was able to get on her feet and have the help of community women, learning to give care to her baby for a year before she moved out on her own. Donna and Chris Rice spent time working with Danny Hill, a young man they met in the church's "Dinner and Discipleship" program. Their involvement with him stimulated his interest in urban ministries and teaching young children, and he became a teacher's aid, working on an elementary education credential at Jackson State. Thus Antioch carries on the process of leadership development in the black community.

As in the Sojourners Community in Washington, D.C., some of Antioch's membership have become identified with magazine publishing. In 1992 the Perkins Foundation began to fund a quarterly, *Urban Family*, to approach the spectrum of inner-city issues from a Christian-values orientation. John was on the masthead as publisher, with Spencer as editor in chief and Chris as managing editor. Nancy became the magazine's production and art manager, and Jennifer Parker, a black Mississippian who had recently graduated from Harvard, became senior editor. The work started out partly in Pasadena but was shortly moved to offices in one of the five Antioch-owned houses on Robinson Street in Jackson. There it grew into a new ministry, largely staffed by Antioch people, but operating separately from Antioch and from VOC.

Urban Family was originally chartered to cover the subject of racial reconciliation as well as the issues and culture of African America. But because they were targeting an inner-city population, the editors decided to devote the magazine exclusively to black concerns. To promote reconciliation as a broader Christian ministry, they started another magazine, *The Reconciler*.

After a few years of marketing *Urban Family*, however, they found it was not drawing the inner-city readership they had been trying to reach. In a mass culture dominated by visual media, magazine subscription, particularly among the less than well-educated, has sharply declined. And *Urban Family* reflected that trend, drawing most of its subscriptions from people in missions and ministries and on Christian college campuses.

After five years' experience in the tough market of little magazines, Spencer and Chris, consulting with the *Christianity Today* staff who was now advising them, decided to move toward combining *Urban Family* and *The Reconciler* and using them as a voice to equip and publicize the reconciliation movement. Support for the new magazine, *Reconcilers,* comes from donors rather than subscribers.

Urban Family, published from 1992 to 1996.

This more reliable arrangement enables the staff to concentrate on turning out a quality magazine as an aspect of their broader ministry rather than having to focus their energies on doing marketing campaigns.

The ministry, now called Reconcilers Fellowship, sponsors a host of activities to further racial healing. Spencer Perkins and Chris Rice have become the chief publicists for what they envision as a national movement. In 1993 the two men wrote a book, *More than Equals,* which weaves their personal stories together around the theme of racial reconciliation. The book made them a popular speaking team on Christian college campuses, in urban ministry networks, and at evangelical churches around the country. Hence they now spend a fair amount of time in travel and speaking engagements, as does Ron Potter, who writes and speaks on African American theology.

Reconcilers Fellowship plans to further their mission through a new training center for racial reconciliation and community development to be built in Jackson. Voice of Calvary's International Study Center, which flourished during the eighties, closed down after the death of Lem Tucker, as Melvin Anderson refocused the resources and energies of the Jackson ministries on "indigenizing."

Lem Tucker was a soft-spoken intellectual who put his own scholarly construction on John's Three Rs in the articulate lectures he presented at the International Study Center. He could have been a seminary professor or, with his keen eye for finance, a corporate executive. In 1985, as he moved to concentrate on developing other black leaders, Lem brought Melvin Anderson on as housing director. And then he made Melvin his assistant, training him in the essentials of management. Though Melvin preferred directing the building crew, he would fill in as executive director when Lem was on the road.

A classmate of Joanie Perkins, Melvin had first been exposed to John's Bible teaching at his elementary school. He would come over to the Perkinses' white house and hang around Vera Mae's kitchen, where she gave him fried chicken or another Southern delicacy and her warm encouragement. Herbert Jones, who was friends with the Anderson family, would come to their house and fill some of the gap left by an absent father. Things had been hard and meager in Melvin's childhood household. His mother and grandmother worked hard for precious little, cleaning the houses of prominent white folks who pressured them to keep Melvin from associating with the radical Perkins ministry. But Melvin remained in VOC's youth program and after he had finished college, while serving as a YMCA administrator, he answered the Jackson Ministries' ad for a new housing director.

Voice of Calvary, as John and then Lem had developed it, had been very much a nationally sponsored ministry. When Lem died, much of the national connection fell away and donations declined by hundreds of thousands of dollars. As part of the new generation of indigenous leaders, Melvin had more local involvements and so he began to emphasize strengthening local relationships and building up the support base around Jackson. He began an extensive network with pastors and businessmen who support the kinds of work VOC does. He hired a new development director and brought in people to do management training. With his housing background, he brought VOC's focus into developing the local neighborhoods.

Under Melvin's leadership the housing ministry began to work out John's dream of an elaborate and systematic plan for Jackson neighborhood reclamation. PDI had made a start in that direction, but its renovated houses were usually sold to VOC staff or rented out. In the eighties home ownership came within reach of inner-city residents as bank financing became more obtainable. Of major help was the Reinvestment Act of 1978, a measure to counter the redlining of poor districts. It required banks to invest a certain percentage of their assets back into the community of residence. At the same time sales of HUD houses and savings and loan foreclosures were making it easier to get bargain prices and good terms.

Melvin transformed VOC's housing ministry from a largely volunteer operation to a professional-level crew, mainly composed of local African Americans. They bought up houses that came on the market, stripped them down to bare frame, and modernized them. Most houses in the once white neighborhood around VOC had been built in the 1920s through the 1940s with three bedrooms, one bath, and a wall heater. Renovation added a second bath, forced-air heating ducts, and washer/dryer hookups. Soon scores of neat cottages, like wild flowers, brightened the neighborhoods around the Four C Center. They had been transformed from rundown rentals into contemporary, affordable homes.

Augmented housing development became the basis of people development in some of Jackson's most blighted neighborhoods. A sea of abandoned, substandard structures, crime, drugs, and despair make Olin Park, on the fringes of the Jackson State campus, one of the worst areas in the city. The cramped duplex row houses were inadequate when they were built there during Jim Crow decades to house the black lower caste of urban day laborers. Lem Tucker harbored a vision of reclaiming this part of the city. He and Ellie lived for a time in the first house VOC bought there. And now Melvin walked the streets, sat on sagging porches, talked with the people, and listened to their ideas about improving the neighborhood. The new director would commit VOC to its most ambitious neighborhood housing program.

The duplexes were made over into more spacious one-family homes. Neighborhood associations were formed and with the help of public authorities they have been able to get law enforcement to help shut down some of the low-life clubs that have acted as magnets for crime and murder. VOC transforms these buildings into family life centers, where healthy social life is reborn and a cluster of revitalization programs are carried on.

Family Challenge, for example, is a set of workshops training people in the life management skills necessary to become home owners. Andy Abrams, an African American with a degree from Moody Bible Institute and years of management experience with Sears, teaches the course. With this kind of neighborhood reclamation emphasis and increasing crosstown networking, Voice of Calvary is working to fulfill John's initial vision: one person, one family, one block, one neighborhood at a time.

Block by block housing transformation in Olin Park brings Jackson's slum dwellers back into a civic environment. Residents learn construction skills working alongside Voice of Calvary workers. Ownership brings dignity and greater community involvement. Neighborhood children get involved in VOC's Good News Clubs and recreation and tutoring programs. Teens gain healthy role models and strong mentoring in the leadership and career development programs.

Typical of neighborhood kids who got a boost from Voice of Calvary was Philip "Pogo" Brown. Coming up in the youth programs, he grew close to Melvin, who mentored him. When he was ready to go to Jackson State, he got help from the VOC scholarship fund. Now nearing thirty, he works as a lab technician and paid commissioner of a city baseball league VOC started. The league, organized with the help of Cincinnati Reds pitcher Jeff Brantley, has as members about 160 boys between the ages of nine and thirteen.

And so the development process John pioneered in Mendenhall and expanded in Jackson continues today, digging deep roots into the neighborhood and renewing the structures and life of the city. Melvin's work to strengthen local ties has born fruit, and by the mid-nineties the local base of support has gone from raising 1 percent to raising 15 percent of Voice of Calvary Ministries' budget.

To sustain VOC's complex operations, continuing to expand its outreach into Jackson's sea of poverty, Melvin, like John, Dolphus, and Lem, spends time traveling, speaking, and developing the national base. Redistribution, which feeds reconciliation as well as development, continues to be a necessary support of the three-legged stool of Christian community development. John has always stressed infusion of outside capital and comingling of people of diverse racial and class backgrounds to spur development and heal our most painful social divisions.

In Pasadena the emphasis has been on instruction and mentoring, and the educational ministries there continue to expand and deepen as a new generation takes over. For some years John had been thinking about creating a school in northwest Pasadena. He designed the programs of Harambee Center to give public school children the close personal guidance and instruction they missed in mass education. But his work has always been about the equipping of African American leaders. He knows that top-level leaders typically come out of the enriched environment and curriculum of preparatory schools. Why not start such a school right there on Navarro Avenue? In the fall of 1995 Harambee Preparatory School opened, with thirty-two-year-old Priscilla Perkins as principal and twenty-one neighborhood children as students.

The work of starting up a quality private school in the inner city was a formidable challenge to the second to youngest of the Perkins children. Priscilla was the quiet, studious Perkins with a capacity for getting a job done and an eye for detail that made her an effective administrator. In her own academy days at Stoneybrook, she had had to study furiously to get up to grade level after coming out of Mississippi's public schools.

Priscilla Perkins, principal of Harambee Preparatory School, 1996.

She started college at Belhaven in Jackson, but the lingering racial frigidity of a white student body caused her to leave for the warmer if more relaxed climate of Jackson State. There she was securely among friends as the Goody Two-shoes they could rely on to be designated driver. She went West to do graduate work at U.C., Santa Barbara, but Harambee needed her, so she settled for commuting to California State, Los Angeles, where she earned her master of education degree.

Running a new school, however, was beyond anything she could have prepared for in the classroom. Colleges of education do not provide training for building an academy in the inner city. Fund-raising, for instance, had to be more extensive and continuous than at other schools, because local families could make only very low tuition payments. To gather the million-dollar endowment that would be necessary to sustain the new school, Priscilla benefited from its high visibility as the latest Perkins ministry. As such, it had a built-in support base among the philanthropists who customarily backed John's projects.

The school fired the imaginations of many resourceful Southern Californians, among them Joe Weller, president of Nestle Chocolate Company, and his wife Carol. The Wellers are a warm, down-to-earth couple who wanted to get personally involved with the ministry. Adept at fund-

Harambee youth at Motown Studios, Detroit, during the 1993 Christian Community Development Association conference. Betty is second from left; Priscilla is second from right.

raising, Carol engineered Harambee's celebrity basketball exhibitions at Pasadena City College. And Joe served on the Perkins Foundation board.

For the school to thrive, it needed a staff closely attuned to the needs of inner-city children and it had that in the three urban missionary women who became its first teachers. Karyn Farrar Perkins, Derek's wife—an experienced public school teacher—and Julie Ragland and Anne Berry, two energetic white women with elementary school teaching credentials, had been on Harambee's staff, working with neighborhood children for years. Priscilla and the three teachers worked together to develop a strong academic curriculum that would also build character in the children. Fortunately they had a powerful model for a quality inner-city school in Marva Collins's West Side Preparatory School in Chicago.

Years ago Collins had taken over an old bank building and with meager facilities had taught skills and breathed a love of learning into ghetto youngsters that had them enthusiastically going through Shakespeare and the classics by the fifth and sixth grades. Her approach recalls that of the tough-minded, warm-spirited teachers, often single women, who peopled the American classroom from frontier days to the mid-twentieth century. Like them, Collins sets firm behavior boundaries, creating an environment of civility, where boisterous, uncouth, or bullying behavior simply have no place. Coming alongside the children, she affirms their abilities and expects quality work, thus instilling self-respect and confidence. In this context, basic-skills training in such things as phonics, to sound out unfamiliar words, becomes an empowering experience.

Harambee's teachers went through Collins's books and they went to her workshops in Chicago, learning to apply her methods. In the midst of an urban environment with so many negative influences, it was vital to build a bastion of learning and mutual respect where the teachers can fortify the minds and spirits of the children they are training to be leaders. Involvement in other Harambee Center activities, like the Tuesday Good News Clubs and the after-school and summer programs, generalize the children's nurture, learning, and values training well beyond the school environment. They become a part of the community Harambee is building. For Harambee to be radically effective it must also transform the children's home environment, and so it is necessary to impact parents and significant elders.

Here the partnering concept that was coming to characterize Christian community development has come into play. Neighborhood Christian Partners, which the Pasadena church association formed to do development and reconciliation, began sponsoring something called the Family Life Investment Program. They set out to implement FLIP within a number of populations, including families with children attending Harambee Preparatory School. Paul Gibson, an African American who graduated from Harvard University and Fuller Seminary and is a Pasadena native, became the program's designer and director. Gibson, with further training in an innovative program at Cal. State, Los Angeles, introduced a multifaceted approach to raising the level of family function.

FLIP was designed to give parents information and training in a variety of relational and practical areas. In relating to their children, parents are taught how to actively listen, resolve conflict, manage anger, and discipline positively through encouragement. A framework for understanding and guiding their children's behavior is given in a presentation on developmental stages. And their own life issues are addressed in segments on self-awareness and self-care. Training in time management and budgeting round out the curriculum, helping harried urban adults set priorities and bring order and a greater sense of mastery to their lives.

Parents of Harambee's twenty-one school children were required to attend FLIP presentations. But Priscilla and her staff did not need to twist any arms, since the program proved to be immensely popular from its start. Hungry for this kind of help, mothers in particular went out of their way to come, and attendance was amazingly always perfect. One pregnant woman went into labor during the class. She left, had her baby, and was back the following week. The seven-week program became so popular that people were asking for more, so they added three supplemental weeks. And when those ended, a group of the people, now bonded with one another, began meeting on their own.

The Family Life Investment Program serves to deepen contact between school and home. As mothers become more involved, Harambee enlists their cooperation in getting the children to turn off the television and develop better study habits. Aware of TV's stifling of thought and its steady diet of killing, casual sex, and hypercommercialism, Harambee staff try to get children to watch less and read more. Mothers record their children's hours of television watching and hours of reading and turn the figures in to the teachers. Harambee teachers assign books over vacation and go to great lengths to make the children into readers.

Harambee's school children have also benefited from sister relationships the school has developed with three other private schools in the Pasadena area. Polytechnic School, across from Cal. Tech., one of the highest rated schools in the country, has students go to Harambee on Thursdays to play musical instruments and tutor children in the classroom. Another sister school, Chandler, shares activities with Harambee children, and Pasadena Christian School shares resources. These relationships together with lots of field trips and news media attention further enrich the children's experience, adding to their sense of personal significance.

For Priscilla the first year of Harambee Preparatory School was a ceaseless round of activity. Fund-raising went well, with a hundred thousand dollars coming out of celebrity basketball alone. Priscilla adopted her parents' habit of "living poor" while investing most of the money that comes in. While this brought rapid progress in financial development, it also caused headaches, as everyday needs sometimes got shortchanged. Harambee's board induced Priscilla to use more money for operating expenses when needed, but her management style, like that of her parents, would always keep a tight rein on finances.

An escalating boundary dispute, including questions of fiscal management, developed between Priscilla and Derek. The school drew the lion's share of attention during its first year, overshadowing Harambee's other ministries. Derek's intense artistic personality sees wholes rather than parts, and his attention rests on inspiration and outreach rather than on the painstaking details of management and finance that so occupy Priscilla. With Harambee's school and its other programs fused under one leadership, Derek's and Priscilla's opposite temperaments and priorities tended to clash and the two commonly found themselves at painful loggerheads.

Derek wanted chief executive authority for Harambee's overall programs, and some of Harambee's board were supportive of his desire. A consensus also existed, which included John and Vera Mae, that Priscilla should retain full executive authority over the school. The board was reluctant to separate Harambee Preparatory School from Harambee Christian Family Center and in the fall of 1995 they decided to give Derek a three-month sabbatical leave to help him reassess his position. He was building a new house diagonally across from the Harambee Center, where he and Rudy Carasco were planning an intentional community similar to Antioch. That project was occupying much of his time.

Carol Weller, director of development for Harambee Preparatory School, and Deborah Perkins, launching the Harambee 100 Campaign of 1997– 98 to raise money for one hundred scholarships.

In the spring of 1996 Derek returned to full-time ministry, and the differences between him and Priscilla were still very much in evidence. Board members now realized they could only resolve the problem by separating the school and having two separate boards of directors. Harambee was fortunate to have a wealth of what John likes to call servant leaders to provide the collective wisdom to resolve this issue. It now appears that the Pasadena ministries, like those in Mendenhall and Jackson are evolving into separate, interrelated clusters. As yet they have no umbrella parish church, but that may evolve out of the new intentional community.

While Derek and Priscilla were establishing their respective roles and sorting out their differences, Betty, the youngest of the Perkins children, was emerging as a key leader in the Pasadena ministry. Along with a team of Harambee's women, including Priscilla, she works with the girls in much the same way Derek and Bryan work with the boys. After the Bible study on Wednesdays, six or seven girls, ranging in age from twelve to nineteen, come for dinner and a sleep-over. As with the boys, this extended time with a small group of girls provides the opportunity for closeness, with individual girls getting warm attention for their special concerns.

Betty is an outgoing person who likes to be in close relationships with her girls. It was hard for her to leave them in the winter of 1996, when she went to Warrenton, Missouri, for three months' intensive training with Child Evangelism Fellowship. Vera Mae, who had received the training in 1982, had long encouraged her to go. But while Betty was gone, a crisis rocked the girls' fellowship at Harambee. Two high school girls and one in her first year of college became pregnant. Before she left, Betty had a dream that one of them was pregnant. She had felt her pulling away. The revelations of pregnancy, as they occurred while she was in Missouri, put her through an emotional upheaval. All she could do finally was give the girls and their pregnancies over to God. And as she was able to release the burden, she felt a reassurance of God's controlling presence.

The Child Evangelism program was a powerful growth experience for Betty. She had been to boarding school for four years at All Saints Episcopal School in Vicksburg, and that had prepared her for academic intensity and classroom and dormitory life in a virtually all-white environment. Much of the time was taken up with Child Evangelism's traditional coursework: learning the biblical basis for each lesson and making the flannel storyboards. Along with these essentials, the program now included training with computer software and a psychological component.

Classes and readings were given in child development, dealing with the issues of the different age groups. They took personality tests to help them gain insight into their own strengths and weaknesses and to increase sensitivity in relating to others with styles different from their own. Talking about themselves on a personal level and talking about dealing with troubled teens and children opened people up to disclosure of their own childhoods and family issues. Many got in touch with personal pain as they became aware of old, unresolved conflicts.

Betty thought about the pressures and deprivations of the Perkinses' missionary lifestyle and about her father's being away from home so much. Then she thought about how he had always returned and she remembered the special attention he had given her. As the training ended, John and Vera Mae traveled to Missouri. They were two proud parents, seeing their youngest child complete her training. John spoke at the graduation exercises, recalling how he had first become aware of God's claims on his life through Spencer's exposure to Child Evangelism.

Returning to California, Betty felt new confidence in herself and was more deeply committed than ever to her work with the girls in Harambee's youth program. She sought out the three girls who were pregnant and spoke to them of God's forgiveness and his love for them and their babies. But it was hard to get them to come back into the group. Betty did her best. She tried to help them past their shame by letting them know they had her unqualified support.

Betty began to get the young women who came on Wednesday nights to talk in depth about their date life. One girl mentioned a boy kissing her in a movie.

"How did you feel?" Betty asked.

"Well I didn't even *like* him," she said.

"And you gave away your precious kisses to somebody you didn't like?" rejoined Betty.

In this kind of frank exchange, the girls paused and thought about what they were doing. Betty thus began to establish a support system to uphold sexual restraint. She felt gratified about the progress her teenagers were making. She introduced the idea of consecrating themselves to God, with a ring as a symbol of their commitment. Five of the girls have taken that spiritual step and others are on the brink of doing so. This welds them together, strengthening them in their commitment to resist sexual license and the shallow self-seeking of the larger society.

In the spring of 1996, as Harambee's first exhausting school year drew to a close, Betty and Priscilla looked forward to visiting their parents in Dallas, and then Joanie, Spencer, and the others in Jackson. Betty was then planning to apply her new skills in the Good News Club that would be a part of Harambee's summer program. And she was beginning to think beyond Northwest Pasadena. She was just turning thirty, and Daddy was encouraging her to think about flying out of Harambee's nest and moving into a youth ministry of her own. With her expansive personality and her credentials to train Child Evangelism teachers, God might be calling her to work with many Harambees. There was that old Perkins prod to step out and risk and grow. John had never been content to hunker down and hold on. He was always looking around the corner for the next challenge. And he knew his youngest daughter had some of that same drive in her.

26

THE BELOVED COMMUNITY

On June 3, 1988, John sat in the front room of his cottage on Navarro Avenue and talked informally about his life's work. The interview was for an article that would be published in *Transformation,* an international magazine of missions and social ethics. Asked what legacy he'd like to leave, he thought a moment and then replied, "I think a concept. I'd like to leave a philosophy of ministry." As he went on to expound this point, he stressed his concern not for forms, but for the ideas that create them. "I think that's what probably stops me from building an empire," he reflected. And then he was reminded of a biblical passage.

"The other morning," he said, "I was doing devotions and it struck me for the first time. I was reading Matthew 24. It says that Jesus had been outside talkin' to them and they return and they go to the temple and the disciples got the feeling from his action and what he told them that they were leavin' the temple for the last time. This is the last visit to the temple. Jesus has convinced them by now he was going die. They are convinced of that. And so they care about the temple, and they show him the temple [as if to say]: 'And don't you say that this is not important. How do you imagine that this is not important?'

"And Jesus says, *'There's not one stone left here that will not be torn down.'* And the idea was, don't put your faith in these things. Don't put your faith in these institutions. Put your faith in something that endures. And I think about the church in China. Look what it's gone through. . . . And look how it's endured, because there's an idea. There's an *idea.*"

John's idea has been encapsulated in his Three Rs of Christian community development. His desire to respond to a God who came alongside him by coming alongside black people in his native Mississippi has led to his living out the process of relocation, reconciliation, and redistribution. He created the model in Mendenhall and as he was creating it, he was already bringing others into it. He proselytized the idea tirelessly while he was in Jackson and then out of Pasadena. And in 1989 the idea went to seed and began pollinating the nation through the Christian Community Development Association.

The experience and the idea that would birth the Christian community development movement was rooted in the history of the African American response to oppression. From the time of slavery, African American thinkers and doers have grappled with the fact of their people's oppressed condition. One of the most prolific reformers, W. E. B. Du Bois, has said the "attitude of the imprisoned group [can take] three main forms: revolt or revenge; adjustment of all thought and action to the greater group; or finally, a determined attempt at self-development, self-realization, in spite of environing discouragements and prejudice." Actually Du Bois's categories are not mutually exclusive but interrelated. An individual or group may have one of the first two tendencies but creatively adapt it into a variety of self-realization.

Malcolm X, for example, had a deep-seated rage at a racist white America, which had always held blacks in subjection. His black nationalist rhetoric scared a lot of whites but it also injected a much needed sense of dignity and pride of heritage into the black community. When he embraced orthodox Islam and made his pilgrimage to Mecca, he had a transforming experience there that opened him to reconciliation and cooperation with whites and non-Muslims. Malcolm then emerged as an inspirational figure with international appeal. His criticism of Euro-American neocolonialism and his identification with the revolutionary aspirations of Third World peoples placed him to the left of mainstream black reformers. But his powerful rhetoric of black self-assertion struck a responsive chord across the spectrum of African America, and he became a beloved folk hero.

If Malcolm X represents a radical, or Left response, Booker T. Washington represents the Right. Emerging in the context of white supremacy, the accommodationist black reform that Washington came to symbolize had stressed vocational and industrial training while downplaying liberal arts education and participation in politics. His autobiography, *Up from Slavery,* was a paean to black success through hard work and self-discipline, akin to the Horatio Alger novels so popular in the age of enterprise. For Washington, confining social structures need not spell defeat. America as he saw it was full of opportunities that anybody with enough grit and moral rectitude could take advantage of. While his position, at least outwardly, acceded to a society of caste, and civil rights advocates like Du Bois justifiably criticized him for it, Washington's philosophy of self-discipline and self-help had merit.

The Tuskegee educator's faith in character development and free market economics continues among conservative evangelicals, whose values and standards echo those of Washington's rural and small town America. When their social conscience is aroused, these Christians give their support to private charities and community development rather than government programs to bring about equality and redistribution.

Neither Washington's nineteenth-century conservatism nor Malcolm X's anticolonial radicalism placed great emphasis on interracial cooperation or integration. Washington worked within a Jim Crow context, while Malcolm X, even as he reached out to white allies after his Mecca experience, favored black separatism in order to get out from under white paternalism. Neither have the spiritual descendants of Malcolm or Washington given much attention to building interracial community. That emphasis has come more from Christian reformers of the Center— Martin Luther King Jr., the liberal, and John Perkins, the evangelical.

When King dramatized conditions in the South or the northern ghettoes, it was liberal America, its media, its government, and its collegiate youth whose support he was seeking to galvanize. At the same time, King knew that government-backed civil rights could not bring the change of heart, the "beloved community," he was so ardently seeking. Without intentional interracial community building, America would continue in its accustomed pattern as two societies—separate, unequal, and deeply divided. King proclaimed his dream of racial reconciliation but he did not get the chance to go beyond the politics of nonviolent demonstrations and government action to bring it about. It has been John Perkins who has put the working clothes on Martin Luther King's dream, building his beloved community.

Perkins agreed with King's liberal belief in engaging federal support for black advancement. In the voting rights campaign and the boycott and demonstrations in downtown Mendenhall he brought the tactics of the civil rights movement to Simpson County. His refusal to hate his Brandon tormentors, and his reorientation of his movement toward racial reconciliation, links him with the redemptive Christianity preached and lived by King.

At the same time Perkin's ideas overlap those of Malcom X and Booker T. Washington. Like Malcolm he has emphasized blacks gaining greater self-determination and power through economic development of their own community. And like the black nationalist leader, he has supported empowerment of Third World peoples. Yet his belief in the disciplinary value of work recall the values of Booker T. Washington. Self-help, ownership, hard work, and character building are as intregral to Voice of Calvary's and Harambee's teaching as to Washington's Tuskegee Institute.

The qualitites Perkins shares with Washington are the ones he has in common with mainstream American evangelicalism. The evangelical businessmen who have always been around him recognize a kinsman. He and they share a love of harnessing the great productive energies of competitive capitalism and using them to develop and empower disadvantaged people. Former business executive Al Whittaker, for example, who has spent much of his life starting small businesses in Third World settings, thinks much the way Perkins does. This kind of compassionate capitalism is what rebuilds the bombed-out inner-city neighborhoods and forges racial reconciliation in CCDA communities.

The resurgent localism of the Christian community developers' neighborhood associations and kids' clubs and church people helping in the elementary schools recalls the habits and values of an older, small town, evangelical America. And the evangelicals of this older America thought in terms of individuals making personal commitments to live out their faith in doing something for the greater good. Today the self-obsessions of a dominant consumer culture have largely stifled the civic spirit among suburbanized evangelicals as they have among the irreligious. But Perkins and the Christian community development movement are renewing evangelical social awareness. And as evangelicals of conscience move to repopulate, reneighbor, and restore America's urban waste places, they recreate a healthy localism.

Set free from the addictions of consumption, the evangelical mind-set tends back toward the nurturance of family and locality. Liberalism, on the other hand, has tended more to make centralized institutions its engine of provision. Perkins has criticized the welfare and housing bureaucracies that do things *for* people, rather than fertilize and water the grass roots, as community development does. Contrast between the two approaches came clear recently in Atlanta, when the community Bob Lupton lives in purchased a public housing project and transformed it into a cooperative. Now formerly listless and uninvolved ghetto residents exhibit pride of ownership and eagerly learn the skills of property management.

At the same time Perkins, who grew up amid the extension of opportunity created by the New Deal, continues to see a positive role for government. During the conservative Reagan administration, he and the others of the Food Assistance Task Force endorsed the federal safety net for society's neediest people but they added that government was especially helpful when it backed privately conceived programs like the food banks. Perkins's support of the government safety net was tempered by his observation of its tendency to become a steel web that ensnares people in dependency, sapping their belief in their own resources.

While he loves the creative energy of competitive capitalism, Perkins, unlike many conservative evangelicals, does not absolutize the free market. Big capital, he recognizes, tends to make its decisions in narrow economic terms that often ignore the public interest. And government regulation is necessary to curb the economic and environmental excesses of capitalism. A piece of banking regulation, for example, the Reinvestment Act, helps in bringing development back to blighted areas. And a host of betterment programs in areas like education and health care make the means of advancement and important services available for people of very limited means.

As a centrist reformer, Perkins has often endorsed government sponsored redistribution. He points out that in America opportunity comes with ownership of capital, and it is exceedingly difficult for a long-impoverished class of people to obtain the skills, education, personal contacts, and access to bank loans that would give them a toehold to climb to success. Hence it is important for the government, as umpire, to enter the game and take positive action to make more opportunities available to those who have been dispossessed. Perkins is aware that the dispossessed are not always black. He recognizes the inequity of giving affirmative action to middle-class and well-to-do African

Americans, while leaving out disadvantaged nonblacks. Hence, he has suggested that affirmative action be modified to include such economic criteria in assessing eligibility.

Government action in itself, however, is insufficient. For John Perkins the key to lasting change is in people's willingness to reoccupy and reclaim the waste places and reneighbor with cast-off people, loving them, teaching them skills, and nurturing their children. Government can help facilitate the process, but the initiative has to come from people themselves of all ethnic backgrounds who have acquired advantage and capital. People of means making the decision to relocate among the underclasses, and suburban churches and businesspeople deciding to partner with inner-city churches and communities, these kinds of deliberate personal commitment are needed to transform America.

Like other evangelicals, Perkins believes that responsibility for positive change rests ultimately in the personal decisions of individuals. People's intentional actions in support of society's dispossessed are the true basis of economic progress, social justice, and racial reconciliation. The mushrooming movement represented by the hundreds of community development associations in CCDA is a tangible testimony to that belief. It began in 1960 when one black refugee from the Deep South, living out the American Dream in California, made the decision to move back among the oppressed in Mississippi.

By the mid-nineties, amid the tensions and antagonisms following the Los Angeles riots and the O. J. Simpson murder trial, evangelical Christians were beginning to awaken from their complacency in regard to racial issues. With CCDA setting the pace, other large bodies of evangelicals across the country began publicly promoting racial reconciliation. The Southern Baptists committed themselves as a denomination to repenting of their racism and seeking reconciled relationships with African Americans. Promise Keepers, a men's movement organized by Bill McCartney, a former University of Colorado football coach, was stressing men's duty to be reconciled and seek friendships across lines of race and ethnicity.

Racial reconciliation is not only one of the seven promises that Promise Keepers make, but it is also a personal issue with McCartney and he has worked to make it central to the movement. Many of the stadium speakers and staff for training pastors are well-known African American ministers, one of them John Perkins. McCartney and Perkins have developed a close working relationship, and at the fall 1995 CCDA Convention in Denver, the former coach gave one of the keynote speeches.

Whether the big stadium rallies and cellular Promise Keeper groups being organized in local churches serve to get many suburban evangelicals involved with the inner city remains to be seen. But at least it can be said that parachurch movements stressing racial reconciliation are at last starting to rouse the dormant conscience of white middle-class evangelicalism.

Flying around the country and speaking constantly to throngs of pastors and urban missionaries and living out of suitcases can get tiring. Vera Mae accompanied John on many of the campaign trips. But when she stayed behind, there was little for her to do in Dallas. She longed to get back to her Child Evangelism classes. Camping in the Dallas apartment between flights, John felt the transiency of the life they were living as he and Gordie worked their American Cities Campaign around the country. John was used to a nomadic existence. He and Vera Mae had lived this way since the sixties. But there had always been a home base, a village they had nourished, a warm familial community they could return to and rest, relax, eat lunch in their backyard with some of the family, visit with friends, and check out the ministries.

Since they had packed up their things and pulled out of Pasadena that June day in 1995, they lacked such a home. Betty and Deborah were living in the little house on Navarro and they had painted, fixed it up, bought new furniture, put their own stamp on it. John would go to Pasadena and stay there from time to time between cities campaigns. And good as it was to stay there with the girls, it still amounted to little more than a pit stop. He and Vera Mae both wanted something more permanent. They thought about going back to Pasadena, but the younger generation, with the help of a broadly equipped Harambee Board, had moved fully into leadership. John and Vera Mae were good to have on hand for consultation, but the school and the ministries were all well-staffed and under their own momentum.

After mulling it over for a number of months, they resolved to move back to Jackson. Vera Mae saw a need there for her to start more Good News Clubs, and John would preside over the new training center they were planning. They decided to live in one of the houses on Robinson Street when they would once again move back to Mississippi.

John liked being in Mississippi. He had become a well-known and well-loved public citizen there and he had close friends all over the state. In the summer of 1996, as the American Cities Campaign was winding down, John and Vera Mae moved back to Jackson during their regular vacation time in Mississippi, settling a few doors down the street from the Antioch household. John would continue his travel as ambassador for the community development movement, but at a less hectic pace than in the American Cities Campaign.

In February 1997, Vera Mae opened a new center for Child Evangelism in another refurbished building there in the Jackson neighborhood. It was called the Veramiah Center, a combination of *Vera Mae* and the name of the Old Testament prophet *Nehemiah*, whose message was one of return and restoration. The benefactor who donated funds to purchase the building had suggested the name Veramiah. The new center would have an eager young director who would take over the reins of leadership from Vera Mae. It was Betty Perkins who returned from Pasadena to head up an expansive new effort to train Child Evangelism teachers to reach unchurched children in Mississippi.

So John and Vera Mae continue in the work they love, surrounded by a younger generation of leaders they trained to take over the ministries. Retirement is a relative term to John. He is an incessantly active man, ever thinking ahead to the next project. On one trip in 1995 John saw Billy Graham's son, Franklin, who is now heading the Graham ministries. Billy Graham has long been John's friend and a warm supporter of Christian community development. Franklin told John that his seventy-seven-year-old father's health wasn't good and he had been encouraging him to retire from doing the crusades. But his dad insisted on continuing to do them, he told John. And John nodded in deep understanding.

Appendix

The African American Church

In the culture and worldview of African Americans, the black church has exercised the most prominent and also the most cryptic presence. It is and has been many different things. As such, it is a series of projections of the black experience in all its many-sided complexity. It is the oldest and for a long time it was the only organized expression of the black community, having originated in slavery. It has spoken with many voices, and these voices have often spoken with ambiguity. In slavery, under the lash of the overseer and the watchful eye of the master, the "invisible institution" was born into a painful and insecure existence.

The black plantation preacher received his call directly from God, and thus he was a charismatic figure, speaking out and interpreting the plight of his people, giving them a sense of meaning and comfort in their joyless lives. The preacher combined elements of African folk religion—a sense that everything is spiritually alive—with a biblical concept of God's salvation and justice. Black preachers often had some literacy gleaned from white clergy and missionaries. From their preachers, slaves were able to gain a sense that the biblical story is one of liberation from the bondage of sin and from every other form of bondage. More than the educated white Christians who controlled their bodies, they understood this truth.

Christianity on the plantations lived under monumental constraints. Slaves were kept from literacy and books. Field slaves spent most of their waking ours at hard stoop labor, and so there was little time to create culture. But human communities will create; they will pour forth the collective upwellings of their souls even amid dire conditions of want and oppression. Indeed the community can gain a depth and purity of faith expression within the grinding jaws of oppression. Such was given witness by the prophets of the ancient Jewish diaspora and the sages of the medieval ghettos. And the spirituality of the African American community would take its form in the context of slavery. Hence it had two poles: one like the North of the compass, pointed to freedom; the other had to make do and serve a downtrodden people's day-to-day needs under the Southern yoke.

One pole was the prophetic call for freedom and human dignity. Rarely was it possible in slavery to directly address these concerns without immediate white retribution. And so all kinds of double entendres pervaded the preacher's exhortations and the spirituals. Most of the references to heavenly freedom thinly cloaked a more material form of deliverance from one's heavy burdens, emancipation. The prophetic side of faith had to remain so masked in slavery, but in 1831 it exploded in lethal violence as the preacher Nat Turner, fired by an apocalyptic vision, led a revolt that killed sixty whites.

As blacks have struggled toward freedom and equality during the time since slavery, this side of the church, with its emphasis on wresting justice from white America, has become more and more prominent. But the other pole of spiritual life, that which had to adapt to and survive under the weight of white supremacy, became the normal church expression.

This was the side of the church that took care of the immediate emotional and practical needs of the people. It was the adaptive response to the distinct pressures on blacks perpetrated by white rulers. Fear and rage were the common emotional base of black life in the Jim Crow South. These emotions worked their destructive way through the black community—husband against wife, parent against child, neighbor against neighbor—the constantly simmering anger periodically boiled over and scalded the people indiscriminately. And it was the church that gave the community an effective valve to let out the hot steam of frustrated lives.

What has always distinguished the black church from the white is the richly emotional texture of its worship. The preacher, traditionally the dominant personage in the black community, is the central figure of a drama that has all the intensive community ritual of a medieval passion play. Because white domination so constricted black public expression, it was all channeled into the one venue of the Sunday meeting. The singing of choral gospel music sets a deeply emotional tone for the service. Black gospel music, with its resonant inflections and its flow of feeling, has a powerful, transporting effect on its listeners.

Woven together with the exciting performance of the sermon, the overall effect is a geyser of feeling. The goings-on up front are orchestrated to get the people "happy" and bring them to shouting. The communal intent was a climactic emotional release, release from the drudgery and the hungry poverty and the hopeless prison of black life. Sunday worship provided a brief haven to elevate the people above their sad, hard lives, so it was not a place for exposition of ideas or theologizing. In the black church service we are in the realm of the performing arts. The message inspired but it was not supposed to make you think.

With the Great Migration, followed by the civil rights movement in the twentieth century, many blacks arriving at middle-class status became critical of the lack of intelligent moral or theological argument in black preaching. The church was condemned as anti-intellectual and regressive, and in a sense it has been. But paradox and contradiction permeate the history of the black church. The poetic, almost operatic form of the black preacher's oratory could be used in a variety of contexts.

Under the dominion of slavery and segregation, he commonly spoke to console and bring hope of ultimate redemption. Preachers often sounded the theme of relief and joy in finally laying one's burden down and being reunited with loved ones on the other shore. They would arouse their congregations' emotional fervor by telling them just what they could expect to experience in heaven: "No rain, no bad weather, no trouble, no sorrow, no crying. Lord! No more lying been said about you, no more tattlin', no more goin' hungry." The preacher gave vent to the deeply felt pain of his people. He spoke to their personal trials and relentless suffering: "*How long?* How long must I labor in the vineyard?" This question was repeated often and echoed by the people. "Talk back" was a vital part of black preaching. Messages were always punctuated with "Amen" or "Preach it" or "All right" or "Tell it like it is" or "Make it plain." With roots in the African call and response, these periodic rhythmic responses helped the preacher feel his message more deeply and drive it home. Talk back spurred on the crescendo, with its powerful outpouring of emotion. The preacher would stoke the bellows of feeling in his people all the more by encouraging such verbal response: "Can I get an Amen?" "Can I get a witness?"

This kind of preaching is a powerful vehicle for giving inspiration and releasing feeling. And it was honed to a fine edge by preachers in the rural South during slavery and segregation. In those days it had strong elements of escapism. It also soothed, encouraged, and gave hope to an oppressed people. It gave strength to endure and that was a deep inner necessity. When times got more hopeful during the civil rights movement, this same format would be adapted to prophetic purposes. Martin Luther King's preaching would rework the old themes to encourage his people to stride toward justice.

In the early spring of 1965, at the conclusion of the heroic march from Selma to Montgomery, Alabama, in the face of massive white resistance, he preached a short sermon. As he neared the end, he intoned: "How long?" Then he answered: "Not long, because no lie can live forever." Then he went on:

How long? Not long, because you still reap what you sow.
How long? Not long, because the arc of the moral universe is long, but it bends toward justice.
How long? Not long, 'cause mine eyes have seen the glory of the coming of the Lord. . . .

Given in the immediate wake of a transforming event where black and white marchers had linked arms under threat of potential violence, this stirring speech is rich with prophetic meaning.

Preaching and the Sunday meeting were the central communal rite of the black church. Nourished in Southern hamlets and transplanted to the urban ghetto, they were adapted to serve the changing state of African American life. But the church was far more than its theatrical worship events. It was the central institution of black America and the organ of its purest expression. Having begun on the plantations as "the invisible institution," it was the chief means of addressing the temporal needs of the people. In slavery it was the preacher himself who would act as a go-between, procuring whatever he could from the white bosses for his people.

In the Southern white culture, evangelical religion was the predominant form, with its call for personal conversion; its emotional, dramatic oratory; and its communal camp meetings. Blacks had originally been attracted to the evangelical expression of Christian faith more than to the more staid and liturgical forms in part because they recalled the spiritual ceremonies of their African past. The white planters recognized the calling of the black preachers in their midst, sometimes allowing them to preach to whites. The preacher functioned as an intermediary, seeking favor with the white bosses as well as from the Almighty. In this sense he worked as the shaman had in Africa, deeply involved in the physical lives, the tangible day-to-day concerns of his people. Blacks never drew the sharp distinction between material and spiritual affairs that whites often did. God was as interested in their freedom and physical well-being as in their eternal salvation. In this sense they were closer to their African roots and closer to the Hebrew culture, which bequeathed the Scripture, than to the white church.

When freedom came, the black church's nurturance of her people could now broaden beyond the office of the preacher. It had already done so north of slavery, beginning in the eighteenth century when racial discrimination caused free blacks to leave the Methodist churches and start their own mutual aid society, which grew into the African Methodist denominations.

The church throughout the South became the womb and cradle of black enterprise. It formed burial, insurance, and banking companies and nurtured whatever business germinated within the black community. Churches also became the chief supporters of education as the best means of advancement for black people. In this endeavor, they created black colleges, vocational schools, and academies. And the pastors solicited aid—conscience money—from white patrons.

They learned to live with segregation, supporting their own separate institutions, and the church became the central clearinghouse for all legitimate black economic and social activity. There were positive and negative effects of the development of the institutional black church. The church became a vested interest. Its pastors were mandarins within the black communities. In the South especially they were their people's advocates and representatives, who petitioned and accommodated the white power structure. Presiding over the tiny empires of segregated churches, they were often a force for conservatism.

By adapting to the existent social structures of a racially discriminatory America, the black church and its clergy became accomplices in upholding those structures, even as they despised them. This was inevitable. Oppressed peoples invariably collaborate with their oppressor and his institutions in order to survive. This collaboration insured the privileged position of black pastors and the established interests of the churches and it kept them from becoming advocates of the radical changes that were necessary to bring real progress to African America.

Despite these limitations, the church remained the embodiment of African American creativity. It was the heart of its spirituality, the chief support of its family life, the base of its enterprise, the nurturing ground of its social relations, and the progenitor of its education. And as the black churches took on their other, prophetic identity in the civil rights movement, they became its primary means for communication and the gathering of support. They invested the movement with spiritual meaning and the power to confront and endure and they provided the institutional apparatus to make it go. Sometimes for worse, but more often for better, the black church has been the hub of the black community.

Among free black people before the Civil War and the freedmen afterward, Baptist and Methodist communions became most common. These were the two most successful evangelical denominations in the nineteenth century and they would ultimately account for six of the seven major black denominations. The seventh, the Church of God in Christ, is the product of the Pentecostal movement, which in turn grew out of the holiness revivals, germinating amid the dislocations of an industrializing America.

Holiness was originally connected with John Wesley and Methodism. Wesley had stressed sanctification, or believers' increasing victory over sin as they mature in faith. Other forms of evangelicalism laid most of the emphasis on the initial conversion, or justification. In the United States between the Revolution and the Civil War there was a tremendous outpouring of spiritual energy and idealism. The Second Great Awakening had produced evangelists like Charles G. Finney, who traversed urban and frontier America preaching a practical, emotional gospel and advocating social reform, including the abolition of slavery.

Following Finney and his convert, abolitionist Theodore Weld, evangelicals of the antebellum period sought to remake America in millennial terms. They crusaded against alcohol, and for Sabbath observance, and for peace, and health foods, and helping the poor, the industrial worker, and the disabled. Some of them even got themselves together into communal societies with unorthodox practices and a strong bent toward perfectionism, or "perfect love."

The most intensely fought of the Protestant crusades of the period was the crusade against slavery. And the denominational persuasion that was spreading most rapidly and was most in tune with the reform-oriented holiness crusade was Wesleyan Methodism. The call to holiness, or perfectionism, which was the final phase of the Second Great Awakening, reached a peak in the year 1858, when there was a nation-wide holiness revival. The revival did not prevent the Civil War from breaking out two years later, however. In fact it may well have accelerated the outbreak of war, since it furthered the antislavery cause, which in turn heightened Southern resistance. Many an evangelical abolitionist would view the war as an Armageddon that would finally eradicate slavery and usher in the Kingdom of Christ in America.

The trauma of bloodletting purged much of the reformist idealism from the country, and the fires of revival died down and almost went out completely. But the embers that remained and were eventually fanned back into flame were holiness embers. Holiness revivals continued after the Civil War, and a number of breakaway holiness denominations were eventually formed.

By the end of the century, when the family farm was in economic trouble, people were moving to the cities, and smokestack industries were working men, women, and children long hours for poverty wages, holiness revivals flared up again. Social and economic frustration turned many of the common people toward spiritual relief. They hungered after hope and the joy and peace that accompany deep faith experience. Many drew the comfort and strength to go on from the holiness churches.

African Americans, always at the bottom of the economic ladder, were particularly hard-hit by the depression of the 1890s. White farmers and tradesmen, on the economic downslide, jealously guarded their status over blacks and often took out their frustrations on them. It was at this time that a rigid segregation became fastened on the South, and other regions saw ever greater discrimination. With their outlook worse than usual, blacks also turned increasingly to healing balm for the spirit. Baptist and Methodist communions were well established. They were not exactly mired in prosperous complacency, but interests were entrenched and conservative, routines were habituated, and little attention was paid to spiritual growth following conversion. Enter Mr. C. P. Jones, a Missionary Baptist in Selma, Alabama, who claimed entire sanctification in 1894.

Now this kind of thing was just not done in Baptist circles, but Reverend Jones was fired by his spiritual vision. On assuming the pastorate at Mt. Helm Baptist Church in Jackson, Mississippi, he began to preach holiness from the pulpit and, to make matters worse, he was determined to spread his message beyond his own congregation. In 1897 he started a series of holiness convocations. This aroused his fellow Baptist pastors to open opposition. They met and expelled him from the denomination. Undaunted, Reverend Jones started the Church of Christ Holiness, U.S.A. as the century turned.

The first decade of the new century saw an upwelling of holiness revivalism nationwide, rural and urban, but with special intensity in some of the newly urbanizing areas such as Houston and Los Angeles. It was in this Southern California city that the most spectacular holiness volcano erupted. In a ramshackle house on Azusa Street, in a rundown industrial part of town, the black holiness preacher William Seymour presided over blacks and whites worshiping together in a nascent American Pentecostalism.

The word *Pentecostal* recalls the outpouring of the Holy Spirit on the primitive church on Pentecost Sunday recorded in the second chapter of Acts. The effects of this spiritual baptism were supernatural gifts, or charisms bestowed on the church, including speaking in tongues, prophesy, healing, and other ecstatic experiences. While the reappearance of Pentecostal experience would have a pervasive and revitalizing influence on worldwide twentieth-century Christianity, its immediate effect was to split the holiness movement into two camps, one of which rejected the supernatural gifts.

One of C. P. Jones's associates in the Church of Christ Holiness, Reverend C. H. Mason, was drawn to Los Angeles where he received the baptism of the Holy Spirit, spoke in tongues, and joined the Pentecostal movement. Jones's reaction was to throw Mason out of the Church of Christ Holiness. Mason went on to found the Church of God in Christ, the black Pentecostal denomination, which would have three and a half million members by 1990.

The non-Pentecostal holiness churches, having recoiled at the direct supernatural manifestations of the Pentecostals did not grow as explosively. But among African Americans, the two holiness traditions remained closely related. Known together as the "sanctified church," these traditions are marked by their ecstatic worship and their emphasis on an ascetic personal code and a life of service.

As the older Baptist and Methodist churches in black urban America grew more formal and genteel, it became the province of the holiness churches, many of which began as storefronts, to reassert vital piety. These churches remained more personal and more rigorous in their adherence to moral structure. Their members were more radical in the way they allowed the faith to permeate their lives. You could join one of the big Baptist or Methodist churches as a badge of identity, the way whites often joined their suburban counterparts. But the act of joining a small, closely knit holiness congregation usually came from a deeper level of being. Hence, John Perkins, as he found faith in Pasadena in 1957, could feel an overall stronger spiritual commitment among the membership at Bethlehem Church of Christ Holiness than he did at the bigger, more institutional Second Baptist.

Bibliographical Notes

Interviews and Field Work

This is primarily a work of oral history, having the bulk of its informational basis in a series of interviews initiated in 1977, when the author first visited Voice of Calvary Ministries in Jackson and Mendenhall, Mississippi. In 1988 John Perkins was re-interviewed in Pasadena for the *Transformation* article cited in chapter 26. And then, beginning in 1993, ongoing interviews were conducted with John Perkins, his family members, people in the ministries he had pioneered, and in the Christian community development movement. This involved return trips to Mississippi to interview the new generation of leaders at Voice of Calvary, Jackson, and at The Mendenhall Ministries. Many of these people, such as Dolphus Weary, Artis Fletcher, and Phil Reed, had been interviewed previously in 1977. The distance between the oral and field research done in the 1970s, the late eighties, and the nineties gives the research process a longitudinal dimension.

Particularly with John Perkins, many hours of recent interviewing have been vital to flesh out his diversity of involvements and add nuance and detail to this work. These were conducted between 1993 and 1996, many of them while the book was being written. To chart the concentric circles of Perkins's life and influence, many interviews were conducted, in person and over the phone, with his compatriots in the movement. Sam Kamaleson, for example, provided important information on Perkins's involvement with World Vision and his work within the international sphere detailed in chapter 22. H. P. Spees, who worked closely with Perkins on his first two books and was integrally involved in the development of Voice of Calvary in Jackson, has also been a major source of information.

In addition to individual interviews, much information was gathered in the field at events such as the two CCDA Annual Conventions: Baltimore in 1994 and Denver in 1995. Between 1993 and 1996, I attended seven day-long meetings and two three-day retreats of the board of directors of the John M. Perkins Foundation for Reconciliation and Development in Pasadena. The meetings of this body, which created CCDA and *Urban Family* magazine, are a rich mine of ideas and debate, a wonderful window on the movement. Many of the individuals on the board have their own organizations and affiliations that feed into the movement. Bud Ipema heads the MidAmerica Leadership Foundation, which does guidance and strategic planning for organizations starting programs in community development. Lula Ballton heads the South Central Community Development Association, linked with the giant West Angeles Church of God in Christ. Bill Greig, who has chaired the Perkins Foundation Board for many years, is president of Gospel Light Publishers (Regal Books), which published *Let Justice Roll Down* and many other books on racial reconciliation and community development.

CHAPTERS 1 AND 2

The basic source of information for Perkins's early family life and for events through the Mendenhall boycott, the Brandon episode, and its aftermath is his autobiographical *Let Justice Roll Down* (Ventura, Calif.: Regal, 1976). Supplementary information on the uncles and Aunt Coot and aspects of his childhood was provided by Perkins in personal interviews.

Perkins's cousin Tom Bass provided information on Emmaline Barnes (Aunt Babe) and her ancestry. And his cousin Rosie Lee Dixon gave a rich, colorful account of John's and her early life together in New Hebron. Dixon's mother, Ethel Noble, provided information about her early life in Mississippi. Both Dixon and her mother presently live in Monrovia, California.

The Perkins family life, in its female prominence and adaptive clanlike structure, represented a common form, with African roots, which the black family took in the rural South. A description of African matrilineal and extended family forms, adapted in America, is in Joseph L. White and Thomas Parham, *The Psychology of Blacks: An African-American Perspective* (Englewood Cliffs, N.J.: Prentice Hall, 1990); and Harriet Pipes McAdoo, ed., *Black Families* (Beverly Hills, Calif.: Sage Publications, 1981). Andrew Billingsley's 1968 study, *Black Families in White America* (Englewood Cliffs, N.J.: Prentice Hall, 1968), is especially illuminating in describing creative black response to the pressures of white domination. In Andrew Billingsley, *Climbing Jacob's Ladder: The Enduring Legacy of African-American Families* (New York: Simon and Schuster, 1992), the author provides an updated and more comprehensive account, detailing the richness and struggle of African American family life and the diverse historical influences that have molded it from its roots in Africa. Herbert G. Gutman, *The Black Family in Slavery and Freedom, 1750–1925* (New York: Random House, 1976) traces the remarkable resilience of the black family during the slavery and Jim Crow eras.

Accounts of the Rural Electrification Administration, its cooperative organization, and its electrical transformation of the rural South are in Frederick W. Muller, *Public Rural Electrification* (Washington, D.C.: American Council on

Public Affairs, 1944); and D. Clayton Brown, *Electricity for Rural America: The Fight for REA* (Westport, Conn.: Greenwood Press, 1980).

Chapter 3

John Perkins's migration to California in 1947 was a part of the post–Second World War phase of successive twentieth-century African American migrations out of the South, beginning at the time of World War I and known collectively as the "Great Migration." Daniel M. Johnson and Rex R. Campbell, *Black Migration in America: A Social Demographic History* (Durham, N.C.: Duke University Press, 1981), place more recent migration within the overall migratory history of African American migration dating from the slave trade. Studies of the Great Migration in terms of contemporary social historiography are in Joe William Trotter Jr., ed., *The Great Migration in Historical Perspective* (Bloomington, Ind.: Indiana University Press, 1991). Causes, process, and consequences of black migration to the Los Angeles area are thoroughly examined in Lawrence Brooks De Graaf, "Negro Migration to Los Angeles, 1930–1950" (Ph.D. diss., UCLA, 1962). Facts of the migration, its background, and consequences, as well as 1946 lynchings in Mississippi, are drawn from this source.

The postwar boom in California is viewed in connection with growth of the military industrial complex in Roger W. Lotchin, *Fortress California, 1910–1961: From Warfare to Welfare* (New York: Oxford University Press, 1992).

Vera Mae Perkins's own account of her marriage and family life is in: "How I Stayed Married for Forty Years," three-part series in *Urban Family* (fall 1992), 28–29; (winter 1993), 20–21; (spring 1993), 26–27.

Chapters 4 and 5

The content of these chapters is largely in *Let Justice Roll Down*. Additional material, such as that on Mama and Papa Wilson, comes from the author's interviews with John Perkins. As indicated at the end of chapter five, a background essay on the African American church is in the appendix, with bibliographical material at the end of the bibliographical notes.

Chapters 6 and 7

The information on R. A. Buckley's life was gathered in an interview at his Mendenhall farm in June 1977 when he was eighty-seven years old. Herbert Jones was interviewed in Jackson in June 1977. Artis Fletcher and Dolphus Weary were interviewed in Mendenhall in June 1977 and again in February 1995. Weary tells his story in *I Ain't Comin' Back* (Wheaton, Ill.: Tyndale, 1990). Jones, Fletcher, and Weary, together with Isaac Newsome, Jesse Newsome, Eugene Walker, and others are quoted at length in John Perkins, *A Quiet Revolution* (Waco, Tex.: Word, 1976).

The most insightful account of the rise of dispensational Fundamentalism is in George Marsden, *Fundamentalism and American Culture: The Shaping of Twentieth-Century Evangelicalism 1870–1925* (New York: Oxford University Press, 1980). An excellent brief summation of the subject is also in Sydney E. Ahlstrom, *A Religious History of the American People* (New Haven: Yale University Press, 1972), 805–16.

Chapter 8

The resource for material in the Martin Luther King Jr. section is David R. Goldfield, *Black, White, and Southern: Race Relations and Southern Culture, 1940 to the Present* (Baton Rouge: Louisiana State University Press, 1990). This is an eloquently written work that emphasizes the civil rights movement's accomplishment in transforming the South so that the races could share what they have in common and make progress together. A good cross section of civil rights writings, which also includes public statements of leading white supremacists, is Peter B. Levy, ed., *Let Freedom Ring: A Documentary History of the Modern Civil Rights Movement* (New York: Praeger, 1992).

Neil R. McMillen, *Dark Journey: Black Mississippians in the Age of Jim Crow* (Urbana, Ill.: University of Illinois Press, 1989), is an excellent in-depth study of Mississippi's caste society before the civil rights movement, viewed "from the bottom up." Robert Fulton Holtzclaw, *Black Magnolias: A Brief History of Afro-Mississippi* (Shaker Heights, Ohio: Keeble Press, 1984), focuses on Reconstruction, the second reconstruction (the modern civil rights movement), and black accomplishment in the face of discrimination and terror. Included are profiles of noted black Mississippians, such as Richard Wright, Medgar Evers, Charles Evers, Aaron Henry, and Fannie Lou Hamer. Charles Evers's book, *Evers,* ed. Grace Halsell (Cleveland, Ohio: World, 1971), compiled from interviews, reveals a tough-minded, business-oriented pragmatist, with qualities similar to many of the strong, irreligious black farmers who supported John Perkins in Mendenhall.

Factual content for the section on Freedom Summer is drawn from William McCord's dramatically written, contemporaneous account, *Mississippi: The Long, Hot Summer* (New York: W. W. Norton, 1965). Charles M. Payne, *I've Got the Light of Freedom: The Organizing Tradition and the Mississippi Freedom Struggle* (Berkeley: University of California Press, 1995), is a useful study of community organizing by indigenous black Mississippians to galvanize the Mississippi civil rights movement.

Chapter 9

John Perkins's second book, *A Quiet Revolution* (Waco, Tex.: Word, 1976), is a good supplement to *Let Justice Roll Down.* It connects evangelism and development with the battle for justice and tells the story of the campaign in Simpson County.

John Perkins's eldest son describes his experiences integrating a white school in Spencer Perkins and Chris Rice, *More Than Equals: Racial Healing for the Sake of the Gospel* (Downers Grove, Ill.: InterVarsity, 1993).

The Deacons for Defense and Justice are strangely absent from historical accounts of the civil rights movement. Two in-depth contemporaneous pieces appeared on them in mass circulation magazines. See Roy Reed, "The Deacons, Too, Ride by Night," *New York Times Magazine* (August 15, 1965): 10–11, 20, 22, 24; and Hamilton Bims, "Deacons for Defense," *Ebony* (September 1965): 25–28, 30. Another magazine article recorded their attempt at becoming a national civil rights organization. See "Deacons Go North: Deacons for Defense and Justice in Chicago," *Newsweek* (May 2, 1966): 20–21.

Chapters 10–13

Interviews with Joanie Perkins and Spencer Perkins supplement their father's account of events in the Mendenhall jail.

Material from court cases growing out of the Mendenhall and Brandon incidents are in *Perkins v. State of Mississippi*, 455 Federal Reporter, 2nd series (1972), 26–151. Descriptions of the events surrounding the Brandon beatings are recorded at length in the dissenting opinion of Chief Judge John Brown. See also Perkins, *Let Justice Roll Down*, 154–96. A telephone interview was also conducted with Perkins's attorney, Constance Slaughter, August 23, 1995.

Chapter 14

Booker T. Washington's address to the International Christian Workers Association convention is taken from Marsden, *Fundamentalism and American Culture*, 81.

On Carl Henry's place as pioneer in returning of twentieth-century evangelicals to social action, see Augustus Cerillo Jr. and Murray W. Dempster, "Carl F. H. Henry's Early Apologetic for an Evangelical Social Ethic," *Journal of the Evangelical Theological Society* 34, no. 3 (September 1991), 365–79.

Freedom Now 1, no. 3 (December 1965) is the early issue with the Perkins family on the cover and containing John Perkins's article. *Freedom Now* 4, no. 3 (May–June 1968) was the memorial issue for Martin Luther King Jr., with the Howard Jones interview on pages 22–25. The first issue under the title *The Other Side* was 5, no. 6 (Nov.–Dec. 1969).

William Pannell's first article was "The High Cost of Loving," *Freedom Now* 4, no. 1 (Jan.–Feb. 1968), 5–6. His first article in the broadened journal was "How Blacks Must Change," *The Other Side* 7, no. 1 (Jan.–Feb. 1971), 16–20. Pannell here quotes Malcom X's statement: "The worst crime the white man has committed has been to teach us to hate ourselves."

The first article by evangelist Tom Skinner was "Black Power," *The Other Side* 8, no. 1 (Jan.–Feb. 1972), 7–11+. Here he makes the case for black empowerment through economic, political, and cultural development. Skinner's early writings, all of which make the case for holistic evangelism, include his autobiographical *Black and Free* (Grand Rapids: Zondervan, 1970); *How Black Is the Gospel* (Philadelphia: Lippincott, 1970); and *Words of Revolution* (Grand Rapids: Zondervan, 1970).

Sojourners began publication as *Post-American* in 1971. Close to a generation senior to Wallis and his collaborators, Perkins became mentor to them. He has been a contributing editor to *Post-American* and then *Sojourners. Post-American* 4, no. 3 (March 1975) features "An Interview with John Perkins" as its cover story. Perkins's articles appeared in *Post-American* 4, no. 5 (June–July 1975); *Sojourners* 5, no. 3 (March 1976); 5, no. 9 (Sept. 1976); 6, no. 5 (May 1977); 6, no. 7 (July 1977); 6, no. 11 (Nov. 1977); and 7, no. 2 (Feb. 1978). More recently *Sojourners* has continued to articulate the cause of African Americans in its reader: *America's Original Sin: A Study Guide on White Racism* (1992).

The rise of an evangelical social gospel in the sixties and seventies, climaxing with the election of Jimmy Carter to the presidency in the "year of the evangelical," is recorded in detail in Robert Booth Fowler, *A New Engagement: Evangelical Political Thought 1966–1976* (Grand Rapids: Eerdmans, 1982). Cerillo and Dempster, *Salt and Light: Evangelical Political Thought in Modern America* (Grand Rapids: Baker, 1989), is a reader that divides recent evangelical thought on public issues into three schools: conservative, liberal, and radical. This volume contains the November 25, 1973, "A Declaration of Evangelical Social Concern," 157–59.

The full citation for David Moberg's book is: *Inasmuch: Christian Social Responsibility in 20th Century America* (Grand Rapids: Eerdmans, 1965). Richard Pierard's book is: *The Unequal Yoke: Evangelical Christianity and Political Conservatism* (Philadelphia: Lippincott, 1970). Paul Jewett's book is: *Man as Male and Female* (Grand Rapids: Eerdmans, 1975). Ronald J. Sider, *Rich Christians in an Age of Hunger: A Biblical Study* (Downers Grove, Ill.: InterVarsity, 1977), also made an important and influential statement.

Fuller Seminary's controversial role in broadening a parochial fundamentalism to a "neo-evangelicalism" strongly emphasizing social ethics is described in George Marsden, *Reforming Fundamentalism: Fuller Seminary and the New Evangelicalism* (Grand Rapids: Eerdmans, 1987).

Chapters 15–19

The content of the specific teachings summarized in chapter fifteen are from a three-part lecture series, *"Introduction to Christian Community Development,"* videotaped at Southern California College in 1983. The three segments were: "The Felt Need Concept," "The Church's Responsibility to the Poor," and "Leadership for Today." While these messages were taped a year after John Perkins left Jackson for Pasadena, the content was the same as what he was teaching at the International Study Center and preaching in colleges and churches around the country while he was based in Jackson.

H Spees's account of the flood in Mendenhall, complete with pictures, is in "The Spirit Hovered over the Water," *The Other Side* 10, no. 3 (May–June 1974), 36–40.

Voice of Calvary's quarterly periodical, *A Quiet Revolution,* published between 1975 and 1994, was a rich source of descriptive and human interest writing on VOC's ministries and their development. John Perkins, Vera Mae Perkins, Spencer Perkins, Joanie Perkins, Lem Tucker, and H Spees, among others, were contributors to QR. It ran for nine years as a newspaper and was changed to magazine format in 1986 and then published irregularly. In that its purpose was to update friends of Voice of Calvary, it served as a good record of change and growth and general goings-on in Mendenhall (until 1980) and Jackson through 1994. The Summer 1980 issue, for example, celebrates "VOC, The First 20 Years." The International Study Center, Thriftco, VOC's Jubilee Celebration, Harambee Christian School of Business, Jean Thomas and Haiti, the VOC health clinics, and People's Development housing ministry are all described in *A Quiet Revolution* articles. QR also served as an outlet for John Perkins's and Lem Tucker's philosophical statements about the Three R's of community development.

John Perkins's third book, *With Justice for All* (Ventura, Calif.: Regal, 1982), describes the Jackson ministries. Gordon Aeschliman, *John Perkins: Land Where My Father Died* (Ventura, Calif.: Regal, 1987), describes Perkins's style of leadership and his principles of community and parish church building. It also contains material on the Mendenhall and Jackson transitions. Dolphus Weary, *I Ain't Comin' Back* (Wheaton, Ill.: Tyndale, 1990), tells the story of Weary's struggles through a poverty-wracked childhood and the VOC, Mendenhall story from Perkins's pioneering days to Weary's and Artis Fletcher's leadership of the present ministries and church. Extensive accounts are included on the development of health care and the traumatic flood incident and the creation of Genesis One school.

Ed McKinley's article, "Submitting to Black Leadership," appeared in *The Other Side* 8, no. 1 (Jan.–Feb. 1972), 29–33.

Material on Phil Reed comes from the 1977 and 1995 interviews and from an oral presentation he did with his wife, Marcia, "Relocation: Living the Good Life," 7th Annual CCDA Convention, November 9–12, 1995, Denver, Colorado.

Material on Lem Tucker comes from February 1995 interviews with VOC President Melvin Anderson and Spencer Perkins. Tucker was memorialized in QR (winter 1989): 3–6. His background and ideas were also described in Angela Elwell Hunt, "Lemuel S. Tucker: Building Bridges to the Inner City," reprint from *Fundamentalist Journal* (Feb. 1987).

Chapters 20 and 21

Moynihan's policy paper, *The Negro Family: The Case for National Action,* provoked a storm of controversy among academics and policy makers over the causes of twentieth-century "urban pathologies" that has continued to rage through the underclass debates of the eighties and nineties. Along with the responses of many black and white leaders and intellectuals, it can be found in Lee Rainwater and William L. Yancey, *The Moynihan Report and the Politics of Controversy* (Cambridge, Mass.: MIT Press, 1967). Moynihan actually borrowed the phrase "tangle of pathology" from *Dark Ghetto: Dilemmas of Social Power* (New York: Haper and Row, 1965) by the well-known black social psychologist Kenneth Clark. Today as teenage motherhood, family disintegration, and antisocial behaviors among youth have ceased to be the peculiar province of the ghetto, Moynihan has come to be regarded as a sage. Says the New York senator, "the instability in the'dark ghettos' that we picked up on our radar now has spread to the majority community." See Daniel Patrick Moynihan, *Miles to Go: A Personal History of Social Policy* (Cambridge, Mass: Harvard University Press, 1996), 168–90.

Debaters of the black underclass question divide into liberal, right, and left positions. William Julius Wilson, a black academic and social democratic liberal, touched off the debate in 1978, much as his white liberal forebear, Pat Moynihan, had in 1965. His book, *The Declining Significance of Race: Blacks and Changing American Institutions,* 2d ed. (Chicago: University of Chicago Press, 1980), tried to attribute the intractable problems of the ghetto more to class than to race, given the emergence of a suburban black middle class in the wake of the civil rights movement and affirmative action. But his title and emphasis provoked a hostile reaction from theorists and activists of the left, who saw it as giving ammunition to those who would cut off race-based remediation.

Wilson's next book, *The Truly Disadvantaged* (Chicago: University of Chicago Press, 1987), further elucidated his economically based position. He acknowledged the existence of self-defeating ghetto pathologies, but unlike theorists of the right, he saw them as the result of the migration of jobs, opportunities, and institutional infrastructure out of the inner cities. The net result Wilson saw was a black underclass trapped and isolated in the inner cities of America, where they were cut off from the possibility of developing the middle-class lifestyles necessary to success.

The conservative side of the debate, elaborated in William Murray, *Losing Ground: American Social Policy 1950–1980* (New York: Basic Books, 1984), blamed governmental policies of welfare statism, particularly changes in eligibility for AFDC, for creating a dependent class of poor. Murray saw mothers choosing welfare over minimum-wage jobs and he favored a laissez-faire solution, which would cut off much of the safety net. He and others on the right do not acknowledge the existence of the structural dislocations Wilson emphasizes, nor do they assign any responsibility to corporate America for creating the problem. They see rehabilitation coming chiefly through the development of self-help resources aided by private sector philanthropy.

Myron Magnet, a critic of liberals and the left, also finds Murray's arguments reminiscent of nineteenth-century classical economics in their depiction of ghetto residents as rationally choosing their poverty. In his *The Dream and the Nightmare: The Sixties' Legacy to the Underclass* (New York: William Morrow, 1993), Magnet disputes Wilson's notion that the underclass is isolated from prevalent American culture norms. Instead, he states that they are all too vulnerable to the dictates of a pathological mainstream culture that has developed since the sixties. He sees a pop culture, readily available and detrimental to all segments of society via media, that has replaced the work ethic and moral restraint with mass narcissism and sensation seeking, fueling antisocial behaviors, which have especially devastating consequences among the urban poor.

Magnet's concept of the culpability of post-sixties cultural change for social deterioration and institutional dysfunction has been advanced by others, including some identified with the left, such as the late Christopher Lasch, *The Culture of Narcissism* (New York: Warner Books, 1979); and Cornel West, "Philosophy and the Urban Underclass," in *The Underclass Question*, ed. Bill Lawson (Philadelphia: Temple University Press, 1992), 191–201. West suggests that a predominant consumer culture's "addiction to stimulation" has done much to cause institutional unraveling among blacks in the inner city.

Wilson's new book, *When Work Disappears: The World of the New Urban Poor* (New York: Random House, 1996), marshals updated, grim poverty statistics to advance his argument that structural changes in society have brought about a chronic inner-city joblessness that causes dysfunctional cultural patterns. His policy recommendations call for massive federal intervention to bring about new job opportunities. A profile of Wilson and summation of his work is in David Remnick, "Dr. Wilson's Neighborhood," *New Yorker* 77, no. 10 (April 29 & May 6, 1996): 96–107.

Magnet, on the other hand, offers the possibility of more locally based approaches. Observing Korean entrepreneurs' consistent success in the inner city, he sees it as the result of strong familial and community support systems and values that continue to emphasize hard work and self-discipline. While Wilson's economic observations have obvious truth, these Korean-Americans suggest an alternative behavior model, which rejects the destructive norms of contemporary consumer culture. John Perkins's community-development movement effectively reintroduces the kinds of values and support systems Magnet describes. That process in Pasadena and its development into a national movement forms the substance of part 3 of this book.

The continuance of economic, social, and cultural factors in America making for the existence of a black underclass and prevalent forms of caste are elucidated in: Obie Clayton, ed., *An American Dilemma Revisited: Race Relations in a Changing World* (New York: Russell Sage Foundation, 1996).

The negative implications of epidemic fatherlessness are set forth in David Blankenhorn, *Fatherless America: Confronting Our Most Urgent Social Problem* (New York: HarperCollins, 1995). Fatherlessness is especially common in the inner city, leaving boys to grow up with no consistent, attached, and loving males to mentor and set behavioral boundaries for young men. A misogynistic street culture, commercialized in rap music, bespeaks the rage young men feel at their fathers' abandonment and resultant dominance of women in their family. Lack of responsible, nurturing fathers to identify with is a root cause of lethal gang violence and the explosion of overall juvenile crime. The Million Man March on Washington in the fall of 1995 testified to African American men's growing recognition of the acute need for them to be husbands and fathers to their families. See Carl F. Ellis Jr., "Why I Marched," *Urban Family* (spring 1996), 9.

Material on the male mentoring in Pasadena comes from extensive interviews with Derek Perkins and Bryan Robinson. Derek and Rudy Carasco are planning a book that describes their youth work.

CHAPTER 22

On the history and politics of the Kenyan revolution, see Carl G. Rosberg Jr. and John Nottingham, *The Myth of Mau Mau: Nationalism in Kenya* (New York: Praeger, 1966). An inside view detailing the content and significance of oathing ceremonies and the like is provided in Donald L. Barnett and Karari Njama, *Mau Mau from Within: An Analysis of Kenya's Peasant Revolt* (New York: Monthly Review Press, 1966).

A personalized account of modern Australia containing an insightful chapter on the plight of the Aborigines is Ross Terrill, *The Australians* (New York: Simon and Schuster, 1987). The evolution of Australian welfare policies toward the Aborigines through 1966 is in A. G. L. Shaw and H. D. Nicolson, *Australia in the Twentieth Century* (Sydney, Australia: Angus & Robertson, 1966).

An account of New Zealand's Maoris, which relates their history in the context of European colonization is in Joan Metge, *The Maoris of New Zealand* (Bristol, England: Routledge & Kegan Paul Ltd., 1967). On Maori culture, see Eric Schwimmer, *The World of the Maori* (Wellington, New Zealand: A. H. & A. W. Reed, 1974).

Material on Jean Thomas and Fond-des-Bancs, Haiti, comes from a 1995 interview with Phil Reed; and Bill Chickering, "The Last Place in the World," *A Quiet Revolution* (winter 1986), 5–7.

CHAPTERS 23 AND 24

Material on the Reagan Task Force on Food Assistance comes from: *Report of the President's Task Force on Food Assistance* (Washington, D.C.: GPO, 1984).

The work of Christian Community Development Association has been highlighted and publicized in its quarterly, *Restorer* (1989–1996), seven volumes.

John Perkins's recent publications on community development include *Beyond Charity: The Call to Christian Community Development* (Grand Rapids: Baker, 1993), which reworks the themes of his earlier *A Quiet Revolution* around more recent events and personalities in Pasadena and various of the CCDA communities; *Resurrecting Hope* (Ventura, Calif.: Regal, 1995), describes ten different Christian community development organizations, including Voice of Calvary

Ministries in Jackson, The Mendenhall Ministries, Lawndale Community Church, and Lake Avenue Congregational Church in Pasadena. Perkins, ed., *Restoring At-Risk Communities: Doing It Together and Doing It Right* (Grand Rapids: Baker, 1995), is a handbook on the different aspects of Christian community development written by participants, including Vera Mae Perkins, Spencer Perkins, Chris Rice, Mary Nelson, Phil Reed, Mark Gornik, Noel Castellanos, and others.

Ray Bakke tells his story and provides historical and cultural insights on the emerging field of urban ministries in *The Urban Christian* (Downers Grove, Ill.: InterVarsity, 1987). The Lawndale story is told enthusiastically, along with some wonderful pictures of participants, in Wayne Gordon, *Real Hope in Chicago: The Incredible Story of How the Gospel Is Transforming a Chicago Neighborhood* (Grand Rapids: Zondervan, 1995). Bob Lupton provides incisive ideas based on his experience of relocating and in community building in inner-city Atlanta. See Lupton, *Theirs Is the Kingdom: Celebrating the Gospel in Urban America* (New York: HarperCollins, 1987); and especially Lupton, *Return Flight: Community Development through Reneighboring Our Cities* (Atlanta: FCS Urban Ministries, 1993). Rock of Salvation Church and Circle Urban Ministries in Chicago are described in the context of the authors' individual stories and their combined process of racial reconciliation in Raleigh Washington and Glen Kehrein, *Breaking Down Walls: A Model for Reconciliation in an Age of Racial Strife* (Chicago: Moody Press, 1993). Spencer Perkins and Chris Rice use a similar format to spread the gospel of racial reconciliation in their *More than Equals* (cited under chapter nine above).

Description of Christian community development in Fresno, California, comes from four interviews with H. P. Spees (1993–95); unpublished printed materials of Youth For Christ; a videotape, *City Builders II* (Fresno, Calif.: Fresno Leadership Foundation, 1996); H. P. Spees, presentation at 6th Annual CCDA Conference, Baltimore, Md., Nov. 17–20, 1994, and presentation at 7th Annual CCDA Conference, Denver, Colo., Nov. 9–12, 1995.

Most information on the American Cities Campaign comes directly from John Perkins. Some material comes from unpublished CCDA publicity broadsides. Material on housing in Grand Rapids comes from Jonathan Bradford, "Housing That Empowers," presentation at 7th Annual CCDA Conference, Denver, Colo., Nov. 9–12, 1995.

CHAPTER 25

Information on Mendenhall Bible Church's Pastor's Development Ministry comes from a February 1995 interview with Rev. Artis Fletcher and from published and unpublished materials of Mendenhall Bible Church and The Mendenhall Ministries, including the syllabus by Artis Fletcher, "National Pastors/Wives Conference, July 9–11, 1992." *TMM Reflections,* the semiannual publication of The Mendenhall Ministries, is the source of much of the information contained in the Mendenhall section of this chapter.

Material on Antioch comes largely from "The Antioch Story," presentations at the Sixth and Seventh Annual CCDA Conferences. Participants in the 1995 presentation included Spencer and Nancy Perkins, Chris and Donna Rice, and Ron Potter and Joanie Perkins Potter. Perkins and Rice, *More Than Equals* also contains information on Antioch. A May 1996 telephone interview with Chris Rice supplemented and clarified information gleaned from these other sources. *Urban Family* was published quarterly from winter 1992 to spring 1996.

The Jackson fieldwork done in February 1995, which updated information on Voice of Calvary Ministries and Voice of Calvary Fellowship, included interviews with Melvin Anderson and Phil Reed, as well as a tour of VOC's housing development work in Olin Park and other locations given by Marcia Reed.

Randall Balmer's chapter, "Mississippi Missions," in his *Mine Eyes Have Seen the Glory* (New York: Oxford University Press, 1993), 176–91, briefly sketches Melvin Anderson and quotes him prior to his becoming director.

Much of the informational basis of the Pasadena segment of this chapter is from 1996 interviews with Priscilla Perkins, Betty Perkins, Julie Ragland, Derek Perkins, Steve Lazarian, Stan Lazarian, and Roland Hinz. Transcription of the February meeting of the board of directors of Harambee Christian Family Center provided another source. A taped presentation on Harambee Preparatory School by Priscilla Perkins, Julie Ragland, and Karyn Farrar Perkins at the Seventh Annual CCDA Conference, Denver, Colorado, was also a source of information. A sense of Harambee's content and spirit was gleaned from Julie Ragland's class at Harambee Preparatory School, Harambee Center's April banquets in 1994, 1995, and 1996, as well as frequent visits to the Harambee Christian Family Center.

Chapter 26

The 1988 interview with John Perkins led to Stephen E. Berk, "From Proclamation to Community: The Work of John Perkins," *Transformation* 6, no. 4 (Oct./Dec. 1989): 1–7.

A good cross-section of Du Bois's work is found in Eric Sundquist, ed., *The Oxford W. E. B. Du Bois Reader* (New York: Oxford University Press, 1996). His statement on "the attitude of the imprisoned group" is from an essay on Booker T. Washington on page 245 of this collection.

The Autobiography of Malcolm X, as told to Alex Haley (New York: Random House, 1965), is Malcolm's own powerful account of his life and inner changes, the essential source for information about him. This book takes its place along with Ralph Ellison's *Invisible Man* and Richard Wright's *Black Boy* and *Native Son* as a universal statement of African American response to oppression. Speeches of Malcolm X and eulogies and articles about him collected at the height of the black power movement are in John Henrik Clarke, ed. *Malcolm X: The Man and His Times* (New York: MacMillan, 1969). A book aimed at youth and looking at Malcolm X in the context of African American history, leadership, and issues and written by a black churchman is Carl Ellis Jr., *Malcolm X: The Man behind the Mask* (Chattanooga, Tenn.: Accord Publications, 1993). It is used as a text for the youth coming to Harambee Christian Family Center.

A fine collection of Martin Luther King documents—books, sermons, speeches, interviews—is James M. Washington Jr., ed., *A Testament of Hope: The Essential Writings and Speeches of Martin Luther King, Jr.* (New York: HarperCollins, 1991). Taylor Branch's exhaustive *Parting the Waters: America in the King Years 1954–1963* (New York: Simon and Schuster, 1989) is a repository of information on King's life, the influences on him, and the movement he led. Branch is working on a second volume depicting King's last five years.

Booker T. Washington's autobiography, *Up from Slavery*, ed. William L. Andrews (New York: W. W. Norton, 1996), is in a "critical edition," which includes an index, letters, and articles about Washington by contemporaries and historians.

Perkins's statement on affirmative action as an important means to establish opportunity for blacks is in *With Justice for All* (1982), 169. In a recent article he finds biblical basis for affirmative action in the Old Testament principle of restitution, wherein "God favored the poor and sometimes took care of the poor at the expense of the rich," and in the New Testament principle of walking the extra mile. The redistribution ideals of biblical Israel would imply using affirmative action more in terms of economic need than race. New Testament conceptions of doing for others implies a spirit of openness of both blacks and whites to the other's point of view. See "Is Affirmative Action Biblically Correct?" *The Reconciler* (fall 1995), 1.

Perkins's recent personal efforts in behalf of racial reconciliation have included a book with former Ku Klux Klan terrorist, Tommy Tarrants, who now pastors a biracial church in the nation's capital. See John Perkins and Thomas A. Tarrants, III, *He's My Brother: Former Racial Foes Offer Strategy for Reconciliation* (Grand Rapids: Chosen, 1995). The book contains both Perkins's and Tarrants's contrasting, dramatic stories. The two men have spoken together on Christian college campuses, and Tarrants was the speaker at the 1995 Harambee banquet.

The handbook for men in Promise Keepers is Bill McCartney, et al., *Seven Promises of a Promise Keeper* (Colorado Springs: Focus on the Family, 1994). Promises make men accountable to "His God," "His Mentors," "His Integrity," "His Family," "His Church," "His Brothers," and "His World." Racial reconciliation is in the category of "His Brothers." At the 1995 CCDA Conference, McCartney spoke movingly of personal experience that led him to commit to racial reconciliation as one of his chief life purposes.

Appendix: The African American Church

The African elements and historic evangelical influence in African American religious expression are delineated in Michael Mullin, *Africa in America: Slave Acculturation and Resistance in the American South and the British Caribbean, 1736–1831* (Urbana, Ill.: University of Illinois Press, 1992), 174–212.

In *The Souls of Black Folk* (1903), W. E. B. Du Bois was one of the first to write objectively about the black church. He sympathetically described "the preacher, the music and the frenzy" and assessed the church's role as "conserver of morals, strengthener of family life and final authority on what is good and right." See H. M. Nelson, R. L. Yokley, and A. K. Nelson, *The Black Church in America* (New York: Basic Books, 1971).

Benjamin Mays and Thomas W. Nicholson, *The Negro's Church* (New York: Institute of Social and Religious Research, 1933), saw the church as a "static," "nonprogressive," and essentially otherworldly institution, which nevertheless has a unique genius, life, and vitality. They point to its control by Negroes themselves and its support of Negro business and education.

E. Franklin Frazier, in his influential essay *The Negro Church in America* (New York: Schoken Books, 1964), originally published in 1949, took a generally negative view of the church, emphasizing its authoritarian and accommodationist qualities and its inhibition of black advancement. Frazier, however, did recognize the church's function as the linchpin of community life and the one institution Negroes could call their own. Hart M. Nelson and Anne Kusener, *The Black Church in the Sixties* (Lexington, KY.: University Press of Kentucky, 1975), underline Frazier's views of the traditional black church, but also see a strong base for community action in the church.

C. Eric Lincoln and Lawrence Mamiya, *The Black Church in the African American Experience* (Durham, N.C.: Duke University Press, 1990), is presently the most comprehensive study of the black church. These authors view the black church in much greater complexity than do other authors. Tracing the African roots of the "invisible institution," Lincoln and Mamiya present a number of different "models" of church function, including a "prophetic" model.

The prophetic role of the black church, in its effect on the civil rights movement through the Southern Christian Leadership Conference, is examined in Aldon Morris, *Origins of the Civil Rights Movement: Black Communities Organizing for Change* (New York: Free Press, 1984).

The art and role of the black preacher and the purpose and structure of the sermon are illuminatingly presented in William H. Pipes, *Say Amen Brother! Old-Time Negro Preaching: A Study in Frustration* (New York: William Frederick Press, 1951). Direct quotes and expostulations from sermons in this chapter come from Pipes. The central, "celebrity" role of the black preacher as representative and spokesperson for the black community is stressed in Charles V. Hamilton, *The Black Preacher in America* (New York: William Morrow, 1972).

A thumbnail history of The Church of Christ Holiness, the denomination in which John Perkins experienced conversion, is in Charles Edwin Jones, *Black Holiness: A Guide to the Participation in Wesleyan Perfectionist and Glossolalic Pentecostal Movements* (Metuchen, N.J.: Scarecrow Press, 1987), 45–47. This is also the source for facts on the founding of the Church of God in Christ. Joseph R. Washington Jr., *Black Sects and Cults* (New York: Doubleday, 1972), sees the holiness movement as responding to people in greater sense of spiritual crisis and producing greater earnestness, vitality, and intensity than the more status-aspiring, mainstream black churches. Jones and Washington are key sources for facts pertaining to the black holiness movement. Cheryl J. Sanders, *Saints in Exile: The Holiness-Pentecostal Experience in African American Religion and Culture* (New York: Oxford, 1996), is an excellent new historical study of the "sanctified" church traditions. Sanders stresses their ecstatic forms of worship and their strong ethic of service.

The leadership of early American evangelicalism in progressive social causes, such as antislavery and the women's rights movement is detailed in Donald W. Dayton, *Discovering an Evangelical Heritage* (New York: Harper & Row, 1976).

Stephen E. Berk is professor of history at California State University, Long Beach. He specializes in American culture and religion and has a particular interest in African American history and Christian community development. He also has training in psychology and is a licensed marriage and family therapist. It was in 1977, as he toured the United States visting Christian communities, that he first met John Perkins. Their relationship continues, and Berk now serves on the board of the John M. Perkins Foundation for Reconciliation and Development.